Third Edition

Essentials of Young Adult Literature

Kathy G. Short
University of Arizona

Carl M. Tomlinson
Northern Illinois University

Carol Lynch-Brown
Florida State University

Holly Johnson
University of Cincinnati

Boston   Columbus   Indianapolis   New York   San Francisco   Upper Saddle River
Amsterdam   Cape Town   Dubai   London   Madrid   Milan   Munich   Paris   Montréal   Toronto
Delhi   Mexico City   São Paulo   Sydney   Hong Kong   Seoul   Singapore   Taipei   Tokyo

Vice President and Editorial Director: Jeff Johnston
Acquisitions Editor: Kathryn Boice
Editorial Assistant: Carolyn Schweitzer
Executive Marketing Manager: Krista Clark
Program Manager: Karen Mason
Project Manager: Cynthia DeRocco
Editorial Production Services and Text Design: Electronic Publishing Services Inc., NYC
Manufacturing Buyer: Linda Sager
Art Rendering and Electronic Page Makeup: Jouve
Cover Designer: Diane Lorenzo
Cover Art: David Wiesner

Credits and acknowledgments borrowed from other sources and reproduced, with permission, in this textbook appear on this page, the appropriate page within text, or on page 292.

Credit: Chapter opener background and A-head child icons: David Wiesner.

Library of Congress Cataloging-in-Publication Data

Short, Kathy Gnagey.
    Essentials of Young Adult Literature / Kathy G. Short, Carl M. Tomlinson, Carol Lynch-Brown, Holly Johnson. — 3rd Edition.
        pages cm
    Includes bibliographical references and index.
    ISBN 978-0-13-352227-3
    1. Young adult literature—History and criticism.   I. Tomlinson, Carl M.   II. Lynch-Brown, Carol.   III. Johnson, Holly.   IV. Title.
    PN1009.A1T55 2014
    809'.892820711—dc23

                                                                                2013038901

10   9   8   7   6   5   4   3   2   1

ISBN 10: 0-13-352227-X
ISBN 13: 978-0-13-352227-3

Contents

Chapter Six   Nonfiction: Biography and Informational Books   105

Chapter Seven   Poetry and Plays   131

Chapter Ten   Experiencing Literature   213

Features

Figures

Preface

Essentials of Young Adult Literature is a brief comprehensive textbook with rich resources—a compendium of information about young adult books. It is tailored to a course in young adult literature but, by virtue of its brevity and affordability, is also suitable as a companion text for a course on teaching reading or literature in middle and high school.

We embrace the idea that the primary focus of a course in young adult literature should be reading actual young adult books, not reading an exhaustive textbook *about* these books. University students need direct experience with young adult books—reading independently, reading aloud to others, discussing, writing, comparing, criticizing, evaluating, and connecting to their lives, as well as exploring ways of sharing these books with young people. We deliberately do not include book reviews and plot summaries within the narrative of the chapters. However, the recommended booklists at the end of each genre chapter contain briefly annotated titles.

One of our goals is to awaken or reawaken the joy of reading for college-level students. This reawakening can happen only if they experience the pleasure and excitement of reading excellent books. At the same time, the body of knowledge about literature and about teaching literature to young adults can be conveyed most efficiently through a textbook. *Essentials of Young Adult Literature* presents this body of knowledge in a clear, concise, direct narrative using brief lists, examples, figures, and tables in combination with prose, thus freeing class time for involvement with literature.

This third edition of *Essentials of Young Adult Literature* heralds a change in authorship as Kathy G. Short and Holly Johnson take on the role of senior authors. Kathy G. Short, professor of children's and young adult literature at the University of Arizona, engages in research about global literature and intercultural understanding, dialogue about literature, and inquiry-based curriculum. Holly Johnson, an associate professor of adolescent literature at the University of Cincinnati, engages in research on adolescents' response to literature, literature across the curriculum, and content analysis of young adult literature.

The field of young adult literature is currently enjoying an explosion of new titles that reflect new formats, genres, styles, and authors. Our goal for this book, however, remains true to Carol's and Carl's initial concept—a comprehensive but brief alternative to compendium textbooks.

Features of *Essentials of Young Adult Literature*

- Comprehensive coverage and content of young adult literature in a brief paperback format
- A genre approach to literature with connections to topics, authors, and notable books
- A logical, well-organized structure

- Useful charts and tables on history, research, read-aloud recommendations, and examples of literature to use across the curriculum
- Notable author features for the genre chapters
- Definitions of terms that appear in bold italics
- Coverage of multicultural and international young adult literature, graphic novels, short stories, novels in verse, and picture books for older readers
- Clearly stated positions on current issues affecting schools and literature: censorship, classics, and standards
- Attention to the needs of resistant readers
- Recommended book lists that are logically organized and briefly annotated
- Awards recognizing young adult literature with listings of the winning titles

Features New to This Edition

- Hundreds of new young adult books in annotated lists and as examples throughout the chapters
- More integration of multicultural and global titles and authors throughout chapters
- Discussion of text complexity, close reading, and other aspects of the Common Core State Standards
- Research on reading interests and discussion of why reading and literature are at risk in our society moved to Chapter 1
- Evaluation and selection criteria in genre chapters revised as questions to facilitate their use as an evaluation tool
- Excellent Books to Read Aloud feature added to the genre chapters
- Types of fantasy and realistic fiction updated to reflect current trends
- Plays and readers theatre added as a genre in the poetry chapter
- Science fiction as a genre
- Chapter 8, "Literature for a Diverse Society," revised to highlight the importance of critically responsive, critically expansive, and culturally critical approaches to literature.
- Previous three chapters in Part Three are reorganized into two chapters

  - Chapter 9, "Literature in the Curriculum," includes the political context of Common Core State Standards, ways of organizing a literature curriculum and developing literature units, and the resources to support this curriculum. The chapter ends with the critical issues to consider in a literature curriculum—censorship, classic texts, and literary criticism.
  - Chapter 10, "Experiencing Literature," begins with a discussion of how to create a literate environment for all readers, especially resistant readers. Teaching strategies and literature engagements are organized into three sections: reading widely for personal purposes, reading critically to inquire about the world, and reading strategically to learn about literature and literacy.

- Expanded discussion of literature circles and literature response engagements
- Additional emphasis on young adult–classic literature pairings
- A discussion of the teaching of literary criticism using young adult literature
- New conceptual planning webs on the forced journeys of refugees and taking responsibility for action in Chapter 9
- Resistant readers addressed in Chapter 10 on experiencing literature through a discussion of the types of adolescent resistant readers and the integration of suggestions for reaching these readers into classroom engagements
- Technology connections integrated across the chapters

Acknowledgments

We are grateful to Aurora Martínez, who made possible the original publication of *Essentials of Young Adult Literature.*

For their generous help, good advice, and valued opinions concerning *Essentials of Young Adult Literature,* we wish to express our appreciation to the following reviewers: Dr. Leslie Crabtree, North Central University; Dr. Thomas Eaton, Southeast Missouri State University; Dr. Julie Gates, Angelo State University; Jeffrey Stuart Kaplan, University of Central Florida; Amy Walsh MacKrell, Simpson College; Dr. Charlotte L. Pass, State University of New York College at Courtland.

We are indebted to illustrator David Wiesner for the cover of this edition of *Essentials of Young Adult Literature.* His images of adolescents who are reaching new heights through literature capture the potential and the challenge that readers experience as they explore ideas and experiences that take them beyond their current understandings and experiences.

Part One

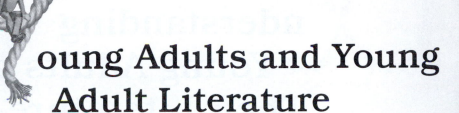

Young Adults and Young Adult Literature

Part One introduces you to the field of young adult literature. These chapters will support you in considering the value of this literature for adolescents and learning how to select and evaluate young adult books, currently the fastest growing area in book publishing.

Chapter 1 begins by defining young adults and young adult literature as well as presenting an overview of the history of young adult literature, including milestones in the evolution of the field and early important works. We discuss the value of this literature for adolescents along with research evidence supporting its benefits for readers and for society. Evaluating and selecting the best books for adolescents involves knowing both readers and books and so includes knowledge about adolescent

reading interests, useful selection sources, and ways of determining text complexity.

Chapter 2 presents important literature concepts, including elements of fiction, fictional literary forms, and aspects of book format, as they connect to young adult literature. The major fictional literary forms of novels and novels in verse, short stories, picture books, and graphic novels are also highlighted.

Although examples are given throughout this text of well-known young adult books as well as recent notable titles, lengthy plot summaries or book reviews are not included. We believe that more is gained from reading and discussing the actual young adult books than from reading *about* the books in a lengthy textbook.

Chapter One

Understanding Young Adults and Their Literature

Change is always accompanied by anticipation, anxiety, excitement, and fear, often felt all at the same time. The years between childhood and adulthood magnify these emotions because they are a time of tremendous change at many levels for young adults as they engage in "becoming" and redefining themselves personally, socially, and culturally. Young adults are old enough to be conscious of this change process and so find reassurance and understanding in the company of those who share their experiences and feelings. That company includes the people in their lives, some of whom are characters in books and the worlds adolescents enter and experience through literature.

Definitions of Young Adult Literature

"Young adult" is a term that has no clear definition, often connoting words such as puberty, adolescence, and teenager, which suggest different things to different people. Even professionals in the fields of sociology, psychology, and education do not agree on the meanings of these terms. In the United States and most other Western countries, young adulthood is associated with biological changes and a growing sense of independence from adults.

Young adults are seen as evolving through a search for self and identity as they grow and change. At some point and for varying economic, social, political, and biological reasons, a child transitions to adulthood, and young adulthood ends. These developments occur at different ages and at different rates for different people, yet the prevalent school configuration in the United States defines middle school as grades 6 through 8 (ages 11 through 14 for most students) and high school as grades 9 through 12 (ages 15 through 18 for most students).

The dominant ideology of adolescence as a life stage that is biologically or psychologically determined by "raging hormones" has been criticized (Flinders, 1999). Adolescence is traditionally viewed as a period of incompleteness when hormonal changes need to be contained during growth toward adulthood, or completeness. Teens are seen as struggling with identity and making risky choices about peer pressure and harmful substances—a perspective that ignores the diverse lives and cultures of adolescents. A social construct view of adolescence supports more complex, contradictory, and multiple portrayals of teens that address the influences of race, gender, social class, and sexuality. In addition, adolescence as a socially constructed life stage recognizes that the concept of adolescence grew out of economic conditions, rather than biological forces, during the Great Depression when teens were pushed out of the workforce and into schools to keep them under control.

Young adult literature, as defined in this text, is literature written for young people ages 12 to 18 and books marketed as "young adult" by a publisher. Our focus is the books that adolescents *choose* to read in contrast to the books they are required to read, with an emphasis on the best of young adult literature while recognizing that a book does not have to be an award winner or receive rave reviews to have value for a reader. Typically young adult literature has these characteristics:

- The main character is an adolescent who is at the center of the plot.
- The events revolve around the adolescent's actions, decisions, and struggle to resolve conflict.
- The events and problems in the plot are related to adolescents, and the dialogue reflects their speech.
- The point of view is that of an adolescent and reflects an adolescent's interpretation of events and people, rather than an adult reflecting back on adolescence.
- The book is written for young adults and marketed to a young adult audience.

Young adult literature is not a *genre* or category of literature, but includes all of the traditional genres from realistic fiction to poetry. It is a body of literature appropriate for individuals at a certain time of life. Chapter 2 includes a discussion of the genres typically found within young adult literature.

History of Young Adult Literature

The history of young adult literature parallels that of adolescence in that books for teens could not precede the concept of adolescence. Until the mid-eighteenth century, the United States was mostly a rural, agrarian society. Children were sent out to work as early as age 7, and by ages 15 or 16 were fully incorporated into the workforce. Independence from parents and families came to young people much earlier than it does today. Schools were scarce, and school attendance was seasonal, sporadic, and short-lived. Consequently, there was little need for books in the general population and the concept of "adolescence" did not exist.

The general acceptance of adolescence as a distinct stage of life emerged in the mid-twentieth century, although its social, economic, and political roots developed earlier, as shown in Table 1.1. The efficiencies of industrialization and modern technology, as well as the passage of child labor laws, removed most children from the workforce and placed them in schools by the early 1900s. Other factors—the Great Depression in the 1930s, a shift away from agriculture to industry, a resulting increase in educational requirements for employment, a demographic shift from rural to urban, and the growth of compulsory school attendance laws—extended this workplace-to-school transition to teens by the 1940s. The National Center for Education Statistics indicates a 72 percent increase in the population of the United States from 1900 to 1940, while the number of high school graduates in the same period increased by more than 1,700 percent (Gopel, 2005). The middle school movement in the 1980s resulted in the inclusion of middle-graders in the definition of young adult.

Of course, young people read and enjoyed books long before there was a body of literature labeled "young adult." Classics such as Emily Brontë's *Wuthering Heights* (1847), Charles Dickens' *Great Expectations* (1861), Jonathan Swift's *Gulliver's Travels* (1726), Jules Verne's *Journey to the Center of the Earth* (1864), and Mark Twain's *The Adventures of Tom Sawyer* (1876) and *The Adventures of Huckleberry Finn* (1884) may have been written for adults, but young people enjoyed them too. After the establishment of juvenile divisions in publishing houses in the 1920s and 1930s, a few noteworthy books such as *Seventeenth Summer* by Maureen Daly (1942) and *The Catcher in the Rye* by J. D. Salinger (1951) were precursors to today's young adult books, although librarians shelved them with books for adults at the time.

Although the forerunners of the young adult book began to appear in the mid-1800s, an emphasis on studying adult classic works of literature in high school dominated the twentieth century, delaying the development of young adult literature. Some of the early important works of young adult literature were published in the late 1960s and early 1970s, but this first flowering of young adult literature was diminished by the simultaneous publication of a plethora of books in which problems overpowered character development and plot. These gloomy problem novels were responsible for a widespread notion that young adult books were categorically poor quality.

In the liberal political climate of the 1960s and 1970s many topics previously considered taboo for young adults (e.g., sex, drug abuse, war, suicide, and pregnancy) were addressed head-on by pioneering young adult authors of contemporary fiction, establishing the first golden age of young adult literature. In response, the number of censorship attempts on books rose steadily throughout the 1970s and 1980s. Nevertheless, due in part

Table 1.1   Milestones in the Concepts of Adolescence and Young Adult Literature

Date/Era	Event	Significance
1892	Formation of the Committee of Ten (mainly presidents of well-known universities)	Promotion of the study of English and literature in high school; established a university-influenced high school canon of classics by basing college entrance exams on knowledge of these books
Early 1900s	Growth of the middle class and educational institutions	Positive view by adults of obedience, self-restraint, dependency, conformity in youth
1904	*Adolescence* by G. Stanley Hall	First formal description of adolescence as a distinct psychological state
1911	National Council of Teachers of English established	Early effort to broaden English curricula beyond the classics to meet the needs of a diverse, democratic society
1920s	Children's divisions established by many publishing houses	Indication of widespread acceptance of the importance of books for young people
1930s	The Great Depression (1929–early 1940s)	Encouragement of teenagers without work to go to high school
1957	Young Adult Services Division established by the American Library Association (now called Young Adult Library Services Association—YALSA)	Recognition of the distinction between childhood and young adulthood and the books appropriate to each group
1960s–1970s	Civil rights and women's liberation movements; more permissive social and sexual climate	Encouragement of books by and about minorities and females and books on topics previously considered taboo for youth
1970s	Publication of many excellent YA books	First golden age of YA literature
1973	Adolescent Literature Assembly of NCTE (ALAN) established	Forum for discussion and advocacy of reading YA books in middle/high schools
1988	Margaret A. Edwards Award established	Acknowledgment of authors for their lifetime achievement in writing YA books popular over a period of time
2000	Michael L. Printz Award for Excellence in Young Adult literature established	National recognition of YA literature as a worthy body of literature

Early Important Works of Young Adult Contemporary Fiction

Date	Literary Work	Significance
1967	*The Outsiders* by S. E. Hinton	Herald of realistic young adult novel; considered by many to be the prototypical young adult book
1967	*The Contender* by Robert Lipsyte	YA book with African-American protagonist
1968	*The Pigman* by Paul Zindel	YA book well received by critics; counters the argument that this literature is poor quality
1969	*My Darling, My Hamburger* by Paul Zindel	One of the first YA novels to address abortion
1970	*Are You There, God? It's Me, Margaret* by Judy Blume	One of the first YA books to feature a frank treatment of female puberty
1971	*Go Ask Alice* by Anonymous (Beatrice Sparks)	One of the first problem novels; controversial topic of drug abuse
1972	*The Man Without a Face* by Isabel Holland	One of the first YA books on homosexuality
1972	*Dinky Hocker Shoots Smack!* by M. E. Kerr	One of the first YA books to realistically portray family dynamics
1973	*A Hero Ain't Nothin' but a Sandwich* by Alice Childress	One of the first YA books to address drug abuse
1974	*The Chocolate War* by Robert Cormier	Set a trend toward "dark" or "bleak" YA novels
1975	*Forever* by Judy Blume	Book on teenage sex challenges taboos against frank discussion of such topics in YA books
1988	*Fallen Angels* by Walter Dean Myers	Signal of growing strength of multicultural authors
1989	*Weetzie Bat* by Francesca Lia Block	One of the first crossover novels; helps open YA writing to innovation and new forms
1998–2007	Harry Potter series by J. K. Rowling	Created a generation of preteen and teen readers and cross over into pop culture and adult readers

to an increase in the number of teens in the 1990s, the field matured and came into its own with the better written, more serious, and more varied young adult books published during the last two decades.

The postmodern movement, which emerged after World War II, significantly influenced young adult literature. This movement responded to the fragmented and multimodal nature of modern society characterized by frequent changes in attitudes, styles, and knowledge. The view that everything is constantly shifting challenged the philosophy and practices of art and literature and rejected fixed ideas about the form and meaning of texts. Postmodernism brought a greater playfulness, cynicism, and unpredictability to books as authors delighted in breaking the rules of convention and giving greater power to readers. A broader range of books were accepted into the mainstream, including graphic novels, novels in verse, docudramas, and novels of mixed genres.

Although postmodern books began as a trend in adult literature, postmodern works continue to grow in number for young adults. Nikolajeva (1998) identifies the defining characteristic of postmodern literary work as genre eclecticism, writing that includes aspects of more than one genre and integrates elements of popular culture such as film and television. Postmodern literature is also characterized by narrative structures that mirror life and may not have distinct beginnings, middles, and endings; emotion-driven rather than event-driven stories; and multiple protagonists, perspectives, and narrators. Inviting readers to consider varied viewpoints on social and personal problems raises issues of equity and identity and the tensions between stability and growth as points of uncertainty, rather than as lessons to be learned—a major shift in young adult literature.

Some postmodern stories include multiple plots or realities with parallel times and places. Authors of postmodern works sometimes encourage readers to take a more active role in the storytelling by using open endings or a choice of endings that invite readers to project subsequent events or by using less authoritative narration that leaves readers to draw their own conclusions. Another interesting feature of postmodern literature is **metafiction,** or having characters or the author talk to the reader about the act of creating the literary work. This technique crosses the line between the imaginary world and real life.

The rising popularity of **crossover novels**—books read and marketed to both young adult and adult audiences—is another manifestation of the trend toward broader definitions of what constitutes young adult literature. Initially, crossover books were published for adults and then crossed over to young adult audiences. These books were often written by young authors, frequently as first novels or a collection of connected stories with protagonists in their teens or twenties who were struggling with right-of-passage issues (Cart, 2004). Recently, the opposite trend has dominated the field, and many adults in their twenties and thirties are reading young adult titles, effectively expanding the young adult market and significantly increasing sales with adults often constituting half of the reading audience for particular books. This trend is most commonly associated with fantasy, especially the Harry Potter, Twilight, and Hunger Games series, and has been accompanied by an increase in movies developed from popular young adult novels.

A developing genre, **New Adult,** is fiction aimed at the 18- to 25-year-old audience with a focus on leaving home, developing sexuality, and negotiating career and educational choices. These novels also cross over to both adult and young adult audiences.

Young adult literature is currently experiencing what many consider its second golden age with new teen imprints at major publishing houses, teen reading groups in bookstores and libraries, and many new exciting authors (Reno, 2008). The increasing sophistication and emotional maturity of adolescents and the freedom of authors to explore almost any topic or issue have led to better writing, more compelling stories, and a tremendous diversity in formats, styles, and content. The separation of teen books from children's books in bookstores and libraries and the use of social media by teens to communicate interactively with each other and with authors have propelled young adult books into the heart of pop culture with television series, movies, video games, and the internet. This golden age was influenced by the Harry Potter books, which created a passion for reading in an entire generation of readers who then moved on to other books and fantasies. The mature content of current young adult books, including sometimes graphic depictions of addiction, sexuality, and violence, has generated controversy and occasional censorship challenges as well as increased readership.

Benefits and Values of Young Adult Literature

Excellent works of young adult literature have a definite place in the lives of adolescents as a source of enjoyment and life experiences. Literature is not written to teach something, but to illuminate what it means to be human and to make accessible the most fundamental experiences of life—love, hope, loneliness, despair, fear, and belonging. Literature is the imaginative shaping of experience and thought into the forms and structures of language. Adolescents read literature to experience life and their experiences inside the world of a story challenge them to think differently about their world. They read because the books are relevant to their lives, addressing their needs and interests.

Young adult literature also has a place in the academic learning of teens in middle and high schools—as class study books in English classes, as reading material in content-area courses, and as independent reading material. Their use is not in competition with the values of classic works of literature, and, in many instances, these two bodies of literature can be used effectively in tandem.

The Value of Literature in the Lives of Young Adults

The primary benefit derived from reading excellent young adult literature is enjoyment. Good young adult books authentically portray the diverse experiences and issues of adolescence and appeal to teens because of the relevance of these books to their lives. Along with enjoyment, reading offers an escape from the pressures of school and personal problems with family or friends, especially with fantasy and humorous stories. Teens also appreciate that many of these books include a focus on sexuality and romantic interest in another person as a major or secondary theme. Young adult books have a social and emotional benefit, offering guidance, comfort, and answers to questions as teens experience romantic feelings and changing relationships.

Another benefit is the contribution of literature to personal and cultural identity. Stories connect adolescents to their past, to the roots of their cultural identities and national heritage, and to the general human condition. When readers find themselves and their families and communities within books, they can explore the multiple connections of their identities, including race, ethnicity, nationality, gender, religion, language, disability, region, family structures, and social class, as well as consider new possible identities in their process of becoming. Books are also the repositories of culture. Knowing the literature, characters, and expressions that are part of the cultural heritage of adolescents allows them to become culturally literate.

Literature based on actual events in the past helps adolescents gain a greater appreciation for what history is and for the people, both ordinary and extraordinary, who made history. By reading stories set in the past, readers can relate on a more personal level with their predecessors and the events that affected their lives. History presented in this way, because it is more interesting, is more memorable and powerful in considering what can be learned from past mistakes.

Literature encourages imagination and transformation. By seeing the world around them in new ways and by considering ways of living other than their own, adolescents are encouraged to think creatively and divergently. Books can provide alternative pathways for understanding the past or imagining the future. As adolescents enter a world through stories that differ from their present, they develop imagination and are inspired to overcome obstacles, consider different perspectives, and formulate personal goals. They transform their understandings of the possibilities for themselves and the world. Often, characters are placed in situations that require them to make difficult life decisions. As the story unfolds and the consequences of characters' choices become apparent, readers can critically consider their decisions and develop their own moral concepts and values.

Literature also offers information and wisdom and so combines the heart and mind, reason and emotion. Informational books provide factual knowledge, whereas fiction and poetry offer insights into life along with information. When a story is so convincingly written that readers feel as though they have lived through an experience or been in that place and time, that book has given them a valuable personal experience beyond the constraints of their current lives. These experiences encourage adolescents to view situations from perspectives other than their own. As they come to see the world around them in new ways and consider ways of living other than their own, adolescents increase their ability to think critically and to better understand the different ways people live.

Literature encourages understanding and empathy through gaining an appreciation of the universality of human needs across history and culture, which makes it possible for adolescents to understand what connects us as human beings as well as what makes each of us unique. Living someone else's life through a story can encourage a sense of social justice and a greater capacity to empathize with others. All readers can benefit from stories that involve them in the lives of characters who struggle with disabilities, politics, or difficult circumstances or whose lives differ because of culture or geography. Literature thus plays an essential role in building intercultural understanding as adolescents immerse themselves in the lives and thinking of characters within global cultures.

The Value of Literature in the Academic Learning of Young Adults

Reading good literature rewards the reader academically by providing interesting relevant texts that encourage learning across all content areas. The proponents of young adult literature, however, have long encountered resistance to the use of these books in schools from administrators, high school teachers, and university professors who rely on history or science textbooks or believe that only the classics are of sufficient literary quality to be taught to young adults in English classes.

The resistance to young adult literature in high schools has been documented in multiple studies that indicate that secondary English teachers believe that young adult literature is only for struggling, reluctant readers or out-of-school recreational reading and that these books lack sophistication and literary merit (Gibbons, Dail, & Stallworth, 2006; Santoli & Wagner, 2004). High school English teachers continue to use classic, canonical works for whole-class instruction, relying on their own experiences in reading these same classics in high school and college and standing by the classics as time-tested works of art. Teachers also cite the time constraints and pressures created by tests and standards and their belief that young adult books are often too controversial to use in class. Tellingly, the most positive attitudes exist among secondary teachers who have read young adult literature, with the less knowledgeable having the most negative perspectives (Stallworth, Gibbons, & Fauber, 2006).

Secondary teachers who have integrated young adult novels into their classrooms find that young adult literature is a vehicle that facilitates learning the same literary elements as found in the classics while also engaging adolescents in thought-provoking discussions and developing a desire to read (Santoli & Wagner, 2004). An analysis of a young adult book can set the stage for analysis of a classic work, and students can explore significant themes or issues across contemporary young adult literature and classics. The breadth and depth of young adult literature today are equal to any genre, with many high-quality pieces of literature that address the life themes found in the classics, but that also connect directly to the lives of adolescents.

Many classics have serious shortcomings when examined through a critical lens and as works suitable for young adults. They tend to be gender and ethnically biased against women and people of color with authors who are primarily male and white. Their language and writing styles are often difficult for adolescents to understand because of arcane expressions and convoluted syntax rarely used today. They are set in the world of the past with abstruse historical references and rarely have teens as main characters. Even if the protagonist is a younger person, the author's point of view is decidedly adult in looking back at adolescence with an adult's interpretation of events and people. Adolescents frequently find classic works difficult and frustrating to read and disconnected from their immediate lives, requiring a teacher's assistance to be understandable. Forcing a steady diet of *only* classic texts can lead to a dislike of reading and work against the goal of creating lifelong readers.

Young adult literature, in contrast, offers well-written books with everyday vocabulary, compressed plots, a limited number of characters, and a focus on a teen protagonist with issues and concerns that engage and resonate with adolescents, making these books accessible and understandable. The books reflect a range of cultural experiences and perspectives and a diversity of writing styles and formats in addition to addressing modern-day issues in the popular culture world in which teens live. Adolescents read more books and more willingly when they can choose reading materials of interest to them, and by reading more, they gain experience and become better readers.

These strengths of young adult literature provide a pathway to discovering and appreciating required classic titles in the curriculum while also creating a community of readers who develop reading habits that will carry them into adulthood. Some classics, of course, continue to hold appeal for adolescents, particularly if taught in an interesting way. In addition, some adolescents are mature beyond their years and prefer adult classic texts. The issue is not either/or but how to integrate classics and young adult literature to provide connection as well as challenge to readers.

The Value of Story in Our Lives

These values of literature for the lives and learning of adolescents are even more significant when considered within the broader frame of story as meaning-making. Stories of all kinds are woven so tightly into the fabric of our everyday lives that it's easy to overlook their significance in framing how we think about ourselves and the world. They fill every part of daily life as we talk about events and people, read books, browse online news, send text messages, listen to music, watch video clips, check in with friends on Facebook, and catch up on a favorite television show. We live storied lives.

Stories are thus much more than a book—they are the way our minds make sense of our lives and world. Stories allow us to move from the chaotic "stuff" of daily life into understanding. An endless flow of experiences surrounds us on a daily basis. We create stories to impose order and coherence on those experiences and to work out their significance (Gotschall, 2012). Stories thus provide a means of structuring and reflecting on our experiences. We tell our stories to invite others to consider our meanings and to construct their own, as well as to better understand those experiences ourselves. We listen to others' stories to try on other perspectives or ways of living in the world.

Story is a mode of knowing—one of the primary ways in which we think and construct meaning from our experiences. Our views of the world are a web of interconnected stories, a distillation of all the stories we have shared. This web of stories becomes our interpretive lens for new experiences and is culturally based. Our human need to story about our experiences may be universal, but there is no one way to tell stories. Our stories are always interwoven with the stories that exist within our own cultures both in content and in the style and structure of the telling.

We also construct stories to make sense of information. Theories can be viewed as just bigger stories. Scientists create a theory by using current information to tell a story that provides an explanation of a natural phenomenon, such as black holes. They change their stories over time as new information and perspectives become available. A story is thus a theory of something—what we tell and how we tell it reveals what we believe (Gotschall, 2012).

Story is at the heart of who we each are as human beings and who we might become. We often treat books as instructional lessons rather than recognizing their broader role as story. The values of literature for adolescents, both inside and outside of school, are interwoven with story as meaning-making.

Evaluating and Selecting Young Adult Literature

Selecting the best available materials for independent reading, literary and literacy instruction, and reading in the content areas is based in a deep knowledge of adolescents as well as books. Finding the right book is always a combination of knowing the reader and knowing the books. This intersection of books and readers develops from knowledge of the reading interests of adolescents and strategies for book selection.

Know the Reader

The best teachers know their students well, both as a group and as individuals. For those who work with adolescents this is no small challenge, since change is such a constant part of the lives of 12- to 18-year-olds and due to the tremendous diversity among adolescents.

The most apparent change is physical growth, with its accompanying awkwardness, self-consciousness, mood swings, and awakening interest in sex. Also apparent are changes in social interaction, primarily the need to be with and communicate with peers and to establish independence from parents and other adults. Less apparent at times is the development of complex and critical thinking and the ability to communicate that thinking to others.

Young adults, if presented with an array of good reading materials by teachers and librarians, are capable of making their own book choices. Peer influence can positively affect these choices through opportunities for adolescents to share their responses to books with each other. Teens who speak up about their reading exert a strong influence on their peers' decisions to select and read certain books.

Book recommendation or selection should include a consideration of students' reading abilities and purpose for reading. Books selected for whole-class assigned reading need to fit many students' needs, interests, and reading levels, keeping in mind that even the most able students who are forced to read uninteresting, irrelevant materials often stop reading voluntarily (Strommen & Mates, 2004). Students reading independently usually fare best with materials that are at or slightly below their reading ability, but keen interest in a topic enables them to read and understand difficult materials.

Another consideration is the experience and maturity of readers. Individual differences and the influence of home, community, and school lead to great variances in maturity within any classroom. For this reason, selections of reading material for whole-class use might be based on the general maturity of a particular group of students, but selections for independent reading material should be determined by an individual's maturity. For example, the treatment of war in Rosemary Wells's *Red Moon at Sharpsburg* (2007) and Margi Preus's *Shadow on the Mountain* (2012) is appropriate for middle-grade classes, but the more graphic treatment of war in Walter Dean Myers's *Sunrise over Fallujah* (2008) and Elizabeth Wein's *Code Name Verity* (2012) is more appropriate for class reading in high school or independent reading for a younger but more mature student.

A person's interests are one of the most powerful forces in motivating reading. Teens' interests, both as a group and individually, are highly diverse and change rapidly, so assessment of student interests must be done regularly to be effective. The first consideration in helping adolescents select books should be the topics they find interesting, particularly for resistant readers. Anderson, Shirey, Wilson, and Fielding (1987) reported the results of four experimental studies where interest accounted for *30* times as much variance in sentence recall as text readability. They also reviewed other studies on interest and concluded that whether or not students find materials interesting had a strong and pervasive effect on learning. Knowledge of adolescents' friends, social activities, skills, and hopes or plans for the future are considerations in recommending books.

Reading interest, reading preference, and reading choice studies provide useful information to those who purchase books or encourage young adults to read. Generally, a reading interest study suggests a feeling one has toward particular reading material; a reading preference implies making a choice from two or more options; a reading choice study investigates the materials that adolescents select and read from a predetermined collection. These studies do not always provide an opportunity for students to express their interests. If, for example, the study does not include graphic novels or dystopias, then students will not be able to select those books as an interest. Although the findings from this body of research can be useful, the results are based on group data or aggregated data and reflect the interests of groups of students, not individuals.

Common sense tells us that adolescents will apply themselves more vigorously to read something they are interested in than something they find uninteresting or boring. Interest generates motivation and engagement, so knowing the reading interests of adolescents makes a difference (Hale & Crowe, 2001). Many studies of adolescent reading interests have been conducted over the past 40 years, indicating the following patterns in reading interests:

- Mysteries and scary stories/horror have a high appeal for many adolescents.
- Adolescent males prefer nonfiction, adventures, sports, and science fiction/fantasy.
- Adolescent females prefer romances and realistic stories, especially novels that connect to their life experiences and that convey the characters' feelings.
- Books of any genre that reflect familiar teen experiences and concerns are a strong draw.
- Recent book sales indicate strong interest in fantasy and dystopias, particularly series books.
- Recent publications are of much higher appeal than older titles.

Research studies continue to show gender differences in reading interests which may be connected to differences in emotional and developmental needs as well as to societal gender expectations. Reading books is considered a female rather than male activity, with boys responding on surveys that they are not reading when, in fact, they are reading a lot of nonfiction and internet materials, but not what they consider "books," which they define as fiction (Hopper, 2005). Another related trend is that females increasingly identify themselves as readers and as valuing reading as they move from middle school through high school, while males' sense of themselves as readers and as valuing reading decreases (Pitcher et al., 2007).

Adolescents are highly influenced by prior knowledge of an author or enjoyment of a particular author's style and often have a favorite genre or author that they search out over and over. They also choose books that their peers have enjoyed and which allow them to claim cultural membership within their peer group. Certain books become part of popular culture with many references integrated within peer talk and so become important referent points and status markers. Adolescents who engage in regular interactions around books with members of their social circles are most likely to see themselves as readers—reading becomes part of their social life (Strommen & Mates, 2004).

Beyond topic or genre, certain characteristics of books are significant for adolescent readers. The patterns across studies (Worthy, Moorman, & Turner, 1999; Smith & Wilhelm, 2002) indicate the appeal of:

- Visual texts, including illustrated books, picture book, comic books, and graphic novels
- Cover illustrations that include teens and provide a context for the content of the book
- Adolescent protagonists that are the age of the reader or slightly older
- Fast-paced and humorous stories
- Books based on movies and television

Identifying the reading interests of resistant readers is particularly significant in order to invite them to move beyond their active avoidance of any reading engagement. Less research has been conducted on the reading materials preferred by resistant adolescent readers, but educators have written about their work (Worthy, Patterson, Salas, Prater, & Turner, 2002; Beers, 2003), indicating that resistant adolescent readers are interested in books with the following characteristics:

- Short books or longer books that have short chapters or sections
- Lots of white space in books; fewer words per page; easy-to-read typeface and font size
- Books with illustrations, photographs, or sketches
- Books *after* seeing the movies
- Comic books and graphic novels or books with comic book—style illustrations
- Series books, especially horror, mystery, or adventure plots

Characteristics of fiction that appeal to, and support, resistant readers include:

- Rapid introduction to main characters with only a few (two to four) characters, each with one name used consistently and each character well delineated
- Characters whose experiences and cultural backgrounds seem similar to their own
- Quick start to the story with action beginning on the first or second page to hook the reader
- Fast pace throughout; less introspection and rumination by characters
- Gripping, memorable stories with emotional impact, especially with a focus on teens' concerns
- Single narrator or single point of view
- Episodic plots or progressive chronological plots that can be easily followed
- Familiar settings that need little description or settings described briefly or shown through illustrations to avoid lengthy descriptions of setting that slow down the pace of the story
- Dialogue with realistic everyday teen talk

Characteristics of nonfiction that appeal to, and support, resistant readers include:

- Heavily illustrated books such as Dorling Kindersley's Eyewitness books
- Trivia books such as the *Guinness Book of World Records,* sports statistics books, and joke books
- Biographies of celebrities, actors, pop musicians, and sports figures
- Game system guides for video and computer games
- Books and magazines about cars, sports, teen advice, and other current topics

Although reading interest research studies report what groups of students like, individual interests often differ from these descriptions. These suggestions of topics and characteristics provide a starting point in collecting and presenting books to groups of adolescents, but do not indicate the interests of a specific adolescent.

Know the Books

Teachers and librarians who are well-read and current with young adult literature are more likely to be able to suggest books that will be of interest to students. Sharing information about books with colleagues, being familiar with notable young adult authors, and reading book reviews are ways to learn about good books. Teachers and librarians will, of course, want to have read any book they plan to use as reading or teaching material with a class.

Knowing the major authors writing for young adults and having a general idea of the kinds of books they write can help a teacher or librarian make good book suggestions. Knowing something interesting about the author—that John Green was a chaplain at a children's hospital and has a funny, frenetic vlog with his brother, or that Libba Bray was in a serious car accident at age 18 that required the reconstruction of her face and that she sings in Tiger Beat, an all-YA author rock band—can motivate a person to read that author's books. Each genre chapter in this text provides a list of notable authors as a starting point to get to know the major authors in the field of young adult literature.

Several book award programs have been established for the purposes of elevating and maintaining the quality of books for young people and for honoring authors whose work is judged by experts in the field to have the greatest literary merit. These award lists can be used as resources for selecting excellent works to share with young adults. Appendix A contains lists of winners of the following major national awards for books for young people:

- *Michael L. Printz Award for Excellence in Young Adult Literature*
- *National Book Award for Young People's Literature* (outstanding literary merit, U.S. author)
- *Newbery Medal* (author of most distinguished contribution in the United States)
- *Sibert Award* (authors and illustrators of distinguished information books in the United States)
- *Orbis Pictus Award* (excellence in writing of nonfiction for young people)
- *YALSA Award for Excellence in Nonfiction for Young Adults* (best nonfiction for young adults)
- *Carnegie Medal* (author of most outstanding book in the United Kingdom)
- *Boston Globe–Horn Book Award* for text (author of poetry or fiction)
- *The Governor General's Literary Award* for text (author of outstanding literature in Canada)
- *Book of the Year for Older Readers Award* (author of outstanding literature in Australia)
- *Coretta Scott King Award* for writing (African-American author)
- *Pura Belpré Award* for writing (Latino author with Latino-themed book)
- *Mildred L. Batchelder Award* (American publisher of an outstanding translated book)
- *Margaret A. Edwards Award* (author's lifetime achievement for young adult books over time)
- *Phoenix Award* (author of a book first published 20 years earlier)

Journals that review young adult literature are an important source of current titles. In addition, these journals contain articles discussing effective strategies for incorporating literature into reading and content-area instruction and for bringing young adults and books together. Each of these publications offers evaluative annotations and age-level recommendations. Review journals that cover the full spectrum of literature from baby books to adult books are not included here:

- *The ALAN Review,* three issues/year, Assembly on Literature for Adolescents, National Council of Teachers of English
- *English Journal,* six issues/year, NCTE
- *The Horn Book Magazine,* six issues/year, Horn Book, Inc.
- *Journal of Adolescent and Adult Literature,* eight issues/year, International Reading Association
- *School Library Journal,* 12 issues/year, Reed Elsevier Inc.
- *Voices from the Middle,* four issues/year, NCTE
- *VOYA–Voice of Youth Advocates,* six issues/year, Scarecrow Press

Annual book lists are developed by library and education organizations and are accessible online. Notable among these related to young adult literature are:

- Best Books for Young Adults, American Library Association (www.ala.org)
- Teachers' Choices, International Reading Association (www.reading.org)
- Alex Award List (books written for adults that appeal to teens), American Library Association (www.ala.org)

Massive amounts of buzz precede the publication of many young adult books, with authors reading the first chapter of an anticipated novel on their blogs and releasing book trailers on YouTube. Teens stay on top of trends at sites like Young Adult Book Central (www.yabooks central.com) and readergirlz (www.readergirlz.com). Teachers and librarians tap into anticipated new books at sites like Reading Rants! (www.readingrants.org) and Guys Lit Wire (http://guyslitwire.blogspot.com).

Know Readers and Books to Examine Text Complexity

The readability and conceptual difficulty of books is another variable in selecting books to meet the reading needs of students and involves knowledge of both readers and text. *Readability* is an estimate of a text's difficulty based on its vocabulary (common versus uncommon words) and sentence structure (short, simple sentences versus long, complex sentences). *Conceptual difficulty* examines the complexity of ideas in the book and how these ideas are presented. Symbolism and lengthy description contribute to the complexity of ideas, just as the use of flashbacks contributes to the complexity of plot presentation.

The reading levels of adolescents differ greatly, making it important to provide materials of varying difficulty. Being able to assess the difficulty of reading materials is helpful; however, for independent reading, adolescents should be encouraged to read books of interest to them regardless of level, so long as they can comprehend the material and want to read it. As adults, we would not appreciate our reading being determined by others who decide that a book is too easy or difficult for us. Adolescent selections for personal reading are balanced with teachers' selections of complex texts for instructional purposes.

The Common Core State Standards (CCSS) focus attention on **text complexity** and the need for students to engage with texts that gradually increase in difficulty of ideas and textual structures. This focus on rigor in reading is based on the goal that students understand the level of texts necessary for success in college and careers by the time they graduate from high school (Fisher, Frey, & Lapp, 2012). Text complexity is determined by consideration of three dimensions in the CCSS (National Governors Association Center for Best Practices and Council of Chief State School Officers, 2010).

1. **Qualitative Dimensions of Text Complexity**—Informed decisions by teachers and librarians about the difficulty of a text based on their judgments about the influences of these aspects on a specific reader:

   a. **Levels of Meaning and Purpose.** Determining greater or less complexity based on how many layers of meaning are in the text and whether the purpose of the text is implicit or clearly stated.

   b. **Structure.** Examining if the text is organized around a simple, well-marked, and conventional structure that readers will quickly recognize or a structure that is unusual and seldom used, such as flashbacks or complex graphics.

   c. **Language Conventionality and Clarity.** Examining whether the text uses clear, literal, contemporary language or relies on figurative, ambiguous, archaic, academic, or unfamiliar language.

   d. **Knowledge Demands.** Evaluating assumptions about the types of life experiences and cultural or content knowledge that readers will bring to a text.

2. **Quantitative Dimensions of Text Complexity**—Computerized readability formulas that rate a text on word familiarity, word length, and sentence length, based on the assumption that unfamiliar words, long words, and long sentences increase complexity.

   a. CCSS recommends the lexile framework (www.lexile.com; Schnick, 2000), but notes that this framework does not provide accurate levels for poetry and complex narrative fiction for young adults.

3. **Reader and Task Considerations Related to the Texts**—Considering the fit between a text and a specific reader who is engaging in a particular task with that text.

   a. **Experiences and strategies of the reader** including cognitive abilities, motivation, interest, knowledge, and experiences.

   b. **Task** that the reader is asked to engage in with a particular text.

Considering all three dimensions of text complexity instead of relying only on quantitative leveling of texts, such as the lexile levels, is essential. Readability formulas may be helpful in selecting books, but they have drawbacks because they do not factor in prior knowledge or interest in a topic. The formulas also have difficulty measuring conceptual difficulty, the complexity of the ideas in a book and how these ideas are presented. Symbolism, abstraction, and figurative language contribute to the complexity of ideas, just as nonlinear plots or shifting points of view contribute to the complexity of the plot. *Skellig* (Almond, 1999) is a novel of magical realism in which two children become involved with an otherworldly being hidden in a garage. The text has easy vocabulary and short sentences with a readability of around grade 3.5. Yet the concepts of spirituality, faith, and prejudice cast the conceptual level of this novel at a higher level, making it more appropriate for students who are 11–15 years old, depending on the background of the specific student. John Stenbeck's *Grapes of Wrath* (1939) scores at a second- to third-grade level on quantitative measures because of the use of dialogue with familiar words and short sentences. The many layers of meaning and mature themes indicate that this book is meant for grades 6 and above. Information on readability can be found through online databases that list lexile reading levels.

The CCSS include a list of Text Exemplars consisting of stories, drama, poetry, and informational texts at each grade level. Excerpts from these texts are provided to help educators explore text complexity. This list of texts is *not* intended as a core reading list for all students; instead these texts are provided as exemplars for teachers to use in understanding text complexity so they can make more effective selections. Students should not be restricted to reading only the books on these lists since many are dated and do not reflect the multicultural or global nature of the world.

Balance and Variety in Book Selections

The balance and variety of books influences the potential academic benefits of literature as well as addresses the wide range of reading interests and abilities among young adults. Many different types of books, including novels, picture books for older readers, collections of short stories and poetry, graphic novels, books of plays, and works of nonfiction, should be available. Balance among *topics, literary forms,* and *genres of literature* is essential.

The *mood* of the books should also be varied to include stories that are sad, humorous, silly, serious, reflective, dramatic, and suspenseful. A steady diet of light, humorous books might, at first, appeal to teens, but eventually, the sameness becomes boring. Reading books with the same dominant emotion ignores the rapid change and growth in personal lives and choices that are the hallmark of young adults. Because their interests are changing, different books help them meet new challenges.

School and classroom collections need a wide range of topics with a gender balance among the main characters. A balance between male and female main characters meets the needs of adolescents and helps them more fully understand perspectives, problems, and feelings across genders. In addition, understanding and empathy for people with physical, emotional, mental, and behavioral disabilities can be gained through their portrayals in books. A positive image of people with disabilities can be conveyed, providing young adults with disabilities the opportunity to see characters like themselves in books.

The representation of people of color as main characters is also essential to presenting a realistic view of society and the world. Through well-written *multicultural literature,* adolescents can see characters from cultural backgrounds similar to their own in leading roles. Characters with whom one can identify permit a deeper involvement in literature and help adolescents understand situations in their lives. Adolescents need to see that someone from a different race, ethnic group, or religion has many of the same needs and feelings as well as come to recognize and value differences in experiences and cultural views. Literature by and about people different from oneself can develop an understanding and appreciation for difference as a resource, not a problem.

Global and international literature, literature set in nations and regions of the world, should also be included in classrooms and libraries in order to encourage the development of global understanding. Through reading books about young adults from global cultures, adolescents can gain cultural literacy on a worldwide basis and develop awareness of global issues and their responsibilities for taking action both locally and globally.

Finding this range of books and staying current with new releases involves familiarity with the major book awards and review journals as well as attending professional conferences to meet authors and illustrators and attend sessions on literature. These resources will help you locate the best in books being published as well as books that meet the specific needs and interests of the diverse group of adolescents who read young adult literature.

So Why Are Literature and Reading at Risk in Our Society?

Given the significant values of story and literature, engaging with all kinds of books for personal reading should be a valued activity in our society. Research indicates that the opposite is true and that voluntary reading is at risk. Newspaper headlines put a spotlight on illiteracy, the number of people who cannot read and write at the levels needed to function in our society, when the much bigger problem is aliteracy, the number of people who can read and choose not to. They read work-related materials, but reading books for personal purposes is not part of their lives.

Voluntary reading of literature in the United States has been monitored by the U.S. Bureau of the Census and the National Endowment for the Arts (NEA) since 1982. From 1982 to 2002, NEA reports show a steady decline in voluntary reading across all age groups in the United States, but particularly among young adults, ages 18–24. The NEA's 2008 report shows that this slide has finally reversed itself and that, for the first time in 25 years, our love of literature has been rekindled with a 7 percent rise in adults reading literature, particularly novels and short stories. Despite this slight rise, there is still cause for concern because only 50.2 percent of Americans report reading *any literature* in 2008, and only 54.3 percent read *a book* that was not related to school or work. The U.S. population now breaks into almost equally sized groups of readers and non-readers, not because the non-readers cannot read but because they are choosing not to read books, either online or in print. The NEA (2008) believes that one reason for the recent slight rise in reading is that parents, teachers, librarians, and civic leaders took action and created thousands of programs for families, schools, and communities based on publicity about the major declines in earlier reports.

The NEA's 2007 report noted that the percentage of 17-year-olds who do *not* read for pleasure doubled over a 20 year period while the amount they read for school (15 or less pages a day) stayed the same. There was also a significant decline from childhood to adolescence from 54 percent to 22 percent for those who read almost daily for pleasure. College attendance is no longer a guarantee of active reading habits with one in three college seniors reading nothing for pleasure in a given week. Our assumption is that high school and college students stop reading for personal purposes because reading becomes associated with textbooks and school work, hardly motivating reading!

On a positive note, researchers at the PEW Research Center (Zickuhr, Rainie, & Purcell, 2013) found that although Americans ages 16 to 29 are heavy technology users with almost all reporting being online, they also read and borrow printed books and value libraries. Readers in this age group report increased use of e-books (25 percent), but their print reading remains steady. They access the online services of libraries and are just as likely as older adults to visit the library, borrow print books, browse the shelves, and use research data-bases. They are also more likely to ask for assistance from librarians and express the need for separate teen hangout spaces in libraries.

The NEA 2007 report details the consequences of the loss of reading for pleasure, not-ing that voluntary reading correlates strongly with academic achievement in reading and that proficient readers have more financially rewarding jobs and opportunities for career growth. Literary readers are three times more likely than non-readers to visit museums, attend plays or concerts, and create artwork, and twice as likely to exercise, volunteer, and vote. Print reading, in contrast to online reading, allows for more of the focused attention and contemplation that is essential to complex communication and insight. The greater academic, professional, and civic benefits associated with higher levels of leisure reading and reading comprehension point to the potential significance of young adult literature in the lives of adolescents.

Books do change lives for the better, and so *you* need to be a reader to engage adoles-cents as readers. Some of you are likely to be among those college students who stopped reading for pleasure due to the lack of relevance in teacher-selected reading materials, dull textbooks, boring instructional practices, lack of time, peer pressure, past failures, a pref-erence for electronic media, and a perception of reading as hard work. Due to the heavy load of coursework, textbook reading, and assigned literature, you may be more likely to watch television or surf the internet, activities that require passive participation, when you have free time. One of our goals is that you re-discover the joys of reading for pleasure and insight through reading lots of young adult books—online and in print, graphic novels, and novels in verse, fantasy in new worlds, and fiction about the past, information about the world, and fiction about the struggles of daily life. If you are to immerse adolescents in reading good books that add to their lives, you need to find those books for your life as well.

As you learn *about* literature in the chapters of this textbook, be sure that you immerse yourself in interesting books. Read picture books and novels, fiction and nonfiction, stories and poems, to reclaim these values for yourself and for the adolescents with whom you will interact. We have kept this textbook concise with many invitations for you as a reader to encourage you to reclaim your reading life. We want you to experience reading as life—not school work.

 # References

Almond, D. (1999). *Skellig*. New York: Delacorte.

Anderson, R. C., Shirey, L., Wilson, P., & Fielding, L. (1987). Interestingness of children's reading material. In R. E. Snow & M. J. Farr (Eds.), *Aptitude, learning, and instruction*, Vol. 3. *Conative and affective process analysis,* pp. 287–299. Hillsdale, NJ: Erlbaum.

Anonymous. (1971). *Go ask Alice*. New York: Harper.

Beers, G. K. (2003). *When kids can't read: What teachers can do*. Portsmouth, NH: Heinemann.

Block, F. L. (1989). *Weetzie Bat*. New York: HarperCollins.

Blume, J. (1970). *Are you there, God? It's me, Margaret*. New York: Bradbury.

———. (1975). *Forever*. New York: Bradbury.

Brontë, E. (2002/1847). *Wuthering Heights*. New York: Penguin.

Cart, M. (2004). Carte blanche: What is young-adult literature? *Booklist, 101*(8), 734.

Childress, A. (1973). *A hero ain't nothin' but a sandwich.* New York: Putnam.

Cormier, R. (1974). *The chocolate war.* New York: Knopf.

Daly, M. (1942). *Seventeenth summer.* New York: Dodd, Mead.

Dickens, C. (2002/1861). *Great expectations.* New York: Penguin.

Fielding, L. G., Wilson, P. T., & Anderson, R. C. (1986). A new focus on free reading: The role of trade books in reading instruction. In T. Raphael (Ed.), *The contexts of school-based literacy,* pp. 149–160. New York: Random House.

Finders, M. J. (1999). Raging hormones: Stories of adolescence and implications for teacher education. *Journal of Adolescent & Adult Literacy, 42*(4), 252–263.

Fisher, D., Frey, N. & Lapp, D. (2012). *Text complexity: Raising rigor in reading.* Newark, DE: IRA.

Gibbons, L., Dail, J., & Stallworth, J. (2006). Young adult literature in the English curriculum today: Classroom teachers speak out. *The ALAN Review, 33*(3), 53–61.

Gopel, E. C. (Ed.). (2005). *The world almanac and book of facts.* New York: World Almanac Books.

Gottschall, J. (2012). *The storytelling animal: How stories make us human.* New York: Houghton Mifflin Harcourt.

Hale, L. A., & Crowe, C. (2001). "I hate reading if I don't have to": Results from a longitudinal study of high school students' reading interests. *ALAN Review, 28*(3), 49–57.

Hall, S. G. (1904). *Adolescence: Its psychology and its relations to physiology, anthropology, sociology, sex, crime, religion and education.* New York: Appleton.

Hinton, S. E. (1967). *The outsiders.* New York: Viking.

Holland, I. (1972). *The man without a face.* New York: Lippincott.

Hopper, R. (2005). What are teenagers reading?: Adolescent fiction reading habits and reading choices. *Literacy, 39*(3), 113–120.

Kerr, M. E. (1972). *Dinky Hocker shoots smack!* New York: Harper.

Lipsyte, R. (1967). *The contender.* New York: HarperCollins.

McMullan, M. (2004). *How I found the strong.* Boston: Houghton.

Myers, W. D. (2008). *Sunrise over Fallujah.* New York: Scholastic.

National Endowment for the Arts. (2007). *To read or not to read: A question of national significance.* Research Division Report #47. Washington, DC: Author.

National Endowment for the Arts. (2008). *Reading on the rise: A new chapter in American literacy.* Retrieved from www.arts.gov/research/ Research_brochures.php.

National Governors Association Center for Best Practices & Council of Chief School Officers. (2010). *Common Core State Standards for English language arts and literacy in history/ social studies, science and technical subjects.* Washington, DC: Authors. http://www. corestandards.org/.

Nikolajeva, M. (1998). Exit children's literature? *The Lion and the Unicorn, 22*(2), 221–236.

Pitcher, S., Albright, L., DeLaney, C., Walker, N., Seunarinesingh, K., Mogge, S., et al. (2007). Assessing adolescents' motivation to read. *Journal of Adolescent & Adult Literacy, 59*(5), 378–396.

Preus, M. (2012). *Shadow on the mountain.* New York: Amulet.

Reno, J. (2008, May 13). Generation R (R is for reader). *Newsweek.*

Rosen, H. (1986). *Stories and meanings.* London: NATE.

Rosenblatt, L. (1978). *The reader, the text, the poem.* Carbondale: Southern Illinois University.

Salinger, J. D. (1951). *The catcher in the rye.* New York: Little, Brown.

Santoli, S., & Wanger, M. (2004). Promoting young adult literature: The other "real" literature. *American Secondary Education, 33*(1), 65–75.

Schnick, T. (2000). *The lexile framework: An introduction for educators.* Durham, NC: MetaMetrics.

Smith, M., & Wilhelm, J. (2002). *Reading don't fix no Chevys: Literacy in the lives of young men.* Portsmouth, NH: Heinemann.

Steinbeck, J. (1939). *The grapes of wrath.* New York: Viking.

Stallworth, J., Gibbons, L., & Fauber, L. (2006). It's not on the list: An exploration of teachers' perspectives on using multicultural literature. *Journal of Adolescent & Adult Literacy, 49*(6), 478–489.

Strommen, L. T., & Mates, B. F. (2004). Learning to love reading: Interviews with older children and teens. *Journal of Adolescent & Adult Literacy, 48*(3), 188–200.

Swift, J. (2003/1726). *Gulliver's travels.* New York: Penguin.

Twain, M. (2002/1876). *The adventures of Tom Sawyer.* Berkeley: University of California Press.

———. (2001/1884). *The adventures of Huckleberry Finn.* Berkeley: University of California Press.

Verne, J. (1995/1864). *Journey to the center of the earth.* New York: Random.

Wein, E. (2012). *Code Name Verity.* New York: Hyperion.

Wells, R. (2007). *Red moon at Sharpsburg.* New York: Viking.

Worthy, J., Patterson, E., Salas, R., Prater, S., & Turner, M. (2002). "More than just reading": The human factor in reaching resistant readers. *Reading Research and Instruction, 41*(2), 177–202.

Worthy, J., Moorman, M., & Turner, M. (1999). What Johnny likes to read is hard to find in school. *Reading Research Quarterly, 34*(1), 12–27.

Zickuhr, K., Rainie, L., & Purcell, K. (2013). *Younger American's library habits and expectations.* Washington, DC: PEW Research Center. http://libraries.pewinternet.org/2013/06/25/younger-americans-library-services/.

Zindel, P. (1968). *The pigman.* New York: Harper.

———. (1969). *My darling, my hamburger.* New York: Harper.

Chapter Two

Learning about Literature

An understanding of how literary elements relate to young adult literature can heighten awareness of literary criticism and provide a vocabulary for expressing responses to books. Literary terms can also be tools that adolescents use to initiate and sustain conversations about literature. By using these terms in your interactions with adolescents, you support them in acquiring a literary vocabulary. An exploration of these literary elements, however, is based in a particular stance about reading and studying young adult literature with adolescents.

The Study of Young Adult Literature

The scholarly study of literature generally focuses on the meaning found in a work of literature and how readers construct that meaning. When readers subject a work to deep analysis through exact and careful reading, it is referred to as *new criticism* or *structural criticism.* In this approach, the analysis of the words and structure of a work is the focus; the goal is to find the "correct" interpretation. Until the 1960s structural criticism dominated middle and high school literature classrooms, and many teachers continue to use this method today. Often teachers using this approach take the view that there is one correct interpretation of any work of literature and so reading is a process of taking from the text only what was put there by the author. The success of young adult readers with any work of literature is determined by how closely their interpretations match the "authorized" interpretation. Students' responses to literature are thus limited to naming (or guessing) the "right" answers to teachers' questions.

Many of you experienced this approach as students and know the frustration and apathy that can result from trying to replicate the teacher's interpretation. You may have even been one of many readers who did not bother with reading the actual book and instead consulted CliffsNotes study guides. Structural approaches do not encourage adolescents to see reading as relevant to their lives outside of school or help them develop confidence in their abilities to construct meaning from a book or connect those meanings to their lives. Often these experiences are so painful that adolescents stop reading books other than to meet school assignments.

Louise Rosenblatt introduced *reader response theory* or the *transactional view of reading* in 1938. She asserted that what the reader brings to the reading act—his or her world of experience, personality, and current frame of mind—is just as important in interpreting the text as what the author writes. Reading is thus a fusion of text and reader. Consequently, any text's meaning will vary from reader to reader and, indeed, from reading to reading of the same text by the same reader. Most of us have experienced reading a book only to discover that a friend has reacted to or interpreted the same book quite differently. Rosenblatt (1978) points out that the text of any book guides and constrains the interpretation that is made, but that a range of personal interpretations are valid and desirable as long as readers can support an interpretation by citing evidence from their lives and the text. Once young adults have made a personal connection, they are more likely to be interested in pursuing a more in-depth analysis of a text.

Readers bring connections from their worlds of experience to a book, including (1) knowledge of various genres and literary forms gained from previous reading that help them understand new, similar books; (2) social relationships that help them understand and evaluate characters' actions and motivations; (3) cultural knowledge that influences their attitudes toward self and others and their responses to story events; and (4) knowledge of the world or topic that can deepen readers' understanding of a text and enrich their response (Beach & Marshall, 1990). Reader response theory, in accepting different interpretations of the same literary work, accommodates both traditional, genre-specific works and genre-eclectic, nonlinear, postmodern literature with its multiple perspectives and plots and demands on the reader to act as coauthor. This coauthorship is based on what the reader brings to the text and interprets from the text, in essence, creating a new text from the one produced by the published author.

Another aspect of Rosenblatt's theory is her focus on the importance of the stance that readers choose related to their purpose for reading. Efferent reading focuses on taking knowledge or information from the text, while aesthetic reading involves living through a literary experience and immersing yourself within the world of the story. Whether people read efferently or aesthetically depends on what they are reading (e.g., a want ad versus a mystery novel) and why they are reading (e.g., for information versus for pleasure). Many teachers encourage an efferent stance toward literature by asking questions on specific details or literary devices, and readers are so preoccupied with reading for those details that they fail to engage with or understand the story itself.

Reading is a fusion of text and reader, so each reading of a particular literary work results in a different transaction. Even a rereading by the same reader will result in a different experience. Rosenblatt (1985) argues that, although the notion of a single correct reading of a literary work is rejected, some readings are more defensible than others once the group has agreed upon certain criteria for evaluating interpretations. Although each reading of a given literary work will be personal and distinct, there are a range of certain generally-agreed-upon interpretations of that work by a community of educated readers. Chapter 10 provides a detailed discussion with suggestions of literature-response engagements, and each genre chapter includes criteria for the evaluation and assessment of that genre.

Many educators fear that the focus on close reading in the Common Core State Standards will result in a return to the painful interrogation of texts to get the "right" interpretation. The authors of the standards seem to have a limited understanding of reader response theory, as only involving personal connections and not recognizing that Rosenblatt argued that personal connections are essential but never sufficient. After sharing initial personal connections, readers are encouraged to examine and challenge their responses with other readers and engage in close reading of both themselves and the text for evidence related to their interpretations. Discussions of the following elements of fiction can provide a vocabulary for this close reading, but should not negate the importance of first sharing personal connections before analyzing how these elements influenced their interpretation of a text.

Elements of Fiction

Learning to evaluate books can best be accomplished by reading as many excellent books as possible. Gradually, your judgment on the merits of individual books will improve. Discussing your responses to these books with students, teachers, and your classmates and listening to their responses will also assist you in becoming a more appreciative critic. Understanding the different parts, or elements, of a piece of fiction and how they work together can help you to become more analytical about literary works and so improve your judgment of literature. A discussion of the elements of poetry is included in Chapter 7, "Poetry," and the elements of nonfiction are included in Chapter 6, "Nonfiction: Biography and Informational Books." The various elements of fiction are discussed separately in the following sections, but it is the unity of all these elements that produces a story.

Plot

The events of a story and the sequence in which they are told constitute the *plot,* what happens in the story. Plot is an important element of fiction to those who want to find excitement in the books they read. A good plot produces conflict to build excitement and suspense to keep the reader involved.

The nature of the *conflict* within the plot can arise from different sources. The basic conflict may be one that occurs within the main character, called *person-against-self.* In this type of story, the main character struggles against inner drives and personal tendencies to achieve some goal. Stories about adolescence will frequently have this conflict as the basis of the story problem. For example, in *Aristotle and Dante Discover the Secrets of the Universe* (2012) by Benjamin Alire Sáenz, 15-year-old Aristotle struggles to know and accept himself and others.

A conflict usually found in survival stories is the struggle of the main character with forces of nature. This conflict is called *person-against-nature.* In *Monument 14* (2013) by Emmy Laybourne, the main characters struggle to survive disasters that are plaguing the earth.

In other stories, the source of the conflict is found between two characters. Conflicts with peers, sibling rivalries, and rebellion against an adult are examples of *person-against-person* conflicts. For example, in *Bucking the Sarge* (2004) by Christopher Paul Curtis, 15-year-old Luther's conflict is with his mother, whose views on right and wrong collide with his own.

Some young adult books present the main character in conflict with society, such as preventing environmental destruction, surviving in an increasingly corporate culture, or coping with political upheaval and war. This conflict is called *person-against-society.* In the historical novel *Traitor* (2010) by Gudrun Pausewang and Rachel Ward, protagonist Anna hides a Russian soldier from her German family and neighbors during World War II. Another example is the thriller *So Yesterday* (2004) by Scott Westerfeld, in which the consumer culture is exposed. Futuristic dystopias, such as *The Hunger Games* (2010) by Suzanne Collins, also create this type of conflict.

In some stories the protagonist faces *multiple conflicts* in which a character may be in conflict with society as well as with other persons. In L. J. Adlington's science fiction novel *Cherry Heaven* (2008), characters are in conflict with the dystopian society in which they find themselves and also in conflict with the former owners of that world as well as with their own inner struggle.

Plots are constructed in many different ways. The most usual structures found in young adult novels are *chronological plots,* which cover a particular period of time and relate the events in order within the time period. For example, if a book relates the events of one week, then Monday's events will precede Tuesday's, and so on. *Lizzie Bright and the Buckminster Boy* (2004) by Gary D. Schmidt has a chronological plot that follows a spiral of disasters that occur when town elders force a poor community of African Americans off a Maine island in order to start a lucrative tourist trade.

There are two distinct types of chronological plots, progressive and episodic. In books with *progressive plots,* the first few chapters are the exposition, in which the characters, setting, and basic conflict are established. Following the expository chapters, the story builds through rising action to a climax. The climax occurs, a satisfactory conclusion (or dénouement) is reached, and the story ends. Figure 2.1 suggests how a progressive chronological plot might be visualized.

Figure 2.1 Diagram of a Progressive Plot

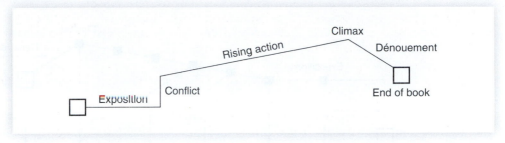

An *episodic plot* ties together separate short stories or episodes, each an entity in itself with its own conflict and resolution. These episodes are typically unified by the same cast of characters and the same setting. Often, each episode comprises a chapter, as in *The Mostly True Adventures of Homer P. Figg* by Rodman Philbrick (2009), in which each chapter is a different incident in Homer's journey to find his brother, who has been sold as a substitute solder in the Civil War. In *The Graveyard Book* by Neil Gaiman (2008), each episodic chapter is a story that traces Bod's growth from a spirited boy to a young man ready to set out into the world. Although the episodes are usually chronological, time relationships among the episodes may be nonexistent or loosely connected. Episodic plots range in complexity from humorous escapades to more dire circumstances. Readers who are new to reading full-length novels may find episodic plot novels especially appealing and easier to negotiate. Figure 2.2 suggests how a chronological episodic plot might be visualized.

With greater frequency young adult novels are appearing with new plot formulations such as *complex multiple plots,* in which the traditional chronology is replaced by nonlinear plots that occur simultaneously. In Matt de la Peña's *Ball Don't Lie* (2005), a basketball story that involves race relations, a disjointed narrative with various viewpoints alternates between past and present and can be seen as a reflection of the internal life of the protagonist. Other stories are told through a multiplicity of protagonists, each of whom has a vantage point from which to unfold some portion of the story being told. Maggie Stiefvater's *The Raven Boys* (2012) and *The Scorpio Races* (2011) both have different characters as narrators who propel the story through multiple plot lines.

Figure 2.2 Diagram of an Episodic Plot

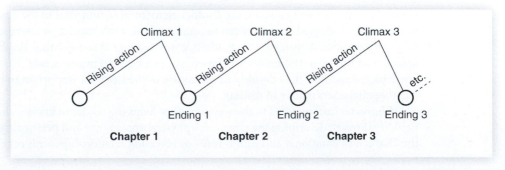

Figure 2.3 Diagram of a Flashback

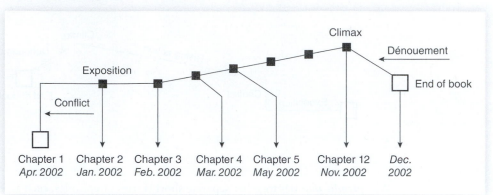

Authors use a **flashback** to convey information about earlier events in a chronological plot—for example, before the beginning of the first chapter. In this case, the chronology of events is disrupted, and the reader is taken back to an earlier time. Flashbacks can occur more than once and in different parts of a story. The use of a flashback permits authors to begin the story in the midst of the action but later fill in the background for full understanding of the present events. Such plots require a higher level of reading comprehension and can be challenging for less able readers. Teachers can help students understand this plot structure by assigning good examples of stories using flashbacks, such as Sharon Draper's *Out of My Mind* (2010), Rick Yancy's *The 5th Wave* (2013), or Libba Bray's *The Diviners* (2012). Class discussion can then focus on the sequence of events and why the author may have chosen to relate the events in this manner. Figure 2.3 illustrates the structure of a book in which some events occurred before the beginning of the book.

A plot device that prepares readers for coming events in a story is **foreshadowing.** This device gives clues to a later event, possibly even the climax of the story. Elizabeth Wein's *Rose under Fire* (2013) begins with a diary entry in which Rose reflects on the crash of a pilot who was attempting to tip a flying bomb, a foreshadowing of the events that lead to her capture by the Nazis. Authors use a range of subtle strategies to prepare readers for the outcomes of stories through foreshadowing.

Characters

Characters, the actors in a story, are another element of fiction vital to the enjoyment of a book. A well-portrayed character can become a friend, a role model, or a temporary parent to a young reader. Although young adults enjoy reading about exciting events, the characters must matter to the reader, or the events no longer seem important. How characters are depicted and how they develop in the course of the story are important to determining whether characters matter to readers.

Characterization refers to the way an author helps the reader to know a character, particularly through describing the character's physical appearance and personality. Portraying the character's emotional and moral traits or revealing relationships with other characters are subtler and more effective techniques. In the most convincing characterizations, we come to know a character through a combination of actions and dialogue, responses of other characters, and narrator descriptions.

Character development refers to the changes, good or bad, that the character undergoes during the course of events in the story. If a character experiences significant life-altering events, readers expect that the character will somehow be different as a result of those events. A character who changes in the course of the story is a known as a *dynamic character.* In Cynthia Kadohata's *Weedflower* (2009), Sumiko finds her world turned upside down when moved to a Japanese internment camp during World War II. As she learns to live in her new environment, she grows as a person and as a member of the community.

In a work of fiction for young adults, there are usually one or two main characters and some minor characters. Ideally, the main character, the *protagonist,* will be a fully described, complex individual who possesses complex good and bad traits, like a real person. Such an individual is called a *round character.* In the historical fiction novel *Code Name Verity* (2012) by Elizabeth Wein, Verity is fully present as a real person who is brave but also is afraid and makes mistakes. The character or force that is in direct opposition to the main character is called an *antagonist.* In Sara Zarr's *Story of a Girl* (2007), Tommy, the former boyfriend, a thoughtless and cruel antagonist, is shown to be vulnerable himself during the course of the story.

Minor or *secondary characters* are described less fully. The extent of description depends on what the reader needs to know about the character for a full understanding of the story. Some of the minor character's traits are described fully, whereas other facets of the character's personality may remain obscure. Because the purpose is to build the story and make it comprehensible, fragmentary knowledge of a minor character may suffice. In *Heat* (2006) by Mike Lupica, a sports novel portraying a positive image of Latino teens competing athletically, secondary character Manny is depicted as the catcher and a loyal mate to talented pitcher Michael Arroyo, the protagonist.

Occasionally, an author will insert a *flat character*—that is, a character described in a one-sided or underdeveloped manner. Although such one-dimensional people do not exist in real life, they may be justified within the story to propel the plot. Sometimes the character is shown as an all-evil or all-frivolous person; folktales, for instance, present flat characters as symbols of good and evil. In some stories, a flat character plays the role of *character foil,* a person who is in direct juxtaposition to another character (usually the protagonist) and who serves to highlight the characteristics of the other individual. A character foil may occur as a flat or a round character. For example, in Gordon Korman's *Born to Rock* (2006), Melinda, childhood friend of the protagonist, Young Republican Leo Caraway, is a flat character who makes Leo aware of the identity of his biological fathers. Melinda also serves as a character foil to Leo in her dislike of Republicans and distaste for Leo's interest in money.

The main characters in an excellent work of fiction for young adults are rounded, fully developed individuals who undergo change in response to life-altering events. Because young adults generally prefer protagonists of their age, or somewhat older, authors of books for young adults often face a dilemma. In real life, young adults usually have restricted freedom of action and decision making within the confines of a family, but a vivid exciting story requires the main characters to be "on their own." Thus, in many young adult novels, authors arrange for parents to be absent, no longer living, or nonfunctioning in the life of that teen.

Setting

The time and place(s) in which the story occurs constitute the ***setting*** of a story. The setting has a more or less important function depending on the story. In historical fiction the authentic re-creation of the period is essential to comprehension of the story's events. In this situation, the setting, fully described both in time and place, is called an ***integral setting.*** The story could not be the same if placed in another setting. For example, in the post-earthquake novel *In Darkness* (2012) by Nick Lake, the setting of Haiti is vital to the authenticity of the story.

By contrast, the setting in folktales is often vague and general. For example, "long ago in a cottage in the deep woods" is meant to convey a universal, timeless tale, one that could have happened anywhere and almost anytime except the present or very recent past. This type of setting is called a ***backdrop setting.*** It simply sets the stage and the mood. The term comes from the theater to refer to scenes performed in front of a curtain or a set painted as a generic street or forest, such as occurs in some of the scenes from Shakespeare.

Theme

The literary ***theme*** of a story is its underlying meaning or significance. The term *theme* should not be confused with *topic* or *theme* as used in the sense of a thematic unit of study. Although we sometimes think of the literary theme as the message or moral of the story, it can just as likely be an aesthetic understanding, such as an appreciation for nature, or a viewpoint on a current societal issue. To identify the theme, think about the author's purpose in writing the story, or what the author is saying through this story.

A theme is better expressed by means of a complete sentence than by a single word. For example, students often suggest survival as a theme found in *Moon over Manifest* by Clare Vanderpool (2011). A better statement of the theme is "Learning to survive takes more than independent effort." The single word *survival* may be a topic found in the story, but it is not an expression of the theme and does not encourage us to consider more complex issues of survival during the Great Depression and the role of family and community for sense of our well-being.

Readers with different life experiences may not identify the same theme, and so students may perceive the underlying meaning of a work in different ways. Indeed most layered works of literature can be argued to have multiple themes. In *Luna* (2006) by Julie Ann Peters, a reader may identify the theme as "People must be free to be themselves" or as "Life is difficult when you don't subscribe to societal norms." A statement of a theme can be a beginning point for students to discuss why they have identified a particular theme, what parts of the novel convinced them of this, and whether they agree personally with a particular theme.

Themes in young adult literature should be worthy of readers' attention and encourage consideration of moral and ethical issues. A theme must not overpower the plot and characters of the story since young adults read fiction primarily for enjoyment, not for enlightenment. Heavy-handed, obvious, and didactic themes detract from a reader's enjoyment of a story. Certainly a well-written book may convey a moral message, but it should also tell a good story from which the message emerges. The theme is thus subtly conveyed to the reader, as in Kirby Larson's *Hattie Big Sky* (2006), which demonstrates that family is not land, nor a home, but a matter of heart.

Often adults write stories not for the enjoyment of readers but to teach lessons in morality. Moralistic stories are often seen as the thinly disguised religious tracts for children and adolescents found in the 1800s, but some authors use young adult literature as a platform to preach about drug abuse, animal rights, or other contemporary issues. If the literary quality of these novels is weak, then the story and characters become secondary to the issue or problem. However, moral values embedded within the fabric of a powerful story may help readers increase their moral reasoning, develop a sense of right and wrong, and make choices for their lives.

Style

Style is the way an author tells the story and so can be viewed as the writing itself, as opposed to the content of the book. However, the style must suit the content of the story; the two are intertwined.

Different aspects of style are considered in evaluating a work of fiction. Most obviously, the **words** chosen to tell the story can be examined—are they long or short, common or uncommon, rhyming or melodic, boring and hackneyed or rich and challenging, impassive or emotional, standard dialect or regional minority dialect? The words should be appropriate to the story being told. As an evaluator of books for young adults, consider: Why did the author choose these words? What effect was the author trying to achieve?

The **sentences** may also be considered. Do they read easily? Do they flow without the reader needing to reread to gain the meaning of the text? Sometimes an author chooses to limit the word choices to write a book that conveys the thought processes and voice of a young narrator. Such books may consequently fall within the lower range of difficulty. Yet in the hands of a gifted writer, the sentences will remain no less melodic, varied in length and structure, and enjoyable to read and hear than sentences in the best books at the highest range of difficulty. An example of a novel written in simple yet powerful language is *Your Own Sylvia* (2007), a portrait of the life of Sylvia Plath, in the form of a novel in verse by Stephanie Hemphill.

With greater frequency, new or unusual forms are appearing in young adult literature, from novels told as a movie script, as in Walter Dean Myers's *Monster* (1999); novels in the form of a diary experimenting with poetic forms, as in Ron Koertge's *Shakespeare Bats Cleanup* (2003); novels in the form of e-mails and phone calls, as in Catherine Stine's *Refugees* (2005); novels in the form of television interviews, radio transcripts, and narrated segments as in Paul Valponi's *The Final Four* (2012); and novels drawing on letters, diary entries, lists, and e-mails, as in Jaclyn Moriarity's *The Year of Secret Assignments* (2004). Styles acceptable in young adult literature have grown far beyond traditional ways of telling a story, as is evident in *Eighth Grade Is Making Me Sick* by Jennifer Holm (2012), where the entire story is told through photo-collages of poems, notes, text messages, comics, food wrappers, and other artifacts of everyday life.

The **organization** of the book may be considered by noting the paragraphs and transitions, length of chapters, headings and chapter titles, preface, endnotes, prologue, epilogue, and length of the book. For many readers chapter length is important. Shorter chapters appeal to students who read more slowly or whose attention spans are shorter. For example, Sharon Creech's *Ruby Holler* (2002) is a 310-page novel with many chapters, but each chapter is only a few pages long. The story's humorous and lighthearted mood, swift action, and quirky characters make it enjoyable for a range of readers.

Chapter titles can provoke interest, as well as provide the reader with clues to predict story events. Some books also provide the readers with a *prologue,* an introductory statement telling events that precede the start of the story. Jane Yolen's and Heidi E. Y. Stemple's *Bad Girls: Sirens, Jezebels Murderesses, Thieves, & Other Female Villains* (2013) contains an informative prologue about the female villains through the ages. They invite readers to become interested in an historical account of female felons and allowing readers to decide how bad these felons were.

Some authors include an *epilogue,* a concluding statement telling events that occur after the story has ended. In *How I Live Now* (2004), Meg Rosoff describes England during a third world war, but then in an epilogue adds a hopeful note of events taking place six years after the conclusion of the story. Occasionally, an author presents information on the sources or historical facts used in the story. In *Yellow Star* (2006), for example, Jennifer Roy places an author's note and a timeline of events in the epilogue.

Point of view is another aspect of an author's style. If the story is told through the eyes and voice of a *third-person narrator* (characterized by the use of *he, she, it*), then the reader can know whatever the narrator knows about the events of the story. In many stories, the narrator is *omniscient* and can see into the minds of all characters and be at many places at the same time. The reader of Lois Lowry's *Son* (2012) can understand and interpret the story from many different perspectives because of Lowry's use of the omniscient point of view. Other stories are narrated from the perspective of only one character in the story. In this case, the story is still told in the third person, but the reader knows only what that particular character can see and understand. This technique is called *limited omniscient* point of view. In Ron Koertge's novel, *Margaux with an X* (2004), the story is told from the viewpoint of Margaux, the cool protagonist who is attracted to uncool Danny.

Other times authors tell the story through a *first-person narrator* (the use of *I*), usually the main character of the story. In such cases the reader gains a sense of closeness to the main character but is not privy to any information unavailable to this character. Some authors have accomplished a first-person point of view by writing as though their main character were writing a diary or letters, as in *The Absolutely True Diary of a Part-time Indian* (2006) by Sherman Alexie. Occasionally, a story is told in first person through the eyes of a minor character. In *The Book Thief* (2007) by Markus Zusak, death is a character who narrates the story of a young book-lover in Nazi Germany.

A *shifting point of view* permits the reader to see events from different characters' points of view. When the point of view shifts, the author cues readers to the changing point of view, as Lynne Rae Perkins does in *Criss Cross* (2005). In this story teen friends offer their varying perspectives on life and on one another during the course of a summer in a small town. The use of several characters as protagonists is being seen more frequently in young adult literature and lends itself to displaying the various ways teenagers perceive one another in a school or social setting.

Symbolism is an artistic convention that authors use to suggest invisible or intangible meanings by analogy to something else through association, resemblance, or convention. Often a *symbol*—a person, object, or situation—represents an abstract or figurative meaning in the story in addition to its literal meaning. Some symbols are universal and can be found repeatedly in literary works; others may be particular to the story. For example, a farm often stands for love and security in works of literature. Some students may read only on a literal level, but they can be helped by teachers to note symbols in the books they are reading. If the symbolic feature recurs in the story, it is referred to as a ***motif.*** The number three is a common motif in folktales, for example.

A ***circular plot structure,*** often seen in adventure novels and quest fantasies, is a narrative device involving setting, character, and theme. Typically a protagonist ventures from home (or the starting place of the story), goes on a journey, often a dangerous one in which many challenges are overcome, and then returns home a changed person. The plot is usually chronological, with the events occurring in a setting that becomes a circle. By returning the character to the place where he started, the author can emphasize the character's growth or change while also highlighting the theme of the story. In Geraldine McCaughrean's *The Kite Rider* (2002), a son trying to save his widowed mother from a horrendous marriage departs on an adventure across China as a circus kite rider. While gaining strength from this experience, he also gains confidence and resolve from his inner journey in which he confronts his beliefs and prejudices before being reunited with his mother. This home/away/home circular structure is challenged in novels, such as *Moon over Manifest* by Clare Vanderpool (2011), where the character has a failed home or parent and abandons that home, instead of leaving a home on a journey, and so has to construct a new home, instead of returning home.

A story must be more than a plot and a character study, however; a story integrates all the elements of fiction into a pleasing whole. In drawing together these elements, authors create new worlds for their readers.

Fictional Literary Forms

In this book we address four fictional literary forms: the novel (including novels in verse), the short story, the picture book, and the graphic novel. Titles of works in these literary forms are noted as such in the list of recommended books at the end of each genre chapter. Collections of short stories are indicated by **(COL)**, picture books are coded as **(PI)**, and graphic novels are noted by **(GR)**. One current trend in novels are novels in verse, coded as **(NV)**.

Novel

The ***novel*** is an extended fictional narrative, generally in prose, with full development of characters, settings, and plots dealing with human experience. Novels have been the mainstay of the literature program in most high schools since the nineteenth century. Middle schools have included novels in the curriculum but have also relied on anthologies of short stories and poems. Novels have the advantage of being able to fully develop the context in which the story is set, the feelings of the characters, and the attitudes of society, as well as the particular events of the story, in the course of the narrative. Major characters are dynamic and rounded, and often the writer may develop multiple characters through overlapping plots while employing complex plot structures. Many young adults enjoy the greater depth, length, and complexity they find in novels, which highlight experiences most readers would not want to miss.

Novels in verse are narratives told through shortened entries that read like verse, but still give the reader a developed sense of setting, characters, and events. Novels in verse focus less on the structure or individuality of single poems that relate to each other, as found in poetry anthologies, and more on the use of the verse format to serve the structure of the novel. These novel-length narratives use different kinds of verse forms, but frequently take the form of free verse as in the groundbreaking novel in verse, Karen Hesse's *Out of the Dust* (1997). Recommended novels can be found in the lists at the end of each genre chapter, with novels in verse marked as (NV).

Short Story

The *short story* is a brief fictional narrative, generally in prose, designed to create a unified impression quickly and forcefully. A short story highlights a particular moment where change occurs, a seminal moment that changes everything so that nothing will be the same again. Short story authors have to choose the right moment and then write into that moment to pull in the reader (Mark, 1988).

The short story has long dominated literature anthologies used in middle schools, but until recently the stories included were written for an adult audience. Today many stories included in anthologies are written for young adults. Contemporary short stories can also be found in magazines for young adults, such as those found in Appendix B. The Paul A. Witty Short Story Award is given annually to an author for an original short story published for the first time in the past year in a periodical for young people. 'Zines are a newer category of media that include short stories teens enjoy and are often produced as e-publications.

In the 1980s, collections of short stories written for and about young adults began to be published. Don Gallo deserves much of the credit for this trend with his 1984 publication of *Sixteen: Short Stories by Outstanding Writers for Young Adults.* Gallo has continued to publish short stories for young adults and other anthologists, and individual writers are creating new anthologies. The best short stories grab the reader's attention with the opening lines, contain lively, readable, honest writing, and give readers something to think about while being entertaining through their focus on the lives and experiences of teens.

Short stories have many advantages for classroom use. Because of their brevity, students have time to explore a variety of topics in a short period of time. Short stories usually take 15 to 20 minutes to read aloud and are ideal for use as an introduction to a unit of study in content-area classes as well as English classes. Short stories can be used to introduce readers to diverse cultures and traditions, to explore new genres in the study of literature, and to serve as models for student writing. Short story collections are coded (COL) in the Recommended Books lists at the ends of the genre chapters.

Picture Book

The *picture book* is a profusely illustrated book in which both words and illustrations contribute to the story's meaning. In a true picture book the story would be diminished without the illustrations, and so the illustrations in picture books are considered integral or essential to the story. At one time picture books were considered appropriate only for young children, but in the 1970s picture books for older readers began to appear. These books are more sophisticated, abstract, or complex in themes and subjects and are written in response to increasingly visual modes of communication now prevalent in society. The advantages in using picture books in middle and high schools include:

- They can be used as teacher read-alouds for introductions and supplements to textbook-based units of instruction and require only a short period of time for sharing the whole text.
- They can be used in text sets (several books on the same subject) for class reading, analysis, and discussion by small groups of students.
- They can stimulate interest in a topic and provoke discussion, leading to deeper understandings of the content, as in *Show Way* by Jacqueline Woodson (2005) with illustrations by Hudson Talbott, to explore the history of African American women from slavery to the present.
- They can demonstrate applications of concepts as D. B. Johnson's *Henry Climbs a Mountain* (2003) does for the concept of civil disobedience.
- They often have factual content that reinforces or enhances that found in textbooks, as Karen Hesse's *The Cats in Krasinski Square* (2004), illustrated by Wendy Watson, does for a unit about the Holocaust by featuring the courage of two Jewish sisters, escapees of the Warsaw ghetto.

Picture books are coded (PI) in the Recommended Books lists at the end of each genre chapter.

Graphic Novel

The **graphic novel** is an extensive book-length narrative in which the text is written in speech bubbles or as captions to comic book–like illustrations. Graphic novels, an extension of earlier comic books, can be of any genre of literature and may be about any theme, topic, or subject. The term *graphic* refers to stories told through images, while *novel* refers to the length of the text regardless of content.

Graphic novels are usually written as sequential frames or panels that go across the page or from top to bottom. Panels are read for both text and picture in order to follow the action. Comics began in the United States, but the comic format also thrived in Europe and Asia. Currently, some of the most popular graphic novels include **manga,** a type of Japanese comic that began as an art form in the early nineteenth century and was influenced by comic books introduced into Japan after World War II. Manga artists typically draw in black and white with characters that frequently have enormous eyes of different shapes combined with distinctive heads of hair. Anime television, which grew out of the manga movement, became very popular in the United States among younger students and sparked young people's growing interest in manga graphic novels. Rarely seen in the United States prior to the 1990s, manga has grown in popularity and represents a new trend in young adult literature.

Graphic novels, with their reliance on illustrations and use of dialogue, can engage students who are visually oriented or struggle with more complex prose. Graphic novels combine excellent, carefully edited text with visuals that are both eye-catching and attention-grabbing, offering a new kind of interactive engagement between reader and text (Cart, 2005). They strongly appeal to a broad audience of adolescents and have greatly increased in popularity and availability.

Graphic novels are now available for all types of readers through new graphic novel imprints from mainstream publishers such as First Second (Roaring Brook Press). Noteworthy graphic novels include:

- *Maus: A Survivor's Tale* (1986) by Art Spiegelman. A Holocaust survivor's story.
- *Bone* (1995) by Jeff Smith. Action-packed adventure of power and evil in a mysterious valley.
- *Persepolis* (2003) by Marjane Satrapi. Author's childhood in Iran during the Islamic Revolution.
- *Chinese Born American* (2007) by Gene Luen Yang. Struggle with identity and belonging.
- *Drama* (2012) by Raina Telgemeier. Middle school musical produces lots of drama.

Graphic novels are coded (GR) in the Recommended Books lists at the end of each genre chapter.

Building Your Knowledge of Literature

The purpose of this text is to introduce you to literature as a discipline so that you become familiar with the genres, literary and visual elements, evaluation and selection criteria, critical issues, and resources along with reading widely from young adult books to interact with a range of authors, illustrators, poets, and titles.

A literature curriculum can be organized by genre, theme or topic, author or illustrator, literary element or device, or notable books. We have organized this text by genre to encourage you to read broadly, but within that genre structure, each chapter is organized around themes and topics and includes discussions of literary elements and lists of authors and notable books and awards.

Genre provides a context for learning about the various types of books and their characteristics, such as historical fiction, fantasy, and poetry. The goal is to expose you to a wide variety of literature and to explore the evaluation and selection criteria for excellent books within each genre.

Theme or topic focuses attention on a book's meaning. Organizing a set of books around particular themes, such as alienation and acceptance by peers or the tension of interdependence in family relationships, encourages critical thinking and in-depth consideration of issues along with more thoughtful connections across books. Organizing books by topic, such as divorce or World War II, can help students find books that interest them for independent reading but often is not as effective for in-depth discussion and inquiry. You are encouraged to explore both themes and topics within the chapters.

An ***author or illustrator*** approach involves organizing books around the people who create books and becoming familiar with their books, creative processes, and life experiences. A list of notable authors for each genre is included in the chapters, and you are encouraged to inquire into the life and work of people whose books particularly intrigue you. Excellent reference sources such as *Something about the Author* provide information about young adult authors, and many biographies and autobiographies are available, such as Walter Dean Myers's *Bad Boy: A Memoir* (2001). An author/illustrator inquiry involves reading books by particular authors or illustrators, examining their writing or artistic style and use of visual and literary elements, noting the themes they explore in their books, locating interviews or articles about their lives, books, and creative process, and exploring the ways in which their lives have influenced their books.

Literary elements and devices are another way to organize a literature curriculum and focus on the literary elements presented in this chapter. Literary devices are particular techniques used by authors for a special effect such as irony, symbolism, or parody. Each genre chapter includes evaluation and selection questions that highlight the role of particular literary elements in that genre.

Organizing around *notable books* involves an in-depth focus on award-winning books or other exemplary classic or contemporary books. The emphasis is on reading a few books closely and engaging in discussions with other readers about your personal connections and the issues you find significant in that book. You can then analyze the features that contribute to their excellence, such as their relevance to readers, unique perspectives or insights, memorable characters, or illustration style. Each chapter includes a list of recommended books for reading aloud and references to award lists that you can consult. You are encouraged to engage in literature discussions around an exemplary book or set of books for each genre to deepen your understandings and ability to evaluate literature.

The Organization of This Text

In Chapters 3 to 8, the main categories of books for young adults are defined and explained, followed by book titles recommended for reading in each of the categories. Chapters 3 to 7 focus on the literary genres, as presented in Table 2.1. The number of the chapter in which each genre of literature is discussed is noted next to the genre. For the purposes of this

Table 2.1 **Genres and Topics of Young Adult Literature**				
Fiction				
Realistic Fiction (3)	**Fantasy and Science Fiction (4)**	**Historical Fiction (5)**	**Nonfiction (6)**	**Poetry and Plays (7)**
Relationships with family and peers	Fantasy based in Folktales and Myths	Beginnings of civilization	Biographies	Lyric poems
Identity and community	Magical realism	Civilizations of the ancient world	Informational books	Narrative poems
Romance and sexuality	Supernatural and paranormal forces	Civilizations of the medieval world		Plays and readers' theatre
Challenges in life	Historical fantasy and time-warps	Emergence of modern nations		
Suspense and survival	Imagined worlds and quests	Development of industrial society		
Sports	Science fiction	World wars in the twentieth century		
		Post–World War II		

textbook, a genre organization, a traditional, though admittedly imperfect, way of grouping literature, is the most practical way to help you make balanced choices in your reading and to demonstrate the wide spectrum of ideas and emotions that can be found in young adult literature. Brief annotations of recommended titles are included at the end of each chapter to encourage your own independent reading in that genre.

Understanding genre characteristics builds a frame of reference for reading a particular genre and can ease the task of comprehension. Furthermore, as you encounter postmodern works of literature that go beyond the traditional boundaries of a genre, knowledge of the traditional literary forms may help you understand what the authors are doing and gain new understandings from the shift in style.

Authors of young adult literature have been experimenting with books that blend characteristics of several genres, and as a result, genre boundaries are increasingly blurred. Magical realism combines realism and fantasy, offering readers new ways to perceive the world, such as Isabel Allende's *City of the Beasts* (2009) and A. S. King's *Please Ignore Vera Dietz* (2010). These novels are discussed in Chapter 4, "Modern Fantasy." Historical fantasy blends historical fiction and modern fantasy, as in Libba Bray's Gemma Doyle series. These works are discussed as fantasy in Chapter 4. Other blended genres include fictionalized biography and informational books that contain elements of both fiction and nonfiction, as in *The Dreamer* (2012) by Pam Muñoz Ryan and Peter Sis, and David Macauly's *Mosque* (2003), found in Chapter 6, "Nonfiction: Biography and Informational Books," and novels written in the style of free verse and other verse forms, such as *The Language Inside* by Holly Thompson (2013). Novels in verse are listed under the particular narrative genre, such as historical fiction or realistic fiction, rather than in the chapter about poetry. These blended-genre works offer readers new perceptions and often provide heightened interest for readers.

Chapter 8, "Literature for a Diverse Society," diverges from the organization of genre and presents books organized by culture. Although multicultural and international books have been placed in a separate chapter to emphasize significant issues of access and availability, many multicultural and global titles are recommended in the genre chapters.

Chapters 9 and 10 focus on literature in the curriculum and the ways in which you might organize a curriculum around literature with adolescents, as well as strategies for engaging them in responding to literature. In addition, these chapters include a discussion of the political context of policies, tests, and standards that affect the ways in which literature is used in classrooms, with a particular emphasis on the Common Core State Standards and their connection to literature.

 # References

Adlington, L. J. (2008). *Cherry heaven*. New York: Greenwillow.

Alexie, S. (2007). *The absolutely true diary of a part-time Indian*. New York: Little, Brown.

Allende, I. (2004). *City of beasts*. Logan, IA: Perfection Learning.

Beach, R., & Marshall, J. (1990). *Teaching literature in the secondary school*. Belmont, CA: Wadsworth.

Bray, L. (2012). *The diviners*. New York: Little, Brown.

Cart, M. (2005). A graphic-novel explosion. *Booklist, 101*(14), 1301.

Collins, S. (2010). *The Hunger Games*. New York: Scholastic.

Creech, S. (2002). *Ruby Holler*. New York: HarperCollins.

Curtis, C. P. (2004). *Bucking the Sarge*. New York: Wendy Lamb.

de la Peña, M. (2005). *Ball don't lie*. New York: Delacorte.

Draper, S. (2012). *Out of my mind*. New York: Atheneum.

Gaiman, N. (2008). *Graveyard book*. New York: Harper.

Gallo, D. (1984). *Sixteen: Short stories by outstanding writers for young adults*. New York: Delacorte.

Helm, J. (2012). *Eighth grade is making me sick: Ginny Davis's year in stuff*. New York: Random.

Hemphill, S. (2007). *Your own, Sylvia: A verse portrait of Sylvia Plath*. New York: Knopf.

Hesse, K. (1997). *Out of the dust*. New York: Scholastic.

———. (2004). *The cats in Krasinski Square*. Illus. by W. Watson. New York: Scholastic.

Johnson, D. B. (2003). *Henry climbs a mountain*. Boston: Houghton Mifflin.

Kadohata, C. (2009). *Weedflower*. New York: Atheneum.

King, A. S. (2010). *Please ignore Vera Dietz*. New York: Knopf.

Koertge, R. (2003). *Shakespeare bats cleanup*. Cambridge, MA: Candlewick.

———. (2004). *Margaux with an x*. Cambridge, MA: Candlewick.

Korman, G. (2006). *Born to rock*. New York: Hyperion.

Lake, N. (2012). *In darkness*. New York: Bloomsbury USA.

Larson, K. (2006). *Hattie Big Sky*. New York: Delacorte.

Laybourne, E. (2013). *Monument 14*. New York: Square Fish.

Lowry, L. (2011). *Son*. New York: Houghton Mifflin.

Lupica, M. (2006). *Heat*. New York: Philomel.

Macauly, D. (2003). *Mosque*. Boston: Houghton Mifflin.

Mark, J. (1988). The short story. *Horn Book Magazine, 64*(1), 42–45.

McCaughrean, G. (2002). *The kite rider*. New York: HarperCollins.

Moriarity, J. (2004). *The year of secret assignments*. New York: Arthur A. Levine.

Myers, W. D. (2001). *Bad boy: A memoir*. New York: Amistad.

———. (1999). *Monster*. New York: Scholastic.

Pausewang, G., & Ward, R. (2010). *Traitor*. New York: Carolrhoda.

Perkins, L. R. (2005). *Criss cross*. New York: Greenwillow.

Peters, J. A. (2006). *Luna*. New York: Little, Brown.

Philbrick, R. (2009). *The mostly true adventures of Homer P. Figg*. New York: Scholastic.

Rosenblatt, L. M. (1978). *The reader, the text, the poem*. Carbondale: Southern Illinois University.

———. (1985). The transactional theory of the literary work: Implications for research. In R. Cooper (Ed.), *Researching response to literature and the teaching of literature: Points of departure* (pp. 33–53). Norwood, NJ: Ablex.

Rosoff, M. (2004). *How I live now*. New York: Wendy Lamb.

Roy, J. (2006). *Yellow star*. Tarrytown, NY: Cavendish.

Ryan, P. M. (2010). *The dreamer*. New York: Scholastic.

Saenz, B. A. (2012). *Aristotle and Dante discover the secrets of the universe*. New York: Simon & Schuster.

Satrapi, M. (2003). *Persepolis*. New York: Pantheon.

Schmidt, G. D. (2004). *Lizzie Bright and the Buckminster boy*. New York: Clarion.

Spiegelman, A. (1986). *Maus: A survivor's tale*. New York: Pantheon.

Stiefvater, M. (2011). *The Scorpio races*. New York: Scholastic.

———. (2012). *The raven boys*. New York: Scholastic.

Stine, C. (2005). *Refugees*. New York: Delacorte.

Telgemeire, R. (2012). *Drama*. New York: Graphix.

Thompson, H. (2013). *The language inside*. New York: Delacorte.

Vanderpool, C. (2011). *Moon over Manifest*. New York: Yearling.

Volponi, P. (2012). *The Final Four*. New York: Viking.

Wein, E. (2012). *Code name Verity*. New York: Hyperion.

———. (2013). *Rose under fire*. New York: Hyperion.

Westerfeld, S. (2004). *So yesterday*. New York: Razorbill.

Woodson, J. (2005). *Show Way*. Illus. by Hudson Talbott. New York: Putman.

Yancey, R. (2013). *The 5th wave*. New York: Putnam Juvenile.

Yang, G. L. (2007). *American born Chinese*. New York: First Second.

Yolen, J., & Stemple, H. (2013) *Bad girls: Sirens, jezebels, murderesses, thieves & other female villains*. Watertown, MA: Charlesbridge.

Zarr, S. (2007). *Story of a girl*. New York: Little, Brown.

Zusak, M. (2007). *The book thief*. New York: Knopf.

Part Two

Genres of Literature

Part Two highlights the genres of young adult literature. Within each genre chapter, the books and trends are organized by topics, historical eras, or types. Organizing by genres is a convenient way for you to locate books and to encourage broad reading, even though literary genres do not have absolute definitions and some books fall between or go across genres. A genre organization also provides criteria for evaluating books and examining how literary elements play out within a particular type of literature.

Many multicultural and global titles are integrated into the relevant genres in Chapters 3 through 7. Chapter 8 focuses on issues related to literature for a diverse society and provides more extensive lists of recommended titles in order to highlight the importance and current status of multicultural and international literature.

The special features in each chapter include a chart of Early Important Works to provide a brief history of the development of each genre. The lists

of Notable Authors highlight well-known creators of literature to facilitate choices for in-depth author studies, while the lists of Excellent Books to Read Aloud provide help in selecting literature for reading aloud to adolescents. The Recommended Books section at the end of each genre chapter includes the best recent books for young adults as well as a few older titles that continue to hold wide appeal. Titles in the Recommended Books lists are organized by the same topics or historical eras as in the body of the chapter to facilitate locating specific types of books. A brief list of films related to each genre follows the Recommended Book lists.

Other recommended titles for young adults can be found in the award lists in Appendix A. These awards were selected specifically for their suitability for young adults. The history, selection criteria, and lists of the winners by year are included for each award.

Chapter Three

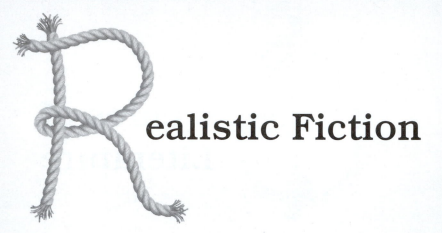

Realistic Fiction

Realistic stories for young adults address difficult life situations where adolescents face times of desolation and misery, often due to the cruelty of other human beings, as well as joyful laughter-filled moments of belonging and love. Young adults search for stories about people who seem like themselves as well as stories that take them beyond themselves to consider the ways that other adolescents experience contemporary life.

Definition and Description

Realistic fiction refers to stories that *could* happen to people, and so these stories are within the realm of possibility for such events to occur. The protagonists are fictitious characters created by the author, but their actions and reactions are quite like those of real people. Sometimes events in these stories are exaggerated or outlandish—hardly probable but definitely possible—and so still fit the definition of realistic fiction. Other times, whether or not a book is realistic fiction depends on interpretation, as in Libba Bray's *Going Bovine,* in which the main character's road trip can either be viewed as an hallucination brought on by illness or a fantasy adventure with an angel and a dwarf.

Realism in literature is a complex, multifaceted concept that includes various components of realism in literature, including factual, situational, emotional, and social (Marshall, 1968). In engaging realistic stories, several of these components occur, with varying degrees of emphasis. *Factual realism* includes descriptions of actual people, places, and events in a book, with facts that are recorded accurately. Accurate descriptions of places are essential to Dana Reinhardt's *The Things a Brother Knows,* the story of a 17-year-old boy who joins his older brother, a recently returned soldier from the Middle East, on a walking trip from Boston to Washington, D.C., in the hopes of learning why his brother has completely withdrawn.

Situational realism is provided by occurrences that are not only possible but also quite likely, often in identifiable locations with characters of an identifiable age and social class, making the plot line believable. The survival story, which often hinges on a life-threatening situation, is an example of a story built on situational realism. Geraldine McCaughrean's *The White Darkness* relates the survival story of a troubled teenage girl who goes on a dangerous secret expedition to Antarctica with an obsessive and manipulative pseudo-uncle.

Emotional realism is provided by the appearance of believable feelings and relationships among characters. Stories that focus on issues of identity often employ emotional realism. John Green's *The Fault in Our Stars* depicts the story of Hazel and Augustus, striving against the odds in both love and cancer, learning that life is lived by moments, not by years.

Social realism provides an honest portrayal of society and its conditions of the moment, including both beneficial and adverse conditions. These stories often involve government, schools, courts, economic systems, and the conditions that are produced from them. In Martine Leavitt's *Heck, Superhero,* Heck finds himself without a home when his mother's life spirals out of control and she abandons him. Heck tries to cope on his own and avoid authorities.

Contemporary realism is a term used to describe stories that take place in the present time and portray attitudes and mores of the present culture, using these components of realism. Unlike early realistic books that depicted only happy families and were never controversial, today's contemporary realism often focuses on societal issues, such as alcoholism, drug use, teen pregnancy, racism, and suicide. These contemporary books still tell of the happy, fun times in young people's lives, but they also include the harsh, unpleasant times. Abuse, neglect, violence, bullying, dysfunctional families, drug abuse, mental illness, disillusionment, and alienation from mainstream society are topics included in contemporary realistic novels.

Authors of contemporary realistic fiction set their stories in the present or recent past. But, in time, features of these stories, such as allusions to popular culture, social practices, and fashion, become dated, and the stories are therefore no longer contemporary, though they remain part of realistic fiction. In some cases the stories may continue to appeal to adolescents because of the power of the storytelling and relevancy of the issues, such as *The Outsiders* by S. E. Hinton.

The ***problem novel*** is a contemporary realistic story that addresses a societal problem and, at times, is used as a synonym for *contemporary realism*. The story is frequently told in the first person or from the point of view of the protagonist, sometimes in a diary form. Dialogue often dominates and represents a particular dialect or teen vernacular, much the way teens would talk, and may include profanity and informal usage.

Problem novel is also sometimes used as a derogatory term to refer to a story in which problems or conflicts overwhelm the plot and characterization. In these cases the novel is written to provide the author with a soapbox from which to lecture or as a vehicle for capitalizing on whatever societal problem is currently at the forefront of the news. Adolescents want and deserve to read books that honestly address issues and topics about which they are concerned or curious, so it is important to locate high-quality literature that tells compelling stories.

Evaluation and Selection of Realistic Fiction

The criteria for evaluating realistic fiction include well-developed characters who manifest change as a result of significant life events, a well-structured plot with sufficient conflict and suspense to hold the reader's interest, a time and place that fit the storyline, and a worthwhile theme that is significant to adolescents. Although these literary elements are basic to any piece of fiction, the following questions are particularly relevant to realistic fiction:

1. **Does the story permit some cause for hope or optimism?** Some realistic novels portray adverse and discouraging social situations, such as homelessness and poverty; yet many of these stories permit cause for optimism. Adolescents often trust that our world can be a good place in which to live and can be made better through their efforts, particularly within some kind of community. Adolescent readers also need to see demonstrations through characters' lives of strategies for overcoming or coping with problems.

2. **Does the message or moral lesson overpower the telling of the story?** Themes in realistic stories often convey moral values, such as the rewards of caring and generosity to others. These moral values must spring naturally from the story, not as the main reason for the story. At times, adults write books for young people with the sole intent of teaching or preaching, and the story is nothing more than a thin disguise for a heavy-handed moral lesson. In fiction, the story is of paramount importance. The moral must not overwhelm the story but may be its logical outcome.

3. **Is the story believable?** Realistic fiction must be believable, even though all aspects may not be probable, as in the unexplained coincidences and mystical messages that

Early Important Works of Realistic Fiction

Date	Literary Work	Significance
1719	*Robinson Crusoe* by Daniel Defoe (England)	One of the first desert island survival adventures
1868	*Little Women* by Louisa May Alcott (United States)	An early family story of great popularity
1876	*The Adventures of Tom Sawyer* by Mark Twain (United States)	Classic adventure story set along the Mississippi
1877	*Black Beauty* by Anna Sewell (England)	One of the first animal stories to deplore inhumane treatment of animals
1883	*Treasure Island* by Robert Louis Stevenson (England)	Classic adventure story with pirates
1934	*The Good Master* by Kate Seredy (United States)	Newbery winner set in Hungary; one of the first realistic stories featuring a global culture
1938	*The Yearling* by Marjorie Kinnan Rawlings (United States)	Classic animal and coming-of-age story
1941	*In My Mother's House* by Ann Nolan Clark (United States)	One of the earliest stories to feature Native Americans
1951	*Catcher in the Rye* by J. D. Salinger (United States)	Novel of teenage rebellion, first published for adults, but later adopted by young adult readers
1964	*Harriet the Spy* by Louise Fitzhugh (United States)	Ushered in the New Realism movement in books for young people
1967	*The Outsiders* by S. E. Hinton (United States)	One of the first young adult books; focuses on gangs, social alienation, and adolescent rebellion
1967	*The Contender* by Robert Lipsyte (United States)	Early young adult book with African-American protagonist
1968/ 1969	*The Pigman and My Darling, My Hamburger* by Paul Zindel (United States)	Romance with alternating chapters by the male and female protagonist and a story addressing abortion
1970/ 1971	*Are You There, God? It's Me, Margaret and Then Again, Maybe I Won't* by Judy Blume (United States)	Early young adult books that feature a frank treatment of sex
1972	*The Man Without a Face* by Isabelle Holland (United States)	One of the first young adult books to feature homosexual protagonists

continued

Early Important Works of Realistic Fiction *(continued)*

Date	Literary Work	Significance
1972	*Dinky Hocker Shoots Smack!* by M. E. Kerr (United States)	Realistic portrayal of family dynamics
1973	*A Hero Ain't Nothin' but a Sandwich* by Alice Childress (United States)	Story addressing drug abuse, African-American protagonist, multiple points of view
1973	*A Day No Pigs Would Die* by Robert Newton Peck (United States)	Rural story about a father–son relationship, coming-of-age story
1974	*The Chocolate War* by Robert Cormier (United States)	Story featuring athletics, religion, gangs, and the pressures to conform

allow three friends to solve art crimes in Blue Balliett's *Chasing Vermeer* and *The Wright 3*. Some authors approach the edge of the believable range to produce a more exciting, suspense-filled story. The sacrifice of some probability for a good story can enhance readers' interest and pleasure. Believability can also be an issue when the events or thinking of characters are outside of the experience of a particular reader, such as a teen's descent into drug addiction and prostitution in Martine Levine's *My Book of Life by Angel*. This author uses a first-person approach where the main character writes her own life story to increase believability.

4. **How does the author use humor to engage readers?** Humor is often found in realistic fiction through characters caught up in outrageous situations or involved in funny predicaments. Adolescents often are amused by the incongruities presented in these escapades, as in Brent Hartinger's *Project Sweet Life*. Other humorous stories draw on wordplay for their humor or in the characters' viewpoint of the situation as in Lynn Rae Perkins's *As Easy as Falling off the Face of the Earth*.

5. **Whose point of view is used to tell the story?** Many realistic works presented through first-person point of view reflect the internal struggles and introspective stances taken by many teenagers as they grow toward adulthood, such as *How to Save a Life* and *Story of a Girl* by Sara Zarr, *Undercover* by Beth Kephart, and *Red Glass* by Laura Resau. Point of view limits what the narrator knows and is able to convey to readers and so first-person is not always the most effective way to tell a particular story.

Controversy involving young adult literature often centers on the treatment of topics in realistic fiction, such as premarital sex, pregnancy, homosexuality, and the use of profanity. Many of these controversial books fall within the types of realism labeled "Romance and Sexuality" and "Identity." Chapter 9 provides a discussion of issues surrounding censorship of these books.

Selection of realistic fiction for classroom and library collections and for class assignments should be balanced among the different topics of realistic stories. A steady diet of serious problem novels does not offer the richness of experience to adolescents that they deserve, nor does it provide for their varied reading interests. The mood of books that are serious and deal with disturbing family situations should be balanced with lighthearted stories with humor or romance. It is also important to include books with female and male protagonists, as well as protagonists from a variety of cultures.

Realistic fiction stories are easy for young adults to relate to and enjoy. They can often see their own lives, or lives much like their own, in these stories, particularly books focused on self-discovery. Many middle school and high school students report a keen interest in sports, adventure, mystery, and romance stories, making it plain that realistic fiction is an important genre for young adults (Hale & Crowe, 2001; Hopper, 2005).

Topics of Realistic Fiction

Realistic fiction includes interactions with self, others, society, or nature and so reflects the joys, challenges, adjustments, anxieties, and satisfactions of human life, as well as relationships with family, peers, and love interests within communities. Realistic fiction also addresses the struggles of many adolescents with issues of identity that may or may not be apparent to others. Many of these books focus on the ways in which characters negotiate conflict and so include more than one aspect of human life; thus, some realistic fiction can be placed in more than one of these categories.

Relationships with Families and Peers

Stories involving relationships with others are often at the heart of realistic fiction. Stories about *families,* both nuclear and extended, often show the struggle between parents and adolescents seeking greater freedom and adolescents' evolving relationships with siblings, such as in *All You Never Wanted* by Adele Griffin and *The Big Nothing* by Adrian Fogelin. One current trend involves books where characters are dealing with the death of a family member, as in *Under the Mesquite* by Guadalupe Garcia McCall. In addition, relationships with trusted extended family members are also prevalent. Aunts, uncles, grandparents, and cousins are important in the lives of many teens, and sometimes a book will tell of an adolescent being raised by a member of the extended family, as in Polly Horvath's *The Canning Season;* other times a relative is portrayed as a supportive family member, as in *Tending to Grace* by Kimberly Newton Fusco.

The **alternative family** of today's world is also depicted, allowing adolescents to see families other than the typical mother, father, and two children. Single-parent families, separation, divorce, and reconstructed families of stepparents and stepchildren as well as temporary family situations, such as foster care, are often the backdrop of stories; *Along for the Ride* by Sarah Dressen and *The Steps* by Rachel Cohn focus on adjustment to a stepfamily.

While many young people are fortunate to have supportive families, others live in families with difficult and abusive situations, as in Nancy Werlin's *The Rules of Survival*. In reading about such harsh situations, adolescents can better understand and deal with their own difficult lives; in other cases such stories help them understand the problems of peers.

Notable Authors of Realistic Fiction

Laurie Halse Anderson, author of novels that depict the raw emotions and turmoil of teenagers. *Speak; Twisted; Prom.* www.writerlady.com

Chris Crutcher, author of realistic sports stories. *Ironman; Angry Management; Staying Fat for Sarah Byrnes; Deadline; Period 8;* and *Athletic Shorts,* a collection of short stories. www.chriscrutcher.com

Matt de la Peña, Mexican-American author of urban novels of diverse teens dealing with difficult life situations. *Balls Don't Lie, Mexican Whiteboy, We Were Here.* www.mattdelapena.com

Sarah Dessen, author who depicts complex relationships between families, friends, and romantic interests. *What Happened to Goodbye; Along for the Ride; The Moon and More.* www.sarahdessen.com

Sharon Draper, author who explores the lives of urban youth as they deal with difficult issues and how much is not seen on the surface. *Out of My Mind; Copper Sun; Just another Hero; November Blues.* www.sharondraper.com

John Green, author of novels in which characters are dying of cancer, contemplating suicide, and falling in and out of love. *The Fault in Our Stars; Will Grayson, Will Grayson; An Abundance of Katherines; Paper Towns.* www.johngreenbooks.com

Ron Koertge, author of many realistic young adult novels that depict universal adolescent concerns, including *Mariposa Blues; The Arizona Kid; Where the Kissing Never Stops; Stoner and Spaz.*

David Levithan, author of novels about the array of teens found within high schools—if we look closely. *Every Day; Every You, Every Me; The Realm of Possibility; Boy Meets Boy.* www.davidlevithan.com

Walter Dean Myers, author of novels about African-American adolescents in urban settings. *Scorpions; Monster; Lockdown; All the Right Stuff.* www.walterdeanmyers.com

Laura Resau, author of books set in Mexico and other global settings; cultural anthropologist. *Red Glass, The Indigo Notebook; The Queen of Water, What the Moon Saw.* www.lauraresau.com

Francisco X. Stork, Mexican-American author who writes of alienated teens trying to rise above their circumstances. *Marcelo in the Real World; Behind the Eyes; The Last Summer of the Death Warriors.* www.franciscostork.com

Nancy Werlin, author of suspenseful mysteries that present delicate issues while, at times, blending fantasy and realism. *The Rules of Survival; Impossible; Black Mirror; Killer's Cousin.* www.nancywerlin.com

Rita Williams-Garcia, author who combines political context, ethical decision-making, and adolescents' lives. *One Crazy Summer; Jumped; No Laughter Here; Like Sisters on the Homefront.* www.ritawg.com

Jacqueline Woodson, African-American author whose novels treat sensitive issues of sexuality, abuse, and race. *I Hadn't Meant to Tell You This; From the Notebooks of Melanin Sun; Beneath a Meth Moon; If You Come Softly.* www.jacquelinewoodson.com

Excellent Realistic Fiction to Read Aloud

Abdel-Fattah, Randa. *Does My Head Look Big in This?* Muslim teen, difference, high school life.

Anderson, Laurie Halse. *Prom.* Friendship, dating, the hypocrisies of high school.

Curtis, Christopher Paul. *Bucking the Sarge.* Mother and son, welfare system fraud.

Dowd, Sioban. *The London Eye Mystery.* Mystery of missing cousin, Asperger's syndrome.

Frost, Helen. *Keesha's House.* Monologues, seven teens looking for shelter.

Gallo, Don, editor. *What Are You Afraid Of? Stories about Phobias.* Short stories about teen phobias.

Green, John. *The Fault in Our Stars.* Romance between two teens with cancer.

Medina, Meg. *Yaqui Delgado Wants to Kick Your Ass.* Bullying, body image, identity.

Myers, Walter Dean. *Darius & Twig.* Friendship, urban violence, and poverty.

Westerfeld, Scott. *So Yesterday.* Ages 15–18. Market-research-trends thriller.

In addition to adapting to one's family situation, adolescents must also learn to cope with their peers. Many realistic stories show adolescents struggling for **acceptance by peers** in a group situation, particularly in school settings, such as in *The Astonishing Adventures of Fanboy and Goth Girl* by Barry Lyga and *How to Say Goodbye in Robot* by Natalie Standiford; Neighborhoods, community centers, and summer camps are other common settings, as in *What They Found: Love on 145th Street* by Walter Dean Myers and *Liar & Spy* by Rebecca Stead. Some books cut across difficult family and school relationships, such as Adam Rapp's *Under the Wolf, Under the Dog,* in which 16-year-old Steve struggles with drug abuse and suicide in response to the breakdown of his family.

Developing **close friendships** is another focus of stories about peer relationships. Friends may be of the same sex or the opposite sex, of the same age or a very different age, or of the same culture or a different culture. A concern for friendship and how to be a good friend are the focus of *Big Mouth & Ugly Girl* by Joyce Carol Oates, *The Year of Secret Assignments* by Jaclyn Moriarty, and *Me and Earl and the Dying Girl* by Jesse Andrews.

Finally, there are the books on **dysfunctional relationships,** addressing violent or abusive relationships that can cause havoc in families and communities. Jennifer Brown's *Hate List* presents the aftermath of a school shooting, while Jay Asher's *Thirteen Reasons Why* focuses on relationships that lead to suicide, and Adam Rapp's *The Children and the Wolves* is an unsettling story of three emotionally disturbed teens who kidnap a child.

Identity and Community

From birth to age 10, most children's lives revolve around family, friends, and classmates, but during adolescence a shift occurs toward self-discovery and independence, along with rapid growth and physical, emotional, moral, and intellectual change. In addition, this is a time when young people come to understand that they have choices to make about their own lives and the way they may want to live that could separate them from family and friends. These changes are reflected in books for adolescents that address issues of identity, as occurred when an adult novel, *Catcher in the Rye* by J. D. Salinger, captured the attention of many young adults and thus became a well-known forerunner to young adult literature. Sometimes books that deal with the struggles encountered during growth from childhood to adulthood are called *rite-of-passage* or *coming-of-age* books.

Coming-of-age stories are also known as **Bildungsroman,** a German term referring to novels that focus on an event leading to the psychological or moral growth of a character who is struggling to move into adulthood, such as in *Pregnant Pause* by Han Nolan, the story of a teen who is pregnant and unhappily married at 16, and *Looking for Alaska* by John Green, in which a teen reexamines his life after a friend's fatal "accident." Adolescent struggles with identity are often magnified within biracial families as in *Mexican Whiteboy* by Matt de la Peña and within immigrant families experiencing a clash of cultures as in An Na's *Wait for Me*. Difficult life situations add another layer of complexity in the short stories of *There Is No Long Distance Now* by Naomi Shihab Nye.

Part of understanding themselves involves adolescents' discovery of their membership in a **community,** a group extending beyond the family. Some young adult books focus on school settings in which students, teachers, administrators, and at times parents comprise the community. Helen Frost's novel told through twenty-two poetic forms, *Spinning through the Universe: A Novel in Poems from Room 214,* shows students, the teacher, and the custodian writing their thoughts about the school. Walter Dean Myers's *Street Love* tackles social class lines in Harlem and their effect on young people, while issues of bullying in schools is the focus of books such as *Jumped* by Rita Williams-Garcia and *The Misfits* by James Howe.

In other books the community setting is the neighborhood. An example is K. L. Going's *Saint Iggy,* in which urban life in housing projects is depicted, a community not often featured in young adult novels. Iggy wants to make something of his life against difficult odds and searches for the parental care that he needs. Janet McDonald's novels follow a community of teen mothers living in urban housing projects.

Community extends beyond neighborhoods to global cultures. With increasing interdependence among countries, young people will likely be more connected to an international community than ever before. Books that highlight life in global cultures can help young adults develop an awareness of and sense of connection with teens from global cultures along with an appreciation for the uniqueness of their cultures, such as the difficulties encountered by an uprooted Ghanaian teen in Adwoa Badoe's *Between Sisters* or the struggles of a Muslim Australian teen in *Does My Head Look Big in This?* by Fanda Abdel-Fattah. The interconnectedness of global community is reflected in *A Long Walk to Water* by Linda Sue Park through the intertwined lives of a young girl in Sudan with a Lost Boy of Sudan who escaped to the United States but returns to search for his family.

Romance and Sexuality

Romance stories are often popular with preteens and teens and, for those interested in romance but shy and confused about relationships with a romantic partner, literature showing romantic encounters can be especially interesting. Some stories depict first loves and romantic relationships as in *My Most Excellent Year* by Steve Kluger, and Rachel Cohn's and

David Levithan's *Nick and Nora's Infinite Playlist.* Other stories, such as Daniel Handler's *Why We Broke Up* and Paul Griffin's *Stay with Me,* reveal the heartbreak that comes with the end of a romantic relationship. Some stories portray abuse in a relationship, as in Chris Lynch's *Inexcusable,* in which a date rape occurs. Others portray characters dealing with pregnancy and teen parenting, such as Sharon Draper's *November Blues* and Angela Johnson's *The First Part Last.*

Young adults become aware of their growing sexuality and its influence on their identities. Stories for older teens often show attraction between members of the opposite sex as well as members of the same sex, with the beginning of sexual activity depicted, such as in Nick Burd's *The Vast Fields of Ordinary.* Stories that portray the struggle of young people coming to terms with their sexual identities are seen more frequently than they were in the past; other stories show the cruelty of society toward young homosexuals, lesbians, bisexuals, and transsexuals as in books like *The Difference between You and Me* by Madeleine George, *The Miseducation of Cameron Post* by Emily Danforth, *I am J* by Cris Beam, and *Boy Meets Boy* by David Levithan.

Challenges in Life

Young people often live with difficult challenges as they attempt to know and be known by others. Some teenagers have disabilities; others have a family member or a friend with a disability. These disabilities may be *physical,* such as scoliosis; *emotional,* such as bipolar disorder, suicidal tendencies, anorexia, or substance abuse; *mental,* such as intellectual or learning disabilities; *behavioral,* such as hyperactivity; or a combination of challenges.

As obesity and eating disorders increase in frequency across society, more stories focus on the physical and emotional health challenges faced by young people dealing with these problems as in *Fat Kid Rules the World* by K. L. Going, *Looks* by Madeleine George, and *Wintergirls* by Laurie Halse Anderson. Addiction is another frequent focus in books, such as *Beneath a Meth Moon* by Jacqueline Woodson on drug addiction and *Burnout* by Adrienne Vrettos on alcoholism.

Authors of young adult books are becoming increasingly sensitive to the need for positive portrayals of individuals with special challenges. As inclusion of special education students into regular classrooms has become a common practice, this trend in young adult literature can be an important resource. Well-written, honest stories of such individuals in books can help adolescents gain an understanding of disabilities, foster an ability to empathize with people who have challenges, and help adolescents understand that they are not alone in their differences. These books include Sharon Draper's *Out of My Mind* on cerebral palsy, Francisco X. Stork's *Marcelo in the Real World* on autism, and Jennifer Roy's *Mindblind* on Asperger's syndrome. Books such as Ned Vizzini's *It's Kind of a Funny Story* and Pete Hautman's *Invisible* deal with mental illness. Other books depict adolescents coping with the mental illness of family members, including parents in *Crazy* by Han Nolan and *Silhouetted by the Blue* by Traci Jones, or a sibling in *Breathless* by Jessica Warman.

Suspense and Survival

Physical danger and violence are external forces that compel adolescents to act with greater maturity and responsibility. Stories of **survival** feature protagonists who must rely on will and ingenuity to survive life-threatening situations. Although traditionally survival stories are set in isolated places, current novels have moved away from the "castaway" plot to stories involving teens who must survive political and racial conflict as in *Endangered* by Eliot Schrefer, set during an uprising in the Congo, and *Now Is a Time for Running* by Michael Williams, set during violence in Zimbabwe. In addition, a growing number of stories are set in cities where gangs, drug wars, prostitution, and abandonment are indeed life threatening, as in *Tyrell* and *Bronxwood* by Coe Booth, *Lockdown* by Walter Dean Myers, and *My Book of Life by Angel* by Martine Leavitt. Adventure stories may be set in any environment where the protagonist faces the challenge of surviving alone or against great odds. Lynne Rae Perkins creates an unusual story of a survival and adventure when a boy gets off a train to make a call and ends up stranded in the middle of nowhere in *As Easy as Falling Off the Face of the Earth*.

Stories of **suspense** can take the form of simple "whodunit" mysteries or complex character stories. The element of suspense is a strong part of the appeal of these stories. In Nancy Werlin's *Black Mirror,* social isolation, mixed race, and suicide at a boarding school contribute to a complex and intriguing mystery. Carl Hiaasen has written mysteries, such as *Hoot, Chomp,* and *Scat*, that combine humor and ecological issues, while Kate Ellison's main character in *The Butterfly Clues* is a girl with obsessive-compulsive disorder who tries to solve the mystery of a shooting.

Many mystery stories are realistic and could happen, but some mysteries have elements of the supernatural and so are considered fantasy. The Edgar Allan Poe Award for Juvenile Mystery Novels (www.mysterywriters.org) can be helpful in selecting good mysteries—one of the most popular story types for intermediate-grade and middle-grade students.

Sports

Sports stories often involve an adolescent protagonist who gains success in a sport but struggles with academics or with interpersonal relationships. John Coy's *Crackback* is a good example of a sports story in which the main character struggles to overcome the harsh criticisms of his coach and his father and to resist peer pressures to use steroids. Some sports stories feature a protagonist who uses sports as an outlet for personal anger and frustration, as in Matt de la Peña's *Ball Don't Lie,* the story of a successful but frustrated 17-year-old basketball player who struggles to overcome poverty and his foster home background. Traditionally written with males as the main characters, a few sports stories feature females as protagonists, such as Kristi Roberts's *My 13th Season* and Catherine Gilbert Murdock's *Dairy Queen.*

Sports books have moved far away from the simplistic hero stories of the past, which primarily consisted of descriptions of adolescents overcoming the odds to win games. These books not only take on complex issues, but include books where authors creatively tell their stories. *Pick-Up Game,* edited by Marc Aronson and Charles R. Smith, contains linked short stories about a game of street basketball, each by a different author, and interspersed with photographs and poems, while Paul Volpani's *The Final Four* focuses on the pressures of the Final Four basketball tournament through television interviews, radio transcripts, and segments narrated by different players that are interspersed between minute-by-minute descriptions of the game.

Stories in the realistic fiction genre present familiar situations with which adolescents can readily identify, reflect contemporary life, and portray settings not so different from the homes, schools, towns, and cities known to today's adolescents. The protagonists of these stories are frequently testing themselves as they grow toward adulthood, encouraging readers to empathize and gain insight into their own predicaments. This genre includes a wide range of books that will entertain, encourage, and inspire adolescents.

 ## References

Hale, L. A., & Crowe, C. (2001). "I hate reading if I don't have to": Results from a longitudinal study of high school students' reading interest. *ALAN Review, 28*(3), 49–57.

Hopper, R. (2005). What are teenagers reading? Adolescent fiction reading habits and reading choices. *Literacy, 39*(3), 113–120.

Marshall, M. R. (1988). *An introduction to the world of children's books* (2nd ed.). Brookfield, VT: Gower.

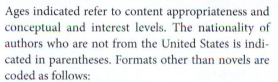 ## Recommended Realistic Fiction Books

Ages indicated refer to content appropriateness and conceptual and interest levels. The nationality of authors who are not from the United States is indicated in parentheses. Formats other than novels are coded as follows:

- **(GR)** Graphic novel
- **(PI)** Picture book
- **(NV)** Novel in Verse
- **(COL)** Short story collection

Relationships with Family

Acampora, Paul. *Defining Dulcie*. Dial, 2006. Ages 12–15. Quirky road trip, grieving father's death.

Banks, Kate. *Walk Softly*, Rachel. Farrar, 2003. Ages 12–16. Diary, death of a sibling, family secrets.

Budhos, Marina. *Ask Me No Questions*. Simon & Schuster, 2006. Ages 12–16. Immigrant Muslim family from Bangladesh after 9/11, secrets, immigration fears, and prejudice.

Cohn, Rachel. *The Steps*. Simon & Schuster, 2003. Ages 10–14. Adjusting to a new stepfamily in Australia.

Creech, Sharon. *Heartbeat*. HarperCollins, 2004. **(NV)** Ages 10–14. Trying to understand mother's pregnancy, grandfather's memory lapses, and best friend's changes.

Dessen, Sarah. *Along for the Ride*. Viking, 2009. Ages 13–18. Effects of divorce, stepfamily, romance.

Fogelin, Adrian. *The Big Nothing*. Peachtree, 2004. Ages 11–14. Parental marital problems and teen anxiety.

——. *Sister Spider Knows All*. Peachtree, 2003. Ages 11–14. Flea market culture, developing an extended family.

Forman, Gayle. *If I Stay*. Dutton, 2009. Ages 14–18. Girl in a coma after the loss of her family in an accident weighs whether to live with grief or die.

Fusco, Kimberly Newton. *Tending to Grace*. Knopf, 2004. Ages 12–15. Finding a home, mother/daughter relationship, stuttering.

Griffin, Adele. *All You Never Wanted*. Knopf, 2012. Ages 14–18. Alternating voices of sibling rivalry and family dysfunction with reflections on socioeconomic class.

Holt, Kimberly Willis. *Keeper of the Night*. Holt, 2003. Ages 11–15. Suicide of a parent, set in Guam.

Horvath, Polly. *The Canning Season*. Farrar, 2003. Ages 12–18. Finding a family, extended family. Humor.

Jocelyn, Marthe. *Would You*. Random, 2008. Ages 15–18. Coping with a sister's accident and coma. (Canadian)

Jones, Kimberly. *Sand Dollar Summer*. Simon & Schuster, 2006. Ages 11–15. Family adjustment to new home.

Kadohata, Cynthia. *The Thing about Luck*. Atheneum, 2013. Ages 12–14. Summer's parents must go to Japan to care for a relative, leaving Summer to work the harvest and care for her brother.

Khan, Rukhsana. *Wanting Mor*. Groundwood, 2009. Ages 12–15. Afghan girl must learn to survive after her father remarries. (Pakistani-Canadian)

Knowles, Johanna. *See You at Harry's*. Candlewick, 2013. Ages 12-15. A flawed but loving family tries to survive a tragedy that tears them apart in grief.

Lawrence, Iain. *The Lightkeeper's Daughter*. Delacorte, 2002. Ages 15–18. Family guilt, reconciliation. (Canadian)

Leavitt, Martine. *Heck, Superhero*. Front Street, 2004. Ages 12–15. Gifted artist dealing with a missing mother and homelessness. (Canadian)

Lindner, April. *Catherine*. Little, Brown, 2013. Ages 14–18. Alternating voices of mother and daughter as Chelsea searches for the mother whom she thought was dead. Modernization of Wuthering Heights. Also *Jane* (2010), an update of Jane Eyre.

Lynch, Chris. *Pieces*. Simon & Schuster, 2013. Ages 14–18. A teen seeks connection with the people who received his brother's donated organs as he struggles with grief and pain.

Mackler, Carolyn. *The Earth, My Butt, and Other Big Round Things*. Candlewick, 2003. Ages 13–18. Disillusionment with not feeling part of the family, weight control, and self-image.

Matson, Margaret. *Second Chance Summer*. Simon & Schuster, 2012. Ages 14–18. Taylor's family has one final summer together before her father dies of cancer. Romance, teen angst, humor, and grief.

Mazer, Norma Fox. *The Missing Girl*. HarperTeen, 2008. Ages 14–18. Abduction and abuse of a girl by a man who has been watching five sisters. Alternating voices.

McCall, Guadalupe Garcia. *Under the Mesquite*. Lee & Low, 2011. **(NV)**. Ages 14–18. Mexican-American girl who copes with family obligations and the loss of her mother.

McCormack, Patricia. *Purple Heart*. Balzer & Bray, 2009. Ages 13–17. Young soldier in Iraq feels guilt over the death of a child.

McKay, Hilary. *Indigo's Star*. Simon & Schuster, 2004. Ages 11–14. Unorthodox English family, dealing with bullies at school. Humor. Casson family series. (British)

Medina, Meg. *Yaqui Delgado Wants to Kick Your Ass*. Candlewick, 2013. Ages 14–18. First-person voice of a girl facing bullying and living in constant fear. Body image, racism, class conflict, questioning of self-worth.

Meldrum, Christina. *Madapple*. Knopf, 2008. Ages 15–18. Family mystery and court trial involve murder and a virgin birth.

Morgenroth, Kate. *Echo*. Simon & Schuster, 2006. Ages 13–18. Depression and mental health issues after a brother's accidental shooting. Psychological thriller.

Mullaly Hunt, Lynda. *One of the Murphys*. Nancy Paulsen, 2012. Ages 11–15. A girl in foster care comes to understand what it means to be part of the family.

Nelson, Theresa. *Ruby Electric*. Simon & Schuster, 2003. Ages 10–13. Father–daughter relationship, single-parent family life.

Pitcher, Annabel. *My Sister Lives on the Mantelpiece*. Little, Brown, 2011. Ages 12–14. A boy tries to cope in a family that has fallen apart after a little sister's death in a terrorist bombing. (British)

Reinhardt, Dane. *The Things a Brother Knows*. Wendy Lamb, 2010. Ages 15–18. A teen follows his brother, an ex-Marine with PTSD, on a walking trip from Boston to Washington DC.

Rice, David. *Crazy Loco*. Dial, 2001. **(COL)** Ages 12–18. Nine short stories about growing up Latino/a, devoted to family and tradition in South Texas.

Saldaña, René. *The Jumping Tree*. Delacorte, 2001. Ages 11–14. Texas border town, Mexican-American family.

Schumacher, Julie. *Black Box*. Delacorte, 2008. Ages 12–18. Sibling's depression, family struggles.

Smith, Hope Anita. *Keeping the Night Watch*. Illus. by E. B. Lewis. Holt, 2008. **(NV)** Ages 11–15.

Relationships within an African-American family. Free verse and sonnets. Sequel to *The Way a Door Closes* (2003).

Sones, Sonya. *One of Those Hideous Books Where the Mother Dies*. Simon & Schuster, 2004. **(NV)** Ages 13–18. Father–daughter relationship, homosexual father.

Stork, Francisco X. *The Last Summer of the Death Warriors*. Scholastic, 2010. Ages 12–16. Love, life, and death are the big ideas in this story of a Mexican-American teen who wants to avenge his sister's death.

Werlin, Nancy. *The Rules of Survival*. Dial, 2006. Ages 14–18. Child abuse by mentally disturbed mother in a suspenseful thriller.

Whaley, John Corey. *Where Things Come Back*. Atheneum, 2011. Ages 14–18. Small town, failed romances, brother's disappearance, and an extinct woodpecker. Grief, second chances, multiple voices. Printz Award.

Whitney, Daisy. *When You Were Here*. Little, Brown, 2013. Ages 14–18. Loss and hope in a Japanese setting. Danny goes to Japan to find answers to his mother's final months before her death from cancer.

Woodson, Jacqueline. *Locomotion*. Putnam, 2003. **(NV)** Ages 9–14. Foster care, surviving death of parents.

Zara, Sara. *How to Save a Life*. Little, Brown, 2011. Ages 14–18. A teen, grieving her father's death struggles with her mother's decision to adopt another teen's baby. Multiple viewpoints.

Relationships with Peers

Andrews, Jesse. *Me and Earl and the Dying Girl*. Amulet, 2012. Ages 14–18. Unlikely friendships of a socially awkward boy who is also a budding filmmaker. Strong first person voice.

Anderson, Laurie Halse. *Twisted*. Viking, 2007. Ages 14–18. Teen boy struggles with the tension between a new social identity and personal integrity.

Brown, Jennifer. *Hate List*. Little, Brown, 2009. Ages 14–18. A teen struggles with the guilt of her role in a school shooting by her boyfriend.

Castellucci, Cecil. *The Plain Janes*. Illus. by Jim Rugg. DC Comics, 2007. **(GR)** Ages 14–18. Forming a secret club in a new school, living in suburbia.

de la Peña, Matt. *We Were Here*. Delacorte, 2009. Ages 14–18. Diary of a biracial teen sentenced to a group home who escapes with two teens and heads to the Mexican border. Friendship and issues of identity.

Dessen, Sarah. *Just Listen*. Viking, 2006. Standing up for self, attempted rape, and alienation from friends.

Fine, Anne. *Up on Cloud Nine*. Delacorte, 2002. Ages 10–14. Attempted suicide, friendship. (British)

Frank, E. R. *Friction*. Simon & Schuster, 2003. Ages 13–18. Teacher–student relationships, peer pressure.

Frost, Helen. *Keesha's House*. Farrar, 2003. **(NV)** Ages 11–18. Seven teens leave home and look for shelter. Monologues.

Hartinger, Brent. *Project Sweet Life*. HarperTeen, 2009. Ages 12–16. Three friends, instructed by their fathers to find summer jobs, devise schemes to make fast money so they can avoid having to work. Humorous.

Hautman, Pete. *Godless*. Simon & Schuster, 2004. Ages 14–18. Creating a new religion that takes on a power of its own among friends.

Hemphill, Stephanie. *Things Left Unsaid*. Hyperion, 2004. **(NV)** Ages 14–18. Girl seeking her own identity, a friend's attempted suicide.

Holm, Jennifer. *Eighth Grade is Making Me Sick: Ginny Davie's Year in Stuff*. Illus. by Elicia Castaldi. Random, 2012. Ages 10–14. Ginny's changing relationships are documented through photocollages of poems, notes, text messages, comics, realia, and food packages.

Hunt, Scott, Illus. *Twice Told: Original Stories Inspired by Original Artwork*. Dutton, 2006. **(COL)** Ages 12–16. Pairs of young adult authors respond to illustrations on many topics, fantastic and realistic.

Johnson, Angela. *A Certain October*. Simon & Schuster, 2012. Ages 14–18. Struggles with guilt and grief after a horrible accident, friendship and autistic younger brother.

Koertge, Ron. *Margaux with an X*. Candlewick, 2004. Ages 14–18. Unexpected friendship, emotional impact of family violence and abuse.

Lubar, David. *Sleeping Freshmen Never Lie*. Dutton, 2005. Ages 13–16. High school freshmen life, first dates, and walking in the halls. Humor.

Lyga, Barry. *The Astonishing Adventures of Fanboy and Goth Girl*. Houghton, 2006. Ages 14–18. Coping with bullying by writing a graphic novel.

Morgenroth, Kate. *Echo*. Simon & Schuster, 2006. Ages 13–18. Depression and mental health issues after an accidental shooting.

Moriarty, Jaclyn. *The Year of Secret Assignments*. Scholastic, 2004. Ages 14–18. Pen pals, romance. Humor. (Austrlian)

Myers, Walter Dean. *Darius & Twig*. Amistad, 2013. Ages 14–18. Two close friends, a runner and a writer, struggle with the violence and poverty of Harlem as they fight for a better future despite limited options.

———. *What They Found: Love on 145th Street*. Wendy Lamb, 2007. (**COL**) Ages 13–18. Fifteen interrelated stories exploring different aspects of love.

Oates, Joyce Carol. *Big Mouth and Ugly Girl*. HarperCollins, 2002. Ages 14–18. Unlikely friendship, finding the courage to fight the system, integrity.

Perkins, Lynne Rae. *Criss Cross*. Greenwillow, 2005. Ages 11–15. Missed communications with different outcomes, contemplative moments among friends. Newbery Award

Rapp, Adam. *33 Snowfish*. Candlewick, 2003. Ages 16–18. Sexually abused runaways, homelessness, drugs.

———. *The Children and the Wolves*. Candlewick, 2012. Ages 14–18. Three emotionally disturbed teens kidnap a young child. Multiple viewpoints.

Saldin, Erin. *The Girls of No-Return*. Scholastic, 2012. Ages 14–18. Clash of three girls in a reform school around friendships, secrets, lies, and betrayals.

Salisbury, Graham. *Island Boyz: Short Stories*. Wendy Lamb, 2002. (**COL**) Ages 13–16. Ten short stories set in Hawaii about bullying and peer pressure.

Sanchez, Jenny Torres. *Death, Dickinson, and the Demented Life of Frenchie Garcia*. Running Press, 2013. Ages 14–18. Frenchie re-creates her one night adventure with Andy to try and understand his suicide.

Schmatz, Pat. *Bluefish*. Candlewick, 2011. Ages 12–15. Difficult relationships with a grandfather and a friend in a new school, struggles with literacy and secrets. Literary allusions.

Schusterman, Neal. *Antsy Does Time*. Dutton, 2008. Ages 11–14. A boy helps a dying friend by giving a month of his own life. Humor.

Smith, Andrew. *Winger*. Simon & Schuster, 2013. Ages 14-18. A self-proclaimed loner at a boarding school and his struggles with relationships. Combines high comedy with tragedy.

Standiford, Natalie. *How to Say Goodbye in Robot*. Scholastic, 2009. Ages 14–18. An intense platonic friendship between a boy and a girl who are both misfits.

Stead, Rebecca. *Liar & Spy*. Wendy Lamb, 2012. Ages 12–14. Spies, games, and friendship accompany a move to a new apartment and family changes.

Wayland, April Halprin. *Girl Coming in for a Landing*. Illus. by Elaine Clayton. Knopf, 2002. (**NV**). Ages 12–16. A year in the life of a teenage girl. Humor.

Wild, Margaret. *Jinx*. Walker, 2002. (**NV**) Ages 15–18. Dealing with the death of friends. (Australian)

Woodson, Jacqueline. *Behind You*. Putnam, 2004. Ages 14–18. Coping with the death of a teenage boy. Alternating voices.

———. *After Tupac and D Foster*. Speak, 2008. Ages 12–15. Friendship, growing up in an unpredictable world and urban environment.

Identity

Abdel-Fattah, Randa. *Does My Head Look Big in This?* Scholastic, 2007. Ages 12–18. A Muslim teen from Palestine copes with issues of faith and identity in her new home in Australia. (Australian)

Alexie, Sherman. *The Absolutely True Diary of a Part-Time Indian*. Little, Brown, 2007. Ages 12–18. Leaving the reservation to go to school and attempting to live in both worlds.

Almond, David. *Raven Summer*. Delacorte, 2008. Ages 14–18. Nature of war, truth, art, and the evil within each person in a complex story set in the British countryside. (British)

Badoe, Adwoa. *Between Sisters*. Groundwood, 2010. Ages 14–18. Teen in Ghana, sent from her village to work as a nanny in a large city, struggles with issues of identity and social class. (Ghanaian)

Bradbury, Jennifer. *Shift*. Atheneum, 2008. Ages 14–18. A coming-of-age story of two friends on a cross-country ride from which one disappears.

Bray, Libba. *Going Bovine*. Delacorte, 2009. Ages 14–18. A teen slacker is diagnosed with "mad cow" disease and goes on a road trip with a dwarf searching for a cure—or is he hallucinating? Satirical treatment of popular culture through dry humor and connections to Don Quixote. Printz Award

Brooks, Kevin. *Lucas*. Scholastic, 2003. Ages 14–17. Dealing with prejudice and bigotry, father–daughter relationship. (British)

Cameron, Emma. *Out of This Place*. Candlewick, 2013. (NV) Ages 14–18. Three teens in difficult life situations struggle to leave "this place" and redefine themselves. Multiple narrators. (Australian)

Canales, Viola. *The Tequila Worm*. Wendy Lamb, 2005. Ages 12–15. Mexican-American teen addresses prejudice by excelling in school.

Cart, Michael, editor. *Rush Hour: Face; A Journal of Contemporary Voices* (Volume 3). Delacorte, 2005. (COL) Ages 15–18. Broad theme of "face" explored in a variety of forms and genres of short stories.

———. *Rush Hour: Reckless; A Journal of Contemporary Voices* (Volume 4). Delacorte, 2006. (COL) Ages 14–18. Stories dealing with the psychology of recklessness in teenagers.

Chambers, Aidan. *Postcards from No Man's Land*. Dutton, 2002. Ages 14–18. Finding parallels between the past of World War II and the present. (British) Printz Award

———. *Dying to Know You*. Amulet, 2012. Ages 14–18. Friendship between an elderly man and a dyslexic boy who is trying to find his own voice. (British)

Cofer, Judith. *If I Could Fly*. Farrar, 2011. Ages 12–16. Doris searches for her place when her mother returns to Puerto Rico, leaving her with her often absent musician father.

Curtis, Christopher Paul. *Bucking the Sarge*. Random, 2004. Ages 13–18. Mother–son relationship, welfare system fraud. Humor.

de la Peña, Matt. *I Will Save You*. Delacorte, 2010. Ages 14–18. Running away to start over, a young man must face his past.

———. *Mexican Whiteboy*. Ember, 2010. Ages 12–16. Baseball player struggles with his biracial identity.

Dessen, Sarah. *What Happened to Goodbye?* Viking, 2011. Ages 13–17. Moved from place to place, a high school student wants friendship and a sense of permanency.

Dorfman, Ariel, and Joaquin Dorfman. *Burning City*. Random, 2005. Ages 15–18. A teen delivers "bad news" messages by bicycle in Manhattan. S (Argentinian-Chilean)

Dowd, Siobhan. *Solace of the Road*. David Fickling, 2009. Ages 14–16. A girl runs away from her foster home in London on a journey of self-discovery, denial, and memory. (Irish)

Fleischman, Paul. *Breakout*. Cricket, 2003. Ages 15–18. Runaway, dealing with foster homes.

French, Simon. *Where in the World*. Peachtree, 2003. Ages 10–14. Adjusting to a new country, relationship between a boy and his grandfather. (Australian)

Green, John. *An Abundance of Katherines*. Dutton, 2006. Ages 14–18. A former child prodigy seeking direction to his life while on a road trip.

———. *Paper Towns*. Dutton, 2008. Ages 15–18. Teen boy trying to understand the mystery of his longtime neighbor, Margo.

Henkes, Kevin. *Olive's Ocean*. Greenwillow, 2003. Ages 11–15. First romance, death of a classmate, journal.

Jacobson, Jennifer. *Stained*. Atheneum, 2005. Ages 15–18. Religious and sexual identities, love and death in a small-town.

Johnson, Maureen. *The Key to the Golden Firebird*. HarperCollins, 2004. Ages 13–18. Sisters struggling with father's death, dealing with drugs, alcohol, and sex.

Johnson, R. Kikuo. *Night Fisher.* Fantagraphics, 2005. **(GR)** Ages 15–18. Alienated teens at a prep school on Maui slip into a life of petty theft and drugs.

Kephart, Beth. *Undercover.* HarperCollins, 2007. Ages 14–18. Personal insights for a girl who ghostwrites love messages for her friends.

Koertge, Ron. *Boy Girl Boy.* Harcourt, 2005. Ages 14–18. An evolving friendship among three teens approaching adulthood.

Magoon, Kekla. *Camo Girl.* Aladdin, 2011. Ages 12–14. A biracial girl struggles with identity and her friendship with the "weird kid" when offered the friendship of a popular new student.

Marchetta, Melina. *Jellicoe Road.* HarperTeen, 2008. Ages 14–18. Intricate structure that connects two narratives across time as a teen in a boarding school pieces together the truth of her past. Printz Award. (Australian)

McCormick, Patricia. *My Brother's Keeper.* Perfection Learning, 2006. Ages 12–14. A family falls apart after the father leaves.

Myers, Walter Dean. *All the Right Stuff.* Amistad, 2012. Ages 14–18. Learning to understand "the social contract," and what it means for a young man just learning about life.

Na, An. *Wait for Me.* Speak, 2006. Ages 14–18. A Korean-American girl struggles with the clash between family expectations and her own dreams.

Nolan, Han. *Pregnant Pause.* Harcourt, 2011. Ages 14–18. A pregnant, married teen searches for who and what she wants to be in her life. Complex character.

Nye, Naomi Shihab. *There is No Long Distance Now.* Greenwillow, 2011. Ages 12–18. Very short stories about teens dealing with difficult life situations in the process of growing up.

Oates, Joyce Carol. *Small Avalanches and Other Stories.* HarperCollins, 2003. **(COL)** Ages 14–18. Twelve stories featuring teenage girls' experiences.

Saldaña, René, Jr. *Finding Our Way: Stories.* Wendy Lamb, 2003. **(COL)** Ages 13–18. Twelve short stories about Latino experiences.

Snell, Gordon, editor. *Thicker Than Water: Coming-of-Age Stories by Irish and Irish-American Writers.* Delacorte, 2001. **(COL)** Ages 14–18.

Twelve stories by well-known writers for young adults.

Sonnenblick, Jordan. *Notes from the Midnight Driver.* Scholastic, 2006. Ages 15–18. A teenage boy's legal problems and his community service at a nursing home. First person narrative, humor.

Tamaki, Mariko. *Emiko Superstar.* Illus. by Steve Rolston. Minx, 2008. **(GR)** Ages 14–18. An Asian-Canadian teen returning home and reflecting on her time in the spotlight as a superstar. (Canadian)

——. *Skim.* Illus. by Jillian Tamaki. Groundwood, 2008. **(GR)** Ages 14–18. After losing her only friend, a misfit faces questions of life, death, identity, and friendship. (Canadian)

Valley, Josanne La. *The Vine Basket.* Clarion, 2013. Ages 12–15. Mehrigul, from a Uyghur tribal group that is scorned by the Chinese government, struggles with poverty and defining her self-worth as a weaver.

Van Draanen, Wendelin. *Runaway.* Knopf, 2006. Ages 12–16. A runaway from foster care learns to cope.

Williams-Garcia, Rita. *No Laughter Here.* HarperCollins, 2004. Ages 12–16. A friend is subjected to female circumcision while visiting Nigeria.

Zarr, Sara. *The Lucy Variations.* Little, Brown, 2013. Ages 14–18. After abandoning a promising piano career, Lucy experiments with new identities and redefines family relationships.

Community

Abirached, Zeina. *A Game for Swallows: To Die, to Leave, to Return.* Translated from French by Edward Gauvin. Graphic Universe, 2012. **(GR).** Ages 14–18. The intertwined stories and relationships of neighbors gathered in a Beirut apartment during bombing. (Lebanese)

Amnesty International. *Free? Stories about Human Rights.* Candlewick, 2009. Ages 12–18. Short stories and poems by top young adult authors, each inspired by articles from the United Nations Declaration of Human Rights.

Anderson, Laurie Halse. *Prom.* Viking, 2005. Ages 14–18. An ordinary high school senior dealing with friendship, dating, and the hypocrisies of high school life.

Berk, Josh. *The Dark Days of Hamburger Halpin.* Knopf, 2010. Mainstreaming, misfits, and murder along with deaf politics all set within high school culture.

Carlson, Lori Marie, editor. *Moccasin Thunder: American Indian Stories for Today.* HarperCollins, 2005. **(COL)** Ages 14–18. Ten stories on the everyday traditions and struggles of Native Americans and their communities.

Craig, Colleen. *Afrika.* Tundra, 2008. Ages 12–15. Search for truth about her father, cruelty of apartheid. South Africa. (Canadian)

Crutcher, Chris. *Period 8.* Greenwillow, 2013. Ages 14–18. A respected teacher sets up Period 8 as a safe place for high school students to talk openly about concerns. Heartbreak, sports, suspense, and a missing student.

Danticat, Edwidge. *Behind the Mountains.* Orchard, 2002. Ages 11–15. Haiti. Immigration to Brooklyn from rural Haiti. Diary entry format.

Fleischman, Paul. *Seedfolks.* HarperCollins, 1997. Ages 11–15. Gardening as an impetus for urban renewal and relationships in a community. Multiple narrators.

Frost, Helen. *Spinning through the Universe: A Novel in Poems from Room 214.* Farrar, 2004. **(NV)** Ages 11–14. Poems considering school and family by a teacher and her students. In poetic forms, explained at the end.

Going, K. L. *Saint Iggy.* Harcourt, 2006. Ages 15–18. New York City housing projects, school suspensions, drug use, 16-year-old Iggy's struggles.

Green, John. *Looking for Alaska.* Dutton Juvenile, 2005. Ages 15–18. A search for answers in the death of a friend, complexity of high school friendships and pranks in a boarding school culture. Printz Award.

Gosselink, John. *The Defense of Thaddeus A. Ledbetter.* Amulet, 2010. Ages 12–14. Thaddeus is in year-long school suspension for organizing an unauthorized school safety drill. Novel is his defense of his actions in the form of a journal, school reports, letters, notes, and illustrations.

Halliday, Ayun. *Peanut.* Schwartz & Wade, 2013. **(GR)** Ages 12–15. Nervous about moving to a new high school, Abby makes herself interesting by claiming to have a peanut allergy.

Howe, James. *The Misfits.* Simon & Schuster, 2001. Ages 10–14. Coping with bullies. Multiple narrators.

Ives, David. *Voss.* Putnam, 2008. Ages 10–16. An undocumented immigrant from Slobovia describes job hunting and other challenges in an American city in letters home to a friend. Humorous.

Laird, Elizabeth, with Sonia Nimr. *A Little Piece of Ground.* Haymarket, 2006. Ages 10–14. A Palestinian boy and his Christian friend work to create a soccer field in the Israeli occupied West Bank. (British)

McDonald, Janet. *Spellbound.* Farrar, 2001. Ages 13–18. Urban housing project, African-American teen mothers drop out of school, forming their own community. Sequels: *Chill Wind* (2002) and *Twists and Turns* (2003).

McGowan, Anthony. *The Knife that Killed Me.* Delacorte, 2008. Ages 14–18. Alienation and reaction within school culture for a teen caught between two groups. (British)

Myers, Walter Dean. *145th Street.* Delacorte, 2000. **(COL)** Ages 12–18. Short stories about Harlem.

Olsen, Sylvia. *The Girl with a Baby.* Sono Nis, 2004. Ages 13–18. A Tsartlip First Nation girl living in British Columbia coping with pregnancy and a new baby. (Canadian)

———. *White Girl.* Sono Nis, 2005. Ages 13–18. An outsider adjusting to a First Nations reserve. (Canadian).

Park, Linda Sue. *A Long Walk to Water.* Clarion, 2010. Ages 12–15. Based on the true story of a Lost Boy of Sudan who escapes and whose life later intersects with the story of a girl searching for clean water in Sudan.

Resau, Laura. *The Indigo Notebook.* Delacorte, 2009. Agers 14–18. Zeeta longs for a normal life after living in 15 countries with her free-spirited mother. Set in Ecuador. Sequels.

———. *What the Moon Saw.* Delacorte, 2006. Ages 10–15. Summer with grandparents in a village in Mexico.

Stine, Catherine. *Refugees.* Delacorte, 2005. Ages 14–18. Dealing with alienation by an Afghan teen and an American teen after the September 11 attack. Told through phone calls and e-mails.

Stratton, Allan. *Chanda's Secrets*. Annick, 2004. Ages 14–18. Living with AIDS in sub-Saharan Africa.

Whitman, Sylvia. *The Milk of Birds*. Atheneum, 2013. Ages 14–18. Alternating first person accounts of two pen pals, one a refugee in the Sudan, and the other a U.S. teen struggling with learning disabilities.

Williams-Garcia, Rita. *Jumped*. HarperTeen, 2009. Ages 14–18. The intertwined lives of three girls during one violent day in an urban high school.

Yang, Gene Luen. *American Born Chinese*. First Second, 2006. **(GR)** Ages 14–18. Three intertwined stories about growing up Chinese American. Mixed genre. Printz Award.

Romance and Sexuality

Anderson, Laurie Halse. *Speak*. Farrar, 1999. Ages 14–18. A girl struggles with becoming a social outcast after calling police to report date rape by a popular boy.

Beam, Cris. *I Am J*. Little, Brown, 2011. Ages 14–18. Teen from a biracial family who is transitioning from female to male.

Burd, Nick. *The Vast Fields of Ordinary*. Dial, 2009. Ages 14–18. Sexual experimentation, coming-out, and a parent's decaying marriage create an honest and dark struggle with identity.

Burgess, Melvin. *Doing It*. Holt, 2004. Ages 14–18. Sexual urges and anxieties of three teenage boys. (British)

Cohn, Rachel and David Levithan. *Nick & Norah's Infinite Playlist*. Ages 14–18. Knopf, 2006. Alternating voices tell the story of one date over one night of two teens recovering from broken hearts and falling in love.

Dalton, Michelle. *Fifteenth Summer*. Simon Pulse, 2013. Ages 12–16. Sweet, realistic tale of a girl's first love.

Danforth, Emily. *The Miseducation of Cameron Post*. Balzere & Bray, 2012. Ages 14–18. A teen is sent to a gay conversion center by her family. Identity and survival.

Deak, Erzsi and Kristin Embry Litchman, editors. *Period Pieces*. HarperCollins, 2003. **(COL)** Ages 10–14. Girls' experiences as they begin menstruation.

Downham, Jenny. *You against Me*. David Fickling, 2010. Mikey falls in love with Ellie, the sister of the boy who his sister claims raped her, causing tension in a forbidden romance. (British)

Draper, Sharon. *November Blues*. Atheneum, 2007. Ages 14–18. A 16-year-old teen deals with pregnancy and the accidental death of her boyfriend.

Freitas, Donna. *The Possibilities of Sainthood*. Farrar, 2008. Ages 14–16. Experiences of first love and family feuds in a Catholic school and an immigrant family.

George, Madeleine. *The Difference between You and Me*. Viking, 2012. Ages 14–18. Complex lesbian relationships and political activism through the voices of three narrators.

Gonzalez, Julie. *Wings*. Delacorte, 2005. Ages 14–18. Falling in love with the wrong people. Two parallel narrators.

Goode, L. *Sister Mischief*. Candlewick, 2011. Ages 14–18. An all-girl hip-hop group of outcasts challenges issues of sexism, racism, religion, and coming out in a small-town high school.

Green, John. *The Fault in Our Stars*. Ages 14–18. Two teens fall in love while dealing with cancer and death.

—— and David Levithan. *Will Grayson, Will Grayson*. Dutton, 2010. Ages 14–18. The alternating voices of two characters with the same name, both struggling with sexuality and relationships. Graphic and humorous.

Griffith, Paul. *Stay with Me*. Dial, 2007. Ages 14–18. Alternating voices tell about the romance between a high school dropout and a straight-A student. Pit bull rescue. (British)

Handler, Daniel. *Why We Broke Up*. Little Brown, 2011. Ages 14–18. The romance and break up of an athlete and a movie fanatic.

Hartinger, Brent. *Geography Club*. HarperTempest, 2003. Ages 14–18. Mutual support among gay and lesbian teenagers in high school.

Horner, Emily. *A Love Story Starring My Best Dead Friend*. Dial, 2010. Ages 14–18. First love between two teen girls and survivors coping with the death of their friend by putting on a musical that she wrote.

Johnson, Angela. *The First Part Last.* Simon & Schuster, 2003. Ages 14–18. Teenage father raising an infant daughter. Printz Award.

King, A.S. *Ask the Passengers.* Little, Brown, 2012. Ages 14–18. Astrid struggles with sexuality, politics, and societal norms in a small town by sending her questions to passengers in planes flying overhead.

Kluger, Steve. *My Most Excellent Year: A Novel of Love, Mary Poppins & Fenway Park.* Dial, 2008. Ages 14–18. Three teens narrate their multiple love stories that include e-mails, text messages, and school assignments.

Koja, Kathie. *Talk.* Farrar, 2005. Ages 14–18. Discovering sexual orientation, high school play, self-perception.

Konigsberg, Bill. *Openly Straight.* Scholastic, 2013. Ages 14–18. Tired of being the token gay kid, Rafe takes on the role of openly straight to become one of the guys in his new school.

Larochelle, David. *Absolutely, Positively Not.* Scholastic, 2005. Ages 12–18. Hilarious coming-out story told as a first-person narrative.

Levithan, David. *Boy Meets Boy.* Knopf, 2003. Ages 14–18. Accepting others and their sexual orientations.

Lockhart, E. *The Disreputable History of Frankie Landau-Banks.* Hyperion, 2008. Ages 15–18. Romance, gender, and power questioned by a girl in an elite boarding school.

Lynch, Chris. *Inexcusable.* Simon & Schuster, 2005. Ages 14–18. Football player rationalizing his actions, date rape.

Madigan, L. K. *Flash Burnout.* Houghton Mifflin, 2009. Ages 14–17. An exploration of the complexities of friendship and romance in the life of Blake, a photographer in training.

McDonald, Abby. *Jane Austen Goes to Hollywood.* Candlewick, 2013. Ages 14–18. Modernized version of *Sense and Sensibility* in which two sisters move to Hollywood after being cut off from the family fortune.

Myers, Walter Dean. *Street Love.* HarperCollins, 2006. **(NV)** Ages 15–18. Hope, love, and anger across social class lines in Harlem. Suitable for readers' theatre.

Orff, Joel. *Waterwise.* Alternative Comics, 2004. **(GR)** Ages 16–18. Recalling the past and life choices with old childhood friends.

Peters, Julie Anne. *Luna.* Little, Brown, 2004. Ages 15–18. Dealing with identity and a transsexual sibling.

Perkins, Stephanie. *Anna and the French Kiss.* Dutton, 2010. Ages 14–18. First love, Paris boarding school, identity and romance.

Resau, Laura. *Red Glass.* Delacorte, 2007. Ages 13–18. First romance on a trip through Mexico and Guatemala.

Rosenberg, Liz. *17: A Novel in Prose Poems.* Cricket, 2002. **(NV)** Ages 14–18. The sexual awakening of a teen intertwined with her struggles with anorexia and depression. Manic depressive mother.

Sanchez, Alex. *Getting It.* Simon & Schuster, 2006. Ages 15–18. Gay and straight friends helping one another.

St. James, James. *Freak Show.* Dutton, 2007. Ages 14–18. Drag queen in small southern town who challenges prejudice by running for Homecoming Queen.

Wild, Margaret. *One Night.* Knopf, 2004. **(NV)** Ages 14–18. Dealing with teen pregnancy and single motherhood. (Australian)

Wilson, Martin. *What They Always Tell Us.* Delacorte, 2008. Ages 14–18. High school student exploring issues of sexual identity, suicide attempt.

Wittlinger, Ellen. *Parrotfish.* Simon & Schuster, 2007. Ages 14–18. A transgendered high school student adjusting to his new identity as a male.

Zarr, Sara. *Story of a Girl.* Little, Brown, 2007. Ages 15–18. A girl's encounter in a backseat of a car results in her being labeled as the school slut and shunned by her father. Small town life.

———. *Sweethearts.* Little, Brown, 2008. Ages 15–18. Two teens confronting a shared abusive sexual situation from seven years earlier.

Challenges in Life

Anderson, Laurie Halse. *Wintergirls.* Viking, 2009. Ages 12–16. Anorexia, guilt, and the death of a friend.

Baskins, Nora Raleigh. *Anything but Typical*. Simon & Schuster, 2009. Ages 11–14. First-person perspective of Jason, an autistic teen, who is a creative writing whiz but at a loss socially.

Book Wish Foundation. *What You Wish For: Stories and Poems for Darfur*. Putnam's, 2011. **(COL)** Ages 12–14. Short stories and poems by well-known authors on the theme of wishing and the dreams of youth.

Brenna, Beverly. *Waiting for No One*. Red Deer Press, 2011. Ages 12–16. A girl with Asperger's Syndrome attempting to find a job and just fit in. (Canadian)

Draper, Sharon. *Out of My Mind*. Perfection, 2012. A brilliant girl with cerebral palsy is assumed to be mentally challenged until technology allows her to speak for the first time.

Gallo, Donald. *What Are You Afraid Of?: Stories about Phobias*. Candlewick, 2006. Ages 12–15. A collection of short stories about facing different kinds of fears.

George, Madeleine. *Looks*. Viking, 2008. Ages 12–18. An unlikely friendship between two high school girls, one anorexic, one obese.

Going, K. L. *Fat Kid Rules the World*. Putnam, 2003. Ages 14–18. Friendship, dealing with obesity, drug abuse.

Hautman, Pete. *Invisible*. Simon & Schuster, 2005. Ages 12–18. Friendship between two high school boys, mental illness.

Hobbs, Valerie. *Defiance*. Farrar, 2005. Ages 11–14. Dealing with cancer, gaining strength through a friendship with an elderly poet.

Hopkins, Ellen. *Impulse*. McElderry, 2007. **(NV)**. Ages 14–18. Three teens connect in a mental hospital after each has attempted suicide.

Jones, Taci. *Silhouetted by the Blue*. Farrar, 2011. Ages 11–14. A teen deals with grief and her father's depression along with adjustment to middle school.

Koertge, Ron. *Stoner and Spaz*. Candlewick, 2002. Ages 14–18. Unlikely romance between a drug user and a teen with cerebral palsy. Also *Now Playing Stoner and Spaz II* (2011).

Nolan, Han. *Crazy*. Harcourt, 2010. Ages 14–18. Teen who is forced to parent his mentally ill father and who ends up in foster care and therapy.

Palacio, R. J. *Wonder*. New York: Knopf. Ages 12–14. A homeschooled boy with a severe facial deformity goes to school for the first time, trying to find his place in middle school life.

Rapp, Adam. *Under the Wolf, Under the Dog*. Candlewick, 2004. Ages 16–18. Living in a therapeutic facility for suicidal and drug-addicted teens.

Rosen, Renee. *Every Crooked Pot*. St. Martin's, 2007. Ages 15–18. Growing up with a disfiguring birthmark and an overly protective father.

Roy, Jennifer. *Mindblind*. Cavendish, 2010. Ages 12–15. A teen with Asperger's Syndrome tries to prove he is a genius by writing songs for his rock band.

Schumacher, Julie. *Black Box*. Delacorte, 2008. Ages 15–18. First person account of a younger sister trying to help her older sister cope with severe depression.

Stork, Francisco X. *Marcelo in the Real World*. Scholastic, 2009. Ages 14–18. An autistic teen, forced to work in his father's mailroom, makes life-changing decisions.

Sullivan, Tara. *Golden Boy*. Putnam's, 2013. Ages 12–16. Born albino in a Tanzanian village, Habo faces tremendous prejudice and must flee poachers who want to sell his body parts.

Vaught, Susan R. *Big Fat Manifesto*. Bloomsbury, 2008. Ages 13–19. Overweight high school senior writing in her school newspaper about being fat in a thin society.

Vrettos, Adrienne. *Burnout*. McElderry, 2011. Ages 14–18. Rebellious teen who has spun out of control and is trying to find her way back from alcoholism.

Vizzini, Ned. *It's Kind of a Funny Story*. Hyperion, 2006. Ages 15–18. A teenage boy battling depression, resorting to drugs, and eventually developing self-awareness.

Warman, Jessica. *Breathless*. Walker, 2009. Ages 14–18. Swimming as an escape from a teen's dysfunctional family and brother's schizophrenia.

Weeks, Sarah. *So B. It*. HarperCollins, 2004. Ages 10–14. Dealing with agoraphobia and the developmental disability of a parent; seeking family origins.

Williams, Carol Lynch. *Waiting*. Simon & Schuster, 2012. **(NV)** Ages 12–18. A teen and her family are devastated by the suicide of her brother, grieving and heartbroken.

Woodson, Jacqueline. *Beneath a Meth Moon*. Nancy Paulsen, 2012. Ages 13–17. Drug abuse to cope with loss and pain as a result of Hurricane Katrina.

Suspense and Survival

Abrahams, Peter. *Down the Rabbit Hole*. Harper-Collins, 2005. Ages 11–15. Amateur actress/story protagonist caught in the middle of a murder mystery.

Allison, Jennifer. *Gilda Joyce: Psychic Investigator*. Dutton, 2005. Ages 10–14. A young detective uncovering the truth behind a family tragedy. Humor.

Alphin, Elaine Marie. *The Perfect Shot*. Carolrhoda, 2005. Ages 13–18. A grieving witness struggling with his responsibilities. Told in flashbacks interspersed with facts from the study of American judicial history.

Balliett, Blue. *Chasing Vermeer*. Illus. by Brett Helquist. Scholastic, 2004. Ages 10–14. Student detectives searching for a missing painting.

———. *The Wright 3*. Illus. by Brett Helquist. Scholastic, 2006. Ages 9–14. Art crime, a Frank Lloyd Wright house, three young sleuths.

Booth, Coe. *Tyrell*. Scholastic, 2006. Ages 14–18. South Bronx in New York City, homelessness, welfare fraud, struggle of 15-year-old Tyrell. First person. Also *Bronxwood* (2011), continuation of Tyrell's story.

Cadnum, Michael. *Flash*. Farrar, 2010. Ages 14–18. Five voices weave together in a scripted drama filled with tension after two brothers bungle a bank robbery, witnessed by a blind man. Thriller, unpredictable.

Cameron, Ann. *Colibrí*. Farrar, 2003. Ages 11–16. Kidnapping, coming of age in Guatemala.

Christopher, Lucy. *Stolen*. Scholastic, 2010. Ages 13–17. Surviving kidnapping and sexual abuse. (British)

Dowd, Siobhan. *A Swift Pure Cry*. Random, 2007. Ages 14–18. Family questioned when a dead baby is found. Remote Irish village. (Irish)

Doyle, Roddy. *Wilderness*. Scholastic, 2007. Ages 12–16. A dual narrative involving a reunion in Dublin with a long-absent mother and a dog-sledding adventure in Finland. (Irish)

Ehrenhaft, Daniel. *Drawing a Blank; or How I Tried to Solve a Mystery, End a Feud, and Land the Girl of My Dreams*. Illus. by Trevor Ristow. HarperCollins, 2006. Ages 13–18. New England prep school, kidnapping, Scotland. Alternating chapters of first person narratives and super-hero comic-strip episodes. Humor.

Ellison, Kate. *The Butterfly Clues*. Egmont, 2012. Ages 14–18. Engaging mystery starring a teen with obsessive-compulsive disorder.

Farish, Terry. *The Good Braider*. Skyscape, 2012. **(NV)** Ages 12–16. Refugee story about a girl and her family who escape Sudan and settle in Portland, Maine. Culture clash.

Hiaasen, Carl. *Chomp*. Knopf, 2012. Ages 10–14. Search for a reality star who disappears in the Everglades.

———. *Hoot*. Knopf, 2003. Ages 10–14. Protecting the environment, owl habitat. Humor.

———. *Scat*. Knopf, 2009. Ages 10–14. The investigation of a missing biology teacher on a school eco-trip.

Leavitt, Martine. *My Book of Life by Angel*. Farrar, 2012. Ages 14–18. Teen struggles to survive a life of prostitution and drugs in Vancouver, BC. Integrates Milton's *Paradise Lost*. (Canadian)

Lyga, Barry. *I Hunt Killers*. Little, Brown, 2012. Ages 15–18. A thriller about a teen whose father is a convicted serial killer and who investigates when someone begins recreating those murders.

McCaughrean, Geraldine. *The White Darkness*. HarperTempest, 2007. Ages 14–18. Survival thriller on an Antarctic expedition. (British) Printz Award.

Morgenroth, Kate. *Jude*. Simon & Schuster, 2004. Ages 14–18. Murder, drugs, and mystery; coming-of-age.

Myers, Walter Dean. *Lockdown*. Amistad, 2010. Reese is serving time in a juvenile detention facility and trying to make the right choices in order to earn early release.

———. *Sunrise over Fallujah*. Scholastic, 2009. Ages 13–18. An account of a young soldier in Iraq.

Perkins, Lynn Rae. *As Easy as Falling Off the Face of the Earth*. Greenwillow, 2010. Ages 12–16. Adventure of a teen who misses his train in the middle of nowhere, out of cell phone range.

Perkins, Mitali. *Bamboo People*. Charlesbridge, 2010. Ages 12–16. Two boys, on opposite sides of the conflict in Burma, tell their stories of trying to survive amidst violence and a repressive regime. Child soldiers.

Petrucha, Stefan. *Nancy Drew: The Demon of River Heights*. Papercutz, 2005. **(GR)** Ages 9–14. Favorite girl detective in a graphic novel with manga-style art.

Sachar, Louis. *Small Steps*. Delacorte, 2006. Ages 11–14. A focus on two of the secondary characters after the closing of Camp Green Lake. Sequel to *Holes* (1998).

Schrefer, Eliot. *Endangered*. Scholastic, 2012. Ages 12–16. Surviving a revolution in the Congo while also saving endangered primates.

Sloan, Holly G. *I'll Be There*. Little, Brown, 2011. Ages 14–18. Sam and his brother struggle to survive a life of crime with his mentally ill father and establish new relationships.

Sonnenblick, Jordan. *After Ever After*. Scholastic, 2010. Ages 12–14. Jeffery has survived leukemia but finds that happily ever after isn't what he expected as he deals with issues of family, friendship, and death.

Sorrells, Walter. *Fake I.D.* Dutton, 2005. Ages 14–18. A missing mother, changing identities, suspense thriller.

Stewart, Trenton Lee. *The Mysterious Benedict Society*. Little, Brown, 2007. Ages 10–14. Four gifted children recruited for a society planning a takeover of the world. Sequels.

Valentine, Jenny. *Me, the Missing, and the Dead*. HarperTeen, 2008. Ages 15–18. Mysterious discoveries about a missing father. Humor. (British)

Venkatraman, Padma. *Island's End*. Putnam's, 2011. Ages 12–16. In an isolated island culture, a girl guides her people into the future, despite main-land influences. Survival of an Indigenous culture. Andaman Islands.

Werlin, Nancy. *Black Mirror*. Speak, 2003. Ages 14–18. Frances investigates her brother's death, ruled a suicide, in the midst of suspicious activities at a boarding school.

Westerfeld, Scott. *So Yesterday*. Penguin, 2004. Ages 15–18. Market-research-trends thriller set in New York City, finding the next "cool thing."

Wynne-Jones, Tim. *Blink & Caution*. Candlewick, 2011. Ages 14–18. Two street kids who get caught in fake kidnapping. Mystery and love story. (Canadian)

Zusak, Markus. *I Am the Messenger*. Knopf, 2005. Ages 15–18. A cab driver receiving mysterious messages that turn him into a hero. (Australian)

Sports

Aronson, Marc, and Charles R. Smith, editors. *Pick-Up Game: A Full Day of Full Court*. Candlewick, 2012. Ages 14–18. Linked short stories, each by a different author, about a game of street basketball, interspersed with poems and photographs.

Coy, John. *Crackback*. Scholastic, 2005. Ages 13–18. High school football player overcoming criticism by his new coach and his father.

de la Peña, Matthew. *Ball Don't Lie*. Delacorte, 2005. Ages 14–18. A talented basketball player dealing with foster homes and surviving in an urban environment.

Deuker, Carl. *Gym Candy*. Houghton, 2007. Ages 13–18. High school football player, steroid use.

———. *Runner*. Houghton, 2005. Ages 12–18. A solitary teen runner dealing with an alcoholic father and crime in an action-packed story.

Feinstein, John. *Vanishing Act*. Knopf, 2006. Ages 11–18. Mysterious disappearance of a female Russian tennis player at the U.S. Open.

FitzGerald, Dawn. *Soccer Chick Rules*. Roaring Brook, 2006. Ages 10–14. A tax levy needed for a winning soccer team's future.

Green, Tim. *Unstoppable*. HarperCollins, 2012. Ages 12–15. A boy in foster care overcomes adversity to become an unstoppable force on the football field.

Jenkins, A. M. *Out of Order*. HarperCollins, 2003. Ages 14–18. High school baseball player trying to cope with academic problems.

Juby, Susan. *Another Kind of Cowboy*. HarperTeen, 2007. Ages 14–18. Two teenage dressage riders, a rich girl, and a closeted 16-year-old boy seeking identity. (Canadian)

Koertge, Ron. *Shakespeare Bats Cleanup*. Candlewick, 2003. Ages 12–15. Coping with an inability to play baseball due to illness. Diary in poetic forms.

Lipsyte, Robert. *Yellow Flag*. HarperTeen, 2007. Ages 14–18. Teen struggling with mixed emotions about his choice: NASCAR racer or trumpet player?

Lupica, Mike. *Heat*. Philomel, 2006. Ages 11–15. Cuban-American Little League ballplayer, his family, his dreams. Humor.

———. *True Legend*. Puffin, 2013. Ages 12–16. Story of a gifted basketball player and the danger of fame.

———. *The Underdogs*. Puffin, 2012. Ages 12–14. A football player tries to keep his team on the field in a small town hit hard by the loss of jobs.

Murdock, Catherine. *Dairy Queen*. Houghton Mifflin, 2006. Ages 14–18. A teen who works hard on her family's dairy farm decides to try out for football. Humor, inner monologues.

Ritter, John H. *The Boy Who Saved Baseball*. Philomel, 2003. Ages 10–14. Saving the town baseball field.

———. *Under the Baseball Moon*. Philomel, 2006. Ages 11–14. Bond between softball player and jazz musician.

Roberts, Kristi. *My 13th Season*. Holt, 2005. Ages 10–14. A girl struggling with her mother's death and challenging a cruel coach who dislikes having a girl baseball player.

Scieszka, Jon, Gordon Korman, Chrise Rylander, Dan Gutman, Anne Ursu, Tim Green, Joseph Bruchac, and Jacqueline Woodson. *Guys Read the Sports Page*. Illus. by Dan Santat. Walden Pond Press, 2012. (**COL**) Ages 11–16. Sports short stories.

Sonnenblick, Jordan. *Curveball: The Year I Lost My Grip*. Scholastic, 2012. Ages 12–15. An injury ends a teen's dreams as a pitcher and moves him into photography and new relationships.

Valponi, Paul. *The Final Four*. Viking, 2012. Ages 12–18. Basketball tournament pressures told through television interviews, radio transcripts, and segments narrated by different players that are incorporated into play-by-play descriptions of the game.

Wallace, Rich. *One Good Punch*. Knopf, 2007. Ages 14–18. Captain of the track team, marijuana.

 ## Related Films and DVDS

Ball Don't Lie. (2008). Author: Matt de la Peña (2005). 102 minutes.

Confessions of a Teenage Drama Queen (2004). Author: Dyan Sheldon (1999). 89 minutes.

Diary of a Wimpy Kid. (2010). Author: Jeff Kinney (2007). 94 minutes.

Flipped. (2010). Author: Wendelin Van Draanen (2003). 90 minutes.

Holes (2003). Author: Louis Sachar (1998). 117 minutes.

Hoot (2006). Author: Carl Hiaasen (2004). 91 minutes.

It's Kind of a Funny Story. (2011) Author: Ned Vizzini (2007). 101 minutes.

Life, Above All. (2011). Author: Allan Stratton. Based on *Chandra's Secret* (2004). 106 minutes.

The Martian Child (2007). Author: David Gerrold (2002). 106 minutes.

The Nanny Diaries (2007). Authors: Emma Laughlin and Nicola Kraus (2002). 106 minutes.

Nick & Norah's Infinite Playlist (2008). Authors: Rachel Cohn and David Levithan (2006). 90 minutes.

Operation Stormbreaker (2006). Author: Anthony Horowitz (2001). 93 minutes.

Perks of Being a Wallflower. (2012). Author: Stephen Chbosky (1999). 103 minutes.

Pitch Perfect. (2012). Author: Mickey Rapkin (2008). 112 minutes.

Precious. (2010). Author: Sapphire (1997). 110 minutes.

P.S. I Love You. (2007). Author: Cecelia Ahern (2003). 126 minutes.

Rabbit-Proof Fence (2002). Author: Doris Pilkington (2002). 93 minutes.

The Perfect Score. (2012). Author: David Levithan (2004). 93 minutes.

The Sisterhood of the Traveling Pants (2005) and *The Sisterhood of the Traveling Pants 2* (2008). Author: Ann Brashares (2001, 2005). 117 minutes; 119 minutes.

Speak (2004). Author: Laurie Halse Anderson (1999). 89 minutes.

Whale Rider (2002). Author: Witi Ihimaera (2003/1987). 101 minutes.

Chapter Four

Fantasy and Science Fiction

Many of the most popular books for adolescents fall into the genres of fantasy and science fiction. *A Wrinkle in Time* and *The Hobbit* immediately come to mind as old favorites, but the massive success of the Harry Potter, Hunger Games, and Twilight series have created a new audience for fantasy and dystopias and a major influx of new books. The creation of stories that are highly imaginative—yet believable—and that present a world that might be, rather than is, are the hallmark of these genres.

Definition and Description

Fantasy refers to stories in which the authors have created events, settings, or characters that are outside the realm of possibility. A fantasy is a story that cannot happen in the real world, and for this reason this genre has been called the literature of the fanciful impossible. Animals talk, inanimate objects come to life, imaginary worlds exist, and fairies and ghosts interact with human characters in stories that are often full of suspense and mystery. Most horror stories fall into this category, as well as popular novels involving vampires, fallen angels, demons, and other metaphysical beings, such as Stephenie Meyer's Twilight Saga and Cassandra Clare's Mortal Instruments series, both of which became best-sellers and were made into movies.

Science fiction is a closely related genre that features scientifically plausible or techno-logically possible future developments that were only imaginary at the time of publication. Futuristic novels, especially dystopias, are popular as reflected in the success of the Hunger Games trilogy by Suzanne Collins, as is steampunk, a subgenre made popular by Philip Reeve's Hungry City Chronicles.

Both genres refuse to accept the world as it is, instead focusing on what could be or what might have been, and so are also known as ***speculative fiction.*** Both create new or different worlds that have internal consistency through rules that are invented by authors. The difference is that the made-up rules of imagined worlds in science fiction have limits that are based in science and technology. In contrast, fantasy employs magic with plots that cannot be explained rationally now or in the future.

In fantasy and science fiction, the **cycle format,** in which one book is linked to another across three or four volumes through characters and settings, is especially prevalent. This format appeals to readers who become attached to certain characters and imagined worlds and delight in reading the next book in the series, such as Veronica Roth's Divergent series and Rick Riordan's Percy Jackson series. Another connection across the two genres is the appeal of the books to adults as well as adolescents so that many young adult fantasies have made a major crossover into adult readership.

Evaluation and Selection of Fantasy

The usual standards for fine fiction must also be met by authors of modern fantasy. Believable and well-rounded characters that develop and change, cohesive plots, detailed settings with internal consistency, a style appropriate to the story, and thought-provoking themes are elements to be expected in all fiction. The motifs, characters, stylistic elements, and themes often come from folklore, since fantasy has its roots in traditional literature. The authors of fantasies are known, and this fact distinguishes the genre from folktales, whose authors are unknown because those stories have been passed down from ancient times through oral traditions. Folklorists are intrigued by the startling similarity of traditional tales around the world. One explanation is that the first humans created these stories and took them along as they populated the globe, the theory of *monogenesis* or "single origin." The other theory, called *polygenesis,* or "many origins," holds that early humans had similar

Early Important Works of Fantasy and Science Fiction

Date	Literary Work	Significance
1726	*Gulliver's Travels* by Jonathan Swift (England)	An adult novel prototype of an adventure story read by young people
1835	*Fairy Tales* by Hans Christian Andersen (Denmark)	First modern folktales
1864	*Journey to the Center of the Earth* by Jules Verne (France)	First science fiction (written for adults)
1865	*Alice's Adventures in Wonderland* by Lewis Carroll (England)	First children's modern fantasy
1897	*Dracula* by Bram Stoker (England)	An adult novel that helped popularize vampires in literature
1910	*Tom Swift and His Airship* by Victor Appleton (United States)	First juvenile science fiction novel
1926	*Amazing Stories,* science fiction magazine (United States)	Recognition of science fiction as a literary genre
1937	*The Hobbit* by J. R. R. Tolkien (England)	Quest adventure with a cult following
1950	*The Lion, the Witch, and the Wardrobe* by C. S. Lewis (England)	First book of the quest series Chronicles of Narnia, told with religious overtones
1962	*A Wrinkle in Time* by Madeleine L'Engle (United States)	Classic science fiction novel for youth
1964	*The Book of Three* by Lloyd Alexander (United States)	First book in the Prydain Chronicles based on medieval Welsh tales
1968	*A Wizard of Earthsea* by Ursula Le Guin (United States)	Classic work about a boy wizard facing evil
1974	*Carrie* by Stephen King (United States)	Adult horror novel that became popular with young adults

urges, needs, doubts, and motives, and created similar stories in response to their world. Regardless of origin, these traditional stories provide a background for understanding and appreciating many types of modern fantasy and the magic, mythical creatures, quests, and personified animals that cross from folklore to fantasy.

The following questions are useful in evaluating fantasy:

- **Does the fantasy have an internal logic or consistency that makes the unreal, strange, paranormal, or magical events believable?** Sometimes, authors will accomplish this purpose by beginning the story in a familiar, ordinary setting with typical contemporary human beings as characters. A transition is then made to the fantasy world, as exemplified in C. S. Lewis's *The Lion, the Witch, and the Wardrobe,* in which the siblings enter a wardrobe in an old house only to discover that the back of the wardrobe leads into the fantasy world of Narnia. Other fantasies begin in the imagined world but manage, through richly described settings and consistent, well-rounded characters, to make this new world believable, as in Marie Lu's *Legend.* Either way, the plot, characters, and setting must be so well developed that the reader is able to suspend disbelief and accept the impossible as real for the duration of the story.

- **Does the author provide a unique setting that is truly imaginative?** In some stories, the setting may move beyond the realistic in both time (moving to the past, future, or holding still) and place (imagined worlds); in other stories only one of these elements (place or time) will go beyond reality. The setting can range from the rich, detailed worlds of Ursula LeGuin's Earthsea or Veronica Roth's dystopic Chicago to the contemporary teen world of David Levithan's *Every Day*, which seems normal in every way, except that the main character awakes each day inside another person's body and life.

Types of Fantasy

The following types of modern fantasy are a starting point for exploring the variety of fantastic stories, motifs, themes, and characters created by authors. Additional types could be listed, and some stories may fit appropriately into more than one type. Mary Hoffman's *Stravaganza: City of Masks* is included as a historical fantasy because of its authentic historical setting, but the inclusion of spirits from the past also makes it a story of the supernatural.

Fantasy Based in Folktales and Myths

Modern folktales, also known as *literary folktales,* are tales told in a form similar to that of a traditional tale with the incorporation of traditional folktale elements: strong, overt conflict; a fast-moving plot with a sudden resolution; a vague setting; and, in some cases, magical elements. Some traditional tales have been expanded into full-length novels, but a known, identifiable author has written these tales. These stories did not spring from the cultural heritage of a group of people through the oral tradition but rather from the mind of one creator. This distinction does not matter to readers, who enjoy these recent tales as much as they do folktales. The tales of Hans Christian Andersen are the earliest and best known of modern folktales, while *Princess Academy* by Shannon Hale is a more recent example. Current trends include mashups, in which characters from a range of folktales are woven into the same story, as in *Enchanted* by Alethea Kontis, and dark, disturbing folktale variations that involve abuse and violence, as in Margo Lanagan's *Tender Morsels.*

Other authors create imagined worlds that draw from mythology, such as the worlds created by Rick Riordan in his Percy Jackson and the Olympian series, where modern teens move into alternative worlds populated by characters from Greek mythology. Others

Notable Authors of Fantasy and Science Fiction

David Almond, British writer noted for magical realism novels for young adults. *Skellig,* Carnegie Medal winner; *Kit's Wilderness; Clay; Slog's Dad.* www.davidalmond.com

Libba Bray, author of stories that span time frames while remaining true to adolescent voices. *The Diviners; Going Bovine; A Great and Terrible Beauty; Beauty Queens.* www.libbabray.com

Nancy Farmer, author known for unusual settings and issue-driven plots, as in *The House of the Scorpion,* a science fiction novel, *The Ear, the Eye, and the Arm; The Sea of Trolls.* www.nancyfarmerwebsite.com

Cornelia Funke, German author of popular fantasy stories including *Dragon Rider, The Thief Lord,* and *Inkheart.* www.corneliafunkefans.com

Margaret Peterson Haddix, an author of fantasies, including science fiction and mysteries with supernatural elements. *Found; Running out of Time; Double Identity; Just Ella; Turnabout.* www.haddixbooks.com

Shannon Hale, an author of modern folktales, including *The Goose Girl; Princess Academy; Book of a Thousand Days;* and *Rapunzel's Revenge,* a graphic novel retelling with Dean Hale. www.squeetus.com

Ursula K. LeGuin, author of the well-known Earthsea quest adventure series and a more recent series about an enslaved town, Annals of the West Shore, including *Gifts; Voices;* and *Powers.* www.ursulakleguin.com

Lois Lowry, winner of the Newbery Medal for *The Giver,* a popular work of science fiction about an apparent utopia that includes the companion novels of *Gathering Blue, The Messenger,* and *Son.* www.loislowry.com

Nnedi Okorafor, Nigerian-American writer of fantasy and science fiction set in Nigeria, including *The Shadow Speaker* and *Akata Witch.* http://nnedi.com/

Terry Pratchett, British author of the Discworld series that includes *The Wee Free Men.* Carnegie Medal for *The Amazing Maurice and His Educated Rodents,* a humorous animal fantasy. www.terrypratchettbooks.com

Philip Pullman, British creator of His Dark Materials, a trilogy comprising *The Golden Compass, The Subtle Knife, The Amber Spyglass,* and the series prequel, *Once upon a Time in the North.* www.philip-pullman.com

Rick Riordan, author of The Heroes of Olympus series, Percy Jackson and the Olympians series, and the Kane Chronicles with titles such as *The Son of Neptune* and *The Serpent's Shadow.* www.rickriordan.com

J. K. Rowling, British author of the popular best-selling series about Harry Potter, a child wizard, that began with *Harry Potter and the Sorcerer's Stone.* www.jkrowling.com

draw from King Arthur legends, as in Philip Reeve's *Here Lies Arthur* and Kevin Crossley-Holland's *The Seeing Stone.*

Magical Realism

Magical realism, a blend of fantasy and realism, is a term applied to a trend in literature that began to appear in the 1950s and 1960s. Magical realism is often associated with Latin

American literary traditions but is now found in literature for young adults from many parts of the world. Magical realism has the appearance of a work of realism, but gradually introduces the fantastic as an integral, and necessary, part of the story. The fantastic is merged into these stories such that the distinction between realism and fantasy is blurred, often leaving the reader in some doubt as to what is real and what is fantasy. Magical realism stories have the feel of realism, but the magical elements that manifest themselves in everyday life cause them to fall outside the definition of realistic fiction. They often have a poetic, mystical tone rather than the adventurous appeal of other fantasies.

Faris (2004) identifies the characteristics associated with magical realism: an unresolved element of magic, placement in the realistic world, doubt remaining for the reader whether what occurred was real or not, a closeness of two worlds, the real and the magical, and disruptions of time, space, and identity. Young adult authors recognized for magical realism include Isabel Allende (*City of the Beasts)*, Francesca Lia Block (*Weetzie Bat* and its sequels), David Almond (*Skellig, Clay, Slog's Dad*), and A. S. King (*Please Ignore Vera Dietz*).

Supernatural and Paranormal Forces

The *supernatural,* a force more powerful than nature, provides the backdrop for many recent fantasies for young adults in which events occur that cannot be explained scientifically. The term *paranormal* is often used synonymously and is considered a more contemporary label for this subgenre. Some use the term *paranormal* to refer to going against scientific laws, such as ghosts or ESP, while *supernatural* refers to going beyond scientific explanation and natural laws, such as demons. Paranormal romances are a strong recent trend. Popular types of supernatural/paranormal tales are mysteries in which supernatural events occur, stories with supernatural characters, stories involving psychic powers, and horror stories.

In *supernatural mysteries* a serious crime is committed, after which clues are gradually revealed by the protagonist. The use of red herrings allows for many characters to appear suspect until one turns out to be the perpetrator of the crime. Many young adult authors write mysteries in which the solution to the crime is partially supernatural or arrived at with supernatural assistance, as in Justine Larbalestier's *Liar,* in which a teen, also a werewolf, is suspected of murdering her boyfriend.

Fantasies for young adults include a myriad of *supernatural characters,* such as vampires, witches, wizards, ghosts, fairies, trolls, werewolves, sorcerers, and demons. The supernatural characters in Lauren Kate's Fallen series are angels who have fallen to earth, Neil Gaiman's *The Graveyard Book* has the protagonist being raised by ghosts, Cassandra Clare's *City of Bones* pits demons against demon hunters, and Maggie Stiefvater's *Scorpio Races* is woven around predatory water horses that emerge from the sea.

Witches are often portrayed as broom-wielding villains of traditional tales, as in the Russian stories about Baba Yaga, but in modern fantasies may be villains, as in Joseph Delaney's *Revenge of the Witch,* or protectors, as in Nnedi Okorafor-Mbachu's *Akata Witch*. Witchcraft and the occult in young adult literature has been a focus of adult criticism because of an upsurge of sects whose members refer to themselves as witches and an increase in fundamentalist religious groups. Some parent groups have attempted to censor young adult books featuring witches and other elements of the occult. Chapter 9 has a discussion on censorship and schools' responsibilities in these situations.

Psychic powers can provide a character with special knowledge that is sometimes dangerous and frightening. Psychic powers include telepathic abilities, extrasensory perception, the ability to communicate with the dead or cross into other worlds, extraordinary mental ability, and clairvoyance. The characters in Maggie Steifvater's new series, The Raven Cycle, use different types of psychic powers in their search for the burial site of an ancient Welsh king.

Horror stories present the struggle against evil and portray tragic and often violent events that are shocking, revolting, and terrifying. Although horror stories may appear to portray reality at its worst, the stories are more about evil that goes beyond natural human behavior and so have an element of the supernatural. The resolution of such stories usually solves the crime, explains how it occurred, and reassures the reader. Stephen King, especially recognized for a large body of horror stories, has avid teenage fans for his adult books, which often feature young protagonists. R. L. Stine is considered the king of horror for young people, and Rick Yancy's popular Monstrumologist trilogy pits a monster hunter against headless violent predators.

Historical Fantasy and Time-Warp Fantasy

Historical fantasy is similar to historical fiction in that the setting, both in time and place, is fully and authentically developed; in addition, an important and usually obvious fantastic element underlies these mixed-genre stories. Libba Bray's *The Diviners* is set in an authentic 1920s New York, but includes a protagonist who uses her power of divination to stop an evil influence and occult murders. An accurate historical novel, this mashup is the beginning of a fascinating series. Another example is Maile Meloy's *The Apothecary,* set in the Cold War of 1952 London with a focus on communism and espionage but with magic elixirs and alchemy thrown in.

In the *time-warp fantasy,* a present-day protagonist goes back in time to a different era. A contrast between the two time periods is shown to readers through the modern-day protagonist's astonishment with earlier customs, as in Jane Curry's *The Black Canary*, in which James moves back and forth through a portal in time from contemporary to 1600 London. These time shifts help James sort out his biracial identity and resentment of the role of music in his family's life.

Imagined Worlds and Quests

High fantasies are set in imagined worlds where the main character is involved in an all-consuming *quest* that concerns the destiny of those worlds. The entire story may be set in that world, as in J. R. R. Tolkein's *The Hobbit* or Ursula LeGuin's Earthsea Cycle, or the characters may move between the real and imagined worlds, as in J. K. Rowling's Harry Potter series and C. S. Lewis's Narnia series. The quest may have a lofty purpose, such as justice or love, or a rich reward, such as a magical power or a hidden treasure. Many are set in medieval times and are reminiscent of the search for the holy grail. The author depicts an imaginary otherworld complete with its own society, history, family trees, geographic location, population, religion, customs, and traditions. Often, characters are drawn from traditional myths and legends and involved in a conflict that centers on the struggle between good and evil. The protagonist is engaged in a struggle against external forces of evil and internal temptations or weaknesses and so the quest represents a journey of self-discovery and personal growth, in addition to the search for the reward. Because of the complex adventures and heroism of these novels, they have a strong appeal for adolescents. Terry Pratchett created an elaborate world, Discworld, which is the setting for multiple characters, novels, and series that he has continued to develop over 30 years. Kristin Cashore's world of three kingdoms involves humans with superhuman gifts who are on a quest for justice and freedom from oppression and strife.

Evaluation and Types of Science Fiction

Science fiction is a form of imaginative literature that projects the future of humankind based on scientifically described discoveries or changes in the earth's environment; it also imagines life on other planets. Because science fiction attempts to portray the world that young people may one day inhabit, it is often called *futuristic fiction.* As in fantasy, these alternative perspectives of reality are explored in a world that must maintain internal consistency with the additional evaluation criteria of scientific plausibility, and so it is important to ask:

- **Does the story appear to be scientifically plausible or technically possible?**
  Hypotheses presented in science fiction should seem believable to the reader because the settings and events are built on extensions of known technologies and scientific concepts.

In novels of science fiction topics such as mind control, genetic engineering, space technologies and travel, visitors from outer space, and future political and social systems all seem possible to readers. Cory Doctorow's *Little Brother*, in a nod to Orwell's *1984*,

---

Excellent Fantasy and Science Fiction to Read Aloud

Anderson, M. T. *Feed.* Dystopia, collapsing environment, technology overload.

Billingsley, Fran. *Chime.* Alternative England, guilt, betrayal, and love.

Doctorow, Cory. *Little Brother.* Terrorism, interrogation by Homeland Security, resistance.

Gaiman, Neil. *Graveyard Book.* Orphan raised by ghosts in graveyard.

Kindl, Patrice. *Keeping the Castle.* Historical fantasy, marrying for money.

Levithan, David. *Every Day.* Waking up each day in a different body and life.

Ness, Philip. *A Monster Calls.* Loss and fear, death of mother, monstrous visitor.

Pratchett, Terry. *Nation.* Alternative world, shipwrecked on an island.

Siefvater, Maggie. *The Scorpio Races.* Romantic adventure, predatory water horses.

Yancy, Rick. *The 5th Wave.* Dystopian thriller, five waves of alien invasion.

challenges the constant surveillance of Homeland Security after a terrorist attack, and Mary Pearson's *The Adoration of Jenna Fox* examines issues of identity, science, and ethics when Jenna awakes from a coma with no memory. These novels especially fascinate young people because they feature characters who must learn to adjust to change and become new people, two aspects of living that adolescents also experience.

Science fiction is commonly associated with **space operas,** exemplified by Star Wars, which involve interstellar empires and intergalactic conflicts, as in Garth Nix's *A Confusion of Princes*. More recently, **dystopias,** existing on the blurred line between fantasy and science fiction, are very popular, as exemplified by the Hunger Games trilogy, because they reflect the truth of the inner lives of adolescents who must survive the arbitrary rules, oppression, and cruelty of high school. A utopian novel presents an imaginary future of ideal social and governmental perfection, whereas a dystopian novel depicts a future place whose people live in fearful, wretched conditions usually in post-apocalyptic urban settings, such as the Chicago setting of Veronica Roth's Divergent trilogy and the Los Angeles setting of Marie Lu's Legend trilogy. Young adult novels such as Gemma Malley's *The Declaration* and Lois Lowry's *The Giver,* open in what seems to be a utopian village, but soon this perfect world is shown to have gone wrong and the characters must either save or flee this dystopian world.

Some dystopias are called **cyberpunk,** because they portray a future where humans are controlled by future technology, such as found in M. T. Anderson's *Feed* featuring a society in which a computer brain implant provides immediate access to entertainment, personal communications, and corporate advertising. **Steampunk** includes the element of anarchy or rebellion (punk), but within the social or technological aspects of the nineteenth century Victorian era (the steam), thus fusing futuristic and antiquated elements. This type of science fiction usually features steam-powered machinery in an alternative history or a post-apocalyptic future where steam power has regained mainstream use, as in Kenneth Oppel's Airborn trilogy and Scott Westerfeld's *Leviathan*.

Science fiction is a significant genre for young adults. Those who are reluctant to read science fiction or who have never read it may want to start with books by Margaret Peterson Haddix (*Double Identity; Turnabout*), Lois Lowry (*The Giver*), or Nancy Farmer (*The House of the Scorpion*).

Fantasy and science fiction appeal to readers with lively imaginations who are willing to go beyond the literal level of a story to its spirit. The many types and topics within these genres offer a breadth of inspiring and thought-provoking stories that meet the needs of adolescents for heroes, justice in the battle with evil, and dreams of love and beauty. The level of conceptual difficulty varies considerably; many books contain multiple levels of meaning and symbolism, and so fantasy and science fiction engage their readers and invite multiple rereadings. Fantasy and science fiction invite us to become greater than we are—and than we hope to be.

 # Reference

Faris, W. B. (2004). *Ordinary enchantments: Magical realism and the remystification of narrative*. Nashville, TN: Vanderbilt Press.

Recommended Fantasy and Science Fiction Books

Ages indicated refer to content appropriateness and conceptual and interest levels. The nationality of authors who are not from the United States is indicated in parentheses. Formats other than novels are coded as follows:

(GR) Graphic novel

(PI) Picture book

(COL) Short story collection

(NV) Novel in verse

Fantasy Based in Folklore and Myth

Bass, L. G. *Sign of the Qin*. Hyperion, 2004. Ages 13–18. A young Starlord's quest to save mankind from destruction by demonic hordes, based on Chinese mythology.

Bedard, Michael. *The Painted Wall and Other Strange Tales*. Tundra, 2003. **(COL)** Ages 12–18. Short stories based on folktales by a 17th century Chinese scholar; ghosts, magicians, haunted monasteries. (Canadian)

Castellucci, Cecil. *The Year of the Beasts*. Roaring Brook Press, 2012. **(GR)** Ages 14–18. A hybrid book that alternates a dark tale of a contemporary family with a graphic retelling of Medusa from Greek mythology.

Crossley-Holland, Kevin. *The Seeing Stone*. Scholastic, 2001. Ages 12–18. King Arthur and the Crusades, Middle Ages. Series includes *At the Crossing Places* and *King of the Middle March*. (British)

Fleischman, Paul. *Dateline: Troy*. Candlewick, 2006. Ages 12–15. A retelling of the legend of the Trojan War interspersed with newspaper clippings of modern events from WWI through the Persian Gulf War.

Geras, Adèle. *Ithaka*. Harcourt, 2006. Ages 15–18. Reimagining *The Odyssey* through young protagonists. Also, *Troy* (Harcourt, 2001) retells *The Iliad* through experiences of two orphaned sisters. (British)

Gidwitz, Adam. *A Tale Dark and Grimm*. Dutton, 2010. Ages 12–14. Several Grimm tales are woven together into a dark humorous book starring Hansel and Gretel. Also *In a Glass Grimmly* (2012).

Gruber, Michael. *The Witch's Boy*. HarperCollins, 2005. Ages 11–14. Literary fairy tale of a witch who takes an abandoned infant into her home.

Hale, Shannon. *Book of a Thousand Days*. Bloomsbury, 2007. Ages 12–15. Retelling of a little known tale by the Grimms, *Maleen Maid,* about two girls imprisoned in a tower in Medieval Mongolia.

———. *The Goose Girl*. Bloomsbury, 2003. Ages 12–16. Retold fairy tale featuring a betrayed princess and human–animal communication. Sequel, *River Secrets* (Bloomsbury, 2006).

———. *Princess Academy*. Bloomsbury, 2005. Ages 10–14. Unusual talents discovered while attending an academy for potential princesses.

Hale, Shannon, and Dean Hale. *Rapunzel's Revenge*. Illus. by Nathan Hale. Bloomsbury, 2008. **(GR)** Ages 10–14. Teaming up Rapunzel and Jack of beanstalk fame in an adventure tale.

Hinds, Gareth. *Beowolf*. Candlewick, 2007. **(GR)** Ages 14–18. A graphic novel adaptation of the classic.

Kontis, Alethea. *Enchanted*. Harcourt, 2012. Ages 14–18. A fairy-tale mashup with characters drawn from many different stories, including a talking frog and a romantic kiss.

Lanagan, Margo. *Tender Morsels*. Knopf, 2008. Ages 15–18. A variation of Snow White and Rose Red in which a young woman escapes terrible abuse in an alternate reality. (Australian) Printz Award.

McCaughrean, Geraldine. *Not the End of the World*. HarperCollins, 2005. Ages 14–18. A thoughtful retelling of the biblical story of Noah's Ark through multiple voices. (British)

McNeal, Tom. *Far, Far Away*. Knopf, 2013. Ages 12–15. Jeremy's ability to speak to the ghost of Jacob Grimm is intertwined with a mystery involving missing children. Allusions to many folktales.

Michaelis, Antonia. *Tiger Moon.* Translated from German by Anthea Bell. Abrams, 2008. Ages 14–18. Set in India in the early 1900s, a young bride awaiting death tells stories drawn from Hindu mythology. (German)

Morpurgo, Michael. *Sir Gawain and the Green Knight.* Illus. by Michael Foreman. Candlewick, 2004. Ages 11–14. A retelling of the medieval tale set in King Arthur's court. (British)

Murdock, Catherine Gilbert. *Princess Ben.* Houghton, 2008. Ages 11–16. A melange of fairy tale favorites including Cinderella, Snow White, and Saint George and the Dragon in novel form.

Myers, Edward. *Storyteller.* Clarion, 2008. Ages 10–14. Elements from familiar stories are woven into a multi-layered story within a story; illuminates the writer's craft and the power of story.

Napoli, Donna Jo. *Bound.* Simon & Schuster, 2004. Ages 12–18. A retelling of the Chinese version of Cinderella, set in northern China.

O'Connor, George. *Olympians: I, Zeus, King of the Gods.* **(GR)** Ages 12–14. A graphic retelling of the Greek myth of Zeus. Extensive backmatter. Olympian Graphic Series.

Pattou, Edith. *East.* Harcourt, 2003. Ages 12–16. A retelling of *East o' the Sun and West o' the Moon.*

Reeve, Philip. *Here Lies Arthur.* Scholastic, 2008. Ages 14–18. A brutal recreation of the Arthurian legend exposing the dark side of Camelot with focus on the power of story. (British)

Riordan, Rick (2005). *The Lightning Thief.* Hyperion, 2005. Ages 12–15. A New York boy learns he is a demigod and is sent on a quest to retrieve Zeus's thunderbolt. Percy Jackson & the Olympians series.

———. *The Lost Hero.* Hyperion, 2010. Ages 12–15. Three students sent to a camp for "bad" kids learn they are demigods and go on a quest to free Hera. Greek and Roman gods. Heroes of Olympus series.

———. *The Red Pyramid.* Hyperion, 2010. Ages 12–15. The father of two teens unleashes an Egyptian god who brings danger to their lives, along with truth about their family. Kane Chronicles.

Stanley, Diane. *Bella at Midnight.* Illus. by Bagram Ibatoulline. HarperCollins, 2006. Ages 10–14. Combines motifs from Cinderella and Arthurian legends to tell the story of a girl who sets out to rescue a prince.

Tomlinson, Heather. *Toad and Diamonds.* Holt, 2010. Ages 12–16. A reimagining of a classic Perrault fairy tale, set in precolonial India where two stepsisters are blessed and cursed by a goddess.

Magical Realism

Allende, Isabel. *City of the Beasts.* HarperCollins, 2002. Ages 14–18. Trying to locate the legendary Beast in the Amazon jungle. (Chilean)

Almond, David. *Clay.* Delacorte, 2006. Ages 11–18. An ordinary altar boy in a small English town and his new friend, a gifted and mysterious artist. (British)

———. *Skellig.* Delacorte, 1999. Ages 10–16. Mysterious stranger in a garage and a grave illness. (British)

———. *Slog's Dad.* Illus. by Dave McKean. Candlewick, 2011. Ages 12–14. Slog is convinced that his dead father has come back to visit him. Short story interspersed with moody pictorial segments. (British)

Barnhill, Kelly. *The Mostly True Story of Jack.* Little, Brown, 2011. Ages 12–14. Mystery, magic, and horror ensue when Jack is sent to live in a small Iowa town where people seem to know him and want to kill him.

Bedford, Marilyn. *Flip.* Wendy Lamb, 2011. Ages 14–18. Alex, an asthmatic clarinet player, wakes up in the body of a good-looking athlete, wondering what has happened to his soul. Thriller.

Block, Francesca Lia. *Weetzie Bat.* Harper & Row, 1989. Ages 14–18. Wild adventures in Los Angeles for Weetzie Bat and her friends. Series.

Brooks, Kevin. *Lucas.* Scholastic, 2003. Ages 13–18. Effects of a mysterious boy on island inhabitants. (British)

Clarke, Judith. *Kalpana's Dream.* Front Street, 2005. Ages 11–15. Unusual occurrences in response to a self-identity essay and the arrival of a great-grandmother from India. (Australian)

Hoffman, Alice. *Green Angel*. Scholastic, 2003. Ages 13–18. Survival in the face of the tragic loss of the entire family. Merges magical realism and dystopia.

King, A. S. *Please Ignore Vera Dietz*. Knopf, 2010. Ages 14–18. Vera is dealing with the sudden death of her estranged best friend, Charlie. Shifting narration, including from ghost Charlie.

Madison, Bennett. *September Girls*. HarperTeen, 2013. Ages 14–18. After his mother leaves, Sam and his family move to a beach town filled with mysterious blonde "Girls." Romance, secrets, mermaids.

McCall, Guadalupe Garcia. *Summer of the Mariposas*. Tu Books, 2012. Ages 14–18. A magical Mexican-American retelling of the *Odyssey*; sisters go on a journey to return a dead man to his family in Mexico.

Medina, Meg. *The Girl Who Could Silence the Wind*. Candlewick, 2012. Ages 14–18. Sonia struggles with the belief of others in her village in Mexico that she has protective powers.

Nilsson, Per. *You & You & You*. Translated from Swedish by Tara Chace. Front Street, 2005. Ages 14–18. Swedish magical realism in a sexually graphic novel of three interconnected misfits. (Swedish)

Richardson, Nigel. *The Wrong Hands*. Knopf, 2006. Ages 12–18. A thrilling mystery set in London merges technology and magical realism. (British)

Supernatural and Paranormal Fantasy

Anderson, Jodi. *Tiger Lily*. HarperTeen, 2012. Ages 14-18. Story of the fierce Tiger Lily and her thorny romance with Peter Pan in a reimagined Neverland. Unrequited love. Postcolonial fable.

Avi. *Strange Happenings: Five Tales of Transformation*. Harcourt, 2006. (COL) Ages 10–15. Five short stories including shape-changers and other bizarre events. Good read-aloud.

Bell, Hilari. *Flame*. Simon & Schuster, 2003. Ages 12–18. A war adventure set in the mythical land of Farsala, partly drawn from Persian legends; ability to control fire, human sacrifice.

Black, Holly. *The Coldest Girl in Coldtown*. Little, Brown, 2013. Walled cities, Coldtowns, are used to quarantine vampires and their victims. Tana must enter that world to save a friend. Revenge, horror, love.

Booraem, Ellen. *Small Persons with Wings*. Dial, 2011. Ages 10–14. Melli's family has a special relationship with creatures who resemble fairies and who have demanded the return of a ring.

Brosgol, Vera. *Anya's Ghost*. First Second, 2011. (GR) Ages 12–16. Anya, a Russian immigrant embarrassed by her accent and body, gains a friend after falling into a well—a ghost with an agenda. Creepy and chilling.

Carey, Janet Lee. *Dragon's Keep*. Harcourt, 2007. Ages 12–16. A princess fulfilling Merlin's prophecy to bring peace to a land plagued by wars with dragons. Sequel, *Dragonwood* (Dial, 2012).

Clare, Cassandra. *City of Bones*. McElderry Books, 2007. Ages 14–18. Urban fantasy; Clary discovers she is a Shadowhunter who fights demons. Sexual tension and fight against evil. Mortal Instruments series.

Constable, Kate. *The Singer of All Songs*. Scholastic, 2004. Ages 12–16. Priestess of ice magic versus a sorcerer.

Crutcher, Chris. *The Sledding Hill*. Ages 11–18. Greenwillow, 2005. Postmodern novel in which the author plays a role and a narrator speaks from beyond the grave; censorship and intellectual freedom, tragic deaths.

Dickinson, Peter. *Angel Isle*. Wendy Lamb, 2006. Ages 14–18. Perilous journey to restore protective magic powers; pursuit by powerful evil magicians. Sequel to *The Ropemaker* (Delacorte, 2001). (British)

——. *The Tears of the Salamander*. Random, 2003. Ages 11–15. A boy is taken by his sorcerer uncle in a mystery involving fire salamanders and a volcano; 18th century Italy and Sicily. (British)

Divakaruni, Chitra Banerjee. *The Conch Bearer*. Millbrook, 2003. Ages 10–14. The return of a magical conch shell to its home in the Himalayan mountains of India.

Dixon, Chuck. *Nightwing: On the Razor's Edge*. Illus. by Greg Land and Drew Geraci. DC Comics,

2005. **(GR)** Ages 13–18. Superhero Nightwing and various villains.

Farmer, Nancy. *The Sea of Trolls*. Atheneum, 2004. Ages 10–14. A Scandinavian hero tale with magic, trolls, and mysterious Norns. Trilogy.

Ferraiolo, Jack. *Sidekicks*. Amulet, 2011. Ages 12–14. Scott, a sidekick to a crime-fighting superhero, is surprised to find out that a girl from his school is the sidekick for his arch-nemesis. Superheroes.

Funke, Cornelia. *Inkheart*. Translated from German by Anthea Bell. Scholastic, 2003. Ages 12–18. Abduction by fictional characters brought to life in this adventure tale. Trilogy. (German)

Gaiman, Neil. *The Graveyard Book*. Illus. by Dave McKean. HarperCollins, 2008. Ages 12–15. An orphan is taken in by the ghosts of a local graveyard. Newbery Award.

———. *The Wolves in the Walls*. Illust. by Dave McKean. HarperCollins, 2003. **(PI)** Ages 10–14. Nightmarish wolves commandeer a home.

Garcia, Kami, and Margaret Stohl. *Beautiful Creatures*. Little, Brown, 2009. Ages 14–18. Southern Gothic romance in which a boy develops a relationship with a girl from a family of spell casters.

Hardinge, Frances. *Well Witched*. HarperCollins, 2008. Ages 10–13. Ancient spirit, powers to fulfill wishes made at a wishing well. (British)

Harris, James S. *Shades of Blue*, vol. 1. Illus. by Cal Slayton. DDP, 2005. **(GR)** Ages 12–16. Female superhero with power to conduct electricity.

Hopkinson, Nalo. *The Chaos*. Margaret McElderry, 2012. Ages 12–18. A biracial girl in Toronto develops black spots and visions in a world gone mad. Caribbean and Russian folklore. (Jamaican-Canadian)

Hurston, Zora Neale. *The Skull Talks Back and Other Haunting Tales*. Adapted by Joyce Carol Thomas. Illus. by Leonard Jenkins. HarperCollins, 2004. **(PI)** Ages 10–13. Illus. retelling of Hurston's supernatural folktales.

Irwin, Jane, and Jeff Verndt. *Vögelein: A Clockwork Faerie*. Fiery Studio, 2003. **(GR)** Ages 11–16. First five issues of *Vögelein* about a mechanical fairy created in the 17th century.

Jones, Diana Wynne. *House of Many Ways*. HarperCollins, 2009. Ages 12–14. A teen house sits for her uncle, a wizard, in a house that bends time and space. Sequel to *Howl's Moving Castle* (Harper, 2001).

Kate, Lauren. *Fallen*. Delacorte, 2009. Ages 14–18. Southern Gothic atmosphere with fallen angels and their interactions with mortal beings. Dark romantic thriller. Series.

Lanagan, Margo. *Black Juice*. HarperCollins, 2005. Ages 15–18. Ten fantasy stories set just outside of reality. Good for class discussions and introduction to fantasy. (Australian)

Larbalestier, Justine. *Liar*. Bloomsbury, 2009. Ages 14–18. Micah, a compulsive liar, is forced to tell the truth when her boyfriend is murdered; werewolves; mysterious thriller. (Australian)

———. *Magic or Madness*. Penguin, 2005. Ages 14–18. The Australian protagonist resists witchcraft, but is transported to New York City. (Australian)

Law, Ingrid. *Savvy*. Dial, 2008. Ages 12–14. Savvy is turning 13, the day she receives her special gift, her "savvy." Coming-of-age saga of a two-day adventure.

Levithan, David. *Every Day*. Knopf, 2012. Ages 14–18. Every morning, "A" wakes up in a different person's body and life, learning not to get attached until A falls in love. Exploration of meaning of love.

McKinley, Robin, and Peter Dickinson. *Water: Tales of Elemental Spirits*. Putnam, 2002. **(COL)** Ages 12–16. A six-story fantasy collaboration with an aquatic theme. Trilogy. (British)

Melling, O. R. *The Hunter's Moon*. Abrams/Amulet, 2005. Ages 14–18. First in a trilogy that blends Irish mythology and geography with a teenage female protagonist. (Irish-Canadian)

Meyer, Stephenie. *Twilight*. Little, Brown, 2005. Ages 14–18. Romance with a tormented vampire. Trilogy.

Ness, Patrick. *A Monster Calls: A Novel*. Illus. by Jim Kay. Candlewick, 2011. Ages 12–18. Moving story of a boy, his seriously ill mother, and a monstrous visitor. Power of story, difficulty of loss, and fear.

Okorafor-Mbachu, Nnedi. *Akata Witch*. Viking, 2011. Ages 12–15. A Nigerian-American girl with albinism moves to Nigeria and discovers she is a Leopard person with magical powers.

Prue, Sally. *Cold Tom*. Scholastic, 2003. Ages 12–16. Half-human boy, rejection by his Elfin tribe. (British)

Rodi, Rob. *Crossovers*. CrossGeneration, 2003. (**GR**) Ages 11–18. Suburban family with an alien collaborator, a superhero, a vampire slayer, and a warrior princess.

Rossetti, Rinsai. *The Girl with Borrowed Wings*. Dial, 2013. Ages 12–18. An isolated girl, controlled by her father, encounters a shape-shifting boy in the desert. Issues of subjugation and freedom. (Thai)

Schusterman, Neal. *The Schwa Was Here*. Dutton, 2005. Ages 11–15. A friend's ability to appear and disappear; feeling unnoticed.

Sfar, Joann. *Little Vampire Does Kung Fu!* Translated from French by Mark and Alexis Siegel. Simon & Schuster, 2003. (**GR**) Ages 12–16. French comics format, bullying, strange monsters, body humor, space travel, and kung fu. (French)

Slade, Arthur. *Dust*. Random, 2003. Ages 12–16. Children missing from Saskatchewan, Canada; mysterious visitor. (Canadian)

Stiefvater, Maggie. *The Raven Boys*. Scholastic, 2012. Three privileged boys and the daughter of a small-town psychic who are immersed in a mystery involving an ancient Welsh king. Raven Cycle quartet.

———. *The Scorpio Races*. Scholastic, 2011. Ages 14–18. Chilling romantic adventure on an island where predatory water horses emerge from the sea.

Thompson, Kate. *Creature of the Night*. Roaring Brook Press, 2008. Ages 14–18. Bobby, in trouble with the law, is forced by his parent to move to rural Ireland and encounters a faerie mystery. (Irish)

Werlin, Nancy. *Impossible*. Dial, 2008. Ages 14–18. A family curse of madness and a pregnancy after a rape on prom night in an interplay of wild magic and contemporary reality. Inspired by the song, Scarborough Fair.

Westerfeld, Scott. *Peeps*. Razorbill, 2005. Ages 15–18. A medical thriller: a vampire and a vampire hunter interspersed with descriptions of actual parasites.

Zevin, Gabrielle. *Elsewhere*. Farrar, 2005. Ages 12–18. An afterlife where aging occurs in reverse.

Horror

Compestine, Ying Chang. *A Banquet for Hungry Ghosts: A Collection of Deliciously Frightening Tales*. Holt, 2009. Ages 12–16. Eight grisly horror stories containing elements of Chinese history and culture. Each tale is followed by historical notes and a recipe that together represent an eight-course banquet.

Delaney, Joseph. *Revenge of the Witch: The Last Apprentice,* Book 1. Illus. by Patrick Arrasmith. Greenwillow, 2005. Ages 10–14. Horror for the apprentice of the local Spook in England of long ago. Series. (British)

Gaiman, Neil. *Coraline*. HarperCollins, 2008. (**GR**) Ages 10–15. Graphic adaptation of horror novel. (British)

Noyes, Deborah, editor. *Gothic!: Ten Original Dark Tales*. Candlewick, 2004. (**COL**) Ages 14–18. Mystery, terror, witches, vampires, demons; payment for the crimes of the past.

Sala, Richard. *Maniac Killer Strikes Again: Delirious, Mysterious Stories*. Fantagraphics, 2004. (**COL, GR**) Ages 14–18. Stories of monsters and secret societies, villains and mad scientists. Humor.

Stine, R. L. *A Midsummer Night's Scream*. Feiwel & Friends, 2013. Ages 12–18. Ambition and murder in the movie industry, a reimagining of *A Midsummer Night's Dream*.

Wooding, Chris. *The Haunting of Alaizabel Cray*. Scholastic, 2004. Ages 12–18. Horror tale set in an alternative Victorian London. (British)

Yancy, Rick. *The Monstrumologist*. Simon & Schuster, 2009. Ages 14–18. In 1888, the United States is plagued by monsters that are headless predators. Told through the diary of an apprentice to a monster hunter. Trilogy.

Historical Fantasy

Beckman, Thea. *Crusade in Jeans*. Translated from Dutch. Front Street, 2003. Ages 11–15. Time travel to Middle Ages, Children's Crusade. (Dutch)

Bray, Libba. *The Diviners*. Little, Brown, 2012. Ages 14–18. Supernatural thriller of occult murders set in 1920s New York. Teens with special abilities, multiple narrators. Trilogy.

Curry, Jane Louise. *The Black Canary*. Simon & Schuster, 2005. Ages 11–15. Time-travel adventure, Elizabethan England, with a biracial protagonist.

Gardner, Sally. *I, Coriander*. Dial, 2005. Ages 11–15. A blend of time and place for a fairy princess, back to 17th century London. (British)

Gavin, Jamila. *The Blood Stone*. Farrar, 2005. Ages 12–16. A search for a father from Europe to Arabia to the Mogul Empire in the 17th century. (British)

Haddix, Margaret Peterson. *Found*. Simon & Schuster, 2008. Ages 10–14. A mystery involving time travel and two opposing forces. Missing Series.

Hautman, Pete. *The Obsidian Blade*. Candlewick, 2011. Ages 14–18. Tucker and his family engage in a religious and ideological battle across time and space through disks that are portals to historical crises. Historical fantasy and science fiction. Klaatu Diskos Trilogy.

Hoffman, Mary. *Stravaganza: City of Masks*. Bloomsbury, 2002. Ages 13–18. Adventures in a parallel world similar to 16th century Venice. Sequels include time travel between modern London and historical Italy.

Kindl, Patrice. *Keeping the Castle: A Tale of Romance, Riches and Real Estate*. Viking, 2012. Ages 14–18. 19th century England tale of a girl who must marry for money. Mirrors *Pride and Prejudice*.

Lagos, Alexander, and Joseph Lagos. *The Sons of Liberty I*. Illus. by Steve Walker. Random, 2010. **(GR)** Ages 12–15. In Colonial United States, two runaway slaves gain unusual powers through experiments by Ben Franklin.

LaFevers, Robin. *Grave Mercy*. Houghton Mifflin, 2012. Ages 14–18. Assassinations, political intrigue, and religion in 15th century Brittany along with honor, valor, and love. Sequel: *Dark Triumph* (2013).

Meloy, Maile. *The Apothecary*. Putnam's, 2011. Ages 12–14. Cold War setting in London, 1952, for a tale of two teens, a mysterious apothecary, missing parents, spies, and a book of secrets. Trilogy.

Meyer, Kai. *The Water Mirror*. Translated from German by Elizabeth D. Crawford. Simon & Schuster, 2005. Ages 10–14. Two orphans apprenticed in medieval Venice to a magical mirror maker. (German)

Phelan, Matt. *The Storm in the Barn*. Candlewick, 2009. **(GR)** Ages 10–14. Jack and his family struggle with the hardships of Dust Bowl America until Jack encounters a supernatural being. Graphic panels.

Schlitz, Laura Amy. *Splendors and Glooms*. Candlewick, 2012. Ages 10–14. London 1860. A gothic thriller involving a kidnapping, orphans, a witch, and an evil puppeteer. Multiple narrators.

Stead, Rebecca. *When You Reach Me*. Wendy Lamb, 2009. Ages 10–14. A girl tries to make sense of mysterious notes. 1980s New York; references to *A Wrinkle in Time*. Newbery Award.

Thal, Lilli. *Mimus*. Translated from German by John Brownjohn. Annick, 2005. Ages 13–18. An apprenticeship to a court jester; depiction of the barbarity of the Middle Ages. (German)

Winters, Cat. *In the Shadow of Blackbirds*. Amulet, 2013. Ages 14–18. San Diego, 1918, during WWI and an influenza outbreak; Mary is involved in séances and spirit photography. Mystery, archival photographs.

Imagined Worlds and Quests

Alexander, Lloyd. *The Book of Three*. Holt, 1964. Ages 10–14. An assistant pig keeper's quest to save his land from evil; based on medieval Welsh myths. Prydain Chronicles.

Billingsley, Franny. *Chime*. Dial, 2011. Ages 14–18. In an alternative England, Briony spins a tale of guilt, mystery, betrayal, and love in a community threatened by the ancient ones. Beautiful language.

Cashore, Kristin. *Graceling*. Harcourt, 2008. Ages 14–18. The adventure of young Lady Katsa possessing a superhuman gift of killing and a young man whose own gift causes her to seek justice. Trilogy.

Flanagan, John. *The Ruins of Gorlan*. Philomel, 2005. Ages 11–16. A group of five orphans, assignments as apprentices, saving the kingdom. Series. (Australian)

Hartman, Rachel. *Seraphina*. Random, 2012. Ages 12–18. A murder disrupts the uneasy peace between humans and dragons in a rich new culture with an odd, but loveable, heroine.

Le Guin, Ursula K. *Gifts*. Harcourt, 2004. Ages 13–16. A parallel world of conflict between occupiers and occupied cultures. Trilogy.

———. *A Wizard of Earthsea*. Parnassus, 1968. Ages 11–18. Apprentice wizard Ged, a quest for self-identity.

Lewis, C. S. *The Lion, the Witch, and the Wardrobe*. Illus. by Pauline Baynes. Macmillan, 1950. Ages 9–14. Good versus evil in a Christian allegory involving an evil witch and a lion. Chronicles of Narnia. (British)

Marchetta, Melina. *Finnikin of the Rock*. Candlewick, 2008. Ages 14–18. A medieval-type world of bloody battles and dark mysteries in which Finnikin works to free his homeland. Lumatere Chronicles. (Australian)

McKinley, Robin. *Pegasus*. Putnam's, 2010. Ages 12–16. In Balsinland, humans are bound to pegasi but unable to communicate until Princess Sylvi connects with pegasus Price Ebon, posing a threat. (British)

Morarity, Chris. *The Inquisitor's Apprentice*. Harcourt, 2011. Ages 12–15. An alternative New York, Sacha works to stop magical crime as an apprentice to an Inquisitor. Sequel: *The Watcher in the Shadows* (2013).

Pratchett, Terry. *Nation*. HarperCollins, 2008. Ages 12–15. An alternative 19th century setting for this adventure on an archipelago after a shipwreck caused by a tsunami. Humor. (British)

———. *The Wee Free Men*. HarperCollins, 2003. Ages 10–14. A witch-to-be, a clan of six-inch men, and a Fairyland invasion. Sequels include *I Shall Wear Midnight* (2010). Discworld. (British)

Pullman, Philip. *The Golden Compass*. Knopf, 1996. Ages 12–18. Abduction of children in an alternate world in which reason and magic vie for power. His Dark Materials trilogy. (British)

Reeve, Philip. *Larklight: A Rousing Tale of Dauntless Pluck in the Farthest Reaches of Space*. Illus. by David Wyatt. Bloomsbury, 2006. Ages 10–15. A pirate space adventure set in 1851. Humor. (British)

Rowling, J. K. *Harry Potter and the Sorcerer's Stone*. Scholastic, 1998. Ages 10–16. A neglected boy with a great destiny as a wizard. Harry Potter series. (British)

Stroud, Jonathan. *The Amulet of Samarkand*. Hyperion, 2003. Ages 12–16. Adventures of an apprentice magician and a demon seeking an amulet in alternative England. Bartimaeus Trilogy. (British)

Tan, Shaun. *The Arrival*. Scholastic, 2007. **(GR)** Ages 12–18. A lone immigrant's journey and adjustment to an unknown fantasy world. Wordless graphic novel. (Australian)

Taylor, Lani. *Daughter of Smoke and Bone*. Little, Brown, 2011. Ages 13–16. Karou, an art student in Prague, was raised by demons and runs errands for a sorcerer in a parallel world with mythical creatures and battles.

Tolkien, J. R. R. *The Hobbit*. Houghton, 1937. Ages 12–18. Adventures of Bilbo Baggins and the wizard Gandalf in Middle Earth. (British)

Science Fiction and Dystopias

Adlington, L. J. *Cherry Heaven*. Greenwillow, 2008. Ages 14–18. Dystopian novel that takes place in a troubled society different, but reminiscent of our own. Alternating narratives. (Australian)

———. *The Diary of Pelly D*. Greenwillow, 2005. Ages 13–18. Dystopian novel featuring Holocaust-like events. Could be paired with historical fiction and nonfiction about the Holocaust. (Australian)

Anderson, M. T. *Feed*. Candlewick, 2002. Ages 15–18. Dystopian novel featuring a collapsing environment and technology overload.

Bacigalupi, Paolo. *Ship Breaker*. Little, Brown, 2010. Ages 12–18. In a dystopian future America, climate change wreaks havoc on a dangerous waterlogged world. Printz Award. Also *The Drowned Cities* (2012).

Brooks, Kevin. *iBoy*. Chicken House, 2010. Ages 14–18. An act of violence leaves an iPhone embedded in Tom's brain, arming him with access to all of cyberspace and a desire for vengeance. (British)

Card, Orson Scott. *Ender's Game*. Starscape, 2002/1977. Ages 14–18. Genetic engineering, war games.

Clements, Andrew. *Things Not Seen*. Putnam/Philomel, 2002. Ages 12–16. Mystery involving an invisible boy and his blind friend.

Collins, Suzanne. *The Hunger Games*. Scholastic, 2008. Ages 15–18. North American dystopia in the near future. Trilogy.

Doctorow, Cory. *Little Brother*. Tor, 2008. Ages 14–18. After a terrorist attack, Marcus is interrogated and fights surveillance of Homeland Security. Tribute to Orwell's *1984*. (Canadian) Sequel: *Homeland* (2013).

DuPrau, Jeanne. *City of Ember*. Random, 2003. Ages 10–15. Futuristic, disintegrating society and dwindling supplies. Trilogy.

Edwards, Janet. *Earth Girl*. Pyr, 2013. Ages 12–16. Abandoned on Earth because she is labeled Handicapped, Jarra works to challenge societal hierarchies. Set in Manhattan in the year 2789. (British)

Farmer, Nancy. *The House of the Scorpion*. Simon & Schuster, 2002. Ages 13–18. A futuristic, corrupt drug empire between Mexico and the United States; ethics of cloning. Sequel, *The Lord of Opium* (2013).

Gagnon, Michelle. *Don't Turn Around*. Harper, 2012. Ages 12–16. A tech-thriller in which teen hackers discover a conspiracy of human experimentation. Near-future dystopia.

Gill, David Mcinnis. *Black Hole Sun*. Greenwillow, 2010. Ages 14–18. Teenage mercenaries hired to protect miners in a dystopian future on Mars. Action, humor, quotes from classical poetry.

Haddix, Margaret Peterson. *Double Identity*. Simon & Schuster, 2005. Ages 10–14. Suspenseful revelations of family secrets and cloning. Also *Double Helix* (2003).

Healey, Karen. *When We Wake*. Little, Brown, 2013. Ages 12-18. Dystopia in which a girl wakes up after being cryogenically frozen for a century.

Johnson, Alaya. *The Summer Prince*. Scholastic, 2013. Ages 14–18. Futuristic Brazil in a thriller around love, death, technology, and art. Class-stratified society.

Klass, David. *Stuck on Earth*. Farrar, Straus, Giroux, 2010. Ages 12–14. An organism on a quest to find a home for his people inhabits the brain of a 14-year-old boy in a dysfunctional family.

Kostick, Conor. *Epic*. Viking, 2007. Ages 13–18. Success is winning in a future gaming world. (British)

Laybourne, Emmy. *Monument 14*. Feiwel & Friends, 2012. Ages 14–18. Natural disasters that are tearing the world apart drive students into a superstore where they create a new social order.

Lowry, Lois. *The Giver*. Houghton, 1993. Ages 11–16. Struggle of conscience for the new receiver of memories in a utopian society. Newbery Award. Also: *Gathering Blue* (2000), *The Messenger* (2004), *Son* (2012).

Lu, Marie. *Legend*. Putnam's, 2011. Ages 14–18. A gripping thriller in dystopic future Los Angeles, told in alternating first person narratives of two teens thrown into direct opposition. Trilogy.

Malley, Gemma. *The Declaration*. Bloomsbury, 2007. Set in 2140 England, this dystopian tale explores overpopulation, global warning, and the ethics of immortality. (British)

Meyer, Marissa. *Cinder*. Feiwel & Friends, 2012. Ages 12–15. A rewriting of Cinderella as a female mechanic who is a cyborg in a plague-ridden future in New Beijing. Lunar Chronicles.

Ness, Patrick. *The Knife of Never Letting Go*. Candlewick, 2008. Ages 14–18. A futuristic all-male society where thoughts are audible, and a coming-of-age journey for two teens. Chaos Walking trilogy.

Nix, Garth. *A Confusion of Princes*. Harper, 2012. Khermi has emerged from years of genetic and technical "remaking" as Prince of the intergalactic Empire. A space opera on what it means to be human. (Australian)

Pearson, Mary. *The Adoration of Jenna Fox*. Holt, 2008. Ages 14–18. Examination of identity, science, and ethics. Jenna awakes from a coma with no memory into a world of secrets. Biotechnology.

Rapp, Adam. *Decelerate Blue*. First Second, 2006. **(GR)** Ages 15–18. Dystopian graphic novel.

Reichs, Kathy. *Virals*. Razorbill, 2010. Ages 12–16. A mysterious virus gives a group of teens uncontrollable new talents. Forensic science and a decades-old murder.

Rossi, Veronica. *Under the Never Sky*. Harper, 2012. Ages 14–18. A dystopian world in which a girl is exiled from a city filled with virtual reality spaces to a dangerous outside wasteland.

Roth, Veronica. *Divergent*. Katherine Tegen, 2011. Ages 14–18. Post-apocalyptic Chicago has structured society into five groups based on specific virtues. Action, romance, difficult choices. Divergent Series.

Strahan, Jonathan. *The Starry Rift: Tales of New Tomorrows*. Viking, 2008. **(COL)** Ages 14–18. Sixteen science fiction stories by well-known writers.

Westerfeld, Scott. *Uglies*. Simon & Schuster, 2005. Ages 12–18. An apparent utopia focused on invasive "nip and tuck," image-obsessed customs. Series.

Yancy, Rick. *The 5th Wave*. Putnam's, 2013. Ages 14–18. A gripping thriller about an earth decimated by the five waves of an alien invasion in the not-too-distant future; moral dilemmas. Trilogy.

Steampunk

Arakawa, Hiromu. *Fullmetal Alchemist 1*. Translated from Japanese, byAkira Watanabe. VIZ Media, 2005. **(GR)** Ages 14–18. Steampunk manga of two brothers in a society pursuing immortality. Series. (Japanese)

Clare, Cassandra. *Clockwork Angel*. Margaret K. McElderry, 2010. Ages 12–15. Steampunk adventure with supernatural elements, set in Victorian England, prequel to Mortal Instruments. Infernal Devices Series.

Link, Kelly, and Gavin Grant, editors. *Steampunk!: An Anthology of Fantastically Rich and Strange Stories*. Candlewick, 2011. Ages 14–18. Fourteen short stories, two in graphic novel form, feature a range of settings and technologies in re-imagining history and exploring new frontiers.

Oppel, Kenneth. *Airborn*. Eoes, 2004. Ages 12–15. Set in Victorian England, an orphan who is a cabin boy for a luxury airship battles with pirates and supernatural forces. Trilogy. (Canadian)

Reeve, Philip. *Mortal Engines*. HarperCollins, 2003. Ages 12–16. A violent future world, where movable and moving cities consume small towns. Hungry Cities Chronicles. (British)

———. *Fever Crumb*. Scholastic, 2009. Ages 12–15. Steampunk set in a future London under invasion; an orphan who is the first female in the Order of Engineers is proclaimed a mutant. Fever Crumb Trilogy. (British)

Slade, Arthur. *The Hunchback Assignments*. Wendy Lamb, 2009. Ages 12–16. A steampunk spy thriller in Victorian England with elements of *Dr. Jekyll and Mr Hyde* and *The Hunchback of Notre Dame*. (Canadian)

Westerfeld, Scott. *Leviathan*. Simon Pulse, 2009. Ages 12–15. A mixture of alternative history and steampunk in a series set in the hostilities surrounding World War I. Bioetechnology versus mechanical technology.

 # Related Films and DVDS

Beautiful Creatures (2013). Authors: Kami Garcia and Margaret Stohl (2009). 124 minutes.

Beowulf (2007). Northern European mythology. 114 minutes.

The Chronicles of Narnia: The Lion, the Witch, and the Wardrobe (2005). Author: C. S. Lewis (1950). 140 minutes. Sequels.

City of Ember (2008). Author: Jeanne DuPrau (2003). 95 minutes.

Coraline (2009). Author: Neil Gaiman (2002).
100 minutes.

Crusade: A March through Time (2008). Author:
Thea Beckman (2003). 100 minutes.

Ella Enchanted (2004). Author: Gail Carson Levine
(1997). 96 minutes.

Ender's Game (2013). Author: Orson Scott Card
(1994). 114 minutes.

Eragon (2006). Author: Christopher Paolini (2003).
104 minutes.

The Golden Compass (2007). Author: Philip
Pullman (1996). 113 minutes.

Harry Potter and the Sorcerer's Stone (2001).
Author: J. K. Rowling (1998). 152 minutes.
Sequels.

The Hobbit: An Unexpected Journey (2012). Author:
J. R. R. Tolkien (1937). 170 minutes.

The Hunger Games (2012). Author: Suzanne Collins
(2008). 143 minutes. Sequels.

Inkheart (2008). Author: Cornelia Funke (2003).
106 minutes.

Journey to Watership Down (2003). Author: Richard
Adams, *Watership Down* (1974). 44 minutes.

Lord of the Rings (2001). Author: J. R. R. Tolkien
(1954–1955). 208 minutes. Sequels.

The Mortal Instruments: City of Bones (2013).
Author: Cassandra Clare (2007). 130 minutes.

Percy Jackson & the Olympians: The Lightning Thief
(2010). Author: Rick Riordan (2005).
119 minutes.

The Seeker: The Dark Is Rising (2007). Author:
Susan Cooper (1973). 99 minutes.

Stardust (2007). Author: Neil Gaiman (1999).
127 minutes.

Twilight (2008). Author: Stephenie Meyer (2005).
122 minutes. Sequels.

The Water Horse (2007). Author: Dick King-Smith.
112 minutes.

 istorical
Fiction

Historical fiction brings history to life, inviting readers to immerse themselves in another time and place. Stories of the past provide us with a sense of humanity and memory. Milton Meltzer (1981) argues that we need history to compare our current experiences with the past in order to make sense of our lives. Without history, we are locked in the current moment, blinded from understanding that moment. We need stories of the past to locate ourselves in the larger continuum of life and to envision reasons for taking action to create change.

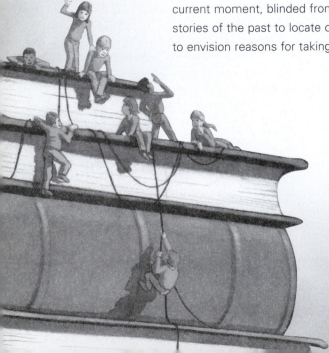

Definition and Description

Historical fiction is realistic fiction set in the past and remote enough from the present to be considered history. Stories about events that occurred at least one generation (twenty years or more) prior to the date of the original publication are included in this chapter. Authors write about time periods in which they did not live or which occurred more than twenty years prior to their books. This distance provides them with contextual perspectives from which to reflect on significance and interpretations of these events. Authors blend historical facts with imaginary characters and an invented plot. The events in their plots must be within the realm of possibility, constructed around actual historical events, authentic period settings, and real historical figures.

In the most common form of historical fiction, the main characters of the story are imaginary, but some secondary characters may be actual historical figures. These stories usually depict a significant historical event, such as a war, an economic depression, or a natural disaster. *Blood on the River, James Town 1607* by Elisa Carbone conveys the story of the Pilgrims' first winter through Samuel Collier, a fictitious character who serves as a page to John Smith. The novel includes historical events, actual people such as Powhatan, Pocahontas, and Smith, and an authentic Jamestown setting.

In another form of historical fiction, the past is described complete with an accurate reconstruction of the physical location and the social traditions, customs, morals, and values of the period, but with no mention of an actual historical event or actual historical figures as characters. *Out of the Easy* by Ruta Sepetys depicts the life of a 1950s teen growing up in New Orleans as she must balance between escaping the French Quarter and becoming entangled in criminal activities.

Another type of historical story is one in which elements of fantasy are found, and therefore the story does *not* qualify as historical fiction. For example, time warps and other supernatural features are found in Mary Hoffman's *Stravaganza* series. These stories are categorized as **historical fantasy** and are included in Chapter 4, "Fantasy and Science Fiction." Adolescents are often limited in their knowledge of history and historical context—the background and environment that surround past events, including how people lived and worked. Reading historical fiction can help them understand the past and appreciate the lives of people who lived in earlier times. By telling the stories of people's everyday lives as well as presenting their triumphs and failures, historical fiction provides the human side of history, making it more real and more memorable. Smith, Monson, and Dobson (1992) found that students in fifth-grade classrooms in which historical novels were used along with textbooks recalled more historical facts and indicated greater enjoyment in their social studies classes than the students in classrooms that had a similar curriculum without the addition of historical novels.

Evaluation and Selection of Historical Fiction

In evaluating historical fiction, the criteria for any well-written piece of literature must be considered, particularly whether the book tells an engaging story involving dynamic, complex characters with whom adolescents can identify. Also of significance is whether the book highlights universal themes that are thought-provoking without being didactic and

Early Important Works of Historical Fiction

Date	Literary Work/Event	Significance
1888	*Otto of the Silver Hand* by Howard Pyle	Early historical fiction
1929	Newbery Medal to *The Trumpeter of Krakow* by Eric Kelly	National recognition for historical fiction
1932–1943	Publication of Little House series by Laura Ingalls Wilder	Classic historical fiction series for children
1944	Newbery Medal to *Johnny Tremain* by Esther Forbes	National recognition for historical fiction
1949–1960	Many historical novels published including *The Door in the Wall* by Marguerite de Angeli, *The Witch of Blackbird Pond* by Elizabeth George Speare, and *The Lantern Bearers* by Rosemary Sutcliff	Dramatic increase in the quality and quantity of historical novels for children and young adults
1961	Newbery Medal to *Island of the Blue Dolphins* by Scott O'Dell	Landmark historical novel with a strong female protagonist from a minority culture
1971	*Journey to Topaz* by Yoshiko Uchida	Early historical work by and about a minority (Japanese American)
1975	*The Song of the Trees* by Mildred Taylor	First in series, African-American family's struggle in Mississippi after the Civil War
1984	*The Sign of the Beaver* by Elizabeth George Speare, Scott O'Dell Award	Scott O'Dell Award is established for historical novels set in North America
1989	Elizabeth George Speare receives the Laura Ingalls Wilder Award for her outstanding works of historical fiction	Recognition of an author of historical fiction for substantial contribution to literature for young people

whether the book is based in accurate historical facts. Historical fiction can be evaluated using these questions:

- *Setting.* **Is the setting described in rich details that are accurate and authentic for that time and place?** A setting must be described in enough detail to provide an authentic sense of a specific time and place without overwhelming the story. Details such as hair and clothing styles, architecture and furnishings, foods and food preparation, and modes of transportation must be subtly woven into the story to provide a convincing, authentic period setting. The characters must act within the traditions and norms of their times.

- *Language.* **Is the dialogue authentic to the time period as well as understandable to adolescents?** Expressing the language or dialect of the period presents a particular challenge to authors, especially in creating dialogue. If the speech of the period is greatly different from that of today, the author must decide whether to remain true to the language of the time, which can cause readers difficulties in comprehending, or change the language to modern phrasing and risk losing the authenticity and sound of the time period. The language should not jar the reader by its obvious inappropriateness or lose the reader by its extreme difficulty. Most authors strive for a middle ground by retaining some flavor of language difference but making modifications to be understandable.

- *Perspective.* **Are multiple perspectives about the events and issues shared through the different characters?** Many adults are unaware that the history they learned many years ago may have been biased or one-sided, highlighting only one group's perspective. Some authors integrate more complex interpretations of historical events by including events and facts that are typically excluded from history textbooks and adding characters who reflect differing experiences and perspectives, especially voices that are often underrepresented in history texts. The challenge is to do so, but still have characters act in historically authentic ways.

Award lists provide sources of recent books that offer readers the human side of history. The Scott O'Dell Award, established in 1982, honors the most outstanding work of children's historical fiction published in the previous year. The work must be written by a U.S. citizen and be set in the New World. The Scott O'Dell Award winners (www.scottodell.com) are a source for selecting outstanding historical fiction. The National Council of Social Studies publishes a list of the most notable trade books in social studies in the May/June issue of *Social Education*. This list, available online at www.socialstudies.org, includes many works of historical fiction and informational books.

Topics of Historical Fiction

Historical fiction can be organized by grouping books around *universal themes* or the *historical periods* in which the books are set.

Universal Themes in Historical Fiction

Common themes that extend across time and place in historical stories can be an approach for selecting historical fiction. For example, a theme such as seeking freedom could be explored using a *text set* of novels set in different times and places. Several themes are listed here, along with books that might be considered to explore that theme. Other themes can be developed through reading historical fiction and considering the common themes or big ideas that go across the books.

The Search for Freedom

Weedflower by Cynthia Kadohata
Catch a Tiger by the Toe by Ellen Levine
Code Name Verity by Elizabeth Wein

Keeping Corner by Kashmira Sheth
Lizzie Bright and the Buckminster Boy by Gary Schmidt
Jefferson's Sons: A Founding Father's Secret Children by Kimberly B. Bradley
The Surrender Tree by Margarita Engle
When My Name Was Keoko by Linda Sue Park
All the Broken Pieces by Ann Burg
The Berlin Boxing Club by Rob Sharenow

Family Closeness in Times of Adversity

Fever 1793 by Laurie Halse Anderson
Out of the Dust by Karen Hesse
A Small White Scar by K. A. Nuzum
Crow by Barbara Wright
One Crazy Summer by Rita Williams-Garcia
Between Shades of Gray by Ruta Sepetys
The Porcupine Year by Louise Erdrich
Moon over Manifest by Clare Vanderpool
Queen of Hearts by Martha Brooks
Okay for Now by Gary Schmidt

The Forced Journeys of Refugees

Secrets in the Fire by Henning Mankell
Flight to Freedom by Ana Veciana-Suarez
Elijah of Buxton by Christopher Paul Curtis
The Braid by Helen Frost
Inside Out and Back Again by Thanhha Lai
Run Far, Run Fast by Timothy Decker
Nory Ryan's Song by Patricia Reilly Giff
My Name Is Not Easy by Debby Edwardson
Never Fall Down by Patricia McCormick
Annexed by Sharon Dogar

Periods of History in Fiction

The natural relationship of historical fiction to the study of history and geography suggests integrating historical fiction novels into world and U.S. history units. The following histori-cal periods provide an idea of how these units might be organized. Historical fiction books set during these eras are listed at the end of this chapter, while biographies of individuals from the same era are found at the end of Chapter 6, "Nonfiction." One issue to note is that the majority of these books continue to view history from a Western perspective.

Beginnings of Civilization Up to 3000 B.C.   This period represents prehistoric cultures and civilizations, including early peoples (Java, Neanderthals, Cro-Magnons) and civilizations in the Middle East and Asia. During this time, Egyptians, Syrians, and Phoenicians developed civilizations, Hebrews produced the religious faith of Judaism, India was the site of Aryan civilizations, and Chinese dynasties created excellent works of art and agricultural systems of irrigation. Few books exist about this time period and most are highly fictionalized due to the lack of detailed records from people in this time. *Thorn* by Betty Levin is set in a fictional prehistoric tribe on the brink of extinction when a strange boat leaves behind a mysterious boy with an atrophied leg.

Civilizations of the Ancient World, 3000 B.C. to A.D. 600 The era of the Greek city-states was followed by Roman rule in Western Europe. Christianity was founded in Jerusalem and spread throughout Europe, while civilizations in ancient Asia produced two remarkable men born about 560 B.C.: the Indian religious leader Buddha and the Chinese philosopher Confucius. The Roman invasion of Carthage is the setting for *Escape by Sea* by I. S. Lawrence, in which a girl and her father are forced into a dangerous sea voyage.

Civilizations of the Medieval World, 600 to 1500 Early African and American civilizations arose independently, while the great civilizations of China, Korea, and Japan continued to flourish, as depicted in Linda Sue Park's *A Single Shard*, about the life of an artistically gifted homeless boy in Korea. The eastern part of the Roman Empire maintained its stability and civilization from the capital of Constantinople. The Byzantine Empire created a distinct culture and branch of the Christian Church—the Orthodox Church—which influenced Russia to adopt the religion and culture. After the fall of the Roman Empire, Western Europe dissolved into isolated separate regions without strong governments. Many of the governing responsibilities were carried out by the Christian Church, which dominated the economic, political, cultural, and educational life of the Middle Ages. These feudal societies eventually gave rise to the nations of modern Europe. Avi's Crispin trilogy portrays medieval life in England and France, while *The Wicked and the Just* by Jillian Coats

Excellent Historical Fiction to Read Aloud

Bradley, Kimberly. *Jefferson's Sons.* Multiple narrators, Jefferson's slave children, early 1800s.

Engle, Margarita. *Surrender Tree: Poems from Cuba's Struggle for Survival.* Novel in verse, Cuba, late 1800s.

Hemphill, Stephanie. *Wicked Girls: A Novel of the Salem Witch Trials.* Voices of the teen accusers, 1692.

Lai, Thanhha. *Inside Out & Back Again.* Vietnamese immigrants, Alabama, 1975.

MacColl, Michaela. *Promise the Night.* British farms in Kenya, 1912. Beryl Markham's childhood.

Park, Linda Sue. *When My Name Was Keoko.* Japanese occupation of Korea, 1940s.

Sepetys, Ruta. *Between Shades of Gray.* Stalin's invasion of Lithuania, Siberian work camps, 1941.

Schmidt, Gary. *Okay for Now.* Abusive father, teen coming to see world as an artist, 1968.

Sheth, Kashmira. *Keeping Corner.* Child widow, women's rights, India, 1918.

Wein, Elizabeth. *Code Name Verity.* Nazi interrogation, female spy, friendship, 1940s.

Notable Authors of Historical Fiction

M. T. Anderson, author and illustrator of children's and young adult books. Noted for the historical fiction series on slavery, The Astonishing Life of Octavian Nothing, Volume I: *The Pox Party* and Volume II: *The Kingdom on the Waves.* Also, *Feed; Whales on Stilts.* www. mt-anderson.com/

Avi [Wortis], author noted for historical fiction novels set in the United States and the British Isles. *Crispin: The End of Time, The True Confessions of Charlotte Doyle, City of Orphans.* www.avi-writer.com

Christopher Paul Curtis, author of realistic and historical fiction novels depicting African-American characters who live near Flint, Michigan. *The Watsons Go to Birmingham 1963; Bud, Not Buddy; Elijah of Buxton.* www. christopherpaulcurtis.com

Karen Cushman, author of acclaimed historical novels set in the Middle Ages. *Catherine, Called Birdy; The Midwife's Apprentice; Matilda Bone.* Also, *Alchemy and Meggy Swan.* www.karencushman.com

Margarita Engle, Cuban-American author of novels in verse about historical events and peoples in Cuba. *The Surrender Tree; Hurricane Dancers; Tropical Secrets; The Firefly Letters.* http://margaritaengle.com/

Karen Hesse, author of the free-verse novels *Out of the Dust* and *Witness.* Also noted for World War II historical books: *Letters from Rifka; The Cats in Krasinski Square.*

Cynthia Kadohata, author of historical fiction about Japanese-American experiences. *Kira-Kira* (Newbery Medal); *Weedflower; Outside Beauty.* www.kira-kira.us/index. html

Iain Lawrence, Canadian author of historical novels including the high-seas adventure trilogy *The Wreckers, The Smugglers,* and *The Buccaneers.* Also, *Lord of the Nutcracker Men,* a World War I novel.

Geraldine McCaughrean, British author of novels set in different countries. *Stop the Train!* in Oklahoma; *The Kite Rider* in China; and *The Pirate's Son* in England to Madagascar. www.geraldinemccaughrean. co.uk

Margi Preus, author and playwright, won a Newbery Honor for her first novel for young people, *Heart of a Samurai,* set in Japan. Also wrote *Shadow on the Mountain,* set in Norway. www.margipreus.com

Graham Salisbury, author of historical and realistic novels set in the Hawaiian Islands where he was raised. *House of the Red Fish; Eyes of the Emperor.* www.grahamsalisbury.com

Gary Schmidt, author of historical fiction novels that focus on difficult social issues and coming-of-age themes. *Lizzie Bright and the Buckminster Boy; The Wednesday Wars; Okay for Now.* www.hmhbooks.com/schmidt

conveys the tension between a Welsh girl and her English mistress during the British occupation of Wales.

Emergence of Modern Nations, 1500 to 1800 The Renaissance, a literary and artistic movement, swept Western Europe, leading to the invention of the printing press, an emphasis on human reason, a reformation of the Christian Church, and advances in science. Shakespeare is an important figure in *The Fool's Girl* (Rees, 2010) which expands on his *Twelfth Night* tale by drawing on palace intrigue. Central governments throughout

Europe increased their power. Spain, and then France, dominated Europe in the 1500s and 1600s, while Russia, Austria, and Prussia rose to power in the 1700s. Europeans explored and settled in Africa, India, and the Americas, with the Portuguese and Spanish taking the lead in exploring and colonizing other countries within East Asia, India, Africa, and the Americas. *The Winter People* by Joseph Bruchac depicts the impact of this colonization on the Abenaki Indians in Canada when they are caught between the British and French. The struggles of the early colonists are portrayed in books such as *Wicked Girls* by Stephanie Hemphill, which is written in the voices of the accusers in the Salem Witch Trials in New England.

Revolutions created new governments and new nations. The American Revolution (1776–1781) created a new nation, while the French Revolution in 1789 affected the direction of governments toward democracy in Europe. Gary Paulsen's *Woods Runner* conveys some of the conflicts within families that arose out of the U.S. Revolutionary War through a format that alternates fiction and nonfiction segments. Napoleon built an empire across Europe, resulting in the uniting of European nations to defeat him. The nations of Latin America began to gain their independence. China expanded gradually under the Ming and Ch'ing dynasties. Japan prospered under the Tokugawa shogunate. The United States and Canada were the sites of rapid population increases due to immigration along the eastern coasts, with the beginning of westward expansion.

Development of Industrial Society, 1800 to 1914   The 1800s were marked by a rapid shift from agricultural societies to industrial societies, with Great Britain as an early site. The factory system developed and prospered, while working and living conditions deteriorated for the worker, especially for the child laborers in Elizabeth Winthrop's *Counting on Grace.* New technology—railroad trains, steamboats, the telegraph, and telephone—affected transportation and communications. Advances in science and medicine helped to explain the world and improved the quality of life. Education developed into an important institution in Western Europe and North America. Europe underwent revolutions that readjusted boundaries and eventually led to the establishment of new nations.

The westward movement in North America was fully realized across the United States and Canada, hastened by the building of railroads. Native Americans struggled for survival in the face of these massive population shifts. In *The Porcupine Year,* Louise Erdich captures some of these tensions for the Ojibwe in Wisconsin. Black slavery had existed in the American colonies from the earliest days, but in the 1800s slavery became a social and economic issue resulting in the Civil War (1861–1865). Julius Lester's *Day of Tears: A Novel in Dialogue* reconstructs the largest slave auction in American history at Savannah, Georgia, through personal accounts of slaves and slave owners. Slavery was abolished and the Union was preserved at the cost of 600,000 lives and a major rift between the North and the South. Rosemary Wells's *Red Moon at Sharpsburg* interweaves war stories from both the North and the South. A depiction of revolution and the brutality of slavery in another context is found in Margarita Engle's *The Surrender Tree,* set in Cuba.

The United States grew in economic and political strength. An age of imperialism resulted in firm control of large areas of the world by other world powers such as England, France, and Belgium. Great Britain dominated India and parts of Africa and continued its influence over Canada, Australia, and New Zealand, while Japan became a powerful force in eastern Asia. Margi Preus's *Heart of a Samurai* tells the story of the first Japanese person to set foot in the United States, while Michaela McColl's *Promise the Night* depicts the childhood of a British girl in colonial Kenya, interspersed with newspaper articles about her later life as a famous aviator.

World Wars in the Twentieth Century, 1914 to 1945   This era includes World War I (1914–1918) in Europe, in which the United States and Canada joined forces with the Allies (Great Britain, France, Russia, Greece, and Romania) against Germany and the Central Powers; the between-wars period that included the Great Depression; Hitler's rise to power in 1933; and World War II (1939–1945) in Europe and Asia, in which Canada and the United States joined forces with England, France, and the Soviet Union to battle Germany, Italy, and Japan. In 1917 the Bolshevik Revolution established a Communist government in Russia. The human cost of the expansion of communism by Russia is conveyed in *Between Shades of Gray* by Ruta Sepetys when a family is sent to Siberia after Stalin's invasion of Lithuania in 1941. Several recent novels have portrayed the effects of World War I, including Geert Spillebeen's *Kipling's Choice* and Monika Schroder's *My Brother's Shadow*.

In 1931, Great Britain recognized Canada, Australia, New Zealand, and South Africa as independent, but each declared their loyalty to the British monarch and continued cultural ties with Great Britain. The atrocities of the Holocaust during World War II—the persecution and killing of Jewish people and others by the Nazi regime—are portrayed in Markus Zusak's *The Book Thief,* recounting the effects of Hitler's rise to power, and Sharon Dogar's *Annexed,* about life with Anne Frank from Peter's point of view. World War II ended shortly after the United States dropped nuclear bombs on Hiroshima and Nagasaki, Japan. Toshi Maruki's *Hiroshima, No Pika,* Sherri Smith's *FlyGirl,* Nancy Bo Flood's *Warriors in the Crossfire,* and Elizabeth Wein's *Code Name Verity* help flesh out young adult's knowledge of World War II while engaging them in believable plot lines and characters. *Weedflower* by Cynthia Kadahota shows how the fear of Japan created by politicians and the press after Pearl Harbor led to the internment of loyal Japanese Americans.

Post–World War II Era, 1945 to 1990   After the war, the United States and Western European nations became involved in a struggle for world influence against Communist nations, particularly the Soviet Union and China, leading to a massive arms buildup. The Korean War (1950–1953) and the Vietnam War (1965–1973) were major conflicts in which the United States fought to contain Communist expansion. The Korean War, combined with the postwar economic recovery of Japan, drew attention to the growing importance of East Asia in world affairs. *All the Broken Pieces* by Ann Burg and *Inside Out and Back Again* by Thanhha Lai describe the impact of the Vietnam War on Vietnamese who had to flee to the United States.

The Soviet Union launched a series of satellites, beginning with Sputnik 1 on October 4, 1957, inaugurating the space age. An explosion of scientific knowledge occurred as a result of massive spending for weapons development and space exploration. The 1950s and 1960s have been described as the Cold War decades because of the hostility between the Soviet Union and the United States. In the 1970s public pressure mounted in the United States to reduce the nation's external military commitments. Alan Armstrong's *Racing the Moon* is the story of a brother and sister who are obsessed with rocket-building and outer space, depicting the peaceful atmosphere of rural postwar America in 1947 but with subtle reminders of the global conflicts that will soon erupt.

During the 1960s a strong civil rights movement, led by Martin Luther King Jr. and other prominent figures of the era, fought for equal treatment of African Americans. The movement led to desegregation of schools, restaurants, transportation, and housing. Another struggle against the policies of racial separation occurred in South Africa in the 1970s and 1980s. Equal rights for women were also sought during the feminist movement in the 1970s. Tensions regarding the Black Panther movement in the 1960s are portrayed in Kekla Magoon's *The Rock and the River* and Rita Williams-Garcia's *One Crazy Summer*. Racism in school contexts is portrayed in the struggle for integration in the South in Robert Sharenow's *My Mother the Cheerleader* and in the boarding schools forced on Native peoples in Alaska in Debby Edwardson's *My Name Is Not Easy*.

Historical fiction offers readers the opportunity to live within the experiences of the past, not just gain knowledge about events and people. They are able to explore the difficult choices and human contradictions that define our world, while maintaining hope for making a change in their present and future worlds through imagining the past.

References

Meltzer, M. (1981). Beyond the span of a single life. In B. Hearne (Ed.), *Celebrating children's books*. New York: Lothrop.

Smith, J. A., Monson, J. A., & Dobson, D. (1992). A case study on integrating history and reading instruction through literature. *Social Education, 56*, 370–375.

Recommended Historical Fiction Books

Ages indicated refer to content appropriateness and conceptual and interest levels. The nationality of authors who are not from the United States is indicated in parentheses. Formats other than novels are coded as follows:

(GR)   Graphic novel

(PI)   Picture book

(COL)   Short story collection

(NV)   Novel in verse

Beginnings of Civilization up to 3000 B.C.

Cowley, Marjorie. *Anooka's Answer*. Clarion, 1998. Ages 10–15. Southern France, Upper Paleolithic era.

Denzel, Justin. *Boy of the Painted Cave*. Philomel, 1988. Ages 10–14. Stone Age, France and Spain, cave paintings. *Return to the Painted Cave* (1997).

Dickinson, Peter. *A Bone from a Dry Sea*. Delacorte, 1993. Ages 11–15. Prehistoric tribe, based on an archaeological dig. (British)

Levin, Betty. *Thorn*. Front Street, 2005. Ages 12–16. Prehistoric times, birth defects.

Williams, Susan. *Wind Rider*. Laura Geringer, 2006. Ages 10-14. Central Asia, 4000 B.C. Taming of horses, gender issues.

Civilizations of the Ancient World, 3000 B.C. to A.D. 600

Lawrence, Caroline. *The Man from Pomegranate Street*. Orion, 2009. Ages 11–15. A.D. 81, Roman Mystery Series. (British)

Lawrence, L. S. *Escape by Sea*. Holiday, 2008. Ages 12–18. Roman Empire, Carthage, Punic War 218–201 B.C. (Australian)

Lester, Julius. *Pharaoh's Daughter*. Houghton Mifflin Harcourt, 2000. Ages 12–18. Moses, Egypt, 332 B.C.

Shecter, Vicky. *Cleopatra's Moon*. Scholastic, 2013. Ages 14–18. Cleopatra's daughter after mother's death.

Sutcliff, Rosemary. *The Eagles of the Ninth*. Square Fish, 2010. Ages 12–16. Roman period, Britain, 125 A.D. (British)

Wein, Elizabeth. *The Lion Hunter*. Viking, 2007. Ages 12–16. Ethiopia, 6th century. Combines myth and history. The Mark of Solomon series.

Winters, Kay. *Voices of Ancient Egypt.* Illus. by Barry Moser. National Geographic, 2003. (**PI**) Ages 9–14. Poems in the voices of ancient Egyptian workers. Egypt, 300 B.C.

Civilizations of the Medieval World, 600 to 1500

Avi. *Crispin: The End of Time*. Balzer & Bray, 2010. Ages 11–15. France and England, 14th century. Also *Crispin: At the Edge of the World* (2006) and *Crispin: The Cross of Lead* (2002).

Coats, Jillian A. *The Wicked and the Just*. Harcourt, 2012. Ages 12–18. British conquest of Wales, 1290s.

Crossley-Holland, Kevin. *Crossing to Paradise*. Scholastic, 2006. Ages 12–16. Pilgrimages in 1189. (British)

Cushman, Karen. *Catherine, Called Birdy*. Clarion, 1994. Ages 12–16. England, manor life, 1290s.

———. *Matilda Bone*. Clarion, 2000. Ages 12–16. Medical practitioner, England, Middle Ages, 1300s.

———. *The Midwife's Apprentice*. Clarion, 1995. Ages 12–16. England, Middle Ages, 1300s. Newbery Award.

Decker, Timothy. *Run Far, Run Fast*. Front Street, 2007. Ages 10–14**. (GR)** Black Plague. Europe, 1348.

Heuston, Kimberley B. *Dante's Daughter*. Front Street, 2003. Ages 14–18. Writer Dante's family. Italy, 1300s.

Hoffman, Mary. *The Falconer's Knot: A Story of Friars, Flirtations, and Foul Play*. Bloomsbury, 2007. Ages 14–18. Murder and romantic intrigue. Italy, 1316. (British)

Jinks, Catherine. *Pagan's Crusade*. Candlewick, 2003. Ages 12–18. A squire with the Templar Knights of Jerusalem, 1187. Sequels *Pagan in Exile* (2004), *Pagan's Vows* (2004), and *Pagan's Scribe* (2005). (Australian)

Karr, Kathleen. *Fortune's Fool*. Knopf, 2008. Ages 12–15. Quest for sanctuary. Medieval Germany, 1300s.

Leeds, Constance. *The Unfortunate Son*. Viking, 2012. Ages 12–14. Apprentice, kidnapping, sold into slavery in Africa. France, 1485–1500.

McCaughrean, Geraldine. *The Kite Rider*. HarperCollins, 2002. Ages 12–16. Ancient China, young man becomes a kite rider in a circus after father's death; eventually comes to the court of Kubla Khan. (British)

Park, Linda Sue. *A Single Shard*. Clarion, 2001. Ages 10–14. Korean potters' village, 1100s. Newbery Award.

Paterson, Katherine. *The Sign of the Chrysanthemum*. Crowell, 1973. Ages 11–14. Political unrest. Japan, 1100s.

Roberts, Judson. *Viking Warrior*. HarperCollins, 2006. Ages 12–16. Denmark, 845. Strongbow Saga.

Yolen, Jane, and Robert Harris. *Girl in a Cage*. Putnam, 2002. Ages 11–15. England, invasion of Scotland, 1306.

Emergence of Modern Nations, 1500 to 1800

Anderson, Laurie Halse. *Chains*. Simon & Schuster, 2008. Ages 12–18. Enslaved teenage sisters sold in 1776 to rich loyalists in New York City. Sequel *Forge* (Atheneum, 2010).

———. *Fever 1793*. Simon & Schuster, 2000. Ages 12–18, Yellow fever epidemic. Philadelphia, 1793.

Anderson, M. T. *The Astonishing Life of Octavian Nothing, Traitor to the Nation*: Volume I: *The Pox Party*. Candlewick, 2006. Volume II: *The Kingdom on the Waves* (2008). Ages 14–18. Revolutionary War, slavery, New England, 1770s.

Avi. *The Fighting Ground*. Lippincott, 1984. Ages 10–14. U.S. Revolutionary War era. New Jersey, 1778.

Bennett, Veronica. *Cassandra's Sister*. Candlewick, 2007. Ages 12–16. Jane Austen, with references to the writing of *Pride and Prejudice* and *Sense and Sensibility*. England, late 1700s. (British)

Bruchac, Joseph. *The Winter People*. Dial, 2002. Ages 12–16. French and Indian War, Abenaki, Canada, 1759.

Cadnum, Michael. *Peril on the Sea*. Farrar, 2009. Ages 12–18. Defeat of the Spanish Armada, adventures on the high seas, writing. England, 1588.

Carbone, Elisa. *Blood on the River: James Town 1607*. Viking, 2006. Ages 12–14. Clash of cultures in the New World through an indentured boy's perspective. Jamestown, VA, 1606.

Cushman, Karen. *Alchemy and Meggy Swan*. Clarion, 2010. Ages 11–14. Physical disability. London, 1573.

Duble, Kathleen Benner. *The Sacrifice*. Simon & Schuster, 2005. Ages 11–15. U.S. Colonial era, Salem witch hunts. Massachusetts, 1692.

Engle, Margarita. *Hurricane Dancers: The First Caribbean Pirate Shipwreck*. Holt, 2011. (NV) Ages 12–16. Multiple voices about issues of captivity and freedom and the age of exploration. Cuba, 1510.

Forbes, Esther. *Johnny Tremain*. Houghton, 1943. Ages 10–13. U.S. Revolutionary War era. Boston, 1770s.

Hearn, Julie. *The Minister's Daughter*. Atheneum, 2005. Ages 14–18. Christianity and old beliefs, pregnancy and witchcraft. England, 1645. (British)

Hemphill, Stephanie. *Wicked Girls: A Novel of the Salem Witch Trials*. Balzer & Bray, 2010. Ages 12–18. (NV) Perspective of the three girls who were the accusers. Massachusetts, 1692.

Ketchum, Liza. *Where the Great Hawk Flies*. Clarion, 2005. Ages 10–14. Relationships between white settlers and Pequot Indians, intermarriage. Vermont, 1782.

Lawrence, Iain. *The Wreckers*. Delacorte, 1998. Ages 10–14. Adventures on high seas; pirates, mystery, 1800s, England, Carribean. The trilogy

includes *The Smugglers* (1999) and *The Buccaneers* (2001). (Canadian)

Meyer, Carolyn. *The Wild Queen: The Days and Nights of Mary, Queen of Scots*. Harcourt, 2012. Ages 12–17. Mary Stuart and her life as queen. Scotland, 1587. Young Royals series.

Paterson, Katherine. *The Master Puppeteer*. Crowell, 1975. Ages 12–16. Poverty and discontent in Osaka, Japan, 1700s.

Paulson, Gary. *Woods Runner*. Wendy Lamb, 2010. Ages 12–15. Wilderness, survival, rescue of parents from British. Alternates fiction and nonfiction segments. Pennsylvania, 1776.

Rees, Celia. *Pirates!* Bloomsbury, 2003. Ages 13–18. Adventure on the high seas. Caribbean, 1725. (British)

———. *The Fool's Girl*. Bloomsbury, 2010. Ages 12–18. Romantic drama, involving Shakespeare with references to *Twelfth Night*. England, Illyria, 1600. (British)

Smith, Charles. *Brick by Brick*. Illus. by Floyd Cooper. Amistad, 2013. (PI) Ages 10–14. A story in verse about the use of slave labor to build the White House.

Speare, Elizabeth George. *The Witch of Blackbird Pond*. Houghton, 1958. Ages 11–14. Girl accused of witchcraft. Connecticut, 1687. Newbery Award

Sturtevant, Katherine. *The Brothers Story*. Farrar, 2009. Ages 12–18. Great Frost, extreme poverty, mental disabilities. London, 1683.

Taylor, Mildred. *The Land*. Phyllis Fogelman, 2001. Ages 11–15. Biracial young man in the South, post–U.S. Civil War, Georgia, 1870s.

Winters, Kay. *Colonial Voices: Hear Them Speak*. Illus. by Larry Day. Dutton, 2008. (PI) Ages 10–14. Poems in the voices of colonists in responding to the Tea Act. Boston Tea Party, 1773.

Development of Industrial Society, 1800 to 1914

Auch, Mary Jane. *Ashes of Roses*. Holt, 2002. Ages 14–18. Fire in shirtwaist factory. New York City, 1911.

Avi. *City of Orphans*. Atheneum, 2011. Ages 12–14. Immigrants, wrongful imprisonment. New York, 1893.

————. *Silent Movie*. Illus. by C. B. Mordan. Atheneum, 2003. **(PI)** Ages 10–14. Swedish immigrants, fledgling film industry, New York City, early 1900s.

————. *The True Confessions of Charlotte Doyle*. Orchard, 1990. Ages 11–15. England, United States, 1830s.

Blackwood, Gary. *Second Sight*. Dutton, 2005. Ages 11–15. Civil War, assassination of Lincoln, United States, 1864.

Boling, Katharine. *January 1905*. Harcourt, 2004. Ages 9–13. Child labor. New England mill town, 1905.

Bradley, Kimberly B. *Jefferson's Sons: A Founding Father's Secret Children*. Dial, 2011. Ages 12–16. Lives of the slave children of Thomas Jefferson and Sally Hemings. Multiple narrators. Virginia, early 1800s.

Brooks, Martha. *Queen of Hearts*. Farrar, 2010. Ages 12–16. French-Canadian girl contracts tuberculosis and is confined to a sanitarium. Manitoba, 1941. (Canadian)

Cadnum, Michael. *Blood Gold*. Viking, 2004. Ages 12–18. Adventure, Panama, California Gold Rush, 1849.

Curtis, Christopher Paul. *Elijah of Buxton*. Scholastic, 2007. Ages 11–14. Runaway slaves in a refuge town, Canada, 1849.

Cushman, Karen. *Rodzina*. Clarion, 2003. Ages 10–14. Orphan train, Chicago to California, 1881.

DeFelice, Cynthia. *Bringing Ezra Back*. Farrar, 2006. Ages 10–13. Dealing with evil, Ohio frontier, 1830s. Sequel to *Weasel* (1990).

Donnelly, Jennifer. *A Northern Light*. Harcourt, 2003. Ages 14–18. Mystery in upstate New York, 1906.

Draper, Sharon. *Copper Sun*. Atheneum, 2006. Ages 14–18. Slave trade, plantation, Carolinas, early 1800s.

Engle, Margarita. *The Firefly Letters: A Suffragette's Journey to Cuba*. Holt, 2010. **(NV)** Ages 12–18. The voices of three women on women's rights—a visitor from Sweden, a slave, and her mistress. Cuba, 1857.

————. *The Surrender Tree: Poems from Cuba's Struggle for Freedom*. Holt, 2008. **(NV)** Ages 14–18. Slavery and rebels in Cuba, 1868–1898.

Erdrich, Louise. *The Porcupine Year*. HarperCollins, 2008. Ages 10–14. Settlers' threats to the Ojibwe way of life. Wisconsin, 1850s. Sequel to *The Birchbark House* (1999) and *The Game of Silence* (2005).

Fradin, Judith, and Dennis Fradin. *The Price of Freedom: How One Town Stood Up to Slavery*. Illus. by Eric Velasquez. Walker, 2013. **(PI)** Ages 10–14. True story of an escaped slave and how he and the townspeople of Oberlin, Ohio, banded together to stand against slave-catchers. Act of protest and heroism.

Frost, Helen. *The Braid*. Farrar, 2006. **(NV)** Ages 12–16. Scottish sisters, separation, Canada, 1850s.

Giff, Patricia Reilly. *Water Street*. Random House, 2006. Ages 10–14. Irish-American immigrants, New York City, 1875. Sequel to *Nory Ryan's Song* (2000) and *Maggie's Door* (2003). Irish potato famine.

Haines, Kathryn Miller. *This Girl is Murder*. Roaring Brook Press, 2011. Ages 14–18. Girl who wants to be a detective like her father, family secrets. New York City, 1942

Holt, Kimberly Willis. *The Water Seeker*. Holt, 2010. Ages 12–15. U.S. frontier, dowsing. Missouri to Oregon, 1833–1859.

Holub, Josef. *An Innocent Soldier*. Translated from German by Michael Hofmann. Scholastic, 2005. Ages 14–18. Napoleon's Russian campaign, 1812. (German)

Ibbotson, Eva. *Journey to the River Sea*. Dutton, 2002. Ages 11–14. Orphan, Amazon adventure. Brazil, 1910. (British)

————. *The Star of Kazan*. Dutton, 2004. Ages 10–14. Abandoned child, Germany/Austria, late 1800s. (British)

Kelly, Jacqueline. *The Evolution of Calpurnia Tate*. Holt, 2009. Ages 11–14. Girl's desire to be a scientist, observations of the natural world, Darwin. Texas, 1899.

Lester, Julius. *Day of Tears: A Novel in Dialogue*. Hyperion, 2005. Ages 12–18. Account of the biggest slave auction in American history. Savannah, Georgia, 1859.

Lewis, J. Patrick. *The Brothers' War: Civil War Voices in Verse*. National Geographic, 2007. Ages 10–14. Poems honoring historical and fictional heroes of the U.S. Civil War. U.S., 1861–1865.

Lowry, Lois. *The Silent Boy*. Houghton, 2003. Ages 10–14. Developmental disability, New England town, 1908–1911.

Major, Kevin. *Ann and Seamus*. Illus. by David Blackwood. Groundwood, 2004. **(NV)** Ages 11–18. Shipwreck and love story. Newfoundland, 1828. (Canadian)

McCaughrean, Geraldine. *Stop the Train!* HarperCollins, 2003. Ages 11–15. Railroad, homesteading. Enid, Oklahoma, 1893. (British)

MacColl, Michaela. *Promise the Night*. Chronicle, 2011. Ages 11–15. British farms in Kenya, Beryl Markham's childhood. Kenya, 1912.

McMullan, Margaret. *How I Found the Strong*. Houghton, 2004. Ages 11–15. A boy witnessing Civil War battlefield slaughter while searching for his father. Mississippi, 1861.

Myers, Anna. *Assassin*. Walker, 2005. Ages 11–15. Alternating narratives by John Wilkes Booth and an assistant seamstress in the White House, assassination of Abraham Lincoln. Washington D.C., 1865.

Myers, Walter Dean. *Riot*. Egmont, 2009. Ages 12–16. Screenplay format, Irish immigrants lash out against African Americans, Civil War Draft Riots. New York City, 1863.

Paterson, Katherine. *Bread and Roses, Too*. Clarion, 2006. Ages 11–15. Mill workers' strike, Massachusetts, 1912.

Pearsall, Shelley. *Crooked River*. Knopf, 2005. Ages 11–14. White pioneers and Indians, Ohio, 1812.

Peck, Richard. *The River between Us*. Dial, 2003. Ages 13–18. Small town, race relations, early Civil War era, humor. Southern Illinois,1861.

———. *The Teacher's Funeral: A Comedy in Three Parts*. Dial, 2004. Ages 10–14. Rural Indiana, 1904.

Philbrick, Rodman. *The Mostly True Adventures of Homer P. Figg*. Blue Sky. 2009. Ages 12–14. U.S. Civil War, slavery, search for brother. Maine, 1860s.

Place, François. *The Old Man Mad about Drawing: A Tale of Hokusai*. Translated from French by William Rodarmor. Godine, 2003. Ages 10–14. Artist Hokusai, the customs of his age. Japan, 1800s. (French)

Preus, Margi. *Heart of a Samurai: Based on the True Story of Nakahama Manjiro*. Amulet, 2010.

Ages 12–15. Japanese–U.S. relationships, shipwreck, Japan, 1841–1851.

Raven, Margot. *Night Boat to Freedom*. Illus. by E. B. Lewis. Farrar, 2006. **(PI)** Ages 10–14. Slavery, escape, fabric arts. Kentucky, late 1800s.

Richards, Jane. *Three Rivers Rising: A Novel of the Johnstown Flood*. Ember, 2011. **(NV)** Ages 14–18 Impact of historical flood on six people, multiple voices. Johnstown, Pennsylvania, 1888–1889.

Schmidt, Gary. *Lizzie Bright and the Buckminster Boy*. Clarion, 2004. Ages 12–18. Race relations, religion, Maine, 1912.

Sedgwick, Marcus. *Revolver*. Roaring Brook Press, 2009. Ages 14–18. Thriller, family threatened due to events during Alaska gold rush. Swedish-Finnish border, 1910. (British)

Siegelson, Kim. *Trembling Earth*. Putnam, 2004. Ages 12–15. Survival story, Okefenokee Swamp, U.S. Civil War era. Georgia, 1860s.

Stolz, Joëlle. *The Shadows of Ghadames*. Translated from French by Catherine Temerson. Delacorte, 2004. Ages 12–15. Muslim traditions, gender roles, Libya, late 1800s. (French)

Tal, Eve. *Double Crossing: A Jewish Immigration Story*. Cinco Puntos, 2005. Ages 11–15. Emigration from the Ukraine in 1905.

Timberlake, Amy. *One Came Home*. Knopf, 2013. Ages 12–15. Search for missing sister. Wisconsin, 1871.

Wells, Rosemary. *Red Moon at Sharpsburg*. Viking, 2007. Ages 12–15. Civil War stories interwoven from both sides, North and South. Battle of Antietam, Virginia, 1862.

Wilson, Diane Lee. *Black Storm Comin'*. Simon & Schuster, 2005. Ages 12–16. Biracial family traveling from Missouri to California; Pony Express; Civil War backdrop, 1860.

Winthrop, Elizabeth. *Counting on Grace*. Random, 2006. Ages 10–15. Laboring in a mill. Vermont, 1910.

Woodson, Jacqueline. *Show Way*. Illus. by Hudson Talbott. Putnam, 2005. **(PI)**. Ages 10–15. History of African-American women from slavery to present, quilts. United States.

Wright, Barbara. *Crow*. Random, 2012. Ages 12–14. Racist uprising of whites against middle class

African Americans. Wilmington, North Carolina, 1898.

Yep, Laurence. *Dragon's Gate*. HarperCollins, 1993. Ages 12–16. Sierra Nevada, transcontinental railroad, Chinese immigrants. California, 1867.

Zimmer, Tracie V. *The Floating Circus*. Bloomsbury, 2008. Ages 12–16. Circus barge, New Orleans, 1850s.

World Wars in the Twentieth Century, 1914 to 1945

Bartoletti, Susan. *The Boy Who Dared*. Scholastic, 2008. Ages 12–18. Resistance, Germany, 1942.

Becker, Jurek. *Jakob the Liar*. Translated from German by Leila Vennewitz. Plum, 1999. Ages 14–18. Set in a German-occupied ghetto, Jakob weaves a web of "good news" lies that create hope. (German)

Bolden, Tonya. *Finding Family*. Bloomsbury, 2010. Ages 12–14. African-American family secrets. Period photographs. West Virginia, 1905.

Couloumbis, Audrey. *War Games: A Novel Based on a True Story*. Random, 2009. Ages 12–14. World War II, Nazi Occupation. Greece, 1941.

Currier, Katrina S. *Kai's Journey to Gold Mountain*. Illus. by Gabhor Utomo. Angel Island, 2005. (**PI**) Ages 10–14. Chinese immigrants, internment. Angel Island, California, 1934.

Curtis, Christopher Paul. *Bud, Not Buddy*. Delacorte, 1999. Ages 9–14. Depression era, Michigan, 1930s.

Davis, Tanita. *Mare's War*. Knopf, 2009. Ages 12–18. Alternates between the present and 1940s, grandmother recounts the challenges she faced as an African American in the Women's Army Corps during World War II.

de la Peña, Matt. *A Nation's Hope: The Story of Boxing Legend Joe Louis*. Illus. by Kadir Nelson. Dial, 2011 (**PI**) Ages 10–14. Fight between Joe Louis and German Max Schmeling, World War II. New York, 1938.

Disher, Garry. *The Divine Wind: A Love Story*. Scholastic, 2002. Ages 14–18. Racism, love, treatment of Japanese Australians, World War II, Australia,1930s and 1940s. (Australian)

Dogar, Sharon. *Annexed*. Houghton Mifflin, 2010. Ages 14–18. Fictional account of life with Anne Frank from Peter's point of view, search for identity. Netherlands, 1942–1944. (British)

Engle, Margarita. *Tropical Secrets: Holocaust Refugees in Cuba*. Holt, 2009. (**NV**) Ages 12–17. Voices of characters involved in decisions about whether to allow entry for Jewish refugees, World War II. Cuba, 1939.

Fitzmaurice, Kathryn. *A Diamond in the Desert*. Viking, 2012. Ages 12–14. Japanese-American boy in the Gila River internment camp, baseball, sister's illness. Composed of brief vignettes. Arizona, 1941.

Flood, Nancy Bo. *Warriors in the Crossfire*. Front Street, 2010. Ages 12–16. World War II, South Pacific, Saipan, 1944.

Frost, Helen. *Crossing Stones*. Farrar, 2009. (**NV**) Ages14–18. Multiple voices, impact of World War I. Michigan, 1917.

Glatsheyn, Yankev. *Emil and Karl*. Translated from Yiddish by Jeffrey Shandler. Roaring Brook, 2006. Ages 10–15. Two boys, one Christian and one Jewish, growing up in pre–World War II Vienna. 1940, Vienna. (Polish)

Hartnett, Sonya. *Thursday's Child*. Candlewick, 2002. Ages 14–18. Depression, Australia, 1930s. (Australian)

Havill, Juanita. *Eyes Like Willy's*. Illus. by David Johnson. HarperCollins, 2004. Ages 12–16. Austrian and French friends on opposite sides, World War I. 1906–1914.

Hesse, Karen. *The Cats in Krasinski Square*. Illus. by Wendy Watson. Scholastic, 2004. (**PI**) Ages 10–14. Nazi occupation of Warsaw, Jewish ghetto, World War II. Free verse. Warsaw, 1942.

———. *Out of the Dust*. Scholastic, 1997. (**NV**) Ages 11–14. Oklahoma, dust bowl, drought, 1930s.

———. *Witness*. Scholastic, 2001. Ages 11–15. (**NV**) Ku Klux Klan, multiple voices in five acts. Vermont, 1924.

Janeczko, Paul B. *Worlds Afire*. Candlewick, 2004. (**NV**) Ages 12–15. Hartford, Connecticut, fire in 1944.

Kadohata, Cynthia. *Weedflower*. Simon & Schuster, 2006. Ages 10–14. Internment camp on the Colorado River Indian reservation in Arizona, Japanese-American family, World War II, 1941.

Kerr, M. E. *Your Eyes in Stars.* HarperCollins, 2006. Ages 14–18. Small town in upstate New York during the Depression. Relationships between Germans and Americans, Jews and Gentiles. New York, 1934.

Larson, Kirby. *Hattie Big Sky.* Delacorte, 2006. Ages 12–16. Homesteading discrimination toward Germans during World War I. Montana, 1918. Sequel *Hattie Ever After* (2012).

Lawrence, Iain. *B for Buster.* Delacorte, 2004. Ages 12–18. Canadian Air Force, World War II, deployment to England for raids over Germany, 1943. (Canadian)

Lisle, Janet Taylor. *The Art of Keeping Cool.* Simon & Schuster, 2000. Ages 10–13. United States and Canada, World War II. Dresden, Germany, 1945. (Canadian)

Maruki, Toshi. *Hiroshima No Pika.* Lothrop, 1980. (PI) Ages 12–15. Effects of nuclear bomb, Hiroshima, 1945. (Japanese)

Morpurgo, Michael. *Private Peaceful.* Scholastic, 2004. Ages 13–18. World War I, England, France, 1916. (British)

———. *An Elephant in the Garden.* Feiwel & Friends, 2011. Ages 10–14. Zookeeper's family keeps an elephant in their backyard during World War II. Dresden, 1945. (British)

Moss, Marissa. *Barbed Wire Baseball.* Illus. by Yuko Shimizu. Abram, 2013. (PI) Ages 10–14. Story of a famous baseball player sent to a Japanese-American internment camp where he created a baseball field.

Myers, Walter Dean. *Harlem Summer.* Scholastic, 2007. Ages 14–18. Harlem Renaissance and Prohibition era, New York City, 1925.

Park, Linda Sue. *When My Name Was Keoko: A Novel of Korea in World War II.* Clarion, 2002. Ages 10–14. Japanese occupation of Korea, 1940s.

Peck, Richard. *Here Lies the Librarian.* Dial, 2006. Ages 12–16. Rural Indiana, 1914.

———. *A Year Down Yonder.* Dial, 2000. Ages 10–15. Depression era, humor. Southern Illinois, 1937.

Preus, Margi. *Shadow on the Mountain.* Amulet, 2012. Ages 14–16. Resistance, World War II. Norway, 1944.

Ray, Delia. *Ghost Girl: A Blue Ridge Mountain Story.* Clarion, 2003. Ages 10–14. Depression era. Virginia, 1929–1932.

Roy, Jennifer. *Yellow Star.* Marshall Cavendish, 2006. Ages 10–15. Nazi occupation of the Lodz ghetto, Poland, 1939–1945.

Ryan, Pam Muñoz. *Esperanza Rising.* Scholastic, 2000. Ages 9–14. Depression era, migrant workers. Mexico and United States, 1930s.

Salisbury, Graham. *Eyes of the Emperor.* Random, 2005. Ages 12–18. Japanese Americans in Army during World War II, prejudice, training scout dogs. Mississippi, 1941.

———. *House of the Red Fish.* Random, 2006. Ages 10–15. Sequel to *Under the Blood-Red Sun* (2005). Japanese Americans, World War II. Hawai'i, 1943.

Schroder, Monika. *My Brother's Shadow.* Farrar, 2011. Post–World War I suffering in Germany, divided loyalties, and simmering resentment create an incendiary political climate. Berlin, 1918. (German)

Selznick, Brian. *The Invention of Hugo Cabret.* Scholastic, 2007. (PI) Ages 12–15. Orphan in a train station, mystery, early filmmaker. Novel in words and pictures. Paris, 1930s.

Sepetys, Ruta. *Between Shades of Gray.* Philemel, 2011. Ages 13–18. Stalin's invasion of Lithuania, family sent to Siberia. Lithuania, 1941.

Sharenow, Rob. *The Berlin Boxing Club.* HarperCollins, 2011. Jewish teen, cartoonist, learning boxing from Max Schmeling. Germany, 1934–1938.

Sheth, Kashmira. *Keeping Corner.* Hyperion, 2007. Ages 12–18. Child widow, women's rights. India, 1918.

Smith, Sherri. *Flygirl.* Speak, 2008. Ages 14–18. African-American girl passes for white to become a pilot, World War II. Louisiana, 1940s.

Spillebeen, Geert. *Kipling's Choice.* Translated from Dutch by Terese Edelstein. Houghton, 2005. Ages 12–16. Son of Rudyard Kipling dies in battle, questioning of war, World War I. France, 1915. (Belgian)

Spinelli, Jerry. *Milkweed.* Random, 2003. Ages 13–18. Persecution of Jews, World War II. Warsaw, 1940s.

Vanderpool, Clare. *Moon over Manifest*. Delacorte, 2010. Ages 12–14. Father's secrets, Depression. Kansas, 1936.

Walters, Eric. *Caged Eagles*. Orca, 2000. Ages 11–15. Internment of Japanese Canadians, World War II. Vancouver, 1940s. (Canadian)

Wein, Elizabeth. *Code Name Verity*. Hypersion, 2012. Ages 14–18. Female friendship of a spy and pilot during World War II, Nazi interrogation and torture of a female Scottish spy. France, 1940s.

———. *Rose Under Fire*. Hyperion, 2013. Ages 14–18. A young American pilot is captured by Nazis and taken to Ravensbruck, the women's concentration camp where medical experimentation occurred. 1939–1945.

Wolf, Joan. *Someone Named Eve*. Clarion, 2007. Ages 11–16. Czechoslovakian child survivor with Aryan features placed in a German family, World War II. Poland, 1942.

Yamasaki, Katie. *Fish for Jimmy: Inspired by One Family's Experience in a Japanese American Internment Camp*. Holiday House, 2013. **(PI)** Ages 10–14. A brother's love and a family's perseverance inside a camp.

Zusak, Markus. *The Book Thief*. Knopf, 2006. Ages 15–18. German foster girl in a working class family during World War II. Narrated by Death. Germany, 1939. (Australian)

Post–World War II Era, 1945 to 1990

Armstrong, Alan. *Racing the Moon*. Random, 2012. Ages 11–14. Two siblings are obsessed with rockets and space travel, set in postwar United States, 1947.

Burg, Ann. *All the Broken Pieces*. Scholastic, 2009. **(NV)** Ages 12–14. A Vietnamese refugee, haunted by his past, interacts with Vietnam veterans, faces prejudice when playing baseball. United States, 1977.

Clinton, Catherine. *A Stone in My Hand*. Candlewick, 2002. Ages 12–18. Palestinian family in crisis when father disappears, brother is drawn into violent protest. Palestine, 1980s.

Compestine, Ying Chang. *Revolution Is Not a Dinner Party*. Holt, 2007. Ages 11–15. Set in 1970s China, this autobiographical novel provides a child's view of the political brutality that invades her home.

Couloumbis, Audrey. *Not Exactly a Love Story*. Random, 2012. Ages 14–17. Vinnie, a loner, engages in late night phone calls to his crush, Patsy, assuming a new identity and gradually building a relationship. 1977.

Curtis, Christopher Paul. *The Watsons Go to Birmingham—1963*. Delacorte, 1995. Ages 10–14. Family trip from Flint, Michigan, to Birmingham, Alabama, U.S. Civil Rights movement. 1963.

Cushman, Karen. *The Loud Silence of Francine Green*. Clarion, 2006. Ages 11–15. McCarthyism in Los Angeles, 1950s.

Edwardson, Debby. *My Name Is Not Easy*. Marshall Cavendish, 2011. Ages 12–15. Inupiaq boy in a Catholic boarding school, five narrators. Alaska, 1960s.

Gantos, Jack. *Dead End in Norvelt*. Farrar, 2011. Ages 11–14. Small town, Pennsylvania, 1960s. Newbery Award. Sequel is *From Norvelt to Nowhere* (2013)

Herrera, Juan Felipe. *Downtown Boy*. Scholastic, 2005. **(NV)** Ages 10–14. Migrant workers, California, 1958.

Houston, Julian. *New Boy*. Houghton, 2005. Ages 13–18. Civil rights struggle, blatant racism, first black student in a boarding school. Connecticut, late 1950s.

Johnston, Tony. *Bone by Bone by Bone*. Roaring Brook, 2007. Ages 11–16. A risky friendship between two boys, one black, one white. Tennessee, 1950s.

Kadohata, Cynthia. *Kira-Kira*. Simon & Schuster, 2004. Ages 12–18. Japanese immigrants, ill sister, small town Georgia in the late 1950s. Newbery Award.

Lai, Thanhha. *Inside Out & Back Again*. Harper, 2011. **(NV)** Ages 10–14. Vietnamese immigrants. Adjusting to language and culture of the United States, Alabama, 1975.

Levine, Ellen. *Catch a Tiger by the Toe*. Viking, 2005. Ages 10–14. McCarthy witch-hunt hearings, Communism, issues of freedom of expression. New York, 1953.

Lyon, George Ella. *Sonny's House of Spies.* Simon & Schuster, 2004. Ages 12–15. Family secrets, homosexual father. Alabama, 1940s and 1950s.

Magoon, Kekla. *The Rock and the River.* Aladdin, 2009. Ages 12–14. Family conflict over differing approaches to Civil Rights Movement; Martin Luther King Jr., Black Panthers. Chicago, 1968. Sequel is *Fire in the Streets* (2012).

Mankell, Henning. *Secrets in the Fire.* Translated from Swedish by Anne Connie Stuksrud. Annick, 2003. Ages 11–14. Land mines, poverty, Mozambique civil war, southern Africa, 1970s and 1980s. (Swedish)

Master, Irfan. *A Beautiful Lie.* Whitman, 2012. Ages 12–15. A boy in India lies to his dying father about the impending partition of India in 1947, separating Muslims and Hindus/Sikhs into different countries. (British)

McCormick, Patricia. *Never Fall Down.* Balzer & Bray, 2012. Ages 12–18. Fictionalized story of Cambodian peace-activist Arn Chom-Pond, surviving the Killing Fields of the Khmer Rouge. Cambodia, 1975–1979.

Nuzum, K.A. *A Small White Scar.* HarperCollins, 2006. Ages 12–15. Caring for a twin brother with Down syndrome. Colorado, 1940s.

Park, Frances, and Ginger Park. *My Freedom Trip: A Child's Escape from North Korea.* Illus. by Debra Reid Jenkins. Boyds Mills, 1998. **(PI)** Ages 10–14. Crossing the 38th parallel prior to the Korean War, late 1940s.

Rowell, Rainbow. *Eleanor & Park.* St. Martin's Griffin, 2013. Ages 14–18. Set across one school year in 1986, story of two alienated misfits who fall in love. Alternating voices.

Schmidt, Gary. *Okay for Now.* Clarion, 2011. Ages 12–14. Teen dealing with cruel father and abusive brother, coming to see the world as an artist. Small town New York, 1968.

Selznick, Brian. *Wonderstruck.* Scholastic, 2011. Ages 12–14. A novel that intertwines the stories of Rose, a deaf child in 1927, told through visual images, and Ben in 1977, told through prose. New York City, 1977.

Sepetys, Ruta. *Out of the Easy.* Philomel, 2013. Ages 14–18. Josie, the daughter of a prostitute, works in a bookstore to create a better life. Friendship, suspense, gangsters. French Quarter, New Orleans, 1950.

Sharenow, Robert. *My Mother the Cheerleader.* HarperTeen, 2007. Ages 13–16. A white family's protest of the court-ordered integration of their daughter's school. New Orleans, 1960.

Veciana-Suarez, Ana. *Flight to Freedom.* Orchard, 2002. Ages 11–18. Cuban immigration to Miami, 1967.

White, Ruth. *The Search for Belle Prater.* Farrar, 2005. Ages 10–14. Search for a boy's missing mother, extended family, friendship, segregation. Virginia, 1955. Sequel to *Belle Prater's Boy* (1996).

———. *Little Audrey.* Farrar, 2008. Ages 10–14. Poverty and hunger in a Virginia coal mining camp, 1948.

Wiles, Deborah. *Countdown.* Scholastic, 2010. Ages 12–14. A family in crisis during the 1962 Cuban Missile Crisis. Incorporates 1960s photos, song lyrics, ads, cartoons, memorabilia. Washington, D.C., 1962.

Williams-Garcia, Rita. *One Crazy Summer.* Amistad, 2010. Ages 10–14. Sisters visit mother who abandoned them, Black Panthers. Oakland, California, 1968.

Wolff, Virginia Euwer. *Bat 6.* Scholastic, 1998. Ages 11–15. Japanese Americans, post–World War II prejudice, multiple voices. California, 1948.

 ## Related Films and DVDS

The December Boys (2007). Author: Michael Noonan (1990/2008). 105 minutes.

The Devil's Arithmetic (1999). Author: Jane Yolen (1988). 97 minutes.

I am David (2004). Author: Ann Holm (1963). 90 minutes.

In the Time of Butterflies (2001). Author: Julia Alvarez (1994). 95 minutes.

Inside Hana's Suitcase (2009). Author: Karen Levine (2002). 90 minutes.

Jakob the Liar (1999). Author: Jurek Becker (1969). 120 minutes.

Lyddie (1995). Author: Katherine Paterson (1991). 90 minutes.

My Louisiana Sky (2001). Author: Kimberly Willis Holt (1998). 98 minutes.

Seabiscuit (2003). Author: Laura Hillenbrand (2001). 141 minutes.

A Separate Peace (2004). Author: John Knowles (1959). 91 minutes.

Standing in the Light (1999). Author: Mary Pope Osborne (1998). Dear America Series. 30 minutes.

Winter of the Red Snow (1999). Author: Kristiana Gregory (1996). Dear America Series. 30 minutes.

Chapter Six

Nonfiction: Biography and Informational Books

Many adolescents are drawn to books about the real world and real people. Today's innovative and inviting works of nonfiction are well-written and feed curiosity and inquiry through combining interesting facts and explanations with provocative questions and issues. Intriguing informational books and biographies with visually interesting graphics can replace dry, bland textbooks that fail to engage adolescents as readers and inquirers.

Definition and Description

Nonfiction usually includes biography and informational books. *Informational books* can be written on any aspect of the social or natural world, including what is known of outer space. These books are literature, not textbooks, and differ in the quality of the writing and illustrations and in their intent. While textbooks are written with the intention of teaching a large body of facts from the view of an expert imparting knowledge, well-written informational books focus on a particular topic or issue from the perspective of one enthusiast sharing with another. Although the roots of nonfiction can be traced to the seventeenth century, much of the growth and development of this genre occurred in the last half of the twentieth century.

Biography gives factual information about the lives of actual people, including their experiences, influences, accomplishments, and legacies. *Partial biographies* detail a particular time period in a person's life, while *collective biographies* chronicle information about groups of people. *Autobiography* is similar in every respect to biography, except that the author tells about his or her own life. *Memoir* also deals with events in the author's life, but this form is used "to experiment, solve puzzles and riddles present in their lives, pose sometimes unanswerable questions, and advance hypotheses and what ifs about their lived experiences" (Kirby & Kirby, 2010, p. 22). The point of memoirs is that authors reveal the meanings of particular events in their lives, not the events themselves. First person narratives and memoirs are so closely related that, without an author's note, a reader may not be able to tell whether the events actually happened to the author.

Nonfiction is often defined in terms of an emphasis on documented fact about the natural world, human behavior, and society with a primary purpose to inform and engage readers with real events or phenomena. In contrast, the content of literary fiction is usually a product of the imagination with a primary purpose of understanding what it means to be human and of serving as entertainment.

Early Important Works of Nonfiction

Date	Literary Work/Event	Significance
1657	*Orbis Pictus* (The World in Pictures) by John Amos Comenius	First known work of nonfiction for young people
1922	*The Story of Mankind* by Hendrik Van Loon	First book to win the Newbery Medal; lively style and creative approach influenced subsequent books
1940	*Daniel Boone* by James H. Daugherty	First biography to win the Newbery Medal
1948	*Story of the Negro* by Arna Bontemps	First book for young people by an African American to win a Newbery Honor
1952	*Diary of a Young Girl* by Anne Frank	Autobiography that raised the public's awareness of the power of this genre; helped many to understand the tragedy of the Jewish Holocaust

Nonfiction writing is often referred to as *expository* writing, or writing that explains, whereas fiction writing is called *narrative* writing, or writing that tells a story. This distinction is overly simplistic as fiction and nonfiction both use narrative and expository writing. A science information book like *The Tarantula Scientist* by Sy Montgomery includes the story of that scientist's life along with information on tarantulas, and Jim Murphy's *An American Plague* tells the stories of people caught up in the panic of the plague and also provides historical information.

Research studies indicate that many young people have trouble reading and writing expository texts, partly because of the lack of early classroom experiences with nonfiction (Duke, 2000; Jeong, Gaffney, & Choi, 2010). Such studies reveal that repeated experiences with a specific genre are essential to learning how to read or write that genre. Many resistant readers prefer nonfiction formats and topics, such as how-to books, books about sports and computer games, and books with highly visual pages of illustrations and graphics. Educators need to be able to select books that match students' interests as well as their academic proficiencies and so must be familiar with a wide variety of nonfiction texts.

Types of Nonfiction

The types of biographies and informational books for young adults are based on several distinct formats and how the information is presented on the page, rather than the information itself:

- *Nonfiction chapter book.* This format highlights a large amount of text organized into chapters, along with graphics and illustrations, such as *Bomb: The Race to Build—and Steal—the World's Most Dangerous Weapon* by Steve Sheinkin and *Charles and Emma: The Darwins' Leap of Faith* by Deborah Heiligman. A recent trend is biographies written in verse form, such as *Your Own Sylvia* by Stephanie Hemphill, a fictionalized biography of Sylvia Plath.

- *Series nonfiction.* This type refers to a set of books published around a common theme, with a focus on personal interests, high-low (high interest, lower reading level), or curriculum-related topics to support student research. Some series books are poorly written and overgeneralize, but other series, such as the Scientists in the Field series and the various Opposing Viewpoints series on controversial topics such as gangs, body image, and drug abuse, are well-written and of strong interest to teens.

- *Nonfiction picture books* and *graphic novels.* Picture books for older readers integrate large illustrations and a brief text to convey information or a life story, such as in *Monsieur Marceau: Actor without Words* by Leda Schubert and *Moonshot: The Flight of Apollo 11* by Brian Floca. Graphic novels use panels of sketches and speech bubbles, such as *Best Shot in the West* by Patricia and Fredrick McKissack, illustrated by Randy DuBurke, to carry the narrative.

- *Photoessay* and *photobiography.* Presentation of information is equally balanced between text and illustration with excellent photographs and a crisp, condensed writing style or in a scrapbook of primary source materials, such as in *Emancipation*

Proclamation: Lincoln and the Dawn of Liberty by Tonya Bolden and *Amelia Lost: The Life and Disappearance of Amelia Earhart* by Candace Fleming.

- *Multigenre books.* These books combine elements of fiction and nonfiction and present accurate factual information alongside an entertaining ribbon of fiction or poetry, such as the combination of biographical poetry, information, and illustrations in *Dare to Dream . . . Change the World,* edited by Jill Corcoran and illustrated by J. Beth Jepson.

- *Fact books* and *reference books.* Fact books present information mainly through lists, charts, and tables in almanacs, sports trivia, and statistics books, and books of world records such as *The Guinness Book of World Records.* Reference books include encyclopedias, dictionaries, and atlases with overall coverage of many facts about a large topic.

Elements of Nonfiction

Understanding the parts, or elements, of nonfiction and how they work together is helpful in becoming more analytical about this kind of literature. Adolescents who understand nonfiction writing and can read it skillfully also improve their reading of other expository texts, including textbooks. Likewise, teachers can use this knowledge to evaluate and select textbooks as well as nonfiction for their students and to more effectively teach nonfiction. Biography, which is more narrative than expository in nature, more closely resembles fiction in its elements.

Structures for Organizing Information

Structure has to do with how the author organizes the information to be presented. Most informational literature is structured in one or more of the following ways. Some works of nonfiction will employ a single text structure; others, particularly longer works, will employ several.

- *Description.* The author gives the characteristics of the topic, with the main topic organized around related subtopics (e.g., *Moonbird: A Year on the Wind with the Great Survivor B95* by Phillip Hoose).

- *Sequence.* The author describes items or events in order, usually chronologically or numerically (e.g., *The War to End All Wars: World War I* by Russell Freedman).

- *Comparison.* The author juxtaposes two or more entities or stances on issues and lists their similarities and differences (e.g., *Body Image,* edited by Laura Scherer).

- *Cause and effect.* The author relates an action and then shows the effect, or result, of this action (e.g., *Sugar Changed the World* by Marc Aronson).

- *Question and answer* or *problem and solution.* The author presents a question, problem, or topic and gives solutions or answers (e.g., *Understanding the Holy Land: Answering Questions about the Israeli–Palestinian Conflict* by Mitch Frank).

Theme and Perspective

Theme in nonfiction is the main point made in the work. Though a work of nonfiction may communicate hundreds of facts about a topic, the theme of the work answers the question, What's the point? Sometimes the theme will be a cognitive concept, such as the way viruses multiply; in other cases, it will be an emotional insight, such as a new or deepened awareness of the strength of the human spirit to challenge social injustice, as in Vaunda Micheaux Nelson's fictional biography, *No Crystal Stair. A Documentary Novel of the Life and Work of Lewis Michaux, Harlem Bookseller.*

Point of view highlights the author's perspective on the person or topic that is the focus of a particular piece of nonfiction. Comparing several biographies on the same person, such as Barry Dennenberg's *Lincoln Shot: A President's Life Remembered,* Candace Fleming's *The Lincolns: A Scrapbook Look at Abraham and Mary,* Russell Freedman's *Lincoln: A Photobiography,* and Harold Holzer's *Father Lincoln: Lincoln and His Sons* provides insight into point of view and counteracts the bias of a particular author. Comparisons of informational books on the same event or time period indicate the particular interests and perspective of an author, such as found in books on the Civil Rights Movement that include Rick Bowers' *Spies of Mississippi,* Larry Dane Brimner's *Birmingham Sunday,* Cynthia Levinson's *We've Got a Job,* and John Stokes' *Students on Strike.*

Style and Features

Style is how authors and illustrators, with their readers in mind, express themselves in their respective media. Sentence length and complexity, word choice, and formal versus conversational tone are stylistic components that writers of nonfiction share with writers of fiction. Technical vocabulary, captions, and graphic elements such as tables, charts, illustrations, photographs, diagrams, maps, and indexes are associated mostly with nonfiction. How authors use these devices is part of their individual style. James Cross Giblin's conversational tone and use of period photographs and political cartoons, quotes, and source notes in his book *The Life and Death of Adolf Hitler* demonstrate how style can make nonfiction more interesting.

The *features* used by authors have different purposes that readers need to be able to use as tools in order to understand nonfiction. Each author uses different combinations of these tools, based on their audience and purpose, in ways that affect the accessibility of a book. Readers spend more time studying these features and illustrations and less time reading text in nonfiction as compared to fiction.

- *Table of contents* overviews the main ideas and organization of the book, while an *index* identifies the specific page where a reader can find a particular topic.
- *Maps*, *diagrams*, and *graphs* provide visual displays of information that show relationships between parts, while *cut-aways* and *cross-sections* let readers look inside something.
- *Glossaries* help readers understand the definitions of important words, while *pronunciation keys* help readers learn how to say a word.
- Pages often have words in a variety of *fonts* and *type sizes,* with bold and italic words signaling importance.

Evaluation and Selection of Nonfiction

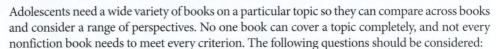

Adolescents need a wide variety of books on a particular topic so they can compare across books and consider a range of perspectives. No one book can cover a topic completely, and not every nonfiction book needs to meet every criterion. The following questions should be considered:

- **Is the book written in a clear, direct, easily understandable style?**
- **Is the information accurate, authoritative, and current?**
- **Are distinctions made between fact, theory, and opinion?**
- **Are multiple perspectives or interpretations of the topic or person presented?**
- **Are the author's qualifications to write on the subject clearly stated in the book?**
- **Is the book visually attractive to readers?** (e.g., covers, illustrations, graphics, less dense text)
- **Is the information presented in ways that support conceptual understanding?** (e.g., known to unknown, general to specific, simple to more complex, explanations as well as facts)
- **Are the captions and labels clearly written and informative?**
- **Is there a clear organizational structure, such as subheadings, that make the text easier to read and comprehend?**
- **Do the reference aids make information easier to find and understand?** (e.g. tables of contents, indexes, pronunciation guides, glossaries, maps)
- **Does the book avoid personification and teleology?** Personification is attributing human qualities to animals, material objects, or natural forces, and teleology is giving humanlike purpose to natural phenomena.

Selecting the best nonfiction for young adults can be a challenge. Several awards and recommended book lists offer good sources for identifying outstanding biographies and informational books.

- Outstanding Science Trade Books for Students K–12: An annual annotated list of notable books in the field of science by the National Science Teachers Association
- Notable Social Studies Trade Books for Young People: An annual annotated list of notable books in the field of social studies by the National Council for the Social Studies
- Orbis Pictus Award for Nonfiction, National Council of Teachers of English (www .ncte.org)
- Robert F. Sibert Informational Book Award and YALSA Award for Excellence in Nonfiction for Young Adults, from the American Library Association (www.ala.org)

Excellent Nonfiction to Read Aloud

Bartoletti, Susan C. *They Called Themselves the KKK: Birth of an American Terrorist Group.* United States, 1860s to present.

Ellis, Deborah. *Kids of Kabul: Living Bravely through a Never-Ending War.* Interviews of young people.

Floca, Brian. *Moonshot: The Flight of Apollo 11.* Pre-flight to splash down.

Lewis, J. Patrick. *The Brother's War: Civil War Voices in Verse.* U.S. Civil War.

Nelson, Kadir. *Heart and Soul: The Story of America and African Americans.* 1700s to present.

Nelson, Vaunda Micheaux. *No Crystal Stair.* Fictionalized biography of Harlem bookseller, Civil Rights era.

Ryan, Pam Muñoz. *The Dreamer.* Illustrated by Peter Sis. Poet Pablo Neruda, Chile, 1904 to 1973.

Sheinkin, Steve. *Bomb: The Race to Build—and Steal—the World's Most Dangerous Weapon.* Nuclear bomb, spies, 1940s.

Swain, Gwenyth. *Hope and Tears: Ellis Island Voices.* Monologues, dialogues, letters, poems.

Turner, Pamela. *The Frog Scientist.* Work of a scientist in the field, effects of pesticides.

Types of Biographies

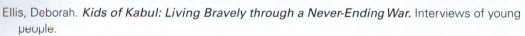

Biographies for young people allow more latitude than adult biographies in fictionalizing some aspects of the person's life. This invention ranges from choosing the aspect of the person's life that the biographer wants to emphasize as the theme of the book (e.g., great energy or love of freedom) to inventing situations and conversation. Biographies can be classified by degree of documentation:

- *Authentic biography.* All factual information is documented through eyewitness accounts, written documents, letters, diaries, and audio and video recordings. Details in the lives of people who lived long ago, such as conversations, are often difficult to document, so biographers use devices such as interior monologue (telling what a person probably thought based on known actions), indirect discourse (reporting the gist of what someone said without using quotation marks), attribution (interpretation of known actions to determine probable motives), and inference to make their stories lively and appealing. An example is *The Notorious Benedict Arnold: A True Story of Adventure, Heroism, & Treachery* by Steve Sheinkin.

- *Fictionalized biography.* The author uses careful research to create dramatic episodes from known facts by using imagined conversation. The conversation is carefully structured around the pertinent facts that are known, but the actual words are invented by the author such as *The Dreamer* by Pam Muñoz Ryan, illustrated by Peter Sis, about the life of Pablo Neruda.

Biographies are organized by era in the recommended book lists at the end of this chapter, using the same categories of time as found in the historical fiction chapter.

Notable Authors of Nonfiction

Susan Campbell Bartoletti, author whose books explore the impact of broad social movements on young people. *Black Potatoes; Hitler Youth; They Called Themselves the KKK.* www.scbartoletti.com

Karen Blumenthal, author of books about often untold history. *Bootleg: Murder, Moonshine, and the Lawless Years of Prohibition; Steve Jobs: The Man Who Thought Different; Let Me Play: The Story of Title IX; Six Days in October: The Stock Market Crash of 1929.* www.karenblumenthal.com

Candace Fleming, author who uses scrapbook formatting for biographies. *Our Eleanor: A Scrapbook Look at Eleanor Roosevelt's Remarkable Life; Amelia Lost: The Life and Disappearance of Amelia Earhart; Ben Franklin's Almanac: Being a True Account of the Good Gentleman's Life.* www.candacefleming.com

Brian Floca, author-illustrator of picture books on historical events. *Locomotive; Moonshot: The Flight of Apollo 11; Lightship; Ballet for Martha.* www.brianfloca.com

Dennis B. and **Judith B. Fradin,** coauthors of biographies of civil rights activists. *Ida B. Wells: Mother of the Civil Rights Movement; The Power of One: Daisy Bates and the Little Rock Nine.*

Russell Freedman, author of photobiographies and informational books about U.S. history. *Lincoln: A Photobiography; The Voice That Challenged a Nation: Marian Anderson and the Struggle for Equal Rights; The War to End All Wars: World War I; Children of the Great Depression.*

James Cross Giblin, author of biographies and informational books about social implications of cultural developments. *When Plague Strikes: The Black Death, Smallpox, AIDS; The Life and Death of Adolf Hitler.*

Jan Greenberg and **Sandra Jordan,** coauthors of picture book biographies about renowned artists. *Andy Warhol: Prince of Pop; Christo and Jeanne-Claude: Through the Gates and Beyond; Ballet for Martha: Making Appalachian Spring.* www.jangreenbergsandrajordan.com

David Macaulay, author-illustrator of mixed-genre books about the construction of monumental buildings and informational picture books. *Cathedral; Building Big; Mosque; How Things Work.* www.davidmacaulay.com

Jim Murphy, author of chapter books about U.S. history events. *Blizzard! The Storm That Changed America; The Crossing: How George Washington Saved the American Revolution.* www.jimmurphybooks.com

Sy Montgomery, author of photoessays on scientists searching for rare or endangered animals in remote global areas. *Quest for the Tree Kangaroo; Kakapo Rescue; The Tarantula Scientist.* www.symontgomery.com

Pamela Turner, author of photoessays on science and nature and scientists in the field, many in global settings. *The Frog Scientist; Gorilla Doctors; Life on Earth—And Beyond.* www.pamelasturner.com/

Topics of Informational Books

Nonfiction is by far the largest single genre in literature in that everything known to humankind is a conceivable topic. Organization of such an enormous variety of topics could, of course, be done in a number of ways, but we have chosen to organize this world of knowledge into the natural sciences, the social sciences, and the humanities. Under each of these broad divisions, books are further organized by *topics of interest and relevance to young adults.* Previously, many of the informational books available for adolescents were series books, some of which are poorly written and list facts with little context or explanation. Recently, there has been an explosion of informational books directed to the young adult audience that are high-quality nonfiction literature.

Natural Sciences

The natural sciences deal with the study of the natural world—biological science (the study of living organisms), physical science (the study of nonliving materials), and practical applications of pure science such as medicine, architecture, and engineering. Examples of topics and books include:

- **The Human Body and Health** (*Chew on This: Everything You Didn't Want to Know about Fast Food* by Eric Schlosser and Charles Wilson)
- **Sex and Sexuality** (*Changing Bodies, Changing Lives* by Ruth Bell)
- **Nature: Earth's Ecosystems, Forces, and Life Forms** (*Tracking Trash: Flotsam, Jetsam and the Science of Ocean Motion* by Loree Burns)
- **Practical Applications in Natural Science** (*Gorilla Doctors: Saving Endangered Great Apes* by Pamela S. Turner)

Social Sciences

The social sciences are concerned with the systematic study of human behavior and society and include topics and books such as:

- **Human and Civil Rights Issues** (*They Called Themselves the KKK* by Susan C. Bartoletti)
- **War and History** (*Titanic: Voices from Disaster* by Deborah Hopkinson)
- **Cultural and Ethnic Diversity** (*The Genius of Islam: How Muslims Made the Modern World* by Bryn Barnard)
- **School-Related Issues** (*Bullying and Hazing,* edited by Jill Hamilton)
- **Sports** (*Let Me Play: The Story of Title IX: The Law that Changed the Future of Girls in America* by Karen Blumenthal)
- **Jobs, Careers, and Money Management** (*Choosing a Career* by Linda Aksomitis)

Humanities

The humanities highlight the visual arts of drawing, filmmaking, painting, and sculpture; the performing arts of dance, music, and acting; and the communicative art of writing. Topics and books include:

- **Music and Dance** (*Rap Music,* edited by Noah Berlatsky)
- **Art and Illustration** (*Making Comics: Storytelling Secrets of Comics, Manga and Graphic Novels* by Scott McCloud)
- **Writing and Film** (*Whatcha Mean, What's in a Zine?* by Esther Watson)

In the late twentieth century, as the stature of nonfiction rose and more top-flight authors and illustrators were engaged in its production, the quality of research, writing, and art in these books improved. A lighter, yet factual, tone balanced with high-quality, informative illustrations and graphics emerged as the preferred nonfiction style. The trend toward more illustrations and less text in nonfiction makes this genre particularly appealing to today's visually oriented young adults.

References

Duke, N. K. (2000). 3.6 minutes a day: The scarcity of informational texts in first grade. *Reading Research Quarterly, 35*(2), 202–225.

Jeong, J., Gaffney, J., & Choi, J. (2010). Availability and use of informational texts in second-, third-, and fourth-grade classroom. *Research in the Teaching of English, 44*(4), 415–456.

Kirby, D. L., & Kirby, D. (2010). Contemporary memoir: A 21st-century genre ideal for teens. *English Journal, 99*(4), 22–29.

Recommended Nonfiction Books

Ages indicated refer to content appropriateness and conceptual and interest levels. The nationality of authors who are not from the United States is indicated in parentheses. Formats other than novels are coded as follows:

(GR) Graphic novel

(PI) Picture book

(COL) Short story collection

(NV) Novel in verse

Biographies are organized by the same historical eras as works of historical fiction (Chapter 5), so that books in these two genres can be matched.

Biography

Civilizations of the Ancient World, 3000 b.c. TO a.d. 600

Bankston, John. *The Life and Times of Alexander the Great.* Lane, 2004. Ages 11–13. 4th century B.C. king of Macedonia.

Freedman, Russell. *Confucius: The Golden Rule.* Illus. Frédéric Clément. Scholastic, 2002.
(PI) Ages 11–14. Life and contributions of 5th century B.C. Chinese philosopher.

Yakin, Boaz. *Marathon.* First Second, 2012. **(GR)** Ages 12–16. Eucles ran the first marathon from Sparta to Athens to inform Athens of the Persian invasion.

Zannos, Susan. *The Life and Times of Socrates.* Lane, 2004. Ages 11–14. 5th century B.C. Athenian philosopher.

Civilizations of the Medieval World, 600 to 1500

Freedman, Russell. *The Adventures of Marco Polo.* Illus. Bagram Ibatoulline. Scholastic, 2006. Ages 11–16. Biography of the 13th century Venetian explorer.

Krull, Kathleen. *Leonardo da Vinci.* Illus. Boris Kulikov. Viking, 2005. Ages 11–14. Life of da Vinci along with some drawings.

Meltzer, Milton. *Columbus and the World around Him.* Watts, 1990. Ages 12–17. Critical examination of the life and influence of Columbus on the New World. 16th century Genoese (Italian) explorer.

Serrano, Francisco. *The Poet King of Tezcoco: A Great Leader of Ancient Mexico.* Illust. Pablo Serrano. Translated by Trudy Balch and Jo Anne Engelbert. Groundwood, 2007. **(PI)** Ages 11–14. Leader who built monuments, libraries, and palaces throughout ancient Mexico.

Shulevitz, Uri. *The Travels of Benjamin of Tudela: Through Three Continents in the Twelfth Century.* Farrar, 2005. **(PI)** Ages 11–14. Poland. 14-year journey of a Spanish Jew in 12th century Europe and Middle East.

Sís, Peter. *Starry Messenger.* Farrar, 1996. **(PI)** Ages 11–14. Galileo, 17th century Italian astronomer physicist.

Stanley, Diane. *Saladin: Noble Prince of Islam.* HarperCollins, 2002. **(PI)** Ages 10–14. Egypt and Syria, 1100s

The Emergence of Modern Nations, 1500 to 1800

Burleigh, Robert. *Napoléon: The Story of the Little Corporal.* Abrams, 2007. **(PI)** Ages 11–14. Picture book on Napoleon filled with facts that address his life, leadership, and military campaign.

Fleming, Candace. *Ben Franklin's Almanac: Being a True Account of the Good Gentleman's Life.* Atheneum, 2003. Ages 11–14. 18th century American statesman, scientist, inventor, and author Benjamin Franklin.

Fradin, Dennis B. *The Founders: The 39 Stories behind the U.S. Constitution.* Illus. Michael McCurdy. Walker, 2005. Ages 11–15. U.S. politics, 1783–1789. Brief sketches of the men who signed the constitution.

———. *The Signers: The 56 Stories behind the Declaration of Independence* (2002). U.S. Revolution, 1775–1783. Brief profiles of the men who signed the Declaration.

Freedman, Russell. *Lafayette and the American Revolution.* Holiday House, 2010. Ages 11–15. The role Lafayette played in the American Revolution to convince the French to support the Americans.

Lasky, Kathryn. *The Man Who Made Time Travel.* Illus. Kevin Hawkes. Farrar, 2003. **(PI)** Ages 10–13. 18th century British clockmaker who solved the problem of tracking longitude in shipboard navigation.

Murphy, Jim. *The Real Benedict Arnold.* Clarion, 2007. Ages 12–16. Evenhanded biography of the American Revolutionary War general best known for his treason.

Nelson, Marilyn. *The Freedom Business: Including a Narrative of the Life and Adventures of Venture, a Native of Africa.* Illus. Deborah Dancy. Boyds Mills, 2008. Ages 14–18. 18th century slave Venture Smith's own narrative paralleled with Nelson's poems.

Price, Sean. *Ivan the Terrible: Tsar of Death.* Scholastic, 2007. Ages 12–15. Story of first tsar of Russia, 1500s.

Reich, Susanna. *Painting the Wild Frontier: The Art and Adventures of George Catlin.* Clarion, 2008. Ages 12–18. Biography of the 18th century painter of Native American life.

Rosen, Michael. *Shakespeare: His Work and His World.* Candlewick, 2001. Ages 11–14. 17th century British dramatist and poet. (British)

Sheinkin, Steve. *The Notorious Benedict Arnold: A True Story of Adventure, Heroism, & Treachery.* Roaring Brook, 2010. Ages 12–15. Arnold as an action hero whose life of adventure and ambition ended in dishonor.

The Development of Industrial Society, 1800 to 1914

Adler, David. *Frederick Douglas: A Noble Life.* Holiday, 2010. Ages 12–16. Influential African-American former slave and journalist during the 1800s.

Atkins, Jeannine. *Borrowed Names: Poems About Laura Ingalls Wilder, Madam C. J. Walker, Marie Curie, and their Daughters.* Henry Holt, 2010. **(NV)** Ages 13–18. Famous U.S. women, poetry 1867–1957.

Blumberg, Rhoda. *York's Adventures with Lewis and Clark: An African-American's Part in the Great Expedition.* HarperCollins, 2004. Ages 11–15.

Clark's slave and member of the Corps of Discovery.

Bolden, Tonya. *Maritcha: A Nineteenth-Century American Girl*. Abrams, 2005. Ages 11–15. A free black child's experiences in New York City before, during, and after the Civil War.

Bruchac, Joseph. *Sacajawea: The Story of Bird Woman and the Lewis and Clark Expedition*. Silver Whistle, 2000. Ages 13–18. William Clark and Sacajawea alternate in describing their experiences on the expedition.

Capaldi, Gina. *A Boy Named Beckoning: The True Story of Dr. Carlos Montezuma, A Native American Hero*. Carolrhoda, 2008. **(PI)** Ages 10–14. Yavapi Indian, Arizona, late 1800s.

Dana, Barbara. *A Voice of Her Own: Becoming Emily Dickinson*. HarperTeen, 2009. Ages 11–15. The girlhood of poet Emily Dickinson.

Dennenberg, Barry. *Lincoln Shot: A President's Life Remembered*. Illus. Christopher Bing. Feiwel & Friends, 2008. Ages 10–15. Large-format biography of Lincoln, set up as commemorative newspaper edition.

Engle, Margarita. *The Poet Slave of Cuba: A Biography of Juan Francisco Manzano*. Illus. Sean Qualls. Holt, 2006. **(NV)** Ages 12–16. How Manzano created poetry in spite of his status as a slave in Cuba.

Fleischman, Sid. *The Trouble Begins at 8: A Life of Mark Twain in the Wild, Wild West*. HarperCollins, 2008. Ages 10–15. Partial biography of the 19th century writer focusing on his travel in the Wild West.

———. *Escape! The Story of the Great Houdini*. Greenwillow, 2006. Ages 11–15. Biography of the world-famous magician who lived from 1874 to 1926.

Fleming, Candace. *Amelia Lost: The Life and Disappearance of Amelia Earhart*. Schwartz & Wade, 2011. Ages 9–14. U.S., women, pilot, 1897–1937. Her life and theories about her disappearance.

———. *The Great and Only Barnum: The Tremendous, Stupendous Life of Showman P. T. Barnum*. Schwartz, 2009. Ages 11–15. 19th century circus showman who brought communities "the greatest show on earth."

———. *The Lincolns: A Scrapbook Look at Abraham and Mary*. Random, 2008. Ages 11–15. Biography of the Lincolns, including Mary Lincoln's life after the president's assassination. Photos and primary documents.

Fradin, Dennis B. *Duel! Burr and Hamilton's Deadly War of Words*. Illus. Larry Day. Walker, 2008. **(PI)** Ages 10–14. Famous Weehawken, New Jersey, duel, 1804.

Fradin, Dennis B., and Judith B. Fradin. *Jane Addams: Champion of Democracy*. Clarion, 2006. Ages 12–14. U.S., woman, social reformer, who worked toward ending child labor laws.

Freedman, Russell. *Lincoln: A Photobiography*. Clarion, 1987. Ages 11–14. 16th U.S. president. Newbery Award.

———. *Abraham Lincoln and Frederick Douglass: The Story Behind an American Friendship*. Clarion, 2012. Ages 11–16. The critical friendship between two influential men during the 1800s.

Giblin, James. *Good Brother, Bad Brother: The Story of Edwin Booth and John Wilkes Booth*. Clarion, 2005. Ages 12–18. The very different lives of the Booth brothers—a preeminent actor and an assassin.

Heiligman, Deborah. *Charles and Emma: The Darwins' Leap of Faith*. Holt, 2010. Ages 11–18. The debate between religion and science within the marriage of Charles and Emma Darwin.

Holzer, Harold. *Father Abraham: Lincoln and His Sons*. Boyds Mills, 2011. Ages 11–16. Exploration of President Lincoln and his relationships with his sons.

Johnson, Dolores. *Onward: A Photobiography of African-American Polar Explorer Matthew Henson*. National Geographic, 2005. Ages 11–14. Henson's role in Robert Peary's expedition to the North Pole in 1909.

Johnson, D. B. *Henry's Night*. Houghton, 2009. **(PB)** Ages 10–14. Henry, a bear, recreates Henry David Thoreau's moonlit walks and love of nature. Series of picture books on Thoreau's philosophy and spirit.

Jurmain, Suzanne. *The Forbidden Schoolhouse: The True and Dramatic Story of Prudence Crandall and Her Students.* Houghton, 2005. Ages 12–14. U.S. educator who dared to teach African-American girls prior to the Civil War and Emancipation.

Kerley, Barbara. *Walt Whitman: Words for America.* Illus. Brian Selznick. Scholastic, 2006. **(PI)** Ages 10–14. U.S. poet, Civil War era, 1819–1892; biography is framed around quotes from his writing.

Kilpatrick, Katherine. *The Snow Baby: The Arctic Childhood of Admiral Robert E. Peary's Daring Daughter.* Holiday House, 2007. Ages 11–15. Living among the Inuit as a young child.

Kraft, Betsy H. *Theodore Roosevelt: Champion of the American Spirit.* Clarion, 2003. Ages 11–14. 26th president of the U.S.

Lutes, Jason, and Nick Bertozzi. *Houdini: The Handcuff King.* Hyperion, 2007. **(GR)** Ages 11–15. Magician, 1908 event in which he jumped from the Harvard Bridge with his hands and feet bound.

McClafferty, Carla K. *Something Out of Nothing: Marie Curie and Radium.* Farrar, 2006. Ages 12–16. Life (1867–1934) of the great Polish research scientist and winner of two Nobel Prizes.

McKissack, Patricia, and Frederick McKissack. *Best Shot in the West: The Adventures of Nat Love.* Illus. Randy DuBurke. Chronicle, 2012. **(GR)** Ages 11–16. The story of the most famous African American cowboy in the U.S.

Nelson, S. D. *Black Elk's Vision: A Lakota Story.* Abrams, 2010. **(PI)** Ages 10–14. U.S. Black Elk, 1863–1950.

Place, François. *The Old Man Mad about Drawing: A Tale of Hokusai.* Translated by William Rodarmor. Godine, 2003. Ages 10–14. Japan, social life, and customs, 1600–1868. (French)

Ray, Deborah Kogan. *Down the Colorado: John Wesley Powell, the One-Armed Explorer.* Farrar, 2007. **(PI)** Ages 8–11. Western exploration in the U.S., 1869.

Reef, Catherine. *The Bronte Sisters: The Brief Lives of Charlotte, Emily, and Anne.* Clarion Books, 2012. Ages 12–18. The turbulent lives of the Bronte sisters as they grew up and became authors.

Rosen, Michael. *Dickens: His Work and His World.* Illus. by Robert Ingpen. Candlewick, 2005. Ages 11–14. The 19th century British author's childhood, influences, and works.

Sandler, Martin W. *Lincoln through the Lens: How Photography Revealed and Shaped an Extraordinary Life.* Walker, 2008. Ages 10–15. Early history of photography and how it affected Lincoln's life and era.

Sís, Peter. *The Tree of Life: Charles Darwin.* Farrar, 2003. **(PI)** Ages 12–14. English evolutionist.

Warren, Andrea. *Charles Dickens and the Street Children of London.* Houghton, 2011. Ages 12–15. 1812–1870.

Wishinsky, Frieda. *What's the Matter with Albert? A Story of Albert Einstein.* Illus. by Jacques Lamontagne. Maple Tree Press, 2002. **(PI)** Ages 10–13. Vignettes of childhood, told from the viewpoint of a young newspaper reporter interviewing Einstein. (German)

World Wars of the Twentieth Century, 1914 to 1945

Bartoletti, Susan Campbell. *Hitler Youth: Growing Up in Hitler's Shadow.* Scholastic, 2005. Ages 11–15. 12 individuals tell of their experiences as members of the Hitler Youth Organization.

Bausum, Ann. *Muckrakers: How Ida Tarbell, Upton Sinclair, and Lincoln Steffens Helped Expose Scandal, Inspire Reform, and Invent Investigative Journalism.* National Geographic, 2007. Ages 12–18. Accounting of how investigative journalism was developed.

Bernier-Grand, Carmen T. *Frida: Viva la vida! Long Live Life!* Illus. by Frida Kahlo. Marshall Cavendish, 2013. **(NV)** Ages 12–18. Biography in free verse poems of the 20th century Mexican painter.

Bryant, Jennifer. *A River of Words: The Story of William Carlos Williams.* Illus. by Melissa Sweet. Eerdmans, 2008. **(PI)** Ages 10–14. U.S. poet and physician, 1883–1963.

Delano, Marfé F. *Genius: A Photobiography of Albert Einstein.* National Geographic, 2005.

Ages 11–14. Einstein's life, personal thoughts, and theories presented with numerous large photographs.

Denenberg, Barry. *Shadow Life: A Portrait of Anne Frank and Her Family.* Scholastic, 2005. Ages 12–14. How the Frank family lived in hiding during the Holocaust.

Fleischman, John. *Black and White Airmen: Their True History.* Houghton Mifflin, 2007. Ages 11–15. The interrelated stories of 2 airmen during WWII.

Fleischman, Sid. *Sir Charlie Chaplin: The Funniest Man in the World.* Greenwillow, 2010. Ages 12–16. England, comedian, 1889–1977.

Fleming, Ann M. *The Magical Life of Long Tack Sam.* Riverhead, 2007. **(GR)** Ages 13–16. Memoir of the author's Chinese great-grandfather who was born in 1885 in China and became a world-class magician.

Fleming, Candace. *Our Eleanor: A Scrapbook Look at Eleanor Roosevelt's Remarkable Life.* Atheneum, 2005. Ages 11–14. U.S. First Lady, 1884–1962.

Giblin, James. *The Life and Death of Adolf Hitler.* Clarion, 2002. Ages 13–18. Austrian-born German dictator and chancellor, and architect of the Jewish Holocaust.

Jiménez, Francisco. *Breaking Through.* Houghton, 2001. Ages 11–14. Mexico. Partial autobiography of a Mexican itinerant farm laborer in California in the 1950s and 1960s.

Katin, Miriam. *We Are on Our Own.* Drawn & Quarterly, 2006. **(GR)** Ages 14–18. Hungary. Author's memoir about escaping from Nazi-occupied Hungary during WWII.

Krinitz, Esther, and Bernice Steinhardt, *Memories of Survival.* Hyperion, 2005. Ages 12–18. A Holocaust survival story in embroidered panels and captions. (Polish)

Maurer, Richard. *The Wright Sister.* Millbrook, 2003. Ages 12–14. Life of Katherine, Orville and Wilbur Wright's sister and 3rd member of the team.

McClafferty, Carla K. *In Defiance of Hitler: The Secret Mission of Varian Fry.* Farrar, 2008. Ages 12–18. How Fry helped 2,000 refugees escape Nazi-occupied France.

Millman, Isaac. *Hidden Child.* Farrar, 2005. **(PI)** Ages 11–14. France. Picture-book autobiography of the author's struggle for survival as a child in Nazi-occupied France.

Phelan, Matt. *Around the World: Three Remarkable Journeys.* Candlewick, 2011. **(GR)** Ages 10–14. Thomas Stevens, Nellie Bly, Joshua Slocum, world travel, 1900s.

Poole, Josephine. *Anne Frank.* Illus. Angela Barrett. Knopf, 2005. **(PI)** Ages 11–13. Introduction to the famous author and her diary.

Rappaport, Doreen. *Beyond Courage: The Untold Story of Jewish Resistance During the Holocaust.* Candlewick, 2012. Ages 12–18. Chronicles the defiance of Jews across Europe during WWII.

Reef, Catherine. *Jane Austen: A Life Revealed.* Clarion, 2011. Ages 13–18. Biography of the unconventional author of *Pride and Prejudice* and *Sense and Sensibility.*

Ryan, Pamela Muñoz. *The Dreamer.* Illus. Peter Sis. Scholastic, 2012. Ages 11–14. Life of poet Pablo Neruda, who won the Nobel Prize.

Sullivan, George. *Berenice Abbott, Photographer: An Independent Vision.* Clarion, 2005. Ages 11–15. Life of the 20th century American pioneer in photography.

———. *Helen Keller: Her Life in Pictures.* Scholastic, 2007. Ages 11–15. Photos of Helen Keller along with information about her life.

Thomson, Ruth. *Terezin: Voices from the Holocaust.* Candlewick, 2011. Ages 11–16. The accounts of those who lived in the Terezin ghetto during WWII.

Weatherford, Carole B. *Becoming Billie Holiday.* Illus. Floyd Cooper. Boyds Mills 2008. **(NV)** Ages 13–18. A fictionalized memoir in verse of the famous African-American jazz singer.

Post–World War II Era, 1945 to 2013

Abirached, Zeina. *A Game for Swallows: To Die, to Leave, to Return.* Graphic Universe, 2012. **(GR)** Ages 12–18. Memoir of life in Lebanon during the 1980s when a religious civil war divided Beirut. (Lebanese)

Ahmed, Leila. *A Border Passage: From Cairo to America—A Woman's Journey.* Penguin, 2012.

Ages 13–18. Egypt. The story of an Egyptian woman who embraces her feminism once she moves to the U.S.

Angel, Ann. *Janis Joplin: Rise Up Singing*. Amulet, 2010. Ages 13–18. The biography of Janis Joplin and her troubled, short life as an icon of the 1960s.

Aronson, Marc. *Master of Deceit J. Edgar Hoover and America in the Age of Lies*. Candlewick, 2012. Ages 13–18. The life of FBI director and the world during the time in which he served as director.

Barakat, Ibtisam. *Tasting the Sky: A Palestinian Childhood*. Farrar, 2007. Israel. A Palestinian woman's memoir of her childhood experience during the Six Days' War (1967).

Bausum, Ann. *Freedom Riders: John Lewis and Jim Zwerg on the Front Lines of the Civil Rights Movement*. National Geographic, 2005. Ages 11–15. Dual biographies of a black man (Lewis) and a white man (Zwerg) who were activists in the civil rights movement.

Beah, Ishmael. *A Long Way Gone: Memoirs of a Boy Soldier*. Farrar, 2007. Ages 16–18. Sierra Leone. Experiences of a 12-year-old recruited as a soldier in Sierra Leone's brutal civil war in the 1990s.

Bernier-Grand, Carmen. *Alicia Alonso: Prima Ballerina*. Illus. Raul Colón. Cavendish, 2011. Cuba, 1921–2012. The life and influence of the famous Cuban ballerina and how she dealt with blindness.

Blumenthal, Karen. *Steve Jobs: The Man Who Thought Different*. Feiwel, 2012. Ages 11–16. The intimate and multiple dimensions of the man behind Apple, Inc.

Brimner, Larry D. *We Are One: The Story of Bayard Rustin*. Boyds Mills, 2007. Ages 11–16. Biography of the architect of the Civil Rights Movement.

———. *Black & White: The Confrontation between Reverend Fred L. Shuttlesworth and Eugene "Bull" Connor*. Calkins Creek, 2011. Ages 12–15. Civil Rights, Birmingham, 1950s and 1960s.

Close, Chuck. *Chuck Close: Face Book*. Abrams Books for Young Readers. Ages 10–14.

American artist who creates oversized portraits despite paralysis.

Corcoran, Jill, editor. *Dare to Dream . . . Change the World*. Illus. J. Beth Jepson. Kane/Miller, 2012. Ages 10–14. Multigenre book of biographical poems and sketches of people who changed the world in some way.

Dendy, Leslie, and Mel Boring. *Guinea Pig Scientists: Bold Self-Experimenters of Science and Medicine*. Holt, 2005. **(COL)** Ages 11–18. Collected biography of people who served as subjects in scientific studies.

Ellis, Deborah. *Our Stories, Our Songs: African Children Talk about AIDS*. Fitzhenry & Whiteside (Canada), 2005. Ages 12–18. Canada. Autobiographical vignettes of African youths whose lives are changed by AIDS.

Fradin, Dennis B. *With a Little Luck: Surprising Stories of Amazing Discovery*. Dutton, 2006. **(COL)** Ages 11–14. Collected biography of 11 scientists who lived during the last 4 centuries.

Fradin, Dennis B., and Judith B. Fradin. *The Power of One: Daisy Bates and the Little Rock Nine*. Clarion, 2004. Ages 14–18. Mentor of the African-American students who integrated Central High School in Little Rock in 1957.

Freedman, Russell. *The Voice That Challenged a Nation: Marian Anderson and the Struggle for Equal Rights*. Clarion, 2011. Ages 11–18. African-American singer.

Greenberg, Jan. *Romare Bearden: Collage of Memories*. Abrams, 2003. Ages 11–14. African-American collage artist.

Greenberg, Jan, and Sandra Jordan. *Andy Warhol: Prince of Pop*. Delacorte, 2004. Ages 13–18. Life and work of the pop art icon.

———. *Christo and Jeanne-Claude: Through the Gates and Beyond*. Roaring Book Press, 2008. Ages 11–16. The installation of the gates project in Central Park.

Hemphill, Stephanie. *Your Own, Sylvia*. Knopf, 2007. **(NV)** Ages 14–18. Fictionalized biography of Sylvia Plath told in poems and multiple voices.

Hoose, Phillip. *Claudette Colvin: Twice toward Justice*. Farrar, 2010. Ages 11–15. The story of a

15-year-old who, prior to Rosa Parks, refused to give up her seat during the Civil Rights Movement.

Kidder, Tracy. *Mountains beyond Mountains: The Quest of Dr. Paul Farmer, a Man who would Cure the World*. Delacorte, 2013. Ages 12–18. Medical doctor who works with the world's most impoverished people.

Lat. *Kampung Boy*. Roaring Brook, 2006. **(GR)** Ages 13–17. Autobiography of the Malaysian cartoonist. (Malaysian)

Lewis, J. Patrick. *Black Cat Bone*. Illus. Gary Kelley. Creative, 2006. **(PI)** Ages 12–18. Picture book biography of blues guitarist Robert Johnson, told in poems.

Li, Moying. *Snow Falling in Spring: Coming of Age in China during the Cultural Revolution*. Farrar, 2008. Ages 12–18. Memoir of harrowing 14 years living in China during the brutal Cultural Revolution.

McClafferty, Carla. *In Defiance of Hitler: The Secret Mission of Varian Fry*. Farrar, 2008. Ages 12–18. American journalist who flew to Europe to help artists and intellectuals flee to freedom.

McKay, Sharon. *War Brothers*. Annick Press, 2013. **(GR)** Ages 12–18. Canada. The story of boys abducted in Uganda to become child soldiers.

Medicine Crow, Joseph, and Herman Viola. *Counting Coup: Becoming a Crow Chief on the Reservation and Beyond*. National Geographic, 2006. Ages 12–18. Autobiography of this 20th-century Native American's life.

Mitchell, Jeff. *Real Justice: Young, Innocent and in Prison: The Story of Robert Baltovich*. Lorimer, 2012. Ages 13–18. Story of a young man accused of murder, imprisoned, and then found innocent.

Myers, Walter Dean. *Bad Boy: A Memoir*. Amistad, 2001. Ages 12–18. Growing up in Harlem, 1940s and 1950s.

Nazario, Sonia. *Enrique's Journey—The True Story of a Boy Determined to Reunite with His Mother*. Random, 2013. Ages 12–16. Overcoming barriers to unite with mother who had immigrated to the U.S.

Nelson, Vaunda Micheaux. *No Crystal Stair: A Documentary Novel of the Life and Work of Lew Michaux, Harlem Bookseller*. Carolrhoda, 2012. Ages 14–18. Fictionalized biography, multiple voices, Civil Rights.

Partridge, Elizabeth. *John Lennon: All I Want Is the Truth*. Viking, 2005. Ages 15–18. Honest but nonjudgmental biography of the influential 20th-century musician.

Pinkney, Andrea Davis. *Hand in Hand: Ten Black Men Who Changed America*. Illus. Brian Pinkney. Disney/Jump at the Sun, 2012. **(COL)** Ages 12–15. Profiles that span U.S. history with introductory poems.

Rembert, Winfred. *Don't Hold Me Back: My Life and Art*. Cricket, 2003. **(PI)** Ages 11–13. Autobiography of the African-American artist.

Roy, Jennifer. *Yellow Star*. Marshall Cavendish, 2006. Ages 10–15. The story of Sylvia Perlmutter, 1 of the 12 children to survive the Lodz ghetto in Poland during WWII.

Rubin, Susan G. Delicious: *The Life and Art of Wayne Thiebaud*. Chronicle, 2007. Ages 11–14. Life of the contemporary painter of everyday objects.

———. *Music Was IT: Young Leonard Bernstein*. Charlesbridge, 2011. How Leonard Bernstein overcame father's biases against Jews to become an influential conductor.

Satrapi, Marjane. *Persepolis: The Story of a Childhood*. Pantheon, 2003. **(GR)** Ages 15–18. Iran. An autobiography of the author's childhood in Iran during the Islamic Revolution. Also *Perspeolis 2* (2004).

Say, Allen. *Drawing from Memory*. Scholastic, 2010. **(PI)** Ages 11–14. Japan. Artist explains his drawing and how it was influenced by his historical context.

Schubert, Leda. *Monsieur Marceau: Actor without Words*. **(PI)** Flashpoint, 2012. Ages 12–17. The life of the world's most famous mime.

Silverstein, Ken. *The Radioactive Boy Scout: The True Story of a Boy and His Backyard Nuclear Reactor*. Random, 2004. Ages 14–18. In the mid-1990s a teenager secretly builds a hazardous nuclear reactor.

Sís, Peter. *The Wall: Growing Up behind the Iron Curtain.* Farrar, 2007. Ages 12–16. Czech Republic. **(PI/GR)** Autobiographical account of growing up in Czechoslovakia under Soviet rule.

Stone, Tanya Lee. *Almost Astronauts: 13 Women Who Dared to Dream.* Candlewick, 2009. **(COL)** Ages 11–14. The stories of 13 women who were admitted to the NASA space program in the 1960s.

Turner, Pamela S. *A Life in the Wild: George Schaller's Struggle to Save the Last Great Beasts.* Farrar, 2009. Ages 11–17. An introduction to conservation that will inspire young people.

Informational Books

Natural Sciences

The Human Body and Health

Farrell, Jeanette. *Invisible Enemies: Stories of Infectious Disease.* Farrar, 2005. Ages 12–18. 7 dreaded human diseases and efforts made to avoid or cure them.

Fleischman, John. *Phineas Gage: A Gruesome but True Story about Brain Science.* Houghton, 2002. Ages 12–14. How a freak accident played an important role in the development of our knowledge of the brain.

Gay, Kathryn. *Am I Fat? The Obesity Issue for Teens.* Enslow, 2006. Ages 13–18. Causes of the epidemic and ways people combat obesity.

Hinds, Maureen J. *Fighting the AIDS and HIV Epidemic: A Global Battle.* Enslow, 2007. Ages 13–18. Explanation of the virus; ways to prevent and treat it; its impact on the world.

Macaulay, David, with Richard Walker. *The Way We Work: Getting to Know the Amazing Human Body.* Houghton, 2008. Ages 12–18. Fully illustrated guide to the human body and its systems.

Murphy, Jim. *An American Plague: The True and Terrifying Story of the Yellow Fever Epidemic of 1793.* Clarion, 2003. Ages 11–18. The history, science, and politics of Philadelphia's harrowing ordeal.

Palid, Thea. *Mixed Messages: Interpreting Body Image and Social Norms.* ABDO, 2008. Ages 11–15. Case studies, critical thinking questions, professional advice, and support for girls.

Scherer, Laura, editor. *Body Image.* Greenhaven, 2013. Essays on teens and body image. Introducing Issues with Opposing Viewpoints series.

———. *Underage Drinking.* Greenhaven, 2013 Essays on various aspects of underage drinking such as binging and parental responsibility. Issues That Concern You series.

Schlosser, Eric, and Charles Wilson. *Chew on This: Everything You Didn't Want to Know about Fast Food.* Houghton/Graphia, 2006. Ages 11–18. The dangers of eating too much fast food.

Shivack, Nadia. *Inside Out: Portrait of an Eating Disorder.* Atheneum, 2007. **(GR)** Ages 14–18. A memoir of the author's battles with anorexia and bulimia.

Simon, Seymour. *Guts: Our Digestive System.* HarperCollins, 2005. Ages 9–14. Photoessay about the workings of the human digestive system.

Wand, Kelly, editor. *Tobacco and Smoking.* Greenhaven, 2012. Ages 12–16. Essays on opinions about issues on tobacco use. Opposing Viewpoints: Current Issues series.

Sex and Sexuality

Belge, Kathy, Marke Bieschke, and Christian Robinson. *Queer: The Ultimate LGBT Guide for Teens.* Zest Books, 2011. Ages 12–18. Guide for helping LGBT students.

Bell, Ruth. *Changing Bodies, Changing Lives: A Book for Teens on Sex and Relationships* (3rd ed.). Three Rivers, 2011. Ages 13–18. Thorough discussion of sexual and emotional changes during the teen years.

Currie-McGhee, Leanne. *Sexually Transmitted Diseases.* ReferencePoint, 2008. Ages 15–18. Current information with color illustrations and drawings. Compact Research: Diseases and Disorders Series.

Eastham, Chad, Bill Farrel, and Pam Farrel. *Guys Are Waffles, Girls Are Spaghetti.* Thomas Nelson, 2009. Ages 12–18. The ways the genders can be different, building healthy relationships.

Forssberg, Mann. *Sex for Guys.* Translated from Swedish by Maria Lunden. Groundwood, 2007. Ages 14–18. An overview of the social issues related to teen males and sex. Groundwork Guides Series.

Haney, Johannah. *The Abortion Debate: Understanding the Issues.* Enslow, 2008. Ages 13–18. Explanation of terms and issues; impact of the issue on politics. Issues in Focus Today.

Harris, Robie H. *It's Perfectly Normal: A Book about Changing Bodies, Growing Up, Sex, and Sexual Health.* Illus. Michael Emberley. Candlewick, 2009. Ages 11–18. Answers to kids' questions on sexuality.

Hasler, Nikol. *Sex: A Book for Teens: An Uncensored Guide to Your Body, Sex, and Safety.* Zest Books, 2010. Ages 16–18. Frank and humorous look at sexuality.

Levithan, David, and Billy Merrill, editors. *The Full Spectrum: A New Generation of Writing about Gay, Lesbian, Bisexual, Transgender, Questioning, and Other Identities.* Knopf, 2006. **(COL)** Ages 13–17. 40 nonfiction pieces by writers under the age of 23.

Nilsson, Lennart. *A Child Is Born.* Photos by Lennart Nilson. Translated from Swedish by Linda Schenck. Delacorte, 2003. Ages 11–18. Fetal development from womb to birth; spectacular microphotography.

Nature: Earth's Ecosystems, Forces, and Life Forms

Burns, Loree G. *Tracking Trash: Flotsam, Jetsam, and the Science of Ocean Motion.* Houghton Mifflin, 2007. Ages 12–15. Describes work of a man who tracks trash in ocean currents. Scientists in the Field series.

Collard, Sneed B. The *Prairie Builders: Reconstructing America's Lost Grasslands.* Houghton, 2005. Ages 11–14. Present-day recreation of the tallgrass prairie in Iowa.

Devlin, Keith. *The Math Instinct: Why You're a Mathematical Genius (along with Lobsters, Birds, Cats and Dogs).* Thunder's Mouth, 2005.

Ages 14–18. Intuitive math solutions by animals to problems.

Gore, Al, and Jane O'Connor. *An Inconvenient Truth: The Crisis of Global Warming.* Viking, 2007. Ages 11–18. Adapted from the documentary, an investigation of the climate issues threatening our planet.

Grace, Catherine. *Forces of Nature: The Awesome Power of Volcanoes, Earthquakes, and Tornadoes.* National Geographic, 2004. Ages 11–14. Causes of these phenomena, their scale, and capacity for destruction.

Hoose, Phillip. *The Race to Save the Lord God Bird.* Farrar, 2004. Ages 11–18. Ivory-billed woodpecker.

———. *Moonbird: A Year in the Wind with the Great Survivor B95.* Farrar, 2012. Ages 11–14. Follows a rufa red knot bird as it flies from the bottom of the world to the top and back again.

Koppes, Steven. *Killer Rocks from Outer Space: Asteroids, Comets, and Meteorites.* Carolrhoda, 2003. Ages 11–14. Information about past and future cosmic collisions.

Murphy, Jim. *Blizzard! The Storm That Changed America.* Scholastic, 2000. Ages 11–18. The 1888 snowstorm that paralyzed the northeastern U.S. for 4 days.

Pringle, Laurence. *Billions of Years, Amazing Changes: The Story of Evolution.* Illus. Steve Jenkins. Boyds Mills, 2011. Ages 12–15. Describes evolution and the history of the study of evolution.

Singer, Marilyn. *Venom.* Darby Creek, 2007. Ages 11–14. Creatures that use venom for attack and defense.

Tanaka, Shelley. *Climate Change.* Groundwood, 2012. Ages 14–18. An overview of the social and political issues related to climate change. Groundwork Guides Series. (Canadian)

Treaster, Joseph B. *Hurricane Force: In the Path of America's Deadliest Storms.* Kingfisher, 2007. Ages 12–16. A scientific and socioeconomic photoessay about hurricanes.

Turner, Pamela S. *Life on Earth—and Beyond: An Astrobiologist's Quest.* Charlesbridge, 2008. Ages 10–13. NASA scientist Christopher

McKay's study of bacteria that live in extreme climatic conditions.

Practical Applications in Natural Science

Aronson, Marc. *If Stones Could Speak: Unlocking the Secrets of Stonehenge.* National Geographic, 2011. Ages 11–14. The exploration of the stones' meanings, excavation of the area, and the importance of archeology.

Abadzis, Nick. *Laika.* Roaring Brook/FirstSecond, 2007. **(GR)** Ages 12–15. First dog in space. (Swedish)

Bishop, Nic. *Digging for Bird Dinosaurs: An Expedition to Madagascar.* Houghton, 2000. Ages 11–14. Photoessay about paleontologist Cathy Forster at work. Scientists in the Field series.

Carson, Mary Kay. *Exploring the Solar System: A History with 22 Activities.* Chicago Review, 2008. Ages 10–14. Space and how it has been explored–history, bios, activities. Also *Beyond the Solar System* (2013).

DeCristifano, Carolyn. *A Black Hole Is Not a Hole.* Charlesbridge, 2012. Ages 12–16. The explanation of black holes and definitions that help explain the phenomenon.

Deem, James. *Faces from the Past: Forgotten People of North America.* Houghton Mifflin, 2012. Ages 11–16. Forensic science in relation to the people who lived in North America over 15,000 years ago.

———. *Bodies from the Ice: Melting Glaciers and the Recovery of the Past.* Houghton Mifflin, 2008. Ages 11–15. The discovery of frozen ancient life in various parts of the world.

Floca, Brian. *Moonshot: The Flight of Apollo 11.* Atheneum, 2009. **(PI)** Ages 10–14. Follows the crew of Apollo 11 from pre-flight to splash down. Beautiful language and illustrations.

Gardner, Robert. *Chemistry Projects with a Laboratory You Can Build.* Enslow, 2007. Ages 11–15. Part of the Build-a-Lab! Science Experiments Series.

Hakim, Joy. *Einstein Adds a New Dimension.* Smithsonian, 2007. Ages 12–18. An account of the development of quantum theory and modern cosmology. The Story of Science.

Innes, Brian. *DNA and Body Evidence.* M. E. Sharpe, 2007. Ages 14–18. History and evolution of DNA and blood analysis and fingerprinting. Forensic Evidence Series.

Larson, Peter, and Kristin Donnan. *Bones Rock! Everything You Need to Know to Be a Paleontologist.* Invisible Cities, 2004. Ages 11–14. The science of paleontology.

Macaulay, David. *The New Way Things Work.* Houghton, 1998. Ages 11–14. A guide to the workings of machines, including digital ones.

———. *Building Big.* Houghton, 2000. **(PI)** Ages 12–18. Design and construction of notable bridges, tunnels, skyscrapers, domes, and dams.

———. *Mosque.* Houghton, 2003. **(PI)** Ages 11–18. Building a mosque in 16th-century Istanbul.

Montgomery, Sy. *Kakapo Rescue: Saving the World's Strangest Parrot.* Photos by Nic Bishop. Houghton, 2010. Ages 11–15. Saving an endangered flightless parrot on an island near New Zealand. Scientists in the Field series.

———. *Quest for the Tree Kangaroo: An Expedition to the Cloud Forest of New Guinea.* Illus. Nic Bishop. Houghton, 2006. Ages 11–15. Expedition to find a rare tree kangaroo. Scientists in the Field series.

———. *The Tarantula Scientist.* Photos by Nic Bishop. Houghton, 2004. Ages 11–14. Tarantulas and the exciting life of a scientist.

O'Connell, Caitlin, and Donna Jackson. *The Elephant Scientist.* Houghton, 2011. Ages 11–14. Observations of African elephants and discoveries of elephant communication. Scientists in the Field series.

Platt, Richard. *Forensics.* Houghton, 2005. Ages 12–16. What the forensic scientist does: evidence collection, DNA analysis, fingerprinting, and more. (British)

Ross, Val. *The Road to There: Mapmakers and Their Stories.* Tundra, 2003. Ages 12–16. Describes the history of map making and the lives of famous cartographers.

Rubalcaba, Jill, and Peter Robertshaw. *Every Bone Tells a Story: Hominin Discoveries, Deductions, and Debates.* Charlesbridge Publishing, 2010. Ages 11–16. Combining archeology and paleontology, the book discusses 4 bone collections and the debates sparked from their discoveries.

Rusch, Elizabeth. *The Mighty Mars Rovers: The Incredible Adventures of Spirit and Opportunity*. Houghton Mifflin, 2012. Ages 11–16. Exploration of Mars using space robots. Scientists in the Field series.

Sullivan, George. *Built to Last: Building America's Amazing Bridges, Dams, Tunnels, and Skyscrapers*. Scholastic, 2005. Ages 11–16. Engineering and construction of major structures. Detailed illustrations.

Thimmesh, Catherine. *Team Moon: How 400,000 People Landed Apollo 11 on the Moon*. Houghton, 2006. Ages 12–15. Chronicles the many who contributed to the mission of Apollo 11. Vintage photos.

Turner, Pamela. *Gorilla Doctors: Saving Endangered Great Apes*. Houghton, 2005. Ages 11–14. Veterinarians' efforts to save mountain gorillas in Rwanda and Uganda. Scientists in the Field series.

———. *The Frog Scientist*. Photos by Andy Comins. Houghton, 2009. Ages 11–14. Work of an African-American scientist to study effects of pesticides on frogs. Scientists in the Field series.

Walker, Sally. *Secrets of a Civil War Submarine: Solving the Mysteries of the H. L. Hunley*. Carolrhoda, 2005. Ages 12–18. The archaeological process in the excavation of a Civil War submarine from Charleston Harbor.

———. *Written in Bone: Buried Lives of Jamestown and Colonial Maryland*. Carolrhoda Books, 2009. Ages 11–15. The discovery of Jamestown remains and the methods of determining their origin.

Social Sciences

Human and Civil Rights Issues

Altman, Linda J. *Bioethics: Who Lives, Who Dies, and Who Decides?* Enslow, 2006. Ages 13–18. Assisted reproduction and abortion, allocation of medical resources, and end-of-life issues. Issues in Focus Today.

———. *Genocide: The Systematic Killing of People*. Enslow, 2008. Ages 13–18. Historic and recent examples of genocide, causes, and ways to avert it in the future. Issues in Focus Today

Bartoletti, Susan C. Black *Potatoes: The Story of the Great Irish Famine, 1845–1850*. Houghton, 2001. Ages 11–18. Impact of the famine on Ireland and the United States.

———. *They Called Themselves the KKK: The Birth of an American Terrorist Group*. Houghton Mifflin, 2010. Ages 12–18. The origin and development of the Klu Klux Klan in the U.S.

Bial, Raymond. *Tenement: Immigrant Life on the Lower East Side*. Houghton, 2002. Ages 11–18. Photoessay describing the gritty life in New York tenements from the early 1800s to 1930.

Bolden, Tonya. *Emancipation Proclamation: Lincoln and the Dawn of Liberty*. Abrams, 2013. Ages 12–15. Issues and tensions surrounding abolition and Lincoln's responses to political, military, and moral arguments.

Bowers, Rick. *Spies of Mississippi: The True Story of the Spy Network That Tried to Destroy the Civil Rights Movement*. National Geographic, 2010. Ages 11–18. How the state of Mississippi commissioned and paid black citizens to infiltrate the NAACP during the 1960s.

Brimner, Larry Dane. *Birmingham Sunday*. Boyds Mills Press, 2010. Ages 11–16. Events at the Birmingham church during the Civil Rights Movement that resulted in the death of four young girls.

———. *Black and White: The Confrontation between Reverend Fred L. Shuttlesworth and Eugene "Bull" Connor*. Boyds Mills, 2011. Ages 11–16. Escalating tensions in Birmingham, Alabama, during Civil Rights.

Freedman, Russell. *In Defense of Liberty: The Story of America's Bill of Rights*. Holiday, 2003. Ages 11–18. Discussion of the Constitution and civil liberties.

Gann, Marjorie, and Janet Wilson. *Five Thousand Years of Slavery*. Tundra, 2011. Ages 14–18. History of the slave trade around the world up to the present. Timelines.

Gay, Kathlyn. *Bigotry and Intolerance: The Ultimate Teen Guide*. Scarecrow Press, 2013. Ages 11–16. Discussion of why people espouse bigotry. It Happened to Me.

Gay, Kathlyn. *Food: The New Gold*. Twenty-First Century, 2013. Ages 14–18. The social, political, and economic issues surrounding food across the world.

Haynes, Charles C., Sam Chaltain, and Susan M. Glisson. *First Freedoms: A Documentary History of the First Amendment Rights in America*. Oxford, 2006. Ages 12–18. History, issues, and people pertinent to the developing notion of free speech.

Herumin, Wendy. *Child Labor Today: A Human Rights Issue*. Enslow, 2007. Ages 12–18. Facts and portraits of the 218,000,000 children forced to work in harsh conditions worldwide. Issues in Focus Today.

Hopkinson, Deborah. *Shutting Out the Sky: Life in the Tenements of New York 1880–1924*. Scholastic, 2003. Ages 11–14. The lives of 5 immigrants living in New York City's tenements.

Kuklin, Susan. *No Choirboy: Murder, Violence, and Teenagers on Death Row*. Holt, 2008. Ages 15–18. A look at prisons, young prisoners, punishment, and the concept of justice in the U.S.

Levinson, Cynthia. *We've Got a Job: The 1963 Birmingham Children's March*. Peachtree, 2012. History through the eyes of four young people who marched in Birmingham during the Civil Rights Movement.

Macy, Sue. *Wheels of Change: How Women Rode the Bicycle to Freedom (With a Few Flat Tires Along the Way)*. National Geographic, 2011. Photoessay of how bicycles gave women freedom to change their lives.

McWhorter, Diane. *A Dream of Freedom: The Civil Rights Movement from 1954 to 1968*. Scholastic, 2004. Ages 10–18. Heroism, idealism, and political turmoil surrounding the Civil Rights Movement.

Nelson, Kadir. *Heart and Soul: The Story of America and African Americans*. Balzer & Bray, 2011. Ages 11–14. How African Americans influenced liberty and justice across U.S. history. Dramatic oil paintings.

Stokes, John A., with Lois Wolfe and Herman Viola. *Students on Strike: Jim Crow, Civil Rights, Brown, and Me*. National Geographic, 2008. Ages 11–16. First person account of the student strike in Virginia in 1951 that was part of the 1954 Brown decision.

War and History

Allen, Thomas B. *George Washington, Spymaster: How the Americans Outspied the British and Won the Revolutionary War*. National Geographic, 2004. Ages 11–14. Role of intelligence and counterintelligence in the Revolutionary War. (British)

Aronson, Marc. *The Real Revolution: The Global Story of American Independence*. Clarion, 2005. Ages 13–18. Global social, political, and economic underpinnings of U.S. move to independence from Great Britain.

———. *Sugar Changed the World: A Story of Magic, Spice, Slavery, Freedom, and Science*. Clarion Books, 2010. Ages 13–18. The ramifications of the growth of the sugar industry.

Balkin, Karen F., editor. *The War on Terrorism*. Greenhaven, 2004. Ages 14–18. 28 authors take pro/con stances on various aspects of terrorism. Opposing Viewpoints: Current Issues series.

Blumenthal, Karen. *Bootleg: Murder, Moonshine and the Lawless Years of Prohibition*. RB Flash Point, 2011. Ages 14–18. Prohibition-era violence and drinking habits of Americans from colonial times to present.

Ellis, Deborah. *Kids of Kabul Living Bravely through a Never-Ending War*. Groundwood Books, 2012. Ages 11–16. Interviews with young people trying to escape the violence of their lives in Kabul.

Floca, Brian. *Locomotive*. Atheneum, 2012. **(PI)** Ages 11–14. Historic journey of family on first passenger train from Omaha to Sacramento. Stunning visual vignettes document the trip and details of the train.

Frank, Mitch. *Understanding the Holy Land: Answering Questions about the Israeli–Palestinian Conflict*. Viking, 2005. Ages 12–18.

Israeli-Palestinian conflict presented in a question-and-answer format.

Freedman, Russell. *Children of the Great Depression.* Clarion, 2005. Ages 11–18. Photoessay about the causes of the economic disaster in the 1920s and 1930s and life during this time.

———. *The War to End All Wars: World War I.* Clarion, 2010. Ages 12–18. Photoessay about the first modern global war that led to mass slaughter. Causes, weaponry, consequences.

———. *Who Was First? Discovering the Americas.* Clarion, 2007. Ages 12–15. A look at various ideas about the discovery of the Americas.

Hampton, Wilborn. *War in the Middle East: A Reporter's Story: Black September and the Yom Kippur War.* Candlewick, 2007. Ages 13–18. Events of the 1970 Jordanian conflict and the 1973 Israeli conflict.

Hopkinson, Deborah. *Up before Daybreak: Cotton and People in America.* Scholastic, 2006. Ages 9–14. How cotton production affected the lives of Americans from the Industrial Revolution to the 1950s.

———. *Titanic: Voices from Disaster.* Scholastic, 2012. Ages 11–16. Narrative about the 1912 disaster with photos, diagrams, and timelines.

Hoose, Phillip. *We Were There, Too! Young People in U.S. History.* Farrar, 2001. Ages 11–14. Contributions of dozens of young people who helped shape our nation.

Janeczko, Paul. *The Dark Game: True Spy Stories.* Candlewick, 2010. Ages 11–16. Short stories about spy elements and historical figures in history who were spies.

Kaufman, Michael T. *1968.* Roaring Brook, 2009. Ages 14–18. France. Argument that the events of 1968 and their impact on people made this a watershed year.

Lewis, J. Patrick. *The Brothers' War: Civil War Voices in Verse.* National Geographic, 2007. Ages 12–18. Poems about those who fought in the American Civil War illustrated with historical photographs.

McPherson, Stephanie. *Iceberg, Right Ahead! The Tragedy of the Titanic.* 21st Century, 2011.

Ages 11–18. Planning and building of the *Titanic* through finding the wreck on the ocean floor.

Murphy, Jim. *The Day the Soldiers Stopped Fighting.* Scholastic, 2009. Ages 12–16. Incident during WWI when soldiers on both sides stopped fighting.

———. *The Crossing: How George Washington Saved The American Revolution.* Scholastic, 2010. Ages 11–16. Washington's role in America's independence.

Nelson, Scott. *Ain't Nothing but a Man: My Quest to Find the Real John Henry.* National Geographic, 2008. Ages 11–14. Search for man behind the John Henry legend. Racial injustice, chain-gang rail workers, 1870s.

O'Brien, Anne S. *After Gandhi: One Hundred Years of Nonviolent Resistance.* Charlesbridge, 2009. Ages 11–15. Profiles 16 activists, resistance groups, and social movements around the world.

Oppenheim, Joanne. *Dear Miss Breed: True Stories of the Japanese American Incarceration during World War II and a Librarian Who Made a Difference.* Scholastic, 2006. Ages 12–16. Librarian who corresponded with children placed in Japanese-American internment camps.

Philbrick, Nathaniel. *The Mayflower & the Pilgrims' New World.* Putnam Juvenile, 2008. Ages 11–15. The account of the Mayflower and Pilgrims' landing in America.

Philip, Neil. *The Great Circle: A History of the First Nations.* Clarion, 2006. Ages 11–15. An explanation of the historical relationship between Native Americans and white settlers.

Rogasky, Barbara. *Smoke and Ashes: The Story of the Holocaust.* Holiday, 2002. Ages 12–18. Anti-Semitism and hate groups from WWII to present.

Schanzer, Rosalyn. *Witches! The Absolutely True Tale of Disaster in Salem.* National Geographic, 2011. Ages 12–15. An account of the witch-hunting hysteria, confusion, and tragedy. Includes courtroom transcripts.

Sheinkin. Steve. *Bomb: The Race to Build—and Steal—the World's Most Dangerous Weapon.* Roaring Brook, 2012. Spies involved in the creation of the first nuclear weapon and the political and scientific context.

Cultural Diversity

Aslan, Reza. *No God but God: The Origins and Evolution of Islam*. Delacorte, 2005. Ages 14–18. Overview of Muslim history and religious beliefs, with links to current concerns, such as jihad and hijab.

Barnard, Bryn. *The Genius of Islam: How Muslims Made the Modern World*. Knopf, 2011. **(PI)** Ages 10–14. Technological and scientific advances during Islamic Golden Age, 7th–12th centuries. Double-page spreads.

Bausman, Ann. *Denied, Detained, Deported: Stories from the Dark Side of American Immigration*. National Geographic, 2009. Ages 12–15. Cycles of arguments for and against immigration across U.S. history.

D'Aluisio, Faith, and Peter Menzel. *What the World Eats*. Tricycle, 2008. Ages 9–13. Details what families eat in 21 countries around the world, how they obtain their food, and what it costs. Eye-catching photos.

Friedman, Lauri, editor. *Discrimination*. Greenhaven, 2009. Ages 12–16. Essays about racial discrimination and profiling, ethnic team names, gay marriage, race-based humor, and affirmative action. Writing the Critical Essay series.

Gaskins, Pearl Fuyo, editor. *What Are You? Voices of Mixed-Race Young People*. Holt, 1999. Ages 13–18. Interviews, essays, and poetry by 40 young adults about their experiences growing up in the U.S.

Hill, Laban C. *Harlem Stomp! A Cultural History of the Harlem Renaissance*. Little, Brown, 2009. Ages 11–18. Early-20th-century African-American migration north; 1920s Harlem.

O'Brien, Tony, and Mike Sullivan. *Afghan Dreams: Young Voices of Afghanistan*. Bloomsbury, 2010. Ages 11–14. First-person interviews that detail the realities and dreams of Afghan children and teens. Photos.

Sloan, Christopher. *Bury the Dead: Tombs, Corpses, Mummies, Skeletons and Rituals*. National Geographic, 2002. Ages 11–18. Funeral rites across time and culture.

St. John, Warren. *Outcasts United: The Story of a Refugee Soccer Team that Changed a Town*. Delacorte, 2012. Ages 11–18. The story of young refugees in Clarkston, Georgia, who form a soccer team.

Swain, Gwenyth. *Hope and Tears: Ellis Island Voices*. Calkins Creek, 2012. Ages 11–14. Fictionalized monologues, dialogues, letters, and poems with real photographs of those who came to Ellis Island.

Weaver, Janice. *From Head to Toe: Bound Feet, Bathing Suits, and Other Bizarre and Beautiful Things*. Illus. Francis Blake. Tundra, 2003. Ages 10–14. Cross-cultural exploration of fashion.

School-Related Issues

Daniels, Peggy, editor. *Zero Tolerance Policies in Schools*. Greenhaven, 2009. Ages 12–16. Essays on pros and cons of zero tolerance policies, including their effect on schools and students. Issues that Concern You series.

Hamilton, Jill, editor. *Bullying and Hazing*. Greenhaven, 2008. Ages 12–16. Essays on opinions about bullying, including female, Internet, and homophobic. Issues that Concern You series.

———. *Electronic Devices in Schools*. Greenhaven, 2007. Ages 12–16. Essays on the pros and cons of iPods, cell phones, camera phones, YouTube, laptops, and PDAs in schools. Issues that Concern You series.

Jacobs, Thomas. *Teen Cyberbullying Investigated: Where Do Your Rights End and Consequences Begin?* Free Spirit, 2010. Ages 12–18. Court cases on cyberbullying and its consequences. Teens and the Law series.

Sonneborn, Liz. *Frequently Asked Questions about Plagiarism*. Rosen, 2011. Ages 12–18. Discussion of plagiarism. FAQ: Teen Life series.

Sports

Beal, Rebecca. *Skateboarding: The Ultimate Guide*. Greenwood, 2013. Ages 11–18. Skateboarding as an extreme sport. Greenwood Guides to Extreme Sports.

Blumenthal, Karen. *Let Me Play: The Story of Title IX: The Law That Changed the Future of Girls in America*. Atheneum, 2005. Ages 12–18. The legislation that gave girls and women equal access to physical education classes, gymnasiums, universities, and graduate schools.

Friedman, Peach. *Diary of an Exercise Addict*. GPP Life, 2008. Ages 12–18. A woman's chronicle of overcoming exercise addiction.

Macy, Sue. *Swifter, Higher, Stronger: A Photographic History of the Summer Olympics*. National Geographic, 2004. Ages 11–18. Fascinating facts, history, controversies, and tragedies surrounding the games.

Nelson, Kadir. *We Are the Ship: The Story of Negro League Baseball*. Hyperion, 2008. **(PI)** Ages 11–15. History, challenges, personalities, and facts surrounding the days of the Negro League.

Willett, Edward. *Frequently Asked Questions about Exercise Addiction*. Rosen, 2009. Ages 12–18. Facts, risky behaviors, and advice for both genders. FAQ: Teen Life series.

Zahensky, Barbara A. Frequently *Asked Questions About Athletes and Eating Disorders*. Rosen, 2008. Ages 12–18. Facts and advice about eating disorders in the lives of athletes. FAQ: Teen Life series.

Jobs, Careers, and Money Management

Aksomitis, Linda, editor. *Choosing a Career*. Greenhaven, 2008. Ages 12–16. Essays on careers: planning, careers for the disabled, nontraditional careers, the military, internships. Issues that Concern You series.

Blackwell, Amy. *Personal Care Services, Fitness, and Education*. Ferguson, 2008. Ages 15–18. Occupations that require a high school diploma only. Great Careers with a High School Diploma series.

Christen, Carol, and Richard Bolles. *What Color Is Your Parachute? For Teens, 2nd Edition: Discovering Yourself, Defining Your Future*. Ten Speed, 2011. Ages 13–18. Discovering strengths and interests.

Ferguson Publications. *Careers in Focus* (53-volume series). Information presented in articles profiling jobs within each field. Examples:

Film (2006), *Automotives* (2009), *Child Care* (2006).

Gay, Kathlyn. *The Military and Teens: The Ultimate Teen Guide*. Ages 14–18. Scarecrow Press, 2008. Discussion of major issues when deciding to join the military. It Happened to Me.

Jackson, Donna M. *ER Vets: Life in an Animal Emergency Room,* Houghton, 2005. Ages 12–14. Explains the processes and the people involved in saving animals.

Denega, Danielle. *Smart Money: How to Manage Your Cash*. Franklin Watts, 2008. Ages 12–15. Overview of money management, including getting a job, budgeting, paying taxes, and investing. Scholastic Choices series.

Monteverde, Matt. *Frequently Asked Questions about Budgeting and Money Management*. Rosen, 2008. Ages 12–18. Facts, risky behaviors, and advice on personal finances. FAQ: Teen Life series.

Humanities

Music and Dance

Berlatsky, Noah, editor. *Rap Music*. Greenhaven, 2012. Ages 13–18. Rap music and issues of censorship, harmful lyrics, violence, and advisory labeling. Introducing Issues with Introducing Issues with Opposing Viewpoints series.

Dagenais, Mande. *Inspired to Dance: Everything You Need to Know about Becoming a Professional Dancer without Breaking a Leg*. iUniverse, 2013. Ages 11–18. What it takes to become a professional dancer.

Fitzgerald, Tamsin. *Hip-Hop and Urban Dance*. Heinemann, 2008. Ages 11–14. Choreography, clothes, fashion, and culture of hip-hop.

Greenberg, Jan, and Sandra Jordan. *Ballet for Martha: Making Appalachian Spring*. Illus. Brian Flores. Flash Point, 2010. **(PI)** Ages 11–14. Collaboration of composer, dancer, and sculptor to create this modern dance.

Helsby, Genevieve. *Those Amazing Musical Instruments!* Sourcebooks, 2007. Ages 9–15. A guide to musical instruments.

Krull, Kathleen. *Lives of the Musicians: Good Times, Bad Times (and What the Neighbors Thought).*

Illus. Kathryn Hewitt. Harcourt, 2011. **(COL)** Ages 10–14. Snapshot biographies of 16 musical greats from classical to ragtime.

Art and Illustration

Ancona, George. *Murals: Walls That Sing.* Marshall Cavendish, 2003. Ages 10–14. How wall paintings represent their communities.

Evans, Dilys. *Show and Tell: Exploring the Fine Art of Children's Book Illustration.* Chronicle, 2008. Ages 12–18. A behind-the-scenes look at how 12 children's book illustrators ply their craft.

Lane, Kimberley. *Come Look with Me: Latin American Art.* Charlesbridge, 2007. Ages 10–14. Come Look with Me series books include African-American, Asian, and American Indian Art as well as women artists.

McCloud, Scott. *Making Comics: Storytelling Secrets of Comics, Manga and Graphic Novels.* Harper, 2006. Ages 11–18. How to make drawings become a story and how cartooning choices communicate meaning.

Peot, Margaret. *Inkblot: Drip, Splat and Squish Your Way to Creativity.* Boyds Mills, 2011. Ages 11–18. The creativity around making inkblots.

Sandler, Martin. *The Dust Bowl through the Lens: How Photography Revealed and Helped Remedy a National Disaster.* Walker, 2009. Ages 10–14. Role of photographers in social change. Vintage photographs.

Sayre, Henry. *Cave Paintings to Picasso: The Inside Scoop on 50 Art Masterpieces.* Chronicle, 2004. Ages 11–14. Art history from 22,000 B.C. to 1964.

Scott, Damion, and Kris Ex. *How to Draw Hip Hop.* Watson-Guptill, 2006. Ages 12–18. Basics of drawing hip hop for graphic novel representations.

Writing and Film

Barry, Lynda. *What It Is.* Drawn & Quarterly, 2008. Ages 14–18. Guide to writing and creativity.

Bodden, Valerie. *Creating the Character: Dialogue and Characterization.* Creative Education, 2008. Ages 12–18. Advice, exercises, and examples from classic and contemporary works. See also in this series *Painting the Picture: Imagery and Description; Setting the Style: Wording and Tone; Telling the Tale: Narration and Point of View.*

Hamlett, Christina. *Screenwriting for Teens: The 100 Principles of Screenwriting Every Budding Writer Must Know.* Michael Wiese, 2006. Ages 13–18. Guide to completing a first short film, including exercises, examples, and a recommended reading list.

Krull, Kathleen. *Lives of the Writers: Comedies, Tragedies (and What the Neighbors Thought).* Illus. Kathryn Hewitt. Harcourt, 2011. **(COL)** Ages 10–13. Brief histories of twenty classic writers.

Lanier, Troy, and Clay Nichols. *Filmmaking for Teens: Pulling Off Your Shorts.* Michael Wiese, 2005. Ages 13–18. A guide to making one's first film.

Levine, Gail Carson. *Writing Magic: Creating Stories That Fly.* HarperCollins, 2006. Ages 12–14. Advice for young writers in short chapters with writing exercises, based on Levine's experiences as a children's author.

Marcus, Leonard S., editor. *The Wand in the Word: Conversations with Writers of Fantasy.* Candlewick, 2006. Ages 12–18. Interviews with 13 writers of fantasy for young people.

Stevens, Chambers, and Renee Rolle-Whatley. *Magnificent Monologues for Teens: The Teens' Monologue Source for Every Occasion!* Sandcastle, 2002. Ages 12–18. Monologues for teens.

——. *Sensational Scenes for Teens: The Scene Study-guide for Teen Actors!* Sandcastle, 2001. Ages 12–18. Age-appropriate scenes for teens to act out.

Watson, Esther. *Whatcha Mean, What's a Zine? The Art of Making Zines and Comics.* Graphia, 2006. Ages 11–18. Description of zines and comics for those interested in creating their own works.

Wolf, Allan. *Immersed in Verse: An Informative, Slightly Irreverent and Totally Tremendous Guide to Living the Poet's Life.* Illus. Tuesday Mourning. Lark Books, 2006. Ages 12–14.

Related Films and DVDs

Many films, videos, and DVDs present biographies of current and historical people from around the world. In addition, cable channels such as the National Geographic Channel, the History Channel, Animal Planet, and Biography provide interesting information about a myriad of topics. This information is just a couple of examples of biographies and nonfiction topics for young adults.

Anne Frank: The Whole Story (2001). Author: Anne Frank (1952). 189 minutes.

Castle (2002); *Cathedral* (1987); *Pyramid* (2000); *Roman City* (1991). Author: David Macaulay. 60 minutes.

Fast Food Nation (2006). Author: Eric Schlosser (2001). 116 minutes.

October Sky (1999). Author: Homer H. Hickman (1998). 108 minutes.

Persepolis (2007). Author: Marjane Satrapi (2003). 96 minutes.

Other sources for biographies and nonfiction/informational media

Kid Info http://www.kidinfo.com/american_history/famous_historical_people.htm

Smithsonian Magazine website http://www.smithsonianmag.com/

Animal Planet Videos http://animal.discovery.com/videos

Biography Channel Videos http://www.biography.com/videos

Discovery Channel Videos http://dsc.discovery.com/videos

History Channel Videos http://www.history.com/videos

National Geographic Videos http://video.nationalgeographic.com/video/

Chapter Seven

Poetry and Plays

Poetry is an enjoyable literary form for many young adults. Poems related to a topic, issue, mood, or emotion can provide a flash of humor or a new perspective. Reading and rereading favorite poems with adolescents on a daily basis and encouraging them to read and write poetry invites them into poetry as a significant way of exploring ideas. By learning more about poetry and the best-loved and respected poets, you can become skillful at selecting and presenting poetry that captures the attention of adolescents.

The second part of this chapter provides a brief overview on plays for young adults, a genre that has often been neglected, but that can actively engage adolescents with characters and oral interpretation. Another form of oral interpretation that allows adolescents to live a piece of literature is readers' theatre.

Definition and Description of Poetry

Poetry is the concentrated expression of ideas and feelings through precise and imaginative words carefully selected for their sonorous and rhythmic effects. Originally, poetry was oral, recited by minstrels as they traversed the countryside, sharing poems and songs to listeners of all ages. The musicality of poetry makes it especially suitable for reading aloud and, at times, putting to music.

Adolescents often believe that rhyme is an essential ingredient of poetry; yet some types of poetry do not rhyme. What distinguishes poetry from prose is the concentration of thought and feeling expressed in succinct, exact, and beautiful language, and an underlying pulse or rhythm.

Not all rhyming, rhythmical language merits the label of poetry. **Verse** is a language form in which simple thoughts or stories are told in rhyme with a distinct beat or meter. Mother Goose and nursery rhymes are good examples of well-known, simple verses. And of course, we are all too aware of the ***jingle,*** a catchy repetition of sounds heard so often in commercials. The lyrics of many popular songs also are examples of verse. The most important features of verses and jingles are their strong rhyme and rhythm with frequent word repetition. Content is often light or even silly. Although verses and jingles can be enjoyable and have a place in the classroom, poetry enriches the lives of adolescents by giving new insights and fresh views on life's experiences and by eliciting strong emotional responses.

Novels in verse for young adults are appearing with greater frequency and represent another instance of ***mashups*** or blending of genres. They are discussed briefly in this chapter, but are integrated in the appropriate genre chapters according to the nature of the story; for example, the free verse novels of Ellen Hopkins on issues of drugs, mental illness, and suicide are in realistic fiction and the free verse novels of Margarita Engle on the history and people of Cuba are found in historical fiction.

Types of Poetry Books

A wide variety of poetry books are available for adolescents, ranging from anthologies and books of poems on special topics and by favorite poets to single illustrated poems in picture book formats. Some will be read independently by adolescents who are often drawn to poetry as a means of expressing deep dark emotions and critiques of adults and society. Other books of poetry will be selected for use in the classroom as bridges between classroom activities, materials for reading, and literature for enjoyment.

Anthologies of Poetry

A large, comprehensive ***anthology*** of poetry is a useful tool for quickly locating a poem to fit a particular need. The better anthologies are organized by subjects for easy retrieval of poems appropriate for almost any occasion. In addition, indexes of poets and titles, or first lines, are usually provided. Works by both contemporary and traditional poets that appeal to a wide age range and use many poetic forms can be found in most anthologies. One notable trend is the inclusion of recordings of poets reading their works along with the book, such as found in *Poetry Speaks Who I Am,* edited by Elise Paschen.

Poetry collections should be judged on the quality of the poetry choices. In addition to quality, consider the illustrations and the appearance of the book. Finding appropriate anthologies will involve careful selections because the majority of anthologies are written for younger audiences or adults with only a few focused on adolescents as their major audience.

Thematic Poetry Books

Thematic poetry books are anthologies that feature poems on one topic or of one poetic form. These specialized collections become important materials for readers who come to love certain kinds of poetry. These collections typically combine poems from current poets with poets from within the canon such as Langston Hughes, William Carlos Williams, and Walt Whitman. Beautifully illustrated thematic collections are available and seem to be especially enjoyed by some students for independent reading. Examples include Naomi Shihab Nye's *What Have You Lost?* and Betsy Franco's *Falling Hard: 100 Love Poems by Teenagers.*

Poetry Books by a Single Poet

A collection of poems by one poet may include the complete works or focus on poems on a particular topic by that poet. *Poetry books by a single poet* invite students to understand and appreciate the works of an individual poet. Many of these books combine poems with evocative illustrations to address the concerns and feelings of young adults, such as *What the Heart Knows* by Joyce Sidman with illustrations by Pamela Zagarenski, as well as to address historical time periods, such as *We Troubled the Waters* by Ntozake Shange with illustrations by Rod Brown on the Civil Rights Movement. Adolescents who identify with favorite poets particularly appreciate this type of poetry book.

Single Illustrated Poetry Books and Graphic Formats

Single illustrated poems are increasingly available in picture book formats, particularly narrative poems. These editions make poetry more appealing and accessible to many adolescents, although the illustrations can interfere with adolescents forming their own mental images from the language created by poets. Several notable examples that bring alive poems by Langston Hughes through visual interpretation include *My People* with expressive sepia photographs by Charles R. Smith, *The Negro Speaks of Rivers* with radiant watercolors by E. B. Lewis, and *I, Too, Am America* with dynamic mixed-media collages by Bryan Collier. Kids Can Press has an excellent series, Visions in Poetry, with picture book versions of classic poems for young adults, such as "Casey at the Bat," "Jabberwocky," "The Highway Man," and "The Raven."

Graphic novels are a strong recent trend in young adult literature, cutting across all genres. Several recent graphic novels interpret epic poems through the use of a graphic format. Gareth Hinds retells Homer's epic poem, *The Odyssey,* in dramatic pencil and watercolor visual images with a judicious minimum of words across various sizes of panels, while Seymour Chwast's *Dante's Divine Comedy* recasts Dante's epic poem through compelling visual imagery and graphic formats.

Novels That Integrate Poetry and Verse

Novels in verse are novel-length narratives told through poetic language, instead of prose, usually in some type of free verse. They differ from narrative poetry as found in Marilyn Nelson's work, for example, in that the individual verses do not each stand alone as poems and are not crafted into specific poetic forms. Novels in verse have become a popular format for conveying difficult topics in succinct verse that does not overwhelm readers with dense printed pages. Some noteworthy examples of such novels are Guadalupe Garcia McCall's *Under the Mesquite* (2011)about a teen dealing with her mother's cancer, Holly Thompsons' *Orchards* (2011) about suicide and guilt, and Ellen Hopkins' *Impulse* (2007) about mental illness.

While fewer books of poetry for young adult audiences are being published, poetry is often integrated into fiction novels for young adults, depicting poetry as a powerful way of reflecting on one's own life. *Shakespeare Bats Clean-up* by Ronald Koertge (2006) is a novel in verse in which a baseball player sidelined by illness begins keeping a journal and writing poetry. *Bronx Masquerade* by Nikki Grimes (2002) reveals the multiple voices of high school students who read their poetry to each other each Friday. Sometimes classic poems are integrated into fiction based in the lives of famous poets, such as *Your Own, Sylvia: A Verse Portrait of Sylvia Plath* by Stephanie Hemphill (2007). *The Language Inside* by Holly Thompson (2013) integrates many references to contemporary poems and approaches to writing poetry in a free verse novel that explores identity in a global world.

These novels in verse and novels where characters use poetry in daily life are not classified within the genre of poetry and so are included in the relevant genre chapters. These books, however, can play a significant role in portraying why poetry matters and the role of poetry in capturing and magnifying the emotions and experiences of life for adolescents.

Elements of Poetry

Just as with a work of fiction, the elements of a poem should be considered if the reader is to understand and evaluate the poem. These parts—meaning, rhythm, sound patterns, figurative language, and sense imagery—work together to express ideas and feelings.

- *Meaning* is the underlying idea, feeling, or mood expressed or implied through the poem. As with other literary forms, poetry is a form of communication; it is the way a particular writer chooses to express emotions and thoughts through the choice and arrangement of words.

- *Rhythm* is the beat or regular cadence of the poem. Poetry, usually an oral form of literature, relies on rhythm to help communicate meaning. A fast rhythm is effected through short lines, clipped syllables, sharp, high vowel sounds, such as the sounds represented by *a, e,* and *i,* and abrupt consonant sounds, such as the sounds represented by *k, t,* and *p.* A fast rhythm can provide the listener with a feeling of happiness, excitement, drama, or even tension and suspense. A slow rhythm is effected by longer lines, multisyllabic words, full or low vowel sounds, such as the sounds represented by *o, oo,* and *u,* and resonating consonant sounds, such as represented by *m, n,* and *l.* A slow rhythm can evoke languor, tranquility, inevitability, and harmony, among other feelings. A change in rhythm during a poem signals the listener to a change in meaning.

- **Sound patterns** are made by repeated sounds and combinations of sounds in the words. Words, phrases, or lines are sometimes repeated in their entirety. Also, parts of words may be repeated, as with rhyme, the most recognized sound device.

  - **Rhyme** occurs when the ends of words (the last vowel sound and any consonant sound that may follow) have the same sounds, such as *vat, rat, that, brat,* and *flat,* or *hay, they, flay, stray,* and *obey.*

  - **Assonance** is a pattern where the same vowel sound is heard repeatedly within a line or a few lines of poetry, such as *hoop, gloom, moon, moot,* and *boots.*

  - **Alliteration** is a pattern in which initial consonant sounds are heard frequently within a few lines of poetry, such as *ship, shy,* and *shape.*

  - **Consonance** is similar to alliteration but usually refers to a close juxtaposition of similar final consonant sounds, as in *flake, chuck,* and *stroke.*

  - **Onomatopoeia** is the use of words that imitate real-world sounds, such as *buzz* for the sound of a bee and *hiss* for snakes.

- **Figurative language** takes many different forms and involves comparing or contrasting one object, idea, or feeling with another one.

  - A **simile** is a direct comparison, typically using *like* or *as* to point out the similarities, as in "The house was *like* a fortress."

  - A **metaphor** is an implied comparison without a signal word to evoke the similarities, as in "The house was a fortress."

  - **Personification** is the attribution of human qualities to animate nonhuman beings or to inanimate objects for the purpose of drawing a comparison between the animal or object and human beings, as in "The *house glared* down haughtily at passersby."

  - **Hyperbole** is an exaggeration to highlight reality or to point out ridiculousness, as in "The house, painted a blinding shade of red, fairly vibrated." Middle schoolers especially enjoy hyperbole because it appeals to their strong sense of the absurd.

- **Sense imagery** is the way in which a poet plays with one or more of the five senses in descriptive and narrative language. **Sight** may be awakened through the depiction of beauty; **hearing** may be evoked by the sounds of a city street; **smell** and **taste** may be recalled through the description of a fish left too long in the sun; and finally, **touch** can be sensitized through describing the gritty discomfort of a wet swimsuit caked with sand from the beach. After listening to a poem, teens can be asked to think about which of the senses the poet is appealing to.

These elements of poetry may be considered to select varied types of poems and group them for sharing. However, teaching each of these elements as separate items to be memorized and used to analyze poems has caused many adolescents to dislike poetry. To help adolescents come to appreciate poetry, it is far better to be enthusiastic, select wisely, read aloud well, and provide many opportunities for them to read and enjoy many kinds of poems.

Evaluation and Selection of Poetry

The criteria to keep in mind when evaluating a poem for use with adolescents are as follows:

- **Are the ideas and feelings expressed in authentic, fresh, and imaginative ways?**
- **Is the expression of the ideas and feelings unique to encourage readers to perceive ordinary things in new ways?** The poem should, in some way, take readers to new insights that go beyond their current views of their lives and feelings.
- **Does the poem present the world through an adolescent's perspective?** The poem should be appropriate to the experiences and age of the adolescents and focus on their lives and as well as on activities that all ages can relate to. Adolescents particularly resist poems that preach to them.

The findings from surveys of students' poetry preferences can be helpful in selecting poems. Terry (1974) and Kutiper and Wilson (1993) studied intermediate-grade students and found:

- A preference for narrative poems over lyric poems and modern over classics.
- An enjoyment of limericks and dislike of haiku and free verse.
- A preference for poems with pronounced sound patterns, especially poems that rhyme or have a regular, distinctive rhythm.
- An interest in humorous poems, poems about animals, and poems about enjoyable, familiar experiences.
- A preference for poems on humor, familiar experiences, unusual people, moments of crisis, and social problems.
- Figurative language in poetry was initially confusing and interfered with understanding the poems.

Abrahamson's (2002) review of earlier studies of poetry preferences of students in grades 7–12 showed:

- Students like narrative poems, humorous poems, and the elements of rhythm and rhyme.
- They prefer more subtle humor and had more appreciation of figurative language.
- The mode of poetry presentation, whether listening to poetry read aloud, listening to it read aloud while reading it, or reading it only, made a difference. Students who listened to the poems while reading them at the same time usually gave the poems the lowest ratings.
- Students especially enjoyed hearing short rhyming poems read aloud and preferred to silently read serious poems or poems without rhyme or obvious rhythm.

A study of school library circulation records in elementary and middle schools indicated that humorous contemporary poetry dominated students' choices (Kutiper & Wilson, 1993). Collections of poetry by poetry award winners did not circulate widely, nor were they widely available in school libraries, even though these poets reflect a higher quality of language than the light verse so popular with students. An interest in poetry that goes beyond humorists can be developed by providing an array of poetry that builds on students' natural interests. A good selection of rhyming narrative poems with distinct rhythms about humorous events and familiar experiences is a good starting point for students who have little experience with poetry. Poems written by adolescents also have the potential for developing interest, such as the collections found in *You Hear Me? Poems and Writings by Teenage Boys,* edited by Betsy Franco, and *Paint Me Like I Am* through Writers Corps.

In selecting poems to read to adolescents, the list of notable poets and the list of poets who have won the National Council of Teachers of English Excellence in Poetry for Children Award are good starting points. The NCTE Award was established in 1977 in the United States to honor living U.S. poets whose poetry has contributed substantially to the lives of young people. This award, now given every other year, is for a poet's entire body of writing for children ages 3 through 13. Although the age range does not cover the entire young adult period, most of these poets have some poetry that is appropriate for teens.

NCTE Excellence in Poetry for Children Award Winners

1977	David McCord	1994	Barbara Juster Esbensen
1978	Aileen Fisher	1997	Eloise Greenfield
1979	Karla Kuskin	2000	X. J. Kennedy
1980	Myra Cohn Livingston	2003	Mary Ann Hoberman
1981	Eve Merriam	2006	Nikki Grimes
1982	John Ciardi	2009	Lee Bennett Hopkins
1985	Lilian Moore	2011	J. Patrick Lewis
1988	Arnold Adoff	2013	Joyce Sidman
1991	Valerie Worth		

In addition, the Poetry Foundation established a Children's Poetry Laureate in 2006, naming Jack Prelutsky, Mary Ann Hoberman, and J. Patrick Lewis to serve two-year terms, and the Lee Bennett Hopkins Poetry Award is given annually to an American poet or anthologist for the most outstanding new book of poetry for children. A reference book, *Young Adult Poetry: A Survey and Theme Guide* (Schwedt & DeLong, 2002) is a useful tool for students and teachers in middle school and high school for locating poems to support the curriculum and to address student interests. This bibliography annotates 198 poetry books and identifies themes in more than 6,000 poems.

Poetry Types and Forms

Poetry can be classified in many ways; one way is to consider two main types that generally differ in purpose. *Lyric poetry* captures a moment, a feeling, or a scene, and is descriptive in nature, whereas *narrative poetry* tells a story or includes a sequence of events. This lyrical poem could also invite a discussion of metaphor:

The Leopard of Loneliness

Loneliness, the leopard,
Stalks the heart;
He captures his prey
And tears it apart.

When he is through,
He goes for the bone;
When he is full,
He leaves you—alone.

—Charles Ghigna

This narrative poem is a contemporary example of using humor to view students' lives.

Evolution

TV came
out of radio,
free verse
came out of rhyme.
I am
coming out of middle school,
changing all the time.
It's time
to lose the water wings,
crawl out of this lagoon.
I want to stand upright.
Get on my feet.
I want it soon.

—Sara Holbrook

Poetry can also be categorized by **poetic form,** which refers to the way the poem is structured or put together. **Couplets, tercets, quatrains,** and **cinquains** refer to the number (two, three, four, and five) of lines in a stanza—a set of lines grouped together. Couplets, tercets, quatrains, and cinquains usually rhyme, though the rhyme schemes may vary; these poetic forms may constitute an entire poem, or a poem may comprise a few stanzas of couplets, tercets, and so on.

Some forms, such as the haiku, have been around for centuries, while others are newly created. Marilyn Singer invented a new poetic form called **reverso,** in which the poems have different meanings in each direction, even though the words used are exactly the same. This form is used in *Mirror Mirror: A Book of Reversible Verse,* to provide new perspectives on well-known fairy tale characters.

Other specific forms frequently found in poetry for young adults are limericks, ballads, haiku, sijo, free verse, and concrete poetry. Two recent collections of poetry, *Poems from Homeroom: A Writer's Place to Start* by Kathi Appelt and *A Kick in the Head* edited by Paul B. Janeczko, feature poems written in many different poetic forms. These collections may be of interest to teachers who wish to encourage students to think about form and how best to express their emotions and thoughts.

Notable Authors of Poetry

Paul Fleischman, poet noted for collections of poems composed and printed for two or more readers to read in unison and solo. *Big Talk; Joyful Noise; I Am Phoenix.* www.paulfleischman.net

Nikki Giovanni, a poet known for free verse about African American experiences. *The Collected Poetry of Nikki Giovanni, 1968–1998; Ego-Tripping and Other Poems for Young People.* www.nikki-giovanni.com

Sara Holbrook, known as a poet and a performer of poetry that appeals to adolescents. *By Definition: Poems of Feelings; Walking on the Boundaries of Change: Poems of Transition.* www.saraholbrook.com

Paul B. Janeczko, a poet and anthologist known for his collections of poems for young adults and for collections that invite participation. *Pocket Poems: Selected for a Journey; A Poke in the I; A Foot in the Mouth; A Kick in the Head; Stone Bench in an Empty Park; Requiem: Poems of the Terezin Ghetto.* www.paulbjaneczko.com

J. Patrick Lewis, a poet recognized for his poems illuminating history. *The Brothers' War: Civil War Voices in Verse; Vherses: A Celebration of Outstanding Women; Monumental Verses.* www.jpatricklewis.com

Marilyn Nelson, a poet who uses a range of poetic forms from requiem to sonnets as reflections on African-American history. *Fortunes Bones; A Wreath for Emmett Till; Sweethearts of Rhythm; The Freedom Business.* www.blueflowerarts.com/marilyn-nelson

Naomi Shihab Nye, a Palestinian-American poet and anthologist whose meditative poems offer global perspectives and whose edited collections include Mexican, Native American, and Middle Eastern poetry. *This Same Sky: A Collection of Poems from around the World; The Space between Our Footsteps: Poems and Paintings from the Middle East; Time You Let Me In: 25 Poets Under 25.*

Joyce Sidman, a poet especially known for vivid poems that explore ecosystems and science information. *Butterfly Eyes and Other Secrets of the Meadow; Song of the Water Boatman and Other Pond Poems; What the Heart Knows—Chants, Charms and Blessings.* www.joycesidman.com

Gary Soto, a poet who captures the experiences of growing up in a Mexican neighborhood in California's Central Valley. *A Fire in My Hands; Partly Cloudy: Poems of Love and Longing.* www.garysoto.com

Patrice Vecchione, an anthologist whose collections address themes and emotions of significance to young adults. *Faith and Doubt; The Body Electric; Revenge and Forgiveness; Truth & Lies.* patricevecchione.com/

A *limerick* is a humorous one-stanza, five-line verse form (usually narrative), in which lines 1, 2, and 5 rhyme and are of the same length and lines 3 and 4 rhyme and are of the same length but shorter than the other lines. Edward Lear popularized this poetic form in the nineteenth century.

A *sonnet* is a fourteen-line poem in two stanzas, an octave and a sestet, or sometimes printed in a single fourteen-line stanza. Sonnets generally rhyme, though the rhyme schemes may vary. A clear break in emotion or thought occurs between the two stanzas or after the middle of the sonnet. Sonnets are often poems of argument or persuasion intended to convince, whether about politics, religion, or love. Sonnets are often thought of as poems of love, and many love sonnets have been written. Marilyn Nelson uses a more complex form, a heroic crown of sonnets, consisting of fifteen interlinked sonnets to tell the story of Emmett Till's brutal murder in *A Wreath for Emmett Till*. In the following poem by Christina Rossetti the speaker asks to be remembered.

Sonnet

> Remember me when I am gone away,
>> Gone far away into the silent land;
>> When you can no more hold me by the hand,
> Nor I half turn to go yet turning stay.
> Remember me when no more day by day
>> You tell me of our future that you planned:
>> Only remember me; you understand
> It will be late to counsel then or pray.
>
> Yet if you should forget me for a while
>> And afterwards remember, do not grieve;
>> For if the darkness and corruption leave
>> A vestige of the thoughts that once I had,
> Better by far that you should forget and smile
> Than that you should remember and be sad.

—Christina Rossetti

A *ballad* is a fairly long narrative poem of popular origin, usually adapted to singing. These traditional story poems are often romantic or heroic, such as "Robin Hood" or "John Henry."

Haiku is a lyric unrhymed poem of Japanese origin with seventeen syllables, usually arranged in three lines with a syllable count of five, seven, and five. Haiku is highly evocative poetry that frequently espouses harmony with and appreciation of nature, such as this traditional haiku from seventeenth-century Japan.

> A weathered skeleton
> in windy fields of memory,
> piercing like a knife

—Matsuo Basho

There are several lesser-known verse forms similar to haiku. *Renga* is a Japanese verse form in which poets alternate turns playing off the previous verse, usually beginning with three lines, followed by two lines in response to start a poetic chain. Examples can be found in *Birds on a Wire* or *A Jewel Tray of Stars* by Paul B. Janeczko and J. Patrick Lewis. *Sijo* is an ancient Korean poetic form with three lines, each fourteen to sixteen syllables, not focused solely on nature, and often with a surprise ending. Examples are found in Linda Sue Park's *Tap Dancing on the Roof: Sijo*.

Free verse is unrhymed poetry with little or light rhythm. Sometimes words within a line will rhyme. The subjects of free verse are often abstract and philosophical; they are always reflective.

Even When

I close my eyes
    the light that was
        you
           burns
                against my lids.

—Christine Hemp

Concrete poetry is written and printed in a shape that signifies the subject of the poem. Concrete poems are a form that must be seen to be fully appreciated. These poems do not usually have rhyme or definite rhythm; they rely mostly on the words, their meanings and shapes, and the way the words are arranged on the page to evoke images. In "Help" the positioning of the words to spell SOS helps convey the meaning through combining humor and misery with a plea for response.

HELP!

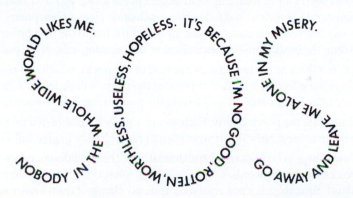

—Robert Froman

Copyright 1974 by Robert Froman. First appeared in *Seeing Things*, published by Thomas Y. Crowell. Reprinted by permission of Curtis Brown, Ltd.

Poetry in the Classroom

Poetry conveys the humor and dark emotions that often characterize the perspectives of adolescents; however, many adolescents have a negative attitude about poetry due to their previous school experiences. Poetry tends to be neglected in school, seldom shared until the dreaded poetry unit comes along and students are bombarded with abstract poems that they are expected to analyze to discover the "hidden meanings." The result is that adolescents can build a lifelong dislike of poetry, instead of being provided with experiences that create a lifelong appreciation of poetry.

Adolescents Listening to and Saying Poems

Teachers and librarians can begin by providing students with many opportunities to hear and say poems. Later, when students have developed a love of poetry and an affinity for the language play in poems, they can read poetry by fine poets and poems by their classmates and write their own poems. In other words, poetry needs to be shared in both oral and written forms.

Poetry should be shared with students often by reading it aloud. Poetry was originally an oral form of literature and so still relies heavily on the auditory perceptions of listeners. Moreover, oral language is the basis of literacy. These two facts combine nicely to make listening to poetry and saying poems a natural introduction to poetry.

Reading Poetry Aloud to Adolescents

Poetry should be read aloud to students often. Brief, positive encounters with one or two poems at a time are best. Too many poems in one sitting may overwhelm students or make the reading tedious. Some points to keep in mind in learning to read poetry include:

- Introduce the poem before reading it aloud, either by tying the poem in with something else or by briefly telling why you chose this poem. Then state the title of the poem and begin to read. After reading the poem, be sure to announce the name of the poet so that students discover the writers they especially enjoy.

- Read poetry for its meaning. Read aloud a poem just as you read aloud prose. Avoid unnatural intonations and follow the punctuation clues. Often, poetry is phrased in such a way that you must continue past the end of the line to the next before pausing. In other words, the breaks must be determined by the meaning units of the poem, not by the lines.

- Do not force or overemphasize the beat of the poem, which can result in an annoying singsong effect. The natural rhythm of the poem will be felt in a more interesting way by reading naturally and letting the poetic language provide the rhythm.

- Enunciate the poem clearly. Each sound and each syllable of a poem must be heard to be appreciated. Slow down your normal reading pace to give full value to each sound.

- Poetry begs to be performed and dramatized. Try out different effects (using different voices, elongating words, singing, shouting, whispering, pausing dramatically) in reading aloud. Your voice is a powerful tool: You may change it from louder to softer to only a whisper; you may start at a deep, low pitch and rise to a medium and eventually high pitch; you may speak very quickly in a clipped fashion and then slow down and drawl out the words. Holbrook's *Wham! It's a Poetry Jam: Discovering Performance Poetry* (2002) offers good suggestions for performing poetry and running a poetry contest.

- Some poems may need to be read aloud a number of times before their many meanings are perceived. Also favorite poems can be enjoyed and savored by hearing them again and again.

- Consider recording poems and making them available along with the poem in print for students to listen to and read. Individual students may enjoy recording a favorite poem for other students' listening. Commercial recordings of popular poets reading their works, accompanied by music, are available and quite popular. Live recordings are also available online. Some teachers have asked school volunteers who are good readers to peruse a poetry anthology, select a favorite poem, and record their reading of the poem.

- After reading a poem aloud, some form of response is occasionally enjoyed. Sometimes the response to a poem is simply the desire to hear it again. Other times, students need a few moments to reflect silently on the poem. Some poems warrant discussion, and students can take the opportunity to think about, How did this poem make you feel? What meaning does this poem have for you?

- Overanalyzing the form, figurative language, and meaning of poems has led to a dislike of poetry. Often, just reading and enjoying the poem is all that is needed. Other times, students can respond to the emotional impact of a poem. Once students have experience with poetry, a careful look at form is appropriate occasionally but only *after* they have an opportunity for personal response. Students can point out parts of the poem that they like and talk about why. They can also be encouraged to explore metaphor, imagery, and sensory language. An analysis of form and language can be integrated into mini-lessons as students write their own poetry and want to make their poems more effective. The major focus, however, should always be on the meaning and emotional impact of a poem.

Choral Poetry

A time-honored technique for saying and hearing poems over and over again, ***choral poetry*** consists of orally interpreting a poem through different arrangements of voices. These poems may be practiced and recited or rehearsed and read aloud. Students enjoy this way of experiencing poetry because they can participate within the safety of a group. The following sections explain how to select choral poems and teach them to students.

1. **Selection.** At first, select short poems (from one to four stanzas) until your students develop some skill with choral reading. Poems that work best as choral readings generally have straightforward meaning and are upbeat and humorous. Poems that contain dialogue or that are composed of couplets and have relatively short lines readily lend themselves to choral arrangements.

2. **Arrangements.** Options for reading a poem chorally include unison, two or three parts, solo voices, cumulative buildup, and simultaneous voices.
   - In unison choral speaking, the students recite the poem together as a group. Two-part or three-part choral poetry is usually based on arranging students into voice types (for example, high, medium, and low) to achieve different effects and by selecting lines of the poem for each group to recite or read.
   - Solo voices can be added to either of these presentations and are sometimes used for asking a question or making an exclamation.
   - Some poems lend themselves to cumulative buildup presentations, such as two voices saying the first line, then two more join in on the second, and then two more, gradually building to a crescendo until the entire class says the last line or stanza.
   - Poetry collections arranged for dramatic choral readings on a particular theme are an interesting variation. Paul Fleischman's *Joyful Noise: Poems for Two Voices; I Am Phoenix: Poems for Two Voices;* and *Big Talk: Poems for Four Voices* are well-known examples. These collections were written to be read aloud by two readers at once, one reading the left half of the page and one reading the right half, as well as certain lines simultaneously. Pairs or groups of four students can each take a different poem from one of these collections for presentation.
   - Many other variations can be developed for choral presentations. As soon as young people learn that poems do not have to be read sedately through exactly as written, they will find excitement and deeper meaning in poetry and become adept at arranging poems inventively.

3. **Performance.** Incorporating action, gestures, body movements, and facial expressions can produce more interesting presentations. Allowing various interpretations of the

same poem is an excellent way to encourage more original and insightful interpretations. Students truly enjoy this nonthreatening way of sharing poetry. Occasionally performing a well-honed choral poem for an audience can bring pride to students.

Adolescents Reading Poems

Adolescents can become engaged with poetry by reading selected poems silently or aloud to others, especially serious poems. Teachers should have one or two comprehensive poetry anthologies for students to browse through for general purposes. In addition, specialized collections by a single poet, such as *A Fury of Motion: Poems for Boys* by Charles Ghigna, and another two or three books of poems on a single topic, such as *Revenge and Forgiveness: An Anthology of Poems,* selected by Patrice Vecchione, are needed. Bringing in new poetry books occasionally over the course of the school year will spark renewed interest in reading poetry. Students can also be encouraged to make copies of their favorite poems from various collections to develop personal, individual anthologies. Many students choose to illustrate these and arrange the poems in new and inventive ways. Other activities to encourage the reading of poetry include:

- Place students in pairs to take turns reading favorite poems to one another. Make video or audio recordings of these readings so students can listen to or watch their own and other students' readings. Teachers have found that when students listen to their own reading of poetry, they note singsong readings and learn to avoid them.

- Place students in pairs with two or three books of poems for each pair. Provide fifteen to twenty minutes for students to read the poems in the books and then select one to read aloud to the class. During the reading time the teacher circulates and assists students in preparing to read poems aloud.

- Ask each student to select three poems by one poet and find something out about the poet; then place students in small groups of five or six to tell briefly about the poet and read the three poems aloud. Janeczko's *The Place My Words Are Looking For: What Poets Say about and through Their Work* (1990) and Sylvia Vardell's *Poetry People* (2007) are excellent resources for this purpose. Information about poets can be found on websites, including www.childrenslit.com.

- Have students find three poems on the same topic, such as hurt feelings, independence, popularity, or friendship, and read them aloud in pairs or small groups.

- Encourage students to find poems that are of the same poetic form (cinquains, limericks, etc.), or that exhibit similar poetic elements (rhyme, alliteration, onomatopoeia, etc.), or that have fast or slow rhythms. These poems can be used for reading aloud that day or week.

- Ask students to bring their collections of poems to class to share. One way to extend this sharing is to have each small group select a poem for a multimodal response by creating a Cin(E)-Poem (Stuart, 2010). Students sketch a storyboard of the poem that integrates images with the language of the poem. They then collect or create digital images, words, sounds, and music.

- An excellent site for ideas and resources for finding and sharing poetry with students is Sylvia Vardell's blog, http://poetryforchildren.blogspot.com/.

- Georgia Heard (2012) provides suggestions for encouraging students to read and appreciate poetry in order to address the Common Core State Standards as related to exemplar poems.

Adolescents Writing Poems   A rich poetry environment stimulates young people's interest in writing their own poems. A book about teaching poetry, *Just People and Other Poems for Young Readers and Paper/Pen/Poem: A Writer's Way to Begin* (Appelt, 1997), may be a natural starting place for helping adolescents to think about poetry and writing poetry. Other books that provide suggestions on how to include poetry in the classroom are *Wordplaygrounds: Reading, Writing, and Performing Poetry in the English Classroom* (O'Connor, 2004); *Awakening the Heart: Exploring Poetry in Elementary and Middle School* (Heard, 1999); *Opening a Door: Reading Poetry in the Middle School Classroom* (Janeczko, 2003); and *Poetry Aloud Here!* (Vardell, 2006)

One way to encourage interest in writing poetry is to introduce students to poets and their visions of poems as those poems are shared in class. *Letters to Poets: Conversations about Poetics, Politics, and Community* by Jennifer Firestone and DanaTeen Lomax (2008) would inspire teens to think more deeply about a poem's genesis as well as inspire them to write their own.

Teachers often start poetry writing as a collaborative effort. The class brainstorms ideas, then composes the poem orally as the teacher writes it on the board, chart paper, or screen. As students become comfortable with writing group poetry, they can branch off and compose poems in pairs or individually. Collections of poems written by young adults can appeal to students and encourage them in their own writing effort, such as Franco's edited collections, *You Hear Me? Poems and Writing by Teenage Boys* (2000) and *Things I Have to Tell You: Poems and Writing by Teenage Girls* (2001). Georgia Heard has collections of poems created from lists and pieces of print found on signs and slips of paper that provide fun ways to ease into writing poetry.

Poetry is a form of communication and so teens can be encouraged to think of an idea, feeling, or event to write about in their poems. They should be reminded that poetry does not have to rhyme and that they should write about something of interest to them. Poetry for young adults follows no absolute rules; perfection of form should not be a goal. Other suggestions to foster poetry writing include:

- Have students compile personal and class anthologies of their own poems or their favorite poems.
- Design displays of students' own poems as well as poems by favorite poets.
- Encourage students to rework a narrative poem into a different genre, such as a newspaper article or a letter. In turn, students may attempt the reverse—take a newspaper article and put it to verse.
- Design posters, individually or in groups, to illustrate a favorite poem.
- Use the works of professional poets as models by attempting imitation of a whole poem or of specific techniques.
- Read aloud several poems of one poetic form; then analyze the form to reveal the characteristics of its structure. Quatrains, cinquains, haiku, concrete poems, and limericks can be used as writing models with students once they have an appreciation for poetry and for specific poetic forms.

- Many teens are performing and publishing their work on websites on poetry jams and slams as spaces where students post their poetry, discuss poetry with young people from around the country and world, and engage in poetry performances. Websites include: Global Writes.org (globalwrites.org); Youth Speaks.org (youthspeaks.org/performances/youth-speaks-teen-poetry-slam) and Poetry Slam.com (www.poetryslam.com). Examples of students performing poetry are also on YouTube.

Some poets have suggested other models and patterns for students to follow in writing poetry. Koch's *Wishes, Lies, and Dreams* (1970/1999), Janeczko's *How to Write Poetry* (1999) and *Seeing the Blue Between: Advice and Inspiration for Young Poets* (2002), Fagin's *The List Poem: A Guide to Teaching and Writing Catalog Verse* (2000), and Jack Prelutsky's *Pizza, Pigs, and Poetry: How to Write a Poem* (2008) are useful resources for teachers who want to encourage students to compose poems.

Poetry and Teaching Ideas

The website www.ReadWriteThink.org is a partnership of the International Reading Association and the National Council of Teachers of English to provide educators with access to high-quality practices and resources through free internet-based content. Lessons and web resources to support the lessons are provided according to grade bands (e.g., 6–8 and 9–12) and areas of literacy.

Two lesson plans from this website with useful ideas for teaching poetry in grade 6 to 8 classrooms are *In the Poet's Shoes: Performing Poetry and Building Meaning* by Beth O'Connor and *Writing Free Verse in the "Voice" of Cesar Chavez* by Dori Maria Jones. Through dramatic readings and exploration of internet resources students develop their own interpretations of a poem's meaning as part of *In the Poet's Shoes* as well as give an oral performance of their own poetry. In *Verse in the "Voice,"* students become familiar with the characteristics of free verse and then write a free verse poem in the voice of labor activist César Chávez after learning about his life and work. As part of this lesson students can compose original poetry books using the website's printing press resource.

The website www.ReadWriteThink.org also has lesson plans for grades 9 to 12. The lesson plan *Ekphrasis: Using Art to Inspire Poetry* by Ann Kelly Cox encourages students to explore ekphrasis—writing inspired by art. Students read and discuss poems inspired by works of art and then search online for artwork that inspires them. The lesson includes links to online resources for research on the poem and the poet, and assignment sheets. In *Stairway to Heaven: Examining Metaphor in Popular Music* by Sue Carmichael, a set of lessons about popular culture is used to help students connect to classical texts. Students explore how lyrics of popular songs contain the same literary elements, such as metaphor, simile, and symbolism, used in the literary texts read in class. With a "literary graffiti tool" provided as part of the lesson students develop their own literary graffiti pictures.

Definition and Description of Plays

Plays, as a literary genre, refer to written dramatic compositions of scripts intended to be acted. A play may be divided into parts, called *acts,* and, in turn, each act may be divided into *scenes.* The script usually has set design, costumes, and stage directions, as well as dialogue provided for each actor. Plays are usually published as *playbooks* or *acting editions* in paperback books by publishers who specialize in plays. Playbooks are inexpensive and can be purchased directly from publishers or ordered through bookstores. Plays are also published in books and magazines.

As with other forms of literature, plays must be interesting to the target audience to be successful. A relevant topic, an interesting character or two, a character to whom the reader can relate, a plot that thickens but is ultimately resolved, conflict, humor, and natural-sounding dialogue all contribute to the interest a play has for young people. Some readers may find the play's stage directions interesting, even if they are not able to produce the play as suggested. Plays may be enjoyed in several ways:

- Read independently
- Read in small groups
- Performed as readers' theatre
- Performed as a formal theatrical presentation before an audience

In selecting plays for classroom use, the distinction between adaptations and original plays is important. Many adaptations, particularly of traditional literature, such as folktales and fables, are available. Far fewer adaptations of contemporary young adult literature are available, and *original plays,* stories originating in play form, are scarce, even though young adults indicate a preference for them. Plays are traditionally categorized within types such as drama, comedy, farce, melodrama, and tragedy, with dramas and comedies most common in plays for youth. In addition, some young adult authors have written their books in screenplay formats, such as *Monster* (1999) and *Riot* (2009) by Walter Dean Myers and *Zap: A Play* by Paul Fleishman (2005), or published a separate edition of the book, such as *Skellig: Two Plays* by David Almond (2005) and *Novio Boy: A Play* by Gary Soto (2006).

The American Alliance for Theatre and Education (AATE) sponsors the Distinguished Play Award, an award that is useful in identifying notable plays for young people. This annual award honors the playwrights and publishers of the works voted as the best original plays for young people published during the preceding year. Category A is for plays primarily for middle school and secondary age audiences. Category C is for the best adaptation of an existing work of literature. For a complete list of award winners, go to www.aate .com/?awardwinners. Other sources include the following:

- Anchorage Press Plays, one of the oldest publishers of plays for youth (www.applays .com)
- Dramatic Publishing Company, a large list of plays (www.dramaticpublishing.com)
- Children's Book and Play Review, an online journal of play reviews (https://ojs.lib .byu.edu)
- International Association of Theatre for Children and Young People, bibliographies of plays and links to resources (U.S. Section www.assitej-usa.org)
- Smith and Kraus, play anthologies for grades 7 through 12, such as 10-minute plays, short monologues, and new plays from a teen point of view (www.smithandkraus.com)
- Eldridge Publishing, one of the oldest children's play publishers (www.histage.com)

Readers' theatre is the oral presentation of literature by two or more actors, and usually a narrator, reading from a script. Unlike plays, there is little or no costuming or movement, no stage sets, and no memorized lines. Literature becomes a lived experience for readers through the use of facial expressions, voice, and a few gestures. For an audience performance, students engage in multiple rereadings to develop a fluent, expression interpretation of a story. Features typically associated with readers' theatre include the following:

- The readers and narrator typically remain on the "stage" throughout the production.
- Readers use little movement; instead, they suggest action with simple gestures and facial expressions.
- Chairs or stools are used for readers and narrator to sit on, and performers usually remain seated throughout the performance. Sometimes, certain readers sit with their backs to the audience to suggest that they are not in a particular scene.
- No costumes or stage settings are necessary and, at most, should be suggestive, rather than complete or literal, to permit the imaginations of the audience to have full rein. The use of sound effects may enhance the performance and give the impression of a radio play.
- Variations may include carefully selected background music, choral poems, and brief scenes from different stories tied together by a common theme.

Scripts adapted from a work of literature can be developed for readers' theatre by students. Short stories readily lend themselves to adaptation, as do well-selected scenes from a favorite novel and novels and nonfiction books written in multiple voices, often in verse. The qualities to seek in a story or scene are natural-sounding dialogue, strong characterization, drama or humor, and a satisfactory ending. If the original work has extensive dialogue, script writing is easy. When dialogue is separated by extensive narration, editing out all but the necessary narrative keeps the script lively, a challenge that can be taken on by students. The script begins with the title of the book or story from which the play is adapted, the name of the author, a list of characters, and usually an opening statement by the narrator. Following the introduction, the dialogue is written into script form. Students will find it useful to see an example of a readers' theatre script before being asked to develop their own. Examples of scripts and tips on scripting, staging, and performing can be found on Aaron Shepard's RT Page (www.aaronshep.com/rt).

Literature to adapt for use as readers' theatre can include virtually any literary genre—picture books for older readers, novels, short stories, biographies, poems, letters, diaries, and journals. Literature that works particularly well for script development includes:

- Novels with strong dialogue, such as *The Boy Who Saved Baseball* by John Ritter (2005) and *Feed* by M. T. Anderson (2002).
- Novels written in verse, such as *Street Love* by Walter Dean Myers (2006) and *Keesha's House* (2003) and *Spinning through the Universe* by Helen Frost (2004).
- Novels with short chapters in different voices, such as *Bull Run* (1993) and *Seedfolks* (1997) by Paul Fleischman, *Witness* by Karen Hesse (2001), *Ringside, 1925: View from the Scopes Trial* by Jennifer Bryant (2008), and *The Final Four* by Paul Valponi (2012).
- Nonfiction books that include short prose or verse pieces in different voices, such as *Voices of Ancient Egypt* (2003) and *Colonial Voices* (2008) by Kay Winters, *Hope and Tears: Ellis Island Voices* by Gwenyth Swain (2012), *Afghan Dreams: Young Voices of Afghanistan* by Tony O'Brien (2010), and *Requiem: Poems of the Terezin Ghetto* by Paul Janeczko (2011).

- Short stories, such as *There is No Long Distance Now* by Naomi Shihab Nye (2011) and *What You Wish For,* edited by Book Wish Foundation (2011).

Readers' theatre presentations give students a good opportunity to strengthen their oral reading abilities and expressive skills. The group typically reads through the script once or twice and then works on refining the interpretive aspects of each performer. Decisions can be made on the arrangement of chairs and speakers for greatest visual effect. Following each presentation, an evaluation is made by the group with the goal of improving future performances.

Readers' theatre does not require a stage or extensive rehearsal time and so is well suited to classroom reenactments of literary experiences. In readers' theatre, students have the opportunity to translate their experiences with a literary work to the medium of drama, thereby deepening their understanding of, and pleasure from, the work.

Plays and readers' theatre encourage imagination as students immerse themselves into a character and story world. Students also develop oral reading fluency and the ability to read smoothly without hesitation and with good comprehension, as well as learning to appreciate language and the richness of dialect.

References

Abrahamson, R. F. (2002). Poetry preference research: What young adults tell us they enjoy. *Voices from the Middle, 10*(2), 20–22.

Anderson, M. T. (2002). *Feed.* Cambridge, MA: Candlewick.

Appelt, K. (1997). *Just people and other poems for young readers & Paper/pen/poem: A young writer's way to begin.* Houston, TX: Absey.

Book Wish Foundation. (2011). *What you wish for: Stories and poems for Darfur.* New York: Putnams.

Bryant, J. (2008). *Ringside, 1925: Views from the Scopes trial.* New York: Yearling.

Fagin, L. (2000). *The list poem: A guide to teaching & writing catalog verse.* New York: Teachers and Writers Collaborative.

Firestone, J., & Lomax, D. (2008). *Letters to poets: Conversations about poetics, politics, and community.* Ardmore, PA: Saturnalia.

Fleishman, P. (1993). *Bull run.* New York: HarperCollins.

———. (1997). *Seedfolks.* New York: HarperCollins.

Froman, R. (1974). SOS. In *Seeing things: A book of poems.* New York: Curtis Brown.

Frost, H. (2003). *Keesha's house.* New York: Farrar.

———. (2004). *Spinning through the universe.* New York: Farrar.

Ghigna, C. (2003). The leopard of loneliness. In C. Ghigna, *A fury of motion.* Honesdale, PA: Boyds Mills.

Grimes, N. (2002). *Bronx masquerade.* New York: Dial.

Heard, G. (1999). *Awakening the heart: Exploring poetry in elementary and middle school.* Portsmouth, NH: Heinemann.

Hemp, C. (1993). Even when. In P. B. Janeczko (Ed.), *Looking for your name.* New York: Orchard.

Hemphill, S. (2007). *Your own, Sylvia: A verse portrait of Sylvia Plath.* New York: Knopf.

Hesse, K. (2001). *Witness.* New York: Scholastic.

Holbrook, S. (2002). *Wham! It's a poetry jam: Discovering performance poetry.* Honesdale, PA: Boyds Mills.

———. (2003). Evolution. In *By definition: Poems of feelings.* Honesdale, PA: Boyds Mills.

Hopkins, E. (2007). *Impulse.* New York: Margaret McElderry.

Janeczko, P. B. (1990). *The place my words are looking for: What poets say about and through their work.* New York: Bradbury.

———. (Ed.). (1999). *How to write poetry*. New York: Scholastic.

———. (Ed.). (2002). *Seeing the blue between: Advice and inspiration for young poets*. Cambridge, MA: Candlewick.

———. (2003). *Opening a door: Reading poetry in the middle school classroom*. New York: Scholastic Professional.

Koch, K. (1999). *Wishes, lies and dreams: Teaching children to write poetry*. New York: Random House. (Original work published 1970)

Koertge, R. (2006). *Shakespeare bats cleanup*. Somerville, MA: Candlewick.

Kutiper, K., & Wilson, P. (1993). Updating poetry preferences: A look at the poetry children really like. *The Reading Teacher, 47*(1), 28–35.

McCall, G. G. (2011). *Under the mesquite*. New York: Lee & Low.

Myers, W. D. (2006). *Street love*. New York: HarperCollins.

Nye, N. S. (2011). *There is no long distance now*. New York: Greenwillow.

O'Brien, T., & Sullivan, M. (2010). *Afghan dreams: Young voices of Afghanistan*. New York: Bloomsbury.

O'Connor, J. S. (2004). *Word playgrounds: Reading, writing, and performing poetry in the English classroom*. Urbana, IL: National Council of Teachers of English.

Prelutsky, J. (2008). *Pizza, pigs, and poetry: How to write a poem*. New York: Greenwillow.

Ritter, J. (2005). *The boy who saved baseball*. New York: Puffin.

Rossetti, C. (1998). Sonnet. In M. Rosen, *Classic poetry: An illustrated collection*. Illus. Paul Howard. Cambridge, MA: Candlewick.

Schwedt, R., & DeLong, J. (2002). *Young adult poetry: A survey and theme guide*. Westport, CT: Greenwood.

Terry, A. C. (1974). *Children's poetry preferences: A national survey of upper elementary grades*. Urbana, IL: National Council of Teachers of English.

Thompson, H. (2011). *Orchards*. New York: Delacorte.

———. (2013) *The language inside*. New York: Delacorte.

Valponi, P. (2012). *The Final Four*. New York: Viking.

Vardell, S. (2006). *Poetry aloud here! Sharing poetry with children*. Chicago: American Library Association.

———. (2007). *Poetry people: A practical guide to children's poets*. Santa Barbara, CA: Libraries Unlimited.

Winters, K. (2008). *Colonial voices: Hear them speak*. New York: Dutton.

———. (2003). *Voices of ancient Egypt*. New York: National Geographic.

 # Recommended Poetry Books and Plays

Ages indicated refer to content appropriateness and conceptual and interest levels. Book formats other than novels are coded as follows:

(GR)   Graphic novel

(PI)   Picture book

(COL)   Collection

Anthologies of Poetry

Collins, Billy. *Poetry 180: A Turning Back to Poetry*. Random House, 2003. Ages 13–18. Compiled by America's poet laureate, an engaging collection of contemporary poems.. See also, *180 More* (2005).

Driscoll, Michael. *A Child's Introduction to Poetry*. Illus. Meredith Hamilton. Black Dog & Leventhal, 2003. Ages 10–14. Discusses poetic forms and individual poets, with examples.

Harrison, Michael, and Christopher Stuart-Clark, editors. *The Oxford Treasury of Classic Poems*. Oxford, 2011. Ages 12–18. A collection of famous traditional poems by mostly British poets.

Johnston, Paula. *World Poetry: Evidence of Life*. Enslow, 2010. Ages 14–18. Introduction to

15 world poets with biographical info on each poet and several analyzed poems. Part of a series, Poetry Rocks!, that includes books on contemporary American poetry, early American poetry, early British poetry, modern American poetry, and modern British poetry, collected for a young adult audience.

Kennedy, Caroline, editor. *A Family of Poems: My Favorite Poetry for Children.* Illus. Jon J. Muth. Hyperion, 2005. Ages 9–14. A varied selection of classic poems from different sources, with luminous watercolor illustrations.

———. *Poems to Learn by Heart.* Illus. Jon J. Muth. Hyperion, 2013. Ages 9–14. A rich diversity of old and new poems, grouped thematically with an explanation of why each was chosen and why memorization is important.

Merchant, Natalie, selector. *Leave Your Sleep: A Collection of Classic Children's Poetry Adapted to Music.* Illus. Barbara McClintock. Frances Foster, 2012. Ages 9–14. 19th- and 20th-century British and American poems with rich visual imagery for the 19 poems and a CD of Merchant's musical compositions for each poem.

Paschen, Elise. *Poetry Speaks Who I Am.* Sourcebooks, 2010. Ages 12–15. Diverse collection of classic and contemporary poetry about the everyday feelings and experiences of teens. CD of poet readings.

Reed, Ishmael. *From Totems to Hip Hop: A Multicultural Anthology of Poetry from across the Americas 1900–2002.* Da Capo Press, 2003. Ages 14–18. Poetry from across cultural traditions and both known and new poets.

Rosenberg, Liz, editor. *The Invisible Ladder: An Anthology of Contemporary American Poems for Young Readers.* Holt, 1996. Ages 12–18. Poets comment on their poems and provide photos of themselves as children and adults.

Thematic Poetry Collections

Adoff, Arnold, editor. *I Am the Darker Brother: An Anthology of Modern Poems by African Americans.* Drawings by Benny Andrews. Simon & Schuster, 2002/1968. Ages 13–18. This revised edition includes 21 new poems and 19 additional African-American poets

Carlson, Lori M., editor. *Cool Salsa: Bilingual Poems on Growing Up Latino in the United States.* Holt, 1994. Ages 13–18. A collection of poems that express Latino youth culture.

———. *Red Hot Salsa: Bilingual Poems on Life, Love, and Victory.* Holt, 2005. Ages 12–18. Another collection of poems about the Latino experience by well-known and emerging poets.

Carlson, Lori, and Carlos Hijuelos, editors. *Burnt Sugar/Cana quemada: Contemporary Cuban Poetry in English and Spanish.* Free Press, 2006. Bilingual compilation of 20th-century poetry that spans the Cuban diaspora.

Clinton, Catherine, editor. *I, Too, Sing America: Three Centuries of African-American Poetry.* Illus. Stephen Alcorn. Houghton, 1998. Ages 11–18. A chronological arrangement of 25 African-American poets, a brief biography, and 1 or more poems for each.

———. editor. *A Poem of Her Own: Voices of American Women Yesterday and Today.* Illus. Stephen Alcorn. Abrams, 2003. Ages 11–18. Poems from 25 American women poets with a biography of each.

Cullinan, Bernice, and Deborah Wooten, editors. *Another Jar of Tiny Stars: Poems by More NCTE Award-Winning Poets.* Boyds Mills, 2009. Ages 9–14. A collection of favorite poems by NCTE Award poets.

Franco, Betsy, editor. *Falling Hard: 100 Love Poems by Teenagers.* Candlewick, 2010. Ages 13–18. Poems written by teens about love.

———. editor. *Things I Have to Tell You: Poems and Writing by Teenage Girls.* Photographs by N. Nickels. Candlewick, 2001. Ages 14–18. Poems, stories, and essays by adolescent girls about the issues in their lives.

———. editor. *You Hear Me? Poems and Writing by Teenage Boys.* Candlewick, 2001. Ages 14–18. Poems, stories, and essays by adolescent boys about the issues in their lives.

Giovanni, Nikki, editor. *Hip Hop Speaks to Children: A Celebration of Poetry with a Beat.* Sourcebooks Jabberwocky, 2008. Range of African-American poetic forms and performance styles with accompanying CD.

Greenberg, Jan. *Heart to Heart: New Poems Inspired by Twentieth Century American Art.* Abrams, 2001. Ages 12–18. A collection of poems by Americans writing about American art.

———. collector. *Side by Side: New Poetry Inspired by Art from around Our World.* Abrams, 2008. Ages 14–18. 30 international poems with the art that inspired them.

Heard, Georgia, editor. *The Arrow Finds Its Mark: A Book of Found Poems.* Illus. Antoine Guilloppe. Roaring Book Press, 2012. Ages 9–14. Poems created out of words and phrases found in everyday places.

———. editor. *Falling Down the Page.* Roaring Brook Press, 2009. Ages 10–14. List poems from contemporary poets that celebrate everyday experiences in a slim vertical volume. Useful for writing projects.

Hopkins, Lee Bennett. *America at War.* Illus. Stephen Alcorn. Simon & Schuster, 2008. Ages 10–16. A reflection on many American experiences during wartime.

———. editor. *My America: A Poetry Atlas of the United States.* Illus. Stephen Alcorn. Simon & Schuster, 2000. Ages 9–14. Poems evocative of seven geographical regions of the United States.

Janeczko, Paul B., selector. *A Foot in the Mouth: Poems to Speak, Sign and Shout.* Illus. Chris Raschka. Candlewick, 2009. Ages 9–14. Poems to read aloud in voices, some bilingual.

———. selector. *A Kick in the Head: An Everyday Guide to Poetic Forms.* Illus. Chris Raschka. Candlewick, 2005. Ages 9–14. A collection of poems of various forms with brief explanations of each form.

———. selector. *Looking for Your Name: A Collection of Contemporary Poems.* Orchard, 1993. Ages 13–18. Poems of social and political conflict.

———. selector. *A Poke in the I: A Collection of Concrete Poems.* Illus. Chris Raschka. Candlewick, 2001. Ages 10–14. A collection of concrete poems.

———. selector. *Stone Bench in an Empty Park.* Photographs by Henri Silberman. Orchard, 2000. Ages 10–13. Contemporary urban haiku with black-and-white photographs.

Janeczko, Paul B., and J. Patrick Lewis. *Birds on a Wire, or, A Jewel Tray of Stars.* Illus. Gary Lippincott. Wordsong, 2008. Ages 8–15. Small town life in springtime described using the ancient Japanese verse form called *renga,* in which 2 or more poets take turns.

Liu, Siyu, and Orel Protopopescu. *A Thousand Peaks: Poems from China.* Illus. Siyu Liu. Pacific View Press, 2001. Ages 12–18. Classical Chinese poetry and a brief cultural history of China.

Morrison, Lillian, compiler. *Way to Go! Sports Poems.* Illus. Susan Spellman. Boyds Mills, 2001. Ages 9–14. 42 poems about a variety of sports.

National Geographic, *Every Human Has Rights: A Photographic Declaration for Kids.* National Geographic, 2009. Ages 10–14. Poems by youth responding to the Universal Declaration of Rights with photographs from around the world.

Nye, Naomi Shihab, editor. *The Space between Our Footsteps: Poems and Paintings from the Middle East.* Simon & Schuster, 1998. Ages 13–18. Poems from the Middle East and North Africa.

———. editor. *This Same Sky: A Collection of Poems from Around the World.* Four Winds, 1992. Ages 11–18. Poems from 69 different countries.

———. editor. *Time You Let Me In: 25 Poets Under 25.* Greenwillow, 2010. Ages 14–18. A wide range of coming-of-age free verse poems from young adult poets, includes short bios of poets.

———. editor. *What Have You Lost?* Photographs by Michael Nye. Greenwillow, 1999. Ages 12–18. Poems about different kinds of loss.

Nye, Naomi Shihab, and Paul B. Janeczko, editors. *I Feel a Little Jumpy around You: A Book of Her Poems and His Poems Collected in Pairs.* Simon & Schuster, 1996. Ages 13–18. Pairs of poems that offer insight to how men and women look at the world.

Rochelle, Belinda. *Words with Wings: A Treasury of African-American Poetry and Art.* Harper-Collins/Amistad, 2001. Ages 10–16. Each of 20 poems is facing a painting in this large-format collection.

Rosenberg, Liz, and Deena November, editors. *I Just Hope It's Lethal: Poems of Sadness, Madness, and Joy.* Houghton, 2005. Ages 14–18.

A collection of 91 poems about emotions, especially depression.

Tadjo, Veronique, editor and illustrator. *Talking Drums: A Selection of Poems about Africa South of the Sahara.* Bloomsbury, 2004. Ages 12–16. The story of Africa through traditional and modern poetry from 16 countries.

Vecchione, Patrice, editor. *The Body Electric: An Anthology of Poems.* Holt, 2002. Ages 13–18. Poems about body image.

——. editor. *Faith and Doubt.* Holt, 2007. Ages 13–18. A themed anthology exploring many facets of faith and doubt in poems from celebrated poets around the world.

——. *Revenge and Forgiveness: An Anthology of Poems.* Holt, 2004. Ages 14–18. Poems about human nature and human emotions.

——. *Truth and Lies.* Holt, 2000. Ages 15–18. A multicultural anthology of 70 poems on truth and lies.

WritersCorps. *Paint Me Like I Am: Teen Poems from WritersCorps.* HarperTempest, 2003. Ages 1418. Anthology of 100 poems from teens in urban areas across the U.S. who took part in WritersCorps.

Poetry Books by a Single Poet

Adoff, Arnold. *Roots and Blues: A Celebration.* Illus. R. Gregory Christie. Clarion, 2011. Ages 11–14. Poems and poetic prose pieces combine with haunting paintings to create a moving meditation on the history of American blues from slavery to the stage. Free verse that often replicates the sounds and rhythms of the blues.

Agard, John. *Half-Caste and Other Poems.* Hodder, 2005. Ages 14–18. A collection of 45 poems that address race and identity. Humor.

Appelt, Kathi. *Poems from Homeroom: A Writer's Place to Start.* Holt, 2002. Ages 12–18. Poems about the experiences of young people with information about how each poem was written and an excellent bibliography of books about writing.

Atkins, Jeanine. *Borrowed Names: Poems about Laura Ingalls Wilder, Madam C.J. Walker, Marie Curie and Their Daughters.* Henry Holt, 2010. Ages 12–16. Poems in the voices of the women and their daughters, retelling their history and difficult mother-daughter relationships. Includes photos, introductions, and afterwords.

Crisler, Curtis L. *Tough Boy Sonatas.* Illus. Floyd Cooper. Boyds Mills, 2007. Ages 14–18. Voices of African-American males growing up in Gary, Indiana, about their difficult life situations.

Dunbar, Paul Laurence. *Jump Back, Honey: The Poems of Paul Laurence Dunbar.* Hyperion, 1999. Ages 10–13. A collection of the best known of the late-19th-century writer's poems.

Fleischman, Paul. *Big Talk: Poems for Four Voices.* Illus. Beppe Giacobbe. Candlewick, 2000. Ages 9–14. Poems to be read aloud by four people, with color-coded text to indicate the reader.

——. *I Am Phoenix: Poems for Two Voices.* Illus. Eric Beddows. Harper, 1985. Ages 9–14. Poems about birds; to be read aloud by two readers.

——. *Joyful Noise: Poems for Two Voices.* Illus. Eric Beddows. Harper, 1988. Ages 9–14. Poems about insects; to be read aloud by two readers.

Ghigna, Charles. *A Fury of Motion: Poems for Boys.* Boyds Mills, 2003. Ages 12–18. Poems to appeal to boys.

Giovanni, Nikki. *The Collected Poetry of Nikki Giovanni, 1968–1998.* Harper, 2007. Ages 12–16. 200 poems written by Giovanni, with extensive notes and afterword.

Glenn, Mel. *Class Dismissed! High School Poems.* Photographs by Michael J. Bernstein. Clarion, 1982. Ages 12–18. 70 poems about the emotional lives of high school students.

Grady, Cynthia. *I Lay My Stitches Down: Poems of American Slavery.* Illus. Michele Wood. Eerdmans, 2012. Ages 10–16. Poems of 10 lines with 10 syllables to symbolize quilt squares convey the agony and dreams of enslaved African Americans. Each poem is accompanied by information on slavery and the quilt-block pattern.

Grandits, John. *Blue Lipstick: Concrete Poems.* Clarion, 2007. Ages 10–18. A humorous collection of 34 concrete poems featuring teenage life.

Holbrook, Sara. *By Definition: Poems of Feelings.* Boyds Mills, 2003. Ages 10–13. Poems about early adolescence.

———. *Walking on the Boundaries of Change.* Boyds Mills, 1998. Ages 11–18. A collection of poems that capture adolescents' feelings about social life.

Holbrook, Sara, and Allan Wolf. *More Than Friends: Poems from Him and Her.* Boyds Mills, 2008. Ages 12–16. Alternating voices of a boy and a girl in the throes of affection. Poetic forms are explained in an addendum.

Janeczko, Paul B. *Requiem: Poems of the Terezin Ghetto.* Candlewick, 2011. Ages 14–18. Disturbing and intense poems in the voices of captives and captors in the infamous concentration camp.

Johnson, Angela. *The Other Side: Shorter Poems.* Orchard, 1998. Ages 11–16. Poems about growing up as an African-American girl in Alabama.

Lawson, JonArno. *Black Stars in a White Night Sky.* Wordsong, 2008. Ages 10–15. Serious, funny, and imaginative poems on a wide range of topics for adolescents who want to explore more complex poetry.

Levithan, David. *The Realm of Possibility.* Knopf, 2004. Ages 14–18. A collection of linked poems in the voices of high school students describing their experiences and relationships. Uses a range of poetic forms.

Lewis, J. Patrick. *The Brothers' War: Civil War Voices in Verse.* National Geographic, 2007. Ages 12–18. Poems honoring historical and fictional heroes.

———. *Edgar Allan Poe's Pie: Math Puzzlers in Classic Poems.* Illus. Michael Slack. Harcourt, 2012. Ages 10–14. Humorous poetry parodies of classic poems that present word problems to solve.

———. *Vherses: A Celebration of Outstanding Women.* Illus. Mark Summers. Creative, 2005. Ages 9–14. Literary portraits of 14 women.

———. *When Thunder Comes: Poems for Civil Rights Leaders.* Illus. various illustrators. Chronicle, 2013. Ages 9–14. Poems on 17 civil rights leaders from around the world in a range of poetry forms and styles. Integrates lesser-known individuals.

Myers, Walter Dean. *Blues Journey.* Illus. Christopher Myers. Holiday, 2003. Ages 10–14. Original poems honoring the blues and its themes.

———. *Here in Harlem: Poems in Many Voices.* Holiday, 2004. Ages 13–18. Poems in the voices of people living and working in Harlem.

———. *Jazz.* Illus. Christopher Myers. Holiday, 2006. Ages 8–12. 15 poems celebrating the stages of jazz.

Nelson, Marilyn. *The Freedom Business.* Illus. Deborah Dancy. Wordsong, 2008. A cycle of poems set in counterpoint against a slave narrative that inspired them. Mixed-media artwork heightens the emotions.

———. *Fortune's Bones: The Manumission Requiem.* Front Street, 2004. **(PI)** Ages 11–16. Poems in multiple voices about an enslaved man whose skeleton became a museum exhibit, includes archival photos and a prose narrative. Raises questions about where humanity lies. Set in 1798.

———. *Sweethearts of Rhythm: The Story of the Greatest All-Girl Swing Band in the World.* Illus. Jerry Pinkney. Dial, 2009. Ages 10–15. Poems in the voices of the band members' instruments with vibrant illustrations that establish the historical context. Includes comprehensive backmatter on the band.

———. *A Wreath for Emmett Till.* Illus. Philippe Lardy. Houghton, 2005. **(PI)** Ages 14–18. An illustrated memorial to the lynched teen through interlocking sonnets in a form called a heroic crown of sonnets.

Nye, Naomi Shihab. *A Maze Me: Poems for Girls.* Illus. Terre Maher. Greenwillow, 2005. Ages 12–18. Free verse poems, newly published, about everyday experiences girls will understand.

Park, Linda Sue. *Tap Dancing on the Roof: Sijo.* Illus. Istvan Banyai. Clarion, 2007. Ages 10–16. Sijo poems, a three-line traditional Korean poetic form, with lighthearted examples.

Reynolds, Jason, and Griffin, Jason. *My Name Is Jason, Mine Too: Our Story, Our Way.* Harper Teen, 2009. Ages 14–18. Autobiographical poetry and art depicting an interracial friendship and staying true to your dreams.

Rylant, Cynthia. *Boris*. Harcourt, 2005. Ages 11–16. Poems speaking to a cat about his life and the life of the narrator. Free verse.

Shange, Ntozake. *We Troubled the Waters*. Illus. Rod Brown. Collins, 2009. Ages 11–14. Collection of art and poetry vignettes from the Civil Rights Movement. Lives of everyday people and major figures.

Sidman, Joyce. *Butterfly Eyes and Other Secrets of the Meadow*. Illus. Beth Krommes. Houghton, 2006. Ages 9–12. An ecosystem of a meadow captured in poems combining riddles and science information.

———. *This Is Just to Say: Poems of Apology and Forgiveness*. Illus. Pamela Zagarenski. Houghton, 2007. Ages 10–16. Fictional students' "sorry" poems with responses from the fictional recipients of the poems.

———. *What the Heart Knows—Chants, Charms and Blessings*. Illus. Pamela Zagarenski. Houghton Mifflin, 2013. Ages 12–16. Poems to provide comfort, courage, and humor at difficult moments of life.

———. *The World According to Dog: Poems and Teen Voices*. Illus. Doug Mindell. Houghton, 2003. Ages 13–18. Poems about dogs and essays by teens about their dogs.

Singer, Marilyn. *Mirror Mirror: A Book of Reversible Verse*. Illus. Josee Masse. Dutton, 2010. Ages 10–14. Short poems, which when reversed, provide new perspectives on fairy tale characters. Introduces reverse as a new form of poetry. See also *Follow Follow: A Book of Reverso Poems* (2013).

Soto, Gary. *A Fire in My Hands*. Harcourt, 2006. Ages 12–15. A revised edition with new poems on the emotions of small moments in everyday life. With notes from the poet on inspirations for poems.

———. *Partly Cloudy: Poems of Love and Longing*. Harcourt, 2009. Ages 12–18. Tender and truthful love poetry.

Spires, Elizabeth. *I Heard God Talking to Me: William Edmondson and His Stone Carvings*. Farrar, Straus, & Giroux, 2009. Ages 12–16. Poems that reflect the hard work and spiritual inspiration of a self-taught African-American sculptor. Combines photography, sculpture, and poetry.

Single Illustrated Poems and Graphic Formats

Chwast, Seymour, adaptor. *Dante's Divine Comedy*. Bloomsbury, 2010. **(GR)** Ages 14–18. A graphic adaptation that distills the poet's classic work into 100 pages of visual imagery and high-level page design.

Hinds, Gareth. *The Odyssey: A Graphic Novel*. Candlewick, 2010. **(GR)** Ages 14–18. Lavish retelling of Homer's epic poem that combines the realistic and the fantastic in lush watercolors, fluid lines, and various sized panels.

Hughes, Langston. *I, Too, Am America*. Illus. Bryan Collier. Simon & Schuster, 2012. **(PI)** Ages 10–16. Classic poem illustrated with collage spreads blending oil paintings with cut paper; focus on African-American porters.

———. *The Negro Speaks of Rivers*. Illus. E. B. Lewis. Disney/Jump at the Sun, 2009. **(PI)** Ages 10–16. Hughes' signature song of the Harlem Renaissance is poignantly expressed through watercolor illustrations.

———. *My People*. Photographs by Charles R. Smith Jr. Atheneum, 2009. Ages 10–16. **(PI)** Artful sepia photographs of faces joyfully celebrate the diversity of African-American culture. Visual images use metaphor and rhythm.

Lewis, Carroll. *Jabberwocky: The Classic Poem from Lewis Carroll's* Through the Looking-Glass and What Alice Found There. Illus. Christopher Myers. Hyperion, 2007. **(PI)** Ages 10–14. A re-imagination of a classic poem as a face-off on an urban basketball court with a hero who has a monstrously outsized hand.

Longfellow, Henry Wadsworth. *Paul Revere's Ride: The Landlord's Tale*. Illus. Charles Santore. HarperCollins, 2003. **(PI)** Ages 9–14. Dramatic illustrations accompany this classic poem.

Noyes, Alfred. The *Highway Man*. Illus. Murray Kimber. Kids Can Press, 2009. **(PI)** Ages 12–16. Depicts the classic poem with an art deco style and a film noir palette through urban imagery and a motorcycle-riding rebel.

Poe, Edgar Allen. *The Raven*. Illus. Ryan Price. Kids Can Press, 2006. **(PI)** Ages 12–16. The tortured mind of the grieving narrator of Poe's classic poem is matched with nightmarish tortured visual imagery. Visions of Poetry series.

Thayer, Ernest. *Casey at the Bat.* Illus. Joe Morse. Kids Can Press, 2010. **(PI)** Ages 12–16. An urban update to this classic poem with angular exaggerated figures that convey an angry energy. Visions of Poetry series.

Plays for Young Adults

Allen, Laurie. *Comedy Scenes for Student Actors: Short Sketches for Young Performers.* Meriwether, 2009. **(COL)** Ages 13–18. 31 short scenes that address issues common to most young adults

Almond, David. *Skellig: Two Plays.* Paw Prints, 2008. Ages 11–15. Based on the book by the same name and includes the play, "Wild Girl, Wild Boy."

Barchers, Suzanne, and Jennifer Kroll. *Classic Readers Theatre for Young Adults.* **(COL)** Libraries Unlimited, 2002. Ages 11–14. 16 scripts useful for readers' theater productions in middle school classrooms.

Brockway-Henson, Amy. *The Hobo Jungle.* AATE Playwrights Network, 2012. Ages 14–18. Based on oral histories of former young hobos traveling the U.S. during the Great Depression.

Bush, Max. *Looking Out.* AATE Playwrights Network, 2012. Ages 13–18. Questioning of how any or all of several groups of boys are involved in an attack on a jogger in a park.

Creech, Sharon. *Replay.* HarperCollins, 2007. Ages 11–15. Novel about a boy who is considered a dreamer by his family, but his life is full of possibilities and stories. Full play at the end of the book.

Daugherty, Linda. *Bless Cricket, Crest Toothpaste, and Tommy Tune.* Anchorage Play Press, 2004. Ages 13–18. Cricket, a high school student, tries to keep her brother with Down syndrome a secret from her friends.

Fleischman, Paul. *Zap: A Play.* Candlewick, 2006. Ages 14–17. An imaginary audience has zappers to change the channel between 7 plays, mixing Shakespeare with Chekhov, Tennessee Williams, and Agatha Christie.

Guehring, Brian. *The Misfits.* AATE Playwrights Network, 2012. Ages 12–16. Adaptation of James Howe's book about four 7th grade misfits

who run for student council. Addresses name-calling and bullying.

Jennings, Coleman. *Theatre for Children: Fifteen Classic Plays.* St. Martin's Press, 2005. **(COL)** Ages 12–15. Includes script for *Witch of Blackbird Pond.*

Myers, Walter Dean. *Monster.* Amistad, 2004. Ages 13–17. Novel written as a screenplay about the trial of a young African-American boy accused of murder.

———. *Riot.* Egmont, 2009. Ages 12–16. Novel written as screenplay about riots of Irish Americans against African Americans in 1863. Focus on Claire, a biracial teen struggling with identity.

Saunders, Dudley. *Abe.* Anchorage Plays Press, 2008. Ages 13–17. Dramatizes period of Abraham Lincoln's life from the ages of 8 to 21, which is largely unknown by the general public.

Schroeder-Arce, Roxanne. *Sangre de un angel/Blood of an Angel.* Anchorage Press Plays, 2008. Ages 13–18. (Bilingual: English/Spanish) Choices and life consequences, immigration, acculturation, identity, and guns.

Shurtz, Raymond King. *Charlie Foster.* Anchorage Press Plays, 2007. Ages 13–18. A coming-of-age story about teens trying to comprehend the life of Charlie Foster, a kid no one knew until he drowned.

Soto, Gary. *Novio Boy: A Play.* Houghton, 2006. Ages 13–17. A comedy about the advice 9th grade Mexican American Rudy gets after asking an 11th grade girl on a date.

Swortzell, Lowell. *Around the World in 21 Plays.* Applause, 2000. **(COL)** Ages 12–17. Plays from around the world that address issues teens face in particular cultures.

Young, Rebecca. *10-Minute Plays for Middle School Performers: Plays for a Variety of Cast Sizes.* Meriwether, 2008. **(COL)** Ages 11–14. Learning how to act, as well as scripts for readers' theatre.

Zeder, Susan. *Doors.* Anchorage Press Plays, 2007. Ages 12–17. Contemporary play about a boy and his parents on the day the parents are separating to get a divorce.

Chapter Eight

Literature for a Diverse Society

We live in a global society, filled with the richness of cultural diversity as well as the oppression of inequity and racism. Literature can provide a pathway to understanding diverse ways of living, valuing our connections as human beings, and challenging inequities. The first part of this chapter, "Multicultural and International Literature," identifies books that highlight cultural diversity around the world and within marginalized groups in the United States. The second part, "An Education That Is Multicultural and Intercultural," focuses on ways educators can make their teaching relevant to students and to the interconnected world in which they live.

Multicultural and International Literature

Multicultural literature and international literature are *not* genres; rather, they are books that occur in all genres. Many references to these books and authors have been integrated into trends and issues, notable author and illustrator lists, and recommended booklists in the genre chapters. In an ideal, culturally integrated world, such inclusion would be sufficient. But the groups and perspectives represented in multicultural literature have, until recently, been absent or misrepresented in books for adolescents and remain underrepresented today. Although international books are growing in availability, they remain a very small percentage of the books published for young adults. Furthermore, neither multicultural nor international literature is well known or fully recognized by the mainstream. These issues gain urgency due to changing demographics in the United States and the globalization of society that increases the need for books to prepare young people for living in a changing and ever more diverse world.

The mismatch between the cultural diversity of adolescents and the books available for them as readers is striking. In 2010, 46 percent of the students in public schools were from minority populations, indicating that the minority will soon become the majority (U.S. Department of Education, 2012). At the same time, the United States is experiencing the largest influx of immigrants since the early 1900s, further increasing the diversity of students. More than 14 million immigrants settled in the United States between 2000 and 2010, coming from all parts of the world, with the majority from Mexico, China and Taiwan, India, Philippines, Vietnam, El Salvador, Cuba, and Korea (U.S. Census Bureau, 2010).

Although the last several decades have seen positive changes in the status of multicultural and international literature in the United States, there is still a marked shortage of both books and authors from within those cultures. The Cooperative Children's Book Center (Homing, Lindgren, & Schliesman, 2013) reported the following statistics from approximately 3,600 new children's and young adult books they reviewed in 2012:

- 119 books (3 percent) had significant African or African-American content of which 55 books were created by a black author and/or illustrator.
- 76 books (2 percent) had significant Asian/Pacific or Asian-/Pacific-American content of which 31 books were created by an author and/or illustrator of Asian/Pacific heritage.
- 54 books (1.5 percent) had significant Latino content and of which 35 were created by a Latino author and/or illustrator.
- 22 books (0.6 percent) featured American Indian themes, topics, or characters of which 7 books were created by an American Indian author and/or illustrator.

A broader indication of the shortage is to note that less than 8 percent of the new children's and adolescent books published in 2012 were by or about people of color, even though these groups represent more than 38 percent of the population (U.S. Census Bureau, 2010). Another problematic indicator is the recent decrease in books depicting people of color, with a decrease from 13 percent of the new books in 2008 to 8 percent in 2012.

In addition, only 2 to 3 percent of the books published for young people are translated books—books originally published in another country in another language and then translated into English and published in the United States These books are a rich source of insider perspectives on global cultures, but very few are available to American readers. This percentage stands in sharp contrast to other countries, where 30 to 50 percent of books are translated.

Since books reflecting multicultural and international perspectives continue to be such a small percentage of the total published books, special efforts are essential to identify and make these books available for adolescents. In addition to not enough books, subtle issues of racism and stereotypes continue to be problematic. All readers have the right to see themselves within a book; to find the truth of their experiences, rather than misrepresentations, and so many challenges remain in the writing and publication of multicultural and international literature.

Definitions and Descriptions

Multicultural literature is defined in various ways by educators and scholars. Some define it broadly as all books about people and their individual or group experiences within a particular culture, including mainstream cultures. Most define it more specifically as literature by and about groups that have been marginalized by dominant European-American cultures in the United States. This definition includes racial, ethnic, religious, and language minorities, those living with physical or mental disabilities, gays and lesbians, and people living in poverty. This chapter highlights literature by and about the racial, religious, and language groups in the United States who have created a substantial body of young adult literature. This includes literature by and about African Americans, Asian/Pacific Americans (including people of Chinese, Hmong, Japanese, Korean, and Vietnamese descent), Latinos (including Cuban Americans, Mexican Americans, Puerto Ricans, and others of Spanish descent), religious cultures (including Buddhist, Hindu, Jewish, and Muslim), and American Indians (a general term referring to the many tribes). Examples of books about these and other marginalized groups are found throughout the genre chapters.

International literature in the United States refers to books that are set in countries outside of the United States. The focus of this chapter is on books originally written and published in countries other than the United States for adolescents of those countries and later published in this country. These books can be subdivided into three categories:

- *English Language Books.* Books originally written in English in another country and then published or distributed in the United States, such as the Harry Potter series (United Kingdom).

- *Translated Books.* Books written in a language other than English in another country, then translated into English and published in the United States, such as *Inkheart* by Cornelia Funke (Germany).

- *Foreign Language Books.* Books written and published in a language other than English in another country, then published or distributed in the United States in that language, such as *Le Petit Prince* by Antoine de Saint-Exupery (France).

The value of international literature is that both the author and the intended readers are insiders to a specific culture, and so these books are an excellent source of insider perspectives on that culture. On the other hand, U.S. readers sometimes struggle with unfamiliar narrative structures, cultural events, people, and terminology, and so may lose interest or struggle with comprehension. Another caution is that readers cannot assume a translated book necessarily reflects an insider perspective. *The Killer's Tears* is a translated book written by Anne-Laure Bondoux, a French author, but the book is set in Chile, an outside culture for that author.

Many authors and illustrators of books set in international contexts are from the United States. These books are written and published in the United States primarily for an audience of U.S. readers, rather than written for adolescents of that specific culture. These books, often referred to as ***global literature,*** have been integrated into other chapters and are not included in this chapter. Global literature is thus a broader term that includes international literature, but also includes the following types of books:

- Books written by immigrants from another country who reside in the United States and write about their country of origin, for example, *Keeping Corner* by Kashmira Sheth (India). Often these authors came as young children or young adults to the United States and so combine insider knowledge of a global culture with knowledge of U.S. readers. One issue is that their insider knowledge may be dated, based in memories of their childhood rather than contemporary life in that culture.

- Books written by U.S. authors who draw from their family's heritage in their country of origin, but whose own experiences have always been in the United States, for example, *The Surrender Tree* by Margarita Engle (Cuba). These authors tap into cultural values and beliefs based in family experiences and have access to family and community resources, but may need to research specific cultural details.

- Books written by U.S. authors who have long-term experiences in another country over time, for example, *This Thing Called the Future* by J. L. Powers (South Africa). Long-term experiences in a culture can develop in-depth understandings of core cultural values and access to resources, providing that the author interacts with insiders from an open-minded perspective, rather than judging the culture through Western views or living in a separate community within that country.

- Books written by U.S. authors who research a particular country and who may or may not visit that country as part of their research, for example, *Endangered* by Eliot Schrefer (Congo) and *The Dreamer* by Pam Muñoz Ryan (Chile). These authors need to engage in careful, in-depth research to avoid inauthentic or inaccurate cultural representations.

- Books written by a U.S. author in collaboration with someone from that culture, for example, *The Queen of Water* by Laura Resau with Maria Virginia Farinango (Ecuador). A current trend is for authors who are outsiders to closely collaborate with an insider who is an informant about cultural details.

One complication is that some authors live and work across global contexts. Cornelia Funke lived and wrote in Germany for many years but now lives in the United States as her primary residence. She still writes her books in German and regularly returns to Germany and so is considered an international author. Books by authors who are immigrants to the United States are not considered international because they often came as children or adolescents and have U.S. citizenship; however, the line between them and authors who retain their citizenship but are long-term residents of the United States is very blurry. In a world where global mobility is becoming the norm, the distinctions between international and global literature may no longer be relevant. The more important issue is considering the range of author experiences and perspectives as related to authenticity under the broader label of global literature.

The Value of Multicultural and International Literature for Young Adults

Multicultural and international literature builds bridges of understanding across countries and cultures, connecting adolescents to their home cultures and to the world beyond their homes. This literature benefits adolescents in the following ways:

- Gives young people who are members of marginalized groups or recent immigrants the opportunity to develop a better sense of who they are and of their agency.
- Develops an understanding of and appreciation for diverse cultures, bringing alive those histories, traditions, and people.
- Addresses contemporary issues of race, religion, poverty, exceptionalities, and sexual orientation from the perspectives of members of those groups to provide more complete understandings of current issues and of people who belong to these groups, thus challenging prejudice and discrimination.
- Adds the perspective of marginalized groups and global cultures to the study of history, thereby giving students a more complete understanding of past events.
- Helps young people realize the social injustices endured by particular peoples in the United States and around the world, both now and in the past, to build a determination to work for a more equitable future.
- Builds young people's interest in people and places and paves the way to a deeper understanding and appreciation of the geographical and historical content encountered in textbooks and content-area studies.
- Provides authenticity through literature written by insiders to a country, region, or ethnic group and allows members of that group to define themselves. These portrayals challenge the typical media coverage of violence and crises.
- Develops a bond of shared experience with young people of other ethnicities and nations and enables young people to acquire cultural literacy from a global perspective.

While textbooks and books can both provide adolescents with information about a country, literature invites them into the world of people from that culture and provides rich details about daily life, human emotions, and relationships, answering the questions that are significant to them. Textbooks may provide facts about a country, but novels about that country show the implications of the facts for adolescents' lives and help readers "live" in the country for a time.

Evaluation and Selection of Multicultural and International Literature

In addition to the requirement that literature have high literary merit, multicultural and international books need to be examined for cultural authenticity, an analysis of the extent to which a book reflects the core beliefs and values and depicts the details of everyday life and language for a specific cultural group. Given the diversity within all cultural groups, there is never one image of life within any culture, and so underlying world views are often more important to consider. Readers from the culture depicted in a book need to be able to identify and feel affirmed that what they are reading rings true in their lives; readers from another culture need to be able to identify and learn something of value about cultural similarities and differences (Fox & Short, 2003). The following criteria should be considered when evaluating and selecting multicultural and international books:

- *Are the cultural beliefs and values authentic from the perspective of that group?* Explore the background of the author and illustrator to determine their experiences and research related to this story (check their websites). Examine the values and beliefs of characters and whether they connect to the actual lives of people from within that culture.

- *Are the cultural details accurate?* Examine the details of everyday life, such as food, clothing, homes, and speech patterns, represented in the text and illustrations and determine whether they fit within the range of experiences of that culture.

- *Is culturally authentic language integrated into the text?* Look for the natural integration of the language or dialect of a specific cultural group, especially within dialogue. Some terms or names in the original language of translated books should be retained, instead of "Americanizing" all of the language and cultural references. A glossary of foreign words found in the text with their meanings and pronunciation is helpful.

- *What kinds of power relationships exist between characters?* Examine which characters are in roles of power or significance in a book, with a particular focus on how the story is resolved and who is in leadership and action roles.

- *Whose perspectives are portrayed and who is the intended audience for the book?* Look at whose perspectives and experiences are portrayed and who tells the story. In particular, consider whether the story is told from a mainstream or European-American perspectives about ethnically or globally diverse characters. Also consider whether the intended audience is adolescents from within that culture or if the book was written to inform a mainstream audience about a culture.

- *What is the balance between historic and contemporary representations across books about this group?* The majority of literature about global and ethnic cultures is found in the genres of traditional literature and historical fiction, creating stereotypes of these cultures as dated and set in the past. Search for books that reflect contemporary images.

- *What is the representation of a particular group across books?* No one book can definitively describe a culture or cultural experience. Look for a range of books that provide multiple representations of a culture and be aware of particular images that are overrepresented—for example, most books depict the Middle East as a rural landscape of sand and camels and as a place of violence and terrorism. These overrepresentations reflect and create stereotypes of a particular group.

Early Important Works of Multicultural Literature

Date	Literary Work/Event	Genre/Significance
1923	*The Voyages of Dr. Dolittle* by Hugh Lofting wins Newbery Medal	Modern fantasy; crudely stereotyped characters accepted as norm
1932	*Waterless Mountain* by Laura Armer wins Newbery Medal	Realistic fiction; positive young adult book about people of color in early 1900s
1946	*The Moved-Outers* by Florence C. Means wins Newbery Honor	Realistic fiction; signaled a departure from stereotyped depiction of people of color
1949	*Story of the Negro* by Arna Bontemps wins Newbery Honor	Informational book; first minority author to win a Newbery Honor
1970–1974	*Sounder* by William Armstrong, *Julie of the Wolves* by Jean C. George, and *The Slave Dancer* by Paula Fox win Newbery Medals	Historical fiction; books by European-Americans with strong multicultural protagonists or themes
1975	*M. C. Higgins, the Great* by Virginia Hamilton wins Newbery Medal	Realistic fiction; first book by an author of color to win the Newbery Medal
1976	*Dragonwings* by Laurence Yep selected as Newbery Honor Book	Historical fiction; first Chinese American to win a Newbery Honor
1977	*Roll of Thunder, Hear My Cry* by Mildred Taylor wins Newbery Medal	Historical fiction; precedent established for members of a culture to write authentically about their own people and culture

Book awards identify high-quality multicultural and international books. The Coretta Scott King Award is given annually to an African-American author and illustrator. The Américas Award and the Pura Belpré Award honor outstanding Latino authors and illustrators of books with Latino content; the Asian Pacific American Award for Literature honors outstanding work by Asian-American authors and illustrators; and the American Indian Youth Literature Awards honors writing and illustrations by and about American Indians. These awards encourage the publication of more and better quality literature highlighting the experiences of diverse cultures.

Awards for international literature include the Mildred L. Batchelder Award, given to a U.S. publisher of the most distinguished translated children's book to encourage the translation and publication of international books. The Outstanding International Books List (www.usbby.org) and Notable Books for a Global Society (www.tcnj.edu/childlit) are annual award lists. The Middle East Book Awards (www.meoc.us) honors books that contribute to understanding the Middle East and its societies and cultures, with a focus on the Arab World, Iran, Israel, Turkey, and Afghanistan. Also, many countries have their own national awards, similar to the U.S. Newbery and Caldecott awards. The Hans Christian Andersen award winners and nominees are a good source of the most outstanding authors and illustrators from around the world (www.ibby.org). Worlds of Words (www.wowlit.org) has a searchable database of international literature available in the United States and two online journals with book reviews of cultural authenticity and the use of this literature in classrooms.

Early Important Works of International Literature

Date	Literary Work	Genre/Country of Origin
1719	*Robinson Crusoe* by Daniel Defoe	Realistic fiction, adventure, survival/England
1726	*Gulliver's Travels* by Jonathan Swift	Modern fantasy, adventure/England
1813	*Pride and Prejudice* by Jane Austen	Realistic fiction/England
1846	*A Book of Nonsense* by Edward Lear	Poetry (limericks)/England
1850, 1861	*Great Expectations* by Charles Dickens	Realistic fiction/England
1864	*Journey to the Center of the Earth* by Jules Verne	Science fiction/France
1865	*Alice's Adventures in Wonderland* by Lewis Carroll	Modern fantasy/England
1883	*Treasure Island* by Robert Louis Stevenson	Realistic fiction, adventure/England
1894	*The Jungle Book* by Rudyard Kipling	Modern fantasy/India (English author)
1908	*Anne of Green Gables* by Lucy M. Montgomery	Realistic fiction/Canada
1937	*The Hobbit* by J. R. R. Tolkien	Modern fantasy/England

In recent years, small presses have been a source of multicultural and international books that are particularly valuable for their cultural points of view.

- Asian American Curriculum Project. Publishes and distributes Asian-American books from small presses. www.asianamericanbooks.com. (Also see Asia for Kids at www.atk.com.)
- Cinco Puntos. Focuses on the U.S./Mexico border region, the Southwest, and Mexico. www.cincopuntos.com
- Piñata Books/Arte Publico. Publishes children's books with a Latino perspective, including many bilingual books. www.latinoteca.com/arte-publico-press/pinata-books
- Just Us Books. Produces African-American books that enhance the self-esteem of African-American children. www.justusbooks.com
- Lee & Low Books. Asian-American-owned company that stresses authenticity in stories for Asian-American, Latino, and African-American children. Also includes

Children's Book Press, an imprint that publishes folktales and contemporary picture books, often bilingual, for Latino, Native American, and Asian-American children. www.leeandlow.com

- Oyate. This Native American organization critically evaluates books with Native themes and distributes books, particularly those written and illustrated by Native people. www.oyate.org. Salina Bookshelf is an example of a small press that focuses on a particular tribe, the Dine. http://www.salinabookshelf.com/

In addition, the United States Board on Books for Young People (USBBY) has a series with extensive annotated bibliographies for children and young adults, the most recent of which is *Bridges to Understanding,* edited by Linda Pavonetti (2011). Evaluating and selecting multicultural and international literature is not enough to ensure that students will actually read the books. Without adult guidance, adolescents tend to choose books about adolescents like themselves, so invite them to explore these books through reading them aloud, giving booktalks, and encouraging discussion in literature circles.

Types of Multicultural Literature

Each ethnic group contains subgroups that differ from one another in characteristics such as country of origin, language, race, traditions, socioeconomic status, and present location. These differences are significant and must be considered in selecting a range of books for a collection in order to guard against presenting these groups as completely uniform or selecting literature that does so. Gross overgeneralization is not only inaccurate but also a form of stereotyping.

African-American Literature　African Americans have produced the largest body of multicultural literature for young people in the United States (Bishop, 2007). A genre particularly well represented is poetry, such as *Sweethearts of Rhythm* by Marilyn Nelson. African Americans have told the stories of their lives in the United States through both historical and realistic fiction. These stories often include painfully harsh but accurate accounts of racial oppression, as in Sharon Draper's historical fiction account of slavery in the Carolinas, *Copper Sun,* or Mildred Taylor's historical fiction saga of the close-knit Logan family, including *Roll of Thunder, Hear My Cry,* and in Jaime Adoff's contemporary realistic novel *The Death of Jayson Porter.* Such stories can be balanced with more positive, encouraging contemporary realistic stories, such as Angela Johnson's *The First Part Last* and Walter Dean Myers' *What They Found.*

African-American nonfiction primarily focuses on the Civil Rights era, such as Elizabeth Partridge's *Marching for Freedom,* and biographies, featuring sports heroes as well as those from a broader spectrum of achievement. For example, see *Hand in Hand: Ten Black Men Who Changed America* by Andrea Pinkney and *Best Shot in the West: The Adventures of Nat Love* by Pat McKissack. Kadir Nelson's *Heart and Soul* combines historical information and biography to create powerful narratives and dramatic images that depict the complex ways in which African Americans contributed to and shaped the history of America.

American Indian and Indigenous Literature　Although much has been written about American Indians, relatively little has been written by members of these cultures, and so this body of literature is dominated by outsider perspectives and issues of authenticity. American Indians who are known for their young adult books include Louise Erdrich,

Notable Authors of Multicultural Literature

African-American

Christopher Paul Curtis, author whose characters cope with life in and around Flint, Michigan. *Bud, Not Buddy; The Watsons Go to Birmingham; Bucking the Sarge.* www.christopherpaulcurtis.com

Sharon Draper, author best known for contemporary African-American characters who confront real-life problems. *Forged by Fire; November Blues; Battle of Jericho.* www.sharondraper.com

Walter Dean Myers, author of gritty, contemporary novels in urban settings and war contexts. *Scorpions; Somewhere in the Darkness; Monster; Street Love; Sunrise over Fallajah.* www.walterdeanmyers.net

Jacqueline Woodson, author noted for introspective novels with strong characterization. *I Hadn't Meant to Tell You This; Miracle's Boys; Locomotion; Beneath a Meth Moon.* www.jacquelinewoodson.com

American Indian

Sherman Alexie, author of penetrating novels and short stories about American Indians. *The Absolutely True Diary of a Part-time Indian; The Toughest Indian in the World.* www.fallsapart.com

Joseph Bruchac, author of fiction and nonfiction about contemporary and historical American Indians. *Code Talker; Winter People; Sacajawea.* www.josephbruchac.com

Louise Erdrich, author of historical fiction novels about Ojibwa life in northern Minnesota, mid-1800s. *The Birchbark House; The Game of Silence; The Porcupine Year.*

Asian-American

Cynthia Kadohata, author of historical fiction about Japanese Americans coping with prejudice and finding strength in family. *Kira-Kira; Weedflower; Outside Beauty.* www.kira-kira.us

Kashmira Sheth, author of historical and contemporary novels about India and Indian-Americans. *Blue Jasmine; Keeping Corner.* http://kashmirasheth.com

Gene Luen Yang, author of comics and graphic novels that combine myth with contemporary identity struggles. *American Born Chinese; Level Up; Boxers; Saints.* http://geneyang.com

Latino

Julia Alvarez, author who writes about life in the Dominican Republic and in the United States. *Before We Were Free; How the Garcia Girls Lost Their Accents* (short stories). www.juliaalvarez.com

Benjamin Alire Sáenz, author and poet who writes about issues of Mexican-American identity, family, and sexuality. *Sammy & Juliana in Hollywood; Aristotle and Dante Discover the Secrets of the Universe.*

Gary Soto, author of contemporary stories about the Mexican-American experience. *Trading Places; Baseball in April and Other Stories; Facts of Life.* www.garysoto.com

Religious Cultures

Rukhsana Khan, Pakistani-Canadian author of picture books and novels with Muslim characters. *Wanting Mor; Big Red Lollipop; Muslim Child.* www.rukhsanakhan.com

Sonia Levitin, author of books about Jewish immigration and experiences. *Journey to America; Silver Days; Strange Relations.* www.sonialevitin.com

Excellent Multicultural Literature to Read Aloud

Alexie, Sherman. *The Absolutely True Diary of a Part-Time Indian.* Junior transfers to an all-white high school.

Budhos, Marina. *Ask Me No Questions.* Muslim family, immigration issues after 9-11.

de la Peña, Matt. *Mexican Whiteboy.* Sports, streets, biracial identity

Draper, Sharon. *Just Another Hero.* Urban teens, struggles at home and school.

Edwardson, Debby. *My Name Is Not Easy.* Indigenous youth in Catholic boarding school, Alaska, 1960s.

Garcia, Cristina. *I Wanna Be Your Shoebox.* Multiracial teen, relationship with grandfather.

Jaramillo, Ann. *La Linea.* Crossing from Mexico to the United States.

Kadohata, Cynthia. *Weedflower.* Japanese-American internment camp.

McCall, Guadalupe Garcia. *Under the Mesquite.* Verse novel, family struggle, death of mother.

Woodson, Jacqueline. *Beneath a Meth Moon.* Addiction, loss and upheaval, Hurricane Katrina.

Sherman Alexie, and Joseph Bruchac. The American Indian Youth Literature Awards honors the best writing and illustrations by and about American Indians.

American Indians have experienced oppression for many years at the hands of European Americans. Consequently, books written from an American Indian perspective often focus on oppression and racism, ranging from historical novels, such as *Sweetgrass Basket* by Marlene Carvell, to contemporary novels, such as *The Absolutely True Diary of a Part-Time Indian* by Sherman Alexie. Appreciation, celebration, and protection of nature—central tenets of Indigenous cultures—are other recurrent themes in this body of literature, such as found in *The Birchbark House* by Louise Erdrich. Indigenous cultures outside of the United States are found in books from Canada, Australia, and New Zealand, such as *Shadows Cast by Stars* by Catherine Knutsson, a post-apocalyptic novel set among the First Nations peoples of the Pacific Northwest.

Another imbalance is that the majority of books continue to be traditional literature and historical fiction, with few contemporary books to challenge stereotypes that American Indians lived "long ago." A further issue is that many tribal nations have few or no children's books available about their specific nation, while others, such as the Dine (Navajos), have a larger body of work. Small tribal presses are producing books for their own young people, but many of these are difficult to access. Oyate (www.oyate.org) provides an online catalog of books from small presses.

Asian-American and Pacific-American Literature Asian-American and Pacific-American literature for young adults is mainly represented by stories about Chinese Americans, Japanese Americans, and Korean Americans, possibly because these groups have lived in the United States longer than others. Recently, works by and about Vietnamese Americans and Indian Americans are appearing. One theme is the oppression that drove people out of their homelands and the prejudice they faced as newcomers in the United States, such as in *Never Fall Down* by Patricia McCormick and *Inside Out and Back Again* by Thanhha Lia. More recently, books are focusing on bicultural identity, learning to appreciate one's cultural heritage as well as developing a strong identity as an American, such as in An Na's realistic story *Wait for Me* and Gene Luen Yang's *American Born Chinese.*

The body of Asian-American young adult literature is rapidly expanding, particularly in realistic and historical fiction with authors such as Linda Sue Park, Cynthia Kadohata, Kashmira Sheth, and Mitali Perkins. Nonfiction, poetry, and fantasy are almost nonexistent, with the exception of Rhoda Blumberg's biography *Shipwrecked! The True Adventures of a Japanese Boy.* The Asian Pacific American Award for Literature, along with small presses and distributors, has also expanded this body of literature. Except for the historical fiction of Graham Salisbury, the Pacific is still not represented well, although Hawai'i has a history of small presses that produce a range of books on Hawaiian culture and history.

Latino Literature   Relatively few Latino books for young adults are published in the United States, despite the fact that Latinos represent an estimated 14 percent of the population and are the fastest-growing segment of the population (U.S. Census Bureau, 2010). The books that are available mainly focus on the experiences of Mexican Americans and Puerto Ricans, with a few books based on Cuban-American experiences. This literature continues to be filled with stereotyped portrayals of Latinos living in poverty and struggling with gang-related violence, with their problems typically solved by European Americans. One notable development is the number of Latino authors and illustrators who are creating books for young adults. Recurrent themes are life in barrios (e.g., *If I Could Fly* by Judith Cofer set in a New Jersey barrio), identifying with one's heritage and American culture (e.g., *Cubanita,* a work of contemporary realistic fiction by Gaby Triana), life under repressive Latin American political regimes (e.g., Julia Alvarez's *Before We Were Free,* set in the Trujillo-era Dominican Republic), and immigration to the United States for economic or political reasons (e.g., Ann Jaramillo's work of contemporary fiction, *La Linea*).

The Américas Award (honoring a U.S. work that authentically presents Latino experiences in Latin America, the Caribbean, or the United States) and the Pura Belpré Award (honoring outstanding Latino authors and illustrators) promote high-quality Latino literature.

Multiracial/Biracial Literature   Many young people today have multiple cultural identities because their families are biracial and multiracial. While multiracial families have become commonplace in the United States, there are still few books which depict multiracial adolescents, such as the main character of Cristina Garcia's *I Wanna Be Your Shoebox* who is Jewish, Japanese, and Cuban. A common theme in the books that do exist is the search for identity and for a way to fit into the multiple cultures of which one is a part, as found in Pearl F. Gaskins' collection of interviews, essays, and poetry by multiracial young adults, *What Are You? Voices of Mixed-Race Young People,* and Claudine O'Heam's collection of first-person accounts of eighteen writers with biracial or bicultural backgrounds, *Half and Half Writers Growing Up Biracial and Bicultural.*

Religious Cultures Literature   As the mainstream religious culture in the United States, Christianity dominates young adult books. Books that portray other religious cultures, including Buddhist, Hindu, Jewish, and Muslim cultures, are difficult to find. Contemporary fiction set within the context of a religious culture and written from the perspective of a member of that religion is especially scarce. Asma Mobin-Uddin's *My Name Is Bilal* is a picture book for older readers that explores fitting into the U.S. mainstream while remaining true to Islamic culture and heritage, while *Wanting Mor* by Rukhsana Kahn focuses on a Muslim girl struggling to find her place in Afghanistan while maintaining her faith. Nonfiction and folklore on the subject of religion are more plentiful, such as *Islam: A Short History* by Karen Armstrong.

The body of Jewish young adult literature is by far the largest produced from nonmainstream religious cultures and mainly focuses on the Jewish Holocaust in Europe during the 1930s and 1940s. The prejudice and cruelty that led to the Holocaust and the devastation of the death camps are recurring themes in both fiction and nonfiction. Since many Jewish people immigrated to the United States as the Nazi threat grew in Europe, much Holocaust literature has been written by eyewitnesses or by authors who base their stories on real people and events, such as *Black Radishes* by Susan Meyer and *Always Remember Me* by Marisabina Russo. Another recent trend is Holocaust novels set in other parts of the world, such as *Tropical Secrets: Holocaust Refugees in Cuba* by Margarita Engle and *A Faraway Island* by Annika Thor about Holocaust refugees in Sweden.

One major concern is the lack of novels reflecting contemporary Jewish-American experiences, although a few are emerging, such as *Ethan, Suspended* by Pamela Ehrenberg. Barry Deutsch's *Hereville: How Mirka Got Her Sword* is a particularly interesting graphic novel about a modern Orthodox Jewish girl who wants to fight dragons. The Jewish community has promoted literary excellence through the National Jewish Book Awards and the Association of Jewish Libraries' Sydney Taylor Awards.

International Books by World Region

The international books that are most often available in the United States have been and continue to be books originally written in English from other English-speaking countries, mainly because they require no translation. The largest numbers of these books come from the United Kingdom, Canada, Australia, and the Republic of South Africa. These books are often edited for spelling, characters' names, place names, and occasionally, titles and cover illustrations before being published in the United States. At best, these alterations make the story more understandable for American readers; at worst, they amount to censorship. Because of cultural similarities between the United States and other English-speaking countries, readers are often surprised to discover that some of their favorite authors are not American, but British, Canadian, or Australian. Many English-language books, however, do feature cultural attitudes and customs not typically found in the United States.

Translated books come to the United States mainly from Europe, and particularly from Germany, France, Switzerland, the Netherlands, Belgium, Sweden, Norway, and Denmark, with a strong focus on historical fiction such as *Daniel Half Human: And the Good Nazi* by David Chotjewitz. Of the Middle Eastern countries, Israel produces the most frequently-translated young adult literature, such as *When I Was a Soldier,* a memoir by Valerie Zenatti. Books from or set in other countries in this region, such as *Tasting the Sky* by Ibtisam Barakat, set in Palestine, and *Persepolis* by Marjane Satrapi, set in Iran, are all the more welcome for their rarity.

Translated young adult literature from Asia originates mostly in Japan, such as *The Friends,* a work of contemporary realistic fiction by Kazumi Yumoto, and a fantasy quest, *Moribito: Guardian of the Spirit,* by Nahoko Uehashio. Recent immigrants from Asian countries have written about their experiences in their homelands, but in English and for an American audience. Both Ji-li Jiang and Ying Chang Compestine, now U.S. residents,

Notable Authors of International Literature

Anne-Laure Bondoux, French author of translated novels dealing with identity and difficult social issues. *The Killer's Tears; A Time of Miracles; Life as It Comes.* www.bondoux.net

Aidan Chambers, British author of sophisticated, multilayered stories of self-discovery for mature readers. *Postcards from No Man's Land; The Toll Bridge; Dying to Know You.* www.aidanchambers.co.uk

Eoin Colfer, Irish author of the five-part fantasy crime Artemis Fowl series. *Artemis Fowl; Benny and Omar; Airman.* www.eoincolfer.com

Cornelia Funke, German author of magical realism and fantasy novels. *The Thief Lord; Inkworld trilogy; Reckless.* www.corneliafunke.com

Margo Lanagan, Australian author known for otherworldly short stories. *Black Juice; White Time; Tender Morsels.* https://twitter.com/margolanagan

John Marsden, Australian author of edgy realism and Tomorrow series about survival during war. *So Much to Tell You; Letters from the Inside; Tomorrow, When the War Began.* www.johnmarsden.com.au

Geraldine McCaughrean, British author of historical fiction and fantasy novels. *A Pack of Lies; The Kite Rider; The White Darkness.* www.geraldinemccaughrean.co.uk

Jean-Claude Mourlevat, French author of novels with moral dilemmas that move between reality and fantasy. *The Pull of the Ocean; Winter's End.*

Beverley Naidoo, South African–born author of novels dealing with the effects of political injustice on youth. *No Turning Back; The Other Side of Truth; Burn My Heart.* www.beverleynaidoo.com

Shaun Tan, Australian author and illustrator of books on social, political, and historical topics, illustrated in a surrealistic style. *The Arrival; Tales from Outer Suburbia; Red Tree; The Lost Thing.* www.shauntan.net

Markus Zusak, Australian author of novels with unusual, enigmatic characters. *I Am the Messenger; The Book Thief.* http://www.randomhouse.com/features/markuszusak/

chronicle their experiences as young people during the Chinese Cultural Revolution in their novels. These books by immigrants about their experiences in their homelands are listed with the recommended multicultural books at the end of this chapter.

African nations, with the exception of the Republic of South Africa, and the developing countries of Central and South America have produced few young adult books that have been exported to the United States, primarily due to economics. Publishing books is expensive, and if books for young people are published, they tend to be textbooks, not trade books. The more developed countries of Brazil and Venezuela have robust publishing industries but still export few young adult books, probably due to a lack of interest by U.S. publishers. Most young adult works of fiction about life in Africa published in the United States have been written by citizens of developed countries who have lived in these places, as did Henning Mankell, author of the docu-novel *Secrets in the Fire* (translated from Swedish), a story about young people and landmines set in Mozambique. British authors are also writing historical fiction about British children growing up in African countries, often based in family history, such as Trilby Kent's *Stones for My Father,* set in South Africa.

Excellent International Literature to Read Aloud

Bondoux, Anne-Laure. *A Time of Miracles.* Translated from French. Eastern European refugee, identity.

Chotjewitz, David. *Daniel Half Human: And the Good Nazi.* Translated from German. World War II, Germany.

Mankell, Henning. *Secrets in the Fire.* Translated from Swedish. Effects of minefields, early 1990s Mozambique.

Master, Irfan. *A Beautiful Lie.* 1947 separation of India and Pakistan.

Morpurgo, Michael. *Private Peaceful.* Brutal trench warfare, World War I, England.

Naidoo, Beverley. *The Other Side of Truth.* Nigerian refugees, abandonment, London.

Pressler, Mirjam. *Let Sleeping Dogs Lie.* Translated from German. Family secrets based in World War II Germany.

Stratton, Allan. *Chanda's Secrets.* Effect of AIDS, South Africa.

Uehashi, Nahoko. *Morbito: Guardian of the Spirit.* Translated from Japanese. Fantasy, woman warrior.

Williams, Michael. *Now Is the Time for Running.* Fleeing Zimbabwe violence for South Africa.

A book's publishing history page is the most reliable source of its country of origin. In most books the publishing history is placed after the title page, but in some cases it is placed at the end of the book. Look for a statement such as "First published in (year) by (name of foreign publisher), (country of origin) as (foreign title)."

An Education That Is Multicultural and Intercultural

Multicultural and international literature is particularly important for young adults, given the cultural diversity of their communities and world, but also because a serious mismatch exists in U.S. schools. On one hand, school curricula and textbooks present predominantly mainstream, European-American perspectives. Moreover, the cadre of U.S. teachers is predominantly (83 percent) from European-American, suburban backgrounds (U.S. Department of Education, 2012). They have been taught to teach in ways that work best with people with similar backgrounds and often have not had close, sustained relationships with individuals from ethnic, cultural, and socioeconomic backgrounds that differ from their own. On the other hand, school populations in the United States are becoming increasingly diverse, with 46 percent of students from minority populations in 2010 (U.S. Department of Education, 2012). At the same time, U.S. classrooms are experiencing a large influx of immigrants, further increasing the diversity of students.

The resulting mismatch has contributed to an education system that is not working for many students. The Office of National Assessment for Educational Progress (2012) reports a continuing reading achievement gap between whites and American Indians, Latinos, and African Americans. In 2011, 15 percent of white eighth graders and 17 percent of Asian-American eighth graders scored below the basic level in reading, which stands in sharp contrast to the percentages for other ethnic groups—41 percent of African Americans, 36 percent of Latinos, and 37 percent of American Indians were below the basic level as eighth graders, and the numbers are much higher for those below proficiency (78 to 85 percent). Clearly, teachers need to become more familiar with the influence of culture on teaching and learning.

Teachers in all parts of the country are increasingly likely to have students from diverse ethnic, racial, national, and language groups in their classrooms, whether in urban, suburban, or rural areas. This diversity is reflected in the global nature of our lives. Adolescents will live and work in a world that is vastly different from the one in which we grew up. Rapid economic, technological, and social changes are connecting us across the globe. Knowledge of the world and of diverse cultures is no longer a luxury, but a necessity. Adolescents need understandings of both the diverse cultural groups within their own country and of global cultures that cross outside of their borders.

An education that is multicultural and intercultural is one in which diverse cultural perspectives are woven throughout the curriculum and school life, instead of being the focus of a special book or unit (Sleeter & Grant, 1987). This orientation includes the following:

- Understanding one's own personal cultural identity
- Valuing the unique perspectives of diverse cultural groups
- Connecting to the universal experiences that are shared across cultures
- Critiquing the inequities and injustices experienced by specific cultural groups
- Developing a commitment to taking action for a more just and equitable world

An education that is multicultural and intercultural is culturally responsive, culturally expansive, and culturally critical. Young adult literature plays a crucial role by providing adolescents with the opportunity to immerse themselves into story worlds and gain insights into how people feel, live, and think. They go beyond a tourist's perspective of simply gaining information about particular cultures to living *within* these cultures through their experiences with literature.

Culturally Responsive Curriculum

All adolescents need to find their lives and cultural experiences reflected within classrooms and the books they read, but this is much more likely to occur for students from mainstream, European-American families. Culturally responsive curriculum focuses on the need to develop teaching strategies and materials that are more consistent with the cultural orientations of ethnically and globally diverse students. Geneva Gay (2010) points out that using the cultural knowledge, experiences, frames of reference, and performance styles of culturally diverse students makes learning more relevant and effective. Teachers are culturally responsive in their use of literature when they:

- ***Find reading materials that are relevant to students' lives.*** Supporting all students as learners means becoming personally acquainted with students and knowledgeable about books that are culturally relevant to their lives. For ethnically and globally diverse students this may be literature about lives and cultures that are similar to their own. For second-language learners this may be the same book in English and in the student's first language, so as to make learning English easier and to signal the value of the student's first language. Students who rarely find their lives reflected in a book may dismiss literacy as irrelevant or even a threat to their cultural identities.

- *Ensure that school and classroom literature collections reflect the cultural diversity of the classroom, school, community, and world.* Even when schools and communities are culturally homogeneous, librarians and teachers should select books that reflect the diversity of the greater world. To do so, they may need to search for books from small presses that focus on particular ethnic groups and for translated books originating from other countries.

- *Invite family members and their funds of knowledge into the classroom.* Encourage students to interview family members and to share the stories that are significant to their history and traditions as resources in the classroom. Use literature that incorporates the actual voices of families and adolescents.

- *Give students a choice in their reading material.* Giving students a choice in what they read acknowledges their lives and interests as significant and relevant within the classroom. Include less conventional formats in selecting reading materials, such as picture books for older readers, audiobooks, and graphic novels, as well as informational materials, such as manuals and magazines.

- *Conference with students about their reading.* Brief one-on-one conversations as students are working or reading give teachers an opportunity to learn about the books students are currently reading and their interests and needs in order to suggest other books.

The search for culturally relevant literature recognizes that all adolescents have multiple cultural identities, including gender, social class, family structure, age, religion, and language, as well as ethnicity and nationality. This broad understanding of culture as ways of living and being in the world that influence our actions, beliefs, and values is essential to understanding why culture matters in our lives. Culture influences how each of us think about ourselves and the world around us. Students from all cultures, including the mainstream, must recognize that they have a particular perspective on the world in order to value as well as critically examine that perspective. This understanding, in turn, supports them in exploring other cultural perspectives.

Culturally Expansive Curriculum

A culturally expansive curriculum builds from awareness of adolescents' own cultural identities to a consideration of points of view that go beyond their own. Literature provides a window to ethnic and global cultures through in-depth inquiries into a particular culture and the integration of multiple cultural perspectives into every classroom study. An inquiry into a particular culture should include a range of books that reflect the diversity and complexity of that culture, for example including contemporary as well as historical novels from different American Indian groups. This range of literature challenges students to go beyond stereotypes to examine shared values and beliefs within a culture as well as the diversity of views and lives that are integral to every cultural group.

A culturally expansive curriculum becomes inclusive of multiple cultural perspectives across all content areas through the integration of literature. The perspectives of those long neglected—American Indians, African Americans, Latinos, and Asian Americans, to name a few—can be integrated into social studies and history. Important contributions by scientists, such as Elijah McCoy, whose inventions revolutionized steam engines, can be included in the science curriculum. Works by authors who reflect a range of ethnic and global backgrounds can be included in the literature curriculum. For example, a literature unit could focus on Francisco Jiménez, a Mexican American whose books describe the struggles of immigrants and their families who work in the California fields, or on the contemporary fiction of Walter Dean Myers, describing situations and problems experienced by many urban African Americans.

One strategy is to read aloud one of the featured author's works while students discuss others by that author in small group literature circles. Another is to start or end class with a poem from collections such as Lori M. Carlson's *Red Hot Salsa* or Naomi Shihab Nye's *The Space between Our Footsteps*. Books by mainstream authors can be paired with multicultural or international literature that is from a similar genre or topic, such as the dystopian Hunger Game novels by Suzanne Collins with the dystopian Indigenous novel, *Shadows Cast by Stars* by Catherine Knutsson, a Metis author. Providing resources and maps so that students can search for information on a culture or country is helpful as is keeping lists of characters or diagrams of relationships and events for complex novels.

The goal of those who write, publish, and promote multicultural and international children's literature is to help young people learn about, understand, and ultimately accept those different from themselves, thus breaking the cycles of prejudice and oppression among peoples of different cultures. Progress toward this goal may well begin when young people read multicultural or international literature and realize how similar they are to adolescents of different cultures and how interesting their differences are. They are also challenged not to consider their own culture as the "norm" against which others are judged as strange or exotic. These books help build bridges and cross borders between people of different cultures (Lehman, Freeman, & Scharer, 2010).

The books that are selected for read-alouds, booktalks, book displays, and text sets for classroom studies or independent reading should reflect the diversity of cultural experiences in the classroom as well as invite exploration of broader ethnic and global cultures. Booktalks, for example, might be used to connect students who read mainstream books with literature from a wider range of cultures that have a similar theme or genre. A collection of multicultural and international books on the theme of identity might include:

The Absolutely True Diary of a Part-Time Indian by Sherman Alexie (Spokane Indian)

American Born Chinese by Gene Luen Yang (Chinese American)

Climbing the Stairs by Padma Venkatraman (India)

Re-Gifters by Mike Carey, Sonny Liew, and Marc Hempel (Korean American)

Strange Relations by Sonia Levitin (Jewish)

Tough Boy Sonatas by Curtis L. Crisler (African American)

Cubanita by Gaby Triana (Cuban American)

Between Sisters by Adwoa Badoe (Ghana)

Culturally Critical Curriculum

Although multicultural education celebrates diversity and cross-cultural harmony, its more important goal has always been to transform society and ensure greater voice, equity, and social justice for marginalized groups (Gay, 2010). Raising issues of inequity, power, and discrimination is central to an education that is multicultural and intercultural. Paulo Freire (1970) believes that students need to critically read the world by questioning "what is" and "who benefits," instead of accepting inequity as just the way things work. Students need to examine why these social problems exist and who benefits from keeping inequities in place. They also need to consider new possibilities by asking "what if," and taking action for social change. Through these questions, students develop a critical consciousness about their everyday world and the ways in which power plays out in their relationships and society.

Literature plays a significant role in social justice education by documenting the history and contemporary stories of marginalized peoples, presenting their perspectives, and providing a way for their voices to be heard. These perspectives are rarely included within textbooks and the standard curriculum. Literature can support students in considering multiple perspectives on complex social issues such as undocumented immigrants, as in *Friends from the Other Side* by Gloria Anzaldua, *The Circuit* by Francisco Jimenez, *La Línea* by Ann Jaramillo, *Ask Me No Questions* by Maria Budhos, *A Time of Miracles* by Anne-Laure Bondoux, and *The Arrival* by Shaun Tan.

A critical literacy or social justice curriculum has four dimensions (Lewison, Leland, & Harste, 2008), all of which can be supported by literature:

- Disrupting the commonplace by looking at the everyday through new lenses that challenge assumptions (e.g., *Outside Beauty* by Cynthia Kadohata or *Does My Head Look Big in This?* by Randa Abdel-Fattah).

- Considering multiple perspectives that may be contradictory or offer alternative interpretations of history or current issues (e.g., *My Name Is Not Easy* by Debby Edwardson or *Daniel Half Human: And the Good Nazi* by David Chotjewitz).

- Focusing on sociopolitical issues to examine societal systems and unequal power relationships and to get at the root causes of social problems (e.g., *La Línea* by Ann Jaramillo or *The Absolutely True Diary of a Part-Time Indian* by Sherman Alexie).

- Taking action to promote social justice by taking a stand against oppression and acting to create change (e.g., *Marching for Freedom* by Elizabeth Partridge or *Iqbal* by Francesco D'Adamo).

One of the challenges in today's society is combating the ignorance that is at the root of racial, cultural, and religious prejudice and intolerance. Young adult literature, particularly the rich multicultural and international selections that are currently available, is a powerful tool in depicting the similarities that connect us as human beings as well as the differences that make us each unique. We are connected by a shared humanity and by the uniqueness that each culture contributes to a richly diverse world. Adolescents need to find their own lives reflected within a book as well as imagine ways of living and thinking beyond their own in order to build bridges of understanding across cultures.

References

Bishop, R. S. (2007). *Free within ourselves: The development of African American children's literature.* Portsmouth, NH: Heinemann.

Fox, D., & Short, K. (2003). *Stories matter: The complexity of cultural authenticity in children's literature.* Urbana, IL: National Council of Teachers of English.

Freire, P. (1970). *Pedagogy of the oppressed.* New York: Continuum.

Gay, G. (2010). *Culturally responsive teaching.* 2nd ed. New York: Teachers College Press.

Homing, K. T., Lindgren, M. V., & Schliesman, M. (2013). *CCBC Choices, 2012.* Madison: University of Wisconsin-Madison.

Lehman, B., Freeman, E., & Scharer, P. (2010). *Reading globally, K-8.* Thousand Oaks, CA: Corwin.

Lewison, M., Leland, C., & Harste, J. (2008). *Creating critical classrooms.* New York: Erlbaum.

Pavonetti, L. (Ed.). (2011). *Bridges to understanding: Envisioning the world through children's books.* Lanham, MD: Scarecrow.

Sleeter, C., & Grant, C. (1987). An analysis of multicultural education in the United States. *Harvard Education Review, 57,* 421–444.

U.S. Census Bureau. (2010). www.census.gov.

U.S. Department of Education. (2012). *The condition of education 2012.* Washington, DC: NCES.

U.S. Department of Education. (2012). *The nation's report card: Reading 2011.* Washington, DC: NCES.

Recommended Multicultural Books

Ages indicated refer to content appropriateness and conceptual and interest levels. Formats other than novels are coded as follows:

(GR)   Graphic novel

(PI)   Picture book

(COL)   Short story collection

(NV)   Novel in verse

African-American Literature

Adoff, Jaime. *The Death of Jayson Porter.* Hyperion, 2008. **(NV)** Ages 15–18. Crushing poverty, neighborhood violence, and lack of family support push a 16-year-old to the edge.

Booth, Coe. *Kendra.* Scholastic, 2008. Ages 14–18. Kendra must deal with her mother's rejection while growing up in the Bronx and Harlem.

———. *Tyrell.* Scholastic, 2006. Ages 14–18. A 15-year-old boy's struggle to survive poverty and temptations in New York City's South Bronx. Sequel is *Bronxwood* (2011).

Crisler, Curtis L. *Tough Boy Sonatas.* Illus. Floyd Cooper. Boyds Mills, 2007. Ages 15–18. 38 gritty poems about growing up male, African-American, and poor in Gary, Indiana.

Curtis, Christopher Paul. *Bucking the Sarge.* Random, 2004. Ages 13–18. A 15-year-old boy seeks self-identity and independence from his overbearing mother.

Draper, Sharon M. *Just Another Hero.* Atheneum, 2009. Ages 15–18. Urban teens struggling with issues at home and at school, including a confrontation with a student who brings a gun to school.

Feelings, Tom. *The Middle Passage: White Ships/ Black Cargo.* Dial, 1995. **(PI)** Ages 11–18. The brutal transatlantic crossing of slaves bound for America told through 64 narrative black-and-white paintings.

Hamilton, Virginia. *The People Could Fly: The Picture Book.* Illus. Leo and Diane Dillon. Knopf, 2004. **(PI)** Ages 11–15. Retelling of a slave escape fantasy.

Johnson, Angela. *The First Part Last*. Simon & Schuster, 2003. Ages 12–16. A 16-year-old father struggles to raise his infant daughter. Prequel to *Heaven*. (1998)

Lester, Julius. *Day of Tears: A Novel in Dialogue*. Hyperion, 2005. Ages 12–15. Fictionalized account of the biggest slave auction in American history (Savannah, Georgia, 1859).

———. *The Old African*. Illus. Jerry Pinkney. Dial, 2005. **(PI)** Ages 11–13. Legend of Ibo slaves in Georgia who walked into the ocean to regain their freedom and spirit.

Myers, Walter Dean. *Autobiography of My Dead Brother*. HarperCollins, 2005. Ages 14–18. 3 young, urban black males follow different paths, one downhill.

———. *Jazz*. Illus. Christopher Myers. Holiday, 2006. **(PI)** Ages 10–15. Poems and illustrations exploring the forms, moods, and styles of jazz.

———. *Street Love*. HarperCollins/Amistad, 2006. (NV) Ages 14–18. Damien and Junice are in love but separated by different social classes and career paths.

Nelson, Kadir. *Heart and Soul: The Story of America and African Americans*. Balzer & Bray, 2011. Ages 12–18. The central place of African Americans in U.S. history using the voice of a grandmother. Oil paintings.

Nelson, Marilyn. *Sweethearts of Rhythm: The Story of the Greatest All-Girl Swing Band in the World*. Illus. Jerry Pinkney. Dial, 2009. **(PI)** Ages 10–14. Poetry and biography of 1940s all-female band.

Nelson, Vaunda Micheaux. *No Crystal Stair*. Illus. R. Gregory Christie. Carolrhoda, 2012. Ages l2–18. Fictionalized documentary of Lewis Michaux, a Harlem bookseller, and his influence on the Civil Rights Movement.

Partridge, Elizabeth. *Marching for Freedom: Walk Together, Children, and Don't You Grow Weary*. Viking, 2009. Ages 10–18. Civil Rights march from Selma to Montgomery. Nonfiction photoessay.

Pinkney, Andrea. *Hand in Hand: Ten Black Men Who Changed the America*. Illus. Brian Pinkney. Disney, 2012. Ages 12–15. 10 biographical vignettes with a poem, watercolor portrait, and profile of their lives and character.

Smith, Hope A. *Keeping the Night Watch*. Illus. E. B. Lewis. Holt, 2008. **(NV)** Ages 10–14. The return of C. J.'s father after a long absence causes resentment. Sequel to *The Way a Door Closes* (2003).

Taylor, Mildred. *Roll of Thunder, Hear My Cry*. Dial, 1976. Ages 11–16. Racial prejudice and injustice against generations of a landowning black family in Mississippi. Part of the Logan Family Saga.

Williams-Garcia, Rita. *Jumped*. HarperCollins, 2009. Ages 14–18. The voices of 3 teen girls in an urban high school across a day that holds the threat of school violence. Literary allusions.

Woodson, Jacqueline. *Beneath a Meth Moon*. Putnam, 2012. Ages 14–18. Laurel's descent into addiction, following family loss and upheaval due to Hurricane Katrina.

American Indian and Indigenous Literature

Alexie, Sherman. *The Absolutely True Diary of a Part-Time Indian*. Little, Brown, 2007. Ages 12–18. Junior, a Spokane Indian, struggles with identity when he transfers to an all-white high school. Semiautobiographical.

Bruchac, Joseph. *Pocahontas*. Silver Whistle, 2003. Ages 12–18. Historically accurate account of the Powhatan girl and her relationship with Captain John Smith.

———. *The Winter People*. Dial, 2002. Ages 12–16. A tale (based on fact) of kidnap and rescue in Quebec in 1759 during the French and Indian War.

Carlson, Lori Marie, editor. *Moccasin Thunder: American Indian Stories for Today*. HarperCollins, 2005. Ages 15–18. **(COL)** 10 contemporary short stories by American Indian writers about American Indian teens.

Carvell, Marlene. *Sweetgrass Basket*. Dutton, 2005. Ages 13–16. 2 Mohawk sisters' terrible experiences at the turn of the 20th century in a boarding school for American Indians.

Edwardson, Debby. *My Name Is Not Easy.* Marshall Cavendish, 2011. Ages 12–16. Life for Indigenous children in a Catholic boarding school in 1960s Alaska. Racism and institutional abuse. Multiple voices.

Erdrich, Louise. *The Porcupine Year.* HarperCollins, 2008. Ages 10–14. Omakaya and her Ojibwe family are displaced by the U.S. government (1857). Sequel to *The Birchbark House* (1999); *The Game of Silence* (2005).

Jordan-Fenton, Christy and Margaret Pokiak-Fenton. *Fatty Legs: A Memoir.* Annick, 2010. Ages 10–14. Memoir of Inuit girl at an oppressive residential school. Sequel is *A Stranger at Home* (2011). (Canadian)

Knutsson, Catherine. *Shadows Cast by Stars.* Atheneum, 2012. Ages 14–18. Dystopia set in First Nations of the Northwest; a plague has devastated the world, except for a tribe on an island off the coast of Canada. (Canadian)

Medicine Crow, Joseph. *Counting Coup: Becoming a Crow Chief on the Reservation and Beyond.* National Geographic, 2006. Ages 12–16. Memoir of the last chief of his people (Absarokee), Custer to present.

Ochoa, Annette, Betsy Franco, and Tracy L. Gourdine, editors. *Night Is Gone, Day Is Still Coming: Stories and Poems by American Indian Teens and Young Adults.* Candlewick, 2003. **(COL)** Ages 12–18. Poems and stories speaking of the past, present, and future.

Olsen, Sylvia. *The Girl with a Baby.* Sono Nis, 2004. Ages 13–18. An Indigenous girl living in British Columbia coping with pregnancy and a new baby. (Canadian)

———. *White Girl.* Sono Nis, 2005. Ages 13–18. An outsider adjusting to a First Nations reserve. (Canadian)

Asian-American and Pacific-American Literature

Blumberg, Rhoda. *Shipwrecked! The True Adventures of a Japanese Boy.* HarperCollins, 2001. Ages 11–14. Manjiro Nakahama, 1st Japanese person to come to the United States.

Budhos, Marina. *Ask Me No Questions.* Atheneum, 2006. Ages 15–18. Nadia, an undocumented Muslim from Bangladesh living in NY, struggles to hold her family together after 9-11.

Carey, Mike. *Re-Gifters.* Illus. Sonny Liew and Marc Hempel. Minx, 2007. **(GR)** Ages 13–18. Korean-American girlfriends learn about life and love during a martial arts tournament.

Desai, Tanjua Hidier. *Born Confused.* Scholastic, 2002. Ages 14–18. Dimple struggles to sort out her bicultural identity as an American and an Indian when her parents introduce her to a "suitable boy."

Kadohata, Cynthia. *Outside Beauty.* Atheneum, 2008. Ages 12–18. Japanese-American sisters are separated and sent to live with their respective fathers when their beautiful mother is critically injured.

———. *Weedflower.* Simon & Schuster, 2006. Ages 11–14. Japanese-American internment, WWII, Arizona.

Lai, Thanhha. *Inside Out & Back Again.* Harper, 2011. **(NV)** Ages 10–14. Vietnamese immigrants. Alabama, 1975.

Na, An. *Wait for Me.* Speak, 2006. Ages 14–18. A Korean-American girl struggles with family expectations and her own dreams.

Perkins, Mitali. *Secret Keeper.* Delacorte, 2009. Ages 14–18. A teen struggles with survival as a female in 1970s India and her love for her sister.

Salisbury, Graham. *Eyes of the Emperor.* Delacorte, 2005. Ages 14–18. A Japanese-American teen from Hawai'i lies about his age to join the Army following Pearl Harbor.

Senzai, N. H. *Shooting Kabul.* Simon & Schuster, 2010. Ages 10–14. A refugee from Afghanistan is plagued with guilt when his little sister is left behind.

Sheth, Kashmira. *Blue Jasmine.* Hyperion, 2004. Ages 11–14. An immigrant from India adjusts to U.S. life.

Tran, G. B. *Vietnamerica: A Family's Journey.* Villard, 2010. **(GR)** Ages 14–18. Graphic memoir of Vietnamese-American artist who visits Vietnam to try to understand his parents.

Woo, Sung. *Everything Asian*. St. Martin's Griffin, 2009. David and his family have recently come from Korea to join his father in New Jersey.

Yang, Gene Luen. *American Born Chinese*. First Second, 2006. **(GR)** Ages 12–18. Postmodern coming-of-age story about self-acceptance.

——. *Level Up*. First Second, 2011. Illus. Thien Pham. **(GR)** Ages 12–18. Dennis turns to video games, but is encouraged by guardian angels to go back to his studies and honor his father's wishes. Magical realism.

Yang, Kao Kalia. *The Latehomecomer: A Hmong Family Memoir*. Coffee House, 2008. Ages 15–18. Story of a woman who emigrated from Laos to Minnesota in 1986 and founded a support service for immigrants.

Yep, Laurence. *Dragon's Gate*. HarperCollins, 1993. Ages 12–16. Chinese-American experiences working on the transcontinental railroad in 1867.

——. *Dragons of Silk*. HarperCollins, 2011. Ages 12–15. Silk binds the lives and struggles of girls from 4 generations across China and the U.S. Conclusion to the Golden Mountain Chronicles.

Yoo, Paula. *Good Enough*. HarperCollins, 2008. Ages 13–16. Korean American Patti Yoon is expected to follow her parents' wishes for success.

Latino Literature

Alvarez, Julia. *Before We Were Free*. Knopf, 2002. Ages 11–14. Life during the Trujillo dictatorship in the Dominican Republic, 1960–1961.

Atkin, S. Beth. *Voices from the Fields: Children of Migrant Farmworkers Tell Their Stories*. Little, Brown, 1993. Ages 10–14. Interviews, poems, and photographs of nine migrant Mexican-American children.

Canales, Viola. *The Tequila Worm*. Random, 2005. Ages 12–15. A Mexican-American girl tries to persuade her parents that she can leave home to go to school and still stay connected to her family and culture.

Carlson, Lori M., editor. *Red Hot Salsa: Bilingual Poems on Being Young and Latino in the United States*. Holt, 2005. Ages 14–18. English/ Spanish. Poems (some by teens) about the challenges of being bicultural.

——. *Voices in First Person: Reflections on Latino Identity*. Atheneum, 2008. **(COL)** Ages 14–18. Short monologues by Latino authors give voice to what it's like to be a Latino teen in the U.S.

Cisneros, Sandra. *The House on Mango Street*. Arte Publico, 1984. Ages 14–18. Growing up Mexican American in the Latino section of Chicago.

Cofer, Judith. *If I Could Fly*. Farrar, 2011. Ages 12–16. Doris searches for her place when her mother returns to Puerto Rico, leaving her with her often absent musician father. New Jersey barrio.

de la Peña, Matt. *We Were Here*. Ember, 2010. Sent to juvenile detention, Miguel keeps a journal— and his crime—from those around him.

Engle, Margarita. *The Wild Book*. Harcourt, 2012. **(NV)** Ages 12–14. A girl struggles with reading in early 1900s Cuba as bandits roam the countryside, kidnapping children. Based on grandmother's story.

Hernandez, Gilbert. *Sloth*. DC Comics/Vertigo, 2006. **(GR)** Ages 15–18. Disillusioned Miguel and friends seek meaning in their small-town lives.

Herrera, Juan Felipe. *Crashboomlove: A Novel in Verse*. University of New Mexico Press, 1999. **(NV)** Ages 14–18. 16-year-old Mexican teen growing up in an American high school.

Jaramillo, Ann. *La Línea* Roaring Brook, 2006. Ages 12–14. A brother and sister cross the Mexican border to find their parents in California, a harsh journey of great risk and danger.

Jiménez, Francisco. *The Circuit: Stories from the Life of a Migrant Child* Houghton, 1999. **(COL)** Ages 11–18. Autobiographical account of the poverty and frustration in the lives of migrant workers. Sequels include *Breaking Through* (2001) and *Reaching Out* (2008).

Manzano, Sonia. *The Revolution of Evelyn Serrano*. Scholastic, 2012. Ages 12–15. 1969 Spanish Harlem and the complex family dynamics in a Puerto Rican family; social activism.

McCall, Guadalupe Garcia. *Under the Mesquite*. Lee & Low, 2008. **(NV)** Ages 14–18. A teen struggles with the responsibility of her Mexican-American family during her mother's battle with cancer.

Medina, Meg. *Yaqui Delgado Wants to Kick Your Ass*. Candlewick, 2013. Ages 14–18. First-person voice of a girl facing bullying and living in constant fear. Body image, racism, class conflict, self-worth.

Nye, Naomi Shihab, editor. *The Tree Is Older Than You Are: A Bilingual Gathering of Poems and Stories from Mexico with Paintings by Mexican Artists*. Simon & Schuster, 1995. **(COL)** Ages 11–18. English/Spanish. Collection of great Mexican poets and painters.

Resau, Laura, and Maria V. Farimango. *The Queen of Water*. Ember, 2011. Ages 14–18. A Quechua Indian girl from a small village in Ecuador is sold as a servant to an upper class urban family. Memoir.

Ryan, Pam Mufioz. *Becoming Naomi Leon*. Scholastic, 2004. Ages 11–15. Naomi's long-absent mother returns, threatening her life with her great-grandmother and brother, and so they go to Mexico to search for her father.

Sáenz, Benjamin Alire. *Aristotle and Dante Discover the Secrets of the Universe*. Simon & Schuster, 2012. Ages 14–18. A poetic novel of the developing relationship between two Mexican-American teens.

———. *Sammy & Juliana in Hollywood*. Cinco Puntos, 2004. Ages 15–18. Dreams and losses while growing up in the Hollywood barrio of Las Cruces, New Mexico, during the late 1960s.

Soto, Gary. *Facts of Life*. Graphia, 2008. **(COL)** Ages 12–18. Short stories on frustrations of growing up Mexican-American.

Stork, Francisco. *The Last Summer of the Death Warriors*. Scholastic, 2012. Ages 14–18. With echoes of Don Quixote, two boys set off to discover the mystery of a sister's death and the cure for the other's cancer.

Triana, Gaby. *Cubanita*. HarperCollins, 2005. Ages 15–18. Cuban-American teen learns to value her heritage.

Weaver, Lila Quintero. *Darkroom: A Memoir in Black and White*. University of Alabama Press, 2012. **(GR)** Ages 14–18. Lila and her family move to Alabama from Argentina in the midst of the 1960s racial strife.

Multiracial/Biracial Literature

Crutcher, Chris. *Whale Talk*. Greenwillow, 2001. Ages 14–18. T.J., an exceptional athlete, bucks the system by organizing a swim team of misfits. Racism, bicultural identity, school violence. Black/Japanese/White.

Curry, Jane Louise. *The Black Canary*. Simon & Schuster, 2005. Ages 11–15. Time-travel adventure to Elizabethan England, with a biracial protagonist who struggles with family expectations and his own identity.

de la Peña, Matt. *Mexican Whiteboy*. Delacorte, 2008. Ages 14–18. Blends sports and street together in a story of a biracial teen struggling with identity. White/Mexican-American.

Garcia, Cristina. *I Wanna Be Your Shoebox*. Simon & Schuster, 2008. Ages 10–14. Yumi, who is Jewish, Japanese, and Cuban, asks her dying grandfather to tell his life story so she can understand her history.

Gaskins, Pearl F., editor. *What Are You? Voices of Mixed-Race Young People*. Holt, 1999. Ages 14–18. Interviews, essays, and poetry by 45 multiracial young people.

Gillan, Maria, and Jennifer Gillan, editors. *Growing Up Ethnic in America: Contemporary Fiction about Learning to Be American*. Penguin, 1999. **(COL)** Ages 15–18. Stories and memoirs about adapting to American ways while holding onto one's native culture.

Hopkinson, Nalo. *The Chaos*. Margaret McElderry, 2012. Ages 12–18. A biracial girl suddenly develops black spots and visions in a world gone mad. Toronto cityscape, Caribbean and Russian folklore. (Canada)

Maia, Love. *DJ Rising*. Little, Brown, 2012. D.J., a black/Puerto Rican teen, makes a name for himself as a disc jockey while dealing with his mother's escalating drug addiction.

O'Hearn, Claudine C. *Half and Half: Writers on Growing Up Biracial and Bicultural*. Pantheon, 1998. Ages 12–18. First-person accounts of 18 writers with biracial or bicultural backgrounds.

Rowell, Rainbow. *Eleanor & Park*. St Martin's Griffin, 2013. Ages 14–18. Set across one school year in 1986, story of two alienated misfits who fall in love. Alternating voices. Korean/White.

Smith, Cynthia Leitich. *Rain Is Not My Indian Name*. HarperCollins, 2001. Ages 11–14. A teen discovers the meaning of her Muskogee Creek Indian heritage as well as her German/Irish heritage.

Smith, Sherri. *Hot, Sour, Salty, Sweet*. Delacorte, 2008. Ages 12–14. Ana's junior-high graduation dinner is filled with cultural collisions and discoveries, especially with her grandparents who are African American and Taiwanese.

Stevenson, Sarah. *The Latte Rebellion*. Flux, 2011. Inspired by a racial insult, Asha and her friends start a social movement to raise awareness of multiracial families. Indian-American/Mexican-Irish-American.

Thompson, Holly. *Orchards*. Delacorte, 2011. (**NV**) Ages 14–18. Kanako, Japanese and Russian Jewish, is sent to Japan to live with relatives after the suicide of a friend.

Religious Cultures Literature

Armstrong, Karen. *Islam: A Short History*. Modern Library, 2002. Ages 12–18. Nonfiction on the history of the Islamic religion up to the present.

Deutsch, Barry. *Hereville: How Mirka Got Her Sword*. Illus. J. Richmond. Amulet, 2010. (**GR**) Ages 10–14. An Orthodox Jewish girl who is a superhero fighting dragons and monsters.

Ehrenberg, Pamela. *Ethan, Suspended*. Eerdmans, 2007. Ages 12–16. Sent to live with his Jewish grandparents in inner-city Washington, DC, Ethan learns much about his own and other cultures in school and at home.

Engle, Margarita. *Tropical Secrets: Holocaust Refugees in Cuba*. Holt, 2009. (**NV**) Ages 12–15. A Jewish refugee is given asylum in Cuba, but political corruption threatens the fate of other refugees aboard a ship.

Gaskins, Pearl F., editor. *I Believe in . . . : Christian, Jewish, and Muslim Young People Speak about Their Faith*. Cricket, 2004. Ages 14–18. The effect of religion on the lives of youth; interviews of 15–24 year olds.

Geras, Adele. *My Grandmother's Stories: A Collection of Jewish Folk Tales*. Illus. Anita Lobel. Knopf, 2003. (**COL**) Ages 11–14. 10 traditional Russian Jewish folktales.

Hesse, Karen. *The Stone Lamp: Eight Stories of Hanukkah through History*. Illus. Brian Pinkney. Hyperion, 2003. (**COL**) Ages 11–13. Poems and narrative. Explanation of eight crucial periods in Jewish history.

Khan, Rukhsana. *Wanting Mor*. Groundwood, 2009. Ages 12–16. When her mother dies, a Muslim girl in Afghanistan faces uncertainty and homelessness but is sustained by her Islamic faith.

Kimmel, Eric. *Wonders and Miracles: A Passover Companion*. Scholastic, 2004. (**COL**) Ages 11–14. Stories, songs, recipes, artwork, prayers, and commentary related to the Jewish holiday.

Levitin, Sonia. *Strange Relations*. Knopf, 2007. Ages 13–17. A 15-year-old Jewish-American girl wrestles with her religious traditions and the issue of faith.

Meyer, Susan. *Black Radishes*. Delacorte, 2010. Ages 11–14. A Jewish family flees Paris to the countryside during WWII. Based on family experiences.

Mobin-Uddin, Asma. *My Name Is Bilal*. Illus. Barbara Kiwak. Boyds Mills, 2005. (**PI**) Ages 11–14. A middle school boy and his sister, the only Muslims in their school, confront prejudice.

Russo, Marisabina. *Always Remember Me: How One Family Survived World War II*. Atheneum, 2005. (**PI**) Ages 11–14. Autobiographical account of a Jewish family's life in Germany and survival of the Holocaust.

Vemick, Shirley. *The Blood Lie*. Cinco Puntos, 2011. Ages 12–16. 1928 New York City where an innocent Jewish boy is accused of murdering a young Christian girl. Based on a true event; anti-Semitism.

Yakin, Boaz, and Nick Bertozzi. *Jerusalem: A Family Portrait*. First Second, 2013. (GR) Ages 14–18. Formation of the Israeli state through 3 generations of a family.

Recommended International Books

Country of original publication is noted.

English-Language Books

Abdel-Fattah, Randa. *Does My Head Look Big in This?* Scholastic, 2007. Ages 12–18. Australia. An Australian/Palestinian teen copes with issues of faith (Muslim) and culture.

Almond, David. *Clay.* Delacorte, 2006. Ages 11–15. England. 3 boys create a huge clay monster that obeys their wishes.

Bardoe, Adwoa. *Between Sisters.* Groundwood, 2010. Ages 14–18. Canada. A Ghanaian teen is sent from her village to work as a nanny in a large city; class stereotypes, meaning of family, identity.

Boyce, Frank C. *Millions.* HarperCollins, 2004. Ages 11–14. England. An enormous, unexpected windfall helps brothers deal with losing their mother.

Brooks, Martha. *Mistik Lake.* Farrar, 2007. Ages 14–18. Canada. 17-year-old Odella comes of age while coping with her mother's death, family secrets, and first romance.

Burgess, Melvin. *Doing It.* Holt, 2004. Ages 14–18. England. Sexual urges and anxieties of three teenage boys.

Buzo, Laura. *Love and Other Perishable Items.* Knopf, 2012. Ages 14–18. Australia. Emotional life of a teen and a young adult through interwoven accounts that show the development of a relationship.

Chambers, Aiden. *Dying to Know You.* Amulet, 2012. Ages 14–18. England. A teen struggling with dyslexia requests an author's help in writing a letter to impress his girlfriend. Uses a variety of literary forms.

Clark, Judith. *Kalpana's Dream.* Front Street, 2005. Ages 12–15. Australia. A girl is helped by her Indian great-grandmother in her search for self-identity.

Colfer, Eoin. *Artemis Fowl.* Hyperion, 2001. Ages 11–14. Ireland. A 12-year-old genius masterminds a gold heist by capturing a fairy and demanding a ransom. Series.

Comish, D. M. *Foundling.* Putnam, 2006. Ages 12–16. Australia. Monster Blood Tattoo series, a survival adventure set in a monster-filled, medieval world. Sequel is *Lamplighter* (2008).

Coates, Jan. *A Hare in the Elephant's Trunk.* Red Deer, 2010. Ages 14–18. Canada. Fictionalized story of Jacob Deng, now living in Canada, who had to flee from his village in the Sudan, becoming one of the Lost Boys.

Craig, Colleen. *Afrika.* Tundra, 2008. Ages 14–18. Canada. Kim, a 13-year-old Canadian, visits South Africa with her South African mother, during the Truth and Reconciliation Hearings about the violence of apartheid.

Crockett, S. D. *After the Snow.* Feiwel & Friends, 2012. Ages 11–16. England. Life after global warming has turned the planet cold.

Crossley-Holland, Kevin. *Crossing to Paradise.* Scholastic, 2006. Ages 12–15. England. A transformational journey for Gatty, a chamber maid, selected to go on a pilgrimage to the Holy Land.

Dhami, Narinder. *Bindi Babes.* Delacorte, 2004. Ages 11–14. England. 3 Indian sisters living in England miss their mother and plot against their aunt.

Dowd, Siobhan. *Bog Child.* Random, 2008. Ages 13–18. Ireland. Intrigue following the discovery of a body buried in a bog in Ireland.

———. *The London Eye Mystery.* Random, 2008. Ages 11–14. England. A boy (possibly with Asperger's syndrome) tries to solve the mysterious disappearance of his cousin.

Doyle, Brian. *Pure Spring.* Groundwood, 2007. Ages 12–16. Canada. Martin is dealing with trouble at work and at home, dealing with his grandfather's dementia. 1950s Ottawa.

Fisher, Catherine. *Incarceron.* Dial, 2010. Ages 12–15. England. Finn is looking for escape from a prison in which he was born and where he will die. Fantasy. Sequel is *Sapphique* (2012).

French, Jackie. *Hitler's Daughter.* HarperCollins, 2003. Ages 11–12. Australia. Ethical questions involving the Jewish Holocaust and Australia's Aboriginal people.

Gee, Maurice. *Salt*. Orca, 2009. Ages 11–15. New Zealand. First book of the Salt Trilogy, which follows Hari as he attempts to rescue his father from imprisonment in the Deep Salt, a place from which no one returns.

Golding, Julia. *The Diamond of Drury Lane*. Roaring Brook, 2008. Ages 14–16. England. Mystery involving a hidden diamond set in early eighteenth-century London's theater district.

Gray, Keith. *Ostrich Boys*. Random House, 2010. Ages 12–17. Scotland. After a friend is killed in an accident, the three remaining friends take his ashes to bury them in Southern Scotland.

Hartnett, Sonya. *Surrender*. Candlewick, 2005. Ages 14–18. Australia. As he is dying, Gabriel recounts his troubled childhood and strange relationship with a dangerous wild boy.

Herrick, Steven. *The Wolf*. Front Street, 2007. Ages 14–18. Australia. Jake and Lucy search for a predator in the Australian mountains, but find something else.

Ibbotson, Eva. *The Star of Kazan*. Dutton, 2004. Ages 11–13. England. A brave heroine encounters sly villains while seeking her true family in early-19th-century Vienna.

Ihimaera, Witi. *Whale Rider*. Harcourt, 2003. Ages 12–16. New Zealand. Maori girl who wants to become the chief of the tribe, a role her grandfather believes is reserved for males.

Jinks, Catharine. *Evil Genius*. Harcourt, 2007. Ages 12–16. Australia. 13-year-old Cadel is being trained by his crooked father to dominate the world. Series.

Jocelyn, Marthe. *How It Happened in Peach Hill*. Random, 2007. Ages 13–18. Canada. 15-year-old Annie rebels against her mother and their life as swindlers in 1920s New York State.

———. *Would You*. Random, 2008. Ages 14–18. Canada. Natalie must cope with the aftermath of her sister being hit by a car.

Kent, Trilby. *Stones for My Father*. Tundra, 2011. Ages 12–15. Canada. Boer War in South Africa, 1900, between Afrikaner colonists and English imperialists. Corlie must survive violence, loss of family, and internment camps.

Lake, Nick. *In Darkness*. Bloomsbury, 2012. Ages 14–18. England. When an earthquake hits Haiti, Shorty is trapped under the rubble in a hospital with memories of violence and visions of a Haitian liberator in 1804. Printz Award.

Lanagan, Margo. *Red Spikes*. Knopf, 2007. (**COL**) Ages 15–18. Australia. 10 stories focusing on what it means to be human.

———. *White Time*. HarperCollins, 2006. (**COL**) Ages 13–18. Australia. 10 stories in a variety of genres.

Laird, Elizabeth, with Sonia Nimr. *A Little Piece of Ground*. Haymarket, 2006. Ages 10–14. England. Israeli occupation of the West Bank; a Palestinian boy and his Christian friend work to create a soccer field.

Leavitt, Martine. *Keturah and Lord Death*. Front Street, 2006. Ages 13–17. Canada. A retelling of Sheherazade.

Little, Jean. *Willow and Twig*. Viking, 2003. Ages 11–14. Canada. Abandoned children try to establish a new home and family.

Lowry, Brigid. *Follow the Blue*. Holiday, 2004. Ages 14–18. New Zealand. A New Zealander tries to find her way in life while living in Australia.

Marchetta, Melina. *Saving Francesca*. Knopf, 2004. Ages 14–18. Australia. Mental depression of a parent.

Marsden, John. *Tomorrow, When the War Began*. Houghton, 1995. Ages 12–18. Australia. (First of 6 books) Teenage guerilla warriors combat the foreign military occupiers of their country.

Master, Irfan. *A Beautiful Lie*. Whitman, 2012. Ages 12–17. England. During the summer of 1947 in India during Partition, Bilal must cope with the changing political environment and his father's impending death.

Matas, Carol. *Sparks Fly Upward*. Clarion, 2002. Ages 11–13. Canada. Coping with anti-Semitism in early 1900s.

McCaughrean, Geraldine. *Cyrano*. Harcourt, 2006. Ages 12–16. England. Retelling of the classic French play.

———. *The White Darkness*. HarperCollins, 2007. Ages 12–16. England. Sym makes some horrifying discoveries about her uncle in Antarctica. Printz Award.

McKay, Hilary. *Forever Rose*. McElderry, 2007. Ages 11–14. England. Final book is a series about 4 sisters, the British Casson family, chaotic family of artists and book lovers.

Michael, Jan. *City Boy*. Clarion, 2009. Ages 10–14. England. Orphaned by AIDs, Sam has to leave the life he knows in urban Malawi for a small remote village without electricity or technology.

Moriarty, Jaclyn. *The Year of Secret Assignments*. Scholastic, 2004. Ages 14–18. Australia. Friendship of 3 girls documented in letters, diaries, lists, e-mail, notes.

———. *A Corner of White*. Arthur A. Levine Books, 2013. Ages 11–15. Australia. Genre-blending book about 2 teens connecting across 2 worlds as both attempt to solve the mysteries of their current life situations.

Morpurgo, Michael. *Private Peaceful*. Scholastic, 2004. Ages 14–18. England. Brutal trench warfare of WWI.

Murray, Martine. *The Slightly True Story of Cedar B. Hartley*. Scholastic, 2003. Ages 11–13. Australia. A girl contemplates a missing brother, a mysterious father, acrobatics, and budding romance.

Naidoo, Beverley. *Burn My Heart*. HarperCollins, 2008. Ages 12–18. South Africa. The Mau Mau uprising in early 1950s Kenya through the eyes of a young white boy and a young Kikuyu boy.

———. *Web of Lies*. HarperColllins, 2006. Ages 12–15. South Africa. Political Nigerian refugees in London face gangs, bullying, and racism. Sequel to *The Other Side of Truth* (2001).

———. *Out of Bounds: Seven Stories of Conflict and Hope*. HarperCollins, 2003. Ages 11–14. South Africa. Living under apartheid in South Africa, 1948–2000.

Nanji, Shenaaz. *Child of Dandelions*. Front Street, 2008. Ages 12–15. Canada. Sabine's wealthy Indian family find themselves in danger when Idi Amin expels all Indians from Uganda. Drawn from family experience.

Nicholls, Sally. *Ways to Live Forever*. Scholastic, 2008. Ages 10–14. England. A boy dying of leukemia keeps a journal of his questions, lists, stories, and pictures.

Nicholson, William. *Seeker*. Harcourt, 2005. Ages 14–18. England. Fantasy world in which 3 teens journey to join a mysterious warrior sect. First book in Noble Warriors series.

Ostlere, Cathy. *Karma*. Razorbill, 2012. **(NV)** Ages 13–18. Canada. Maya, raised in Canada, travels to India with her father to bury her mother in 1984, a time of racial conflict in India.

Peacock, Shane. *Eye of the Crow*. Tundra, 2007. Ages 12–15. Canada. A young Sherlock Holmes.

Peet, Mal. *Tamar*. Candlewick, 2007. Ages 14–18. England. Tamar searches for answers to the mystery surrounding her grandfather's role as a resistance fighter in 1945 Netherlands.

Perera, Anna. *The Glass Collector*. Whitman, 2012. Ages 14–18. England. A teen lives among the garbage piles in the slums of Cairo, collecting broken glass to build a better future.

Powers, J. L., editor. *That Mad Game: Growing Up in a War Zone*. Cinco Puntos, 2012**. (COL)** Ages 14–18. Essays by authors who recount their experiences growing up in war zones all over the world.

Pratchett, Terry. *Nation*. HarperCollins, 2008. Ages 12–16. England. 2 teens from different cultures are brought together when a tidal wave inundates an island. Fantasy.

Pullman, Philip. *The Golden Compass*. Knopf, 1996. Ages 12–16. England. Quest fantasy pitting a young heroine against ruthless soul–thieves. His Dark Materials trilogy.

Rees, Celia. *This Is Not Forgiveness*. Bloomsbury, 2012. Ages 14–18. England. Love triangle between 2 brothers and a girl involved with political anarchists. Mental illness, psychological thriller.

Reeve, Philip. *Here Lies Arthur*. Scholastic, 2008. Ages 12–16. England. A new perspective on the events and characters in the Arthurian legend.

Robert, Na'ima B. *Far from Home*. Frances Lincoln, 2011. Ages 14–18. England. 2 girls in Zimbabwe 25 years apart, both evicted from their homes, one by white colonists and the other by African revolutionaries.

Rosen, Michael. *Michael Rosen's Sad Book*. Illus. Quentin Blake. Candlewick, 2005. **(PI)**

Ages 10–16. England. A father struggles through the stages of grief after the death of his son.

Rosoff, Meg. *How I Live Now*. Wendy Lamb, 2004. Ages 14–18. England. A near-future novel of a teen caught up in an invasion of England that leads to chaos and fear, ripping apart a family and a land. Printz Award.

Rowling, J. K. *Harry Potter and the Sorcerer's Stone*. Scholastic, 1998. Ages 11–13. England. A young wizard battling a local evil in the real world and a cosmic evil in a fantasy world. Harry Potter fantasy series.

Scott, Michael. *The Alchemyst*. Delacorte, 2007. Ages 12–15. Ireland. Fantasy which borrows from history, legend, and mythology, but set in modern times when 2 twins enter an alternative fantasy world. Series.

Sedgwick, Marcus. *Midwinter Blood*. Roaring Brook, 2013. Ages 14–18. England. Fantasy with 7 linked vignettes of horror and passion across time on a Scandinavian island.

Selvadurai, Shyam. *Swimming in the Monsoon Sea*. Tundra, 2005. Ages 14–17. Canada. When his Canadian cousin visits, a 13-year-old Sri Lankan boy learns much about his family and himself.

Slade, Arthur. *Dust*. Wendy Lamb, 2003. Ages 11–14. Canada. Drought, missing children, and a stranger are mysteriously related.

Stratton, Allan. *Chanda's Secrets*. Annick, 2004. Ages 14–18. Canada. The effect of AIDS on the lives of children and young adults in South Africa.

Sutcliffe, William. *The Wall*. Walker, 2013. Ages 12–16. England. Joshua's town is surrounded by a wall to keep the community safe from their enemies, but he finds a tunnel. Fable of Israeli/Palestinian conflict.

Tamaki, Mariko. *Skim*. Groundwood, 2008. **(GR)** Ages 12–17. Canada. Life at an all-girls school where issues such as suicide, sexuality, and fitting in are addressed.

Tan, Shaun. *The Arrival*. Scholastic, 2007. **(GR, wordless)** Ages 12–18. Australia. Visual narrative of the immigrant experience of arriving in a strange new country.

———. *Tales from Outer Suburbia*. Scholastic, 2009. **(COL)** Ages 12–18. Australia.

15 illustrated stories about strange situations in suburbia and how people react to them.

Thompson, Kate. *The New Policeman*. Greenwillow, 2007. Ages 12–16. England. Teen visits an alternate world to repair a cosmic time leak. Sequels include *The Last of the High Kings* (2008) and *The White Horse Trick* (2010).

Updale, Eleanor. *Montmorency*. Scholastic, 2004. Ages 12–16. England. Suspense-filled Victorian London spy drama. Series.

Valentine, Jenny. *Me, the Missing, and the Dead*. HarperTeen, 2008. Ages 14–18. England. While learning about a deceased concert pianist, Lucas solves the mystery of his missing father.

Wallace, Jason. *Out of Shadows*. Holiday House, 2011. Ages 11–15. England. Set in the 1980s, Robert finds himself faced with the racial and political issues that plague Zimbabwe after moving there from London.

Weber, Lori. *If You Live Like Me*. Lobster Press, 2009. Ages 13–17. Canada. Accompanying her parents on their research trip to Newfoundland, Cheryl finds community in an isolated town.

Wild, Margaret. *Fox*. Illus. Ron Brooks. Kane/Miller, 2001. **(PI)** Ages 11–14. Australia. Modern fable of friendship and betrayal.

Williams, Michael. *Now Is the Time for Running*. Little, Brown, 2011. Ages 12–15. South Africa. A massacre in Zimbabwe sends a boy and his mentally disabled brother fleeing to South Africa.

Wynne-Jones, Tim. *Blink & Caution*. Candlewick, 2011. Ages 14–18. Canada. 2 street kids get tangled up in high-profile kidnapping. Relationships, suspense.

Yee, Paul. *Money Boy*. Groundwood, 2011. Ages 14–18. Canada. Ray is kicked out of his house and must survive on the streets of Toronto when his Chinese father discovers he is gay.

Zusak, Markus. *The Book Thief*. Knopf, 2007. Ages 14–18. Australia. Stolen books help a girl cope with life and death in Nazi-era Germany.

Translated Books

Abirached, Zeina. *A Game for Swallows: To Die, to Leave, to Return*. Translated from French by Edward Gauvin. Graphic Universe, 2012. **(GR)** Ages 14–18. France. The intertwined stories and relationships of neighbors gathered in a Beirut apartment during bombing in the 1984 civil war in Lebanon.

Blackcrane, Gerelchimeg. *Black Flame*. Translated from Chinese by Anna Holmwood. Ages 12–14. China. Adventures of a fiercely powerful Tibetan mastiff and his encounters with people across Tibet, Mongolia, and China.

Bondoux, Anne-Laure. *The Killer's Tears*. Translated from French by Y. Maudet. Delacorte, 2006. Ages 14–18. France. Awakening of conscience as a boy is forced to live with his parents' murderer in Chile.

———. *A Time of Miracles*. Translated from French by Y. Maudet. Delacorte, 2011. Ages 12–16. France. A boy leaves his war-torn home in the Caucasus and journeys as a refugee to France in search of his identity.

Buchholz, Quint. *The Collector of Moments*. Translated from German by Peter F. Niemeyer. Farrar, 1999. **(PI)** Ages 11–13. Germany. The stories found in art and their power to affect the viewer's life.

Chen, Jiang Hong. *Mao and Me: The Little Red Guard*. Translated from French by Caludai Zoe Bedrick. Enchanted Lion, 2008. **(GR, PI)** Ages 12–14. France. Memoir of an artist's life during the Chinese Cultural Revolution.

Chotjewitz, David. *Daniel Half Human: And the Good Nazi*. Translated from German by Doris Orgel. Atheneum, 2004. Ages 14–18. Germany. Relationship of two boys, one Jewish and the other a Hitler Youth, WWII.

Combres, Elizabeth. *Broken Memory: A Novel of Rwanda*. Translated from French by Sheila Tanaka. Groundwood, 2009. Ages 12–15. France. A girl who survives the Rwandan massacre returns home to heal from the memories.

D'Adamo, Francesco. *Iqbal: A Novel*. Translated from French by Ann Leonori. Atheneum, 2003. Ages 10–14. France. Fictionalized story of the life of a Pakistani boy who led a child labor movement in the 1990s.

de Saint-Exupery, Antoine. *Le Petit Prince*. Harcourt, 1943/2001. Ages 6 and up. France. Childlike but profound views on life and human nature. French language version.

Duman Tak, Bibi. *Soldier Bear*. Illus. Philip Hopman. Translated from Dutch by Laura Watkinson. Eerdmans, 2011. Ages 10–14. Netherlands. Fictionalized true story of Polish soldiers during WWII who adopted a bear cub that traveled with them in Iran and Italy.

Erlings, Fridrick. *Fish in the Sky*. Translated from Icelandic. Candlewick, 2012. Ages 13–16. Iceland. Josh is attempting to grow up, including understanding his new sexual feelings.

Funke, Cornelia. *Reckless*. Translated from German by Oliver Latsch. Little, Brown, 2010. Ages 12–16. Germany. Fantasy adventure in Mirrorworld, where Jacob, a treasure seeker, must rescue his brother. Series.

Gandolfi, Silvana. *Aldabra, or the Tortoise Who Loved Shakespeare*. Translated from Italian by Lynne Schwartz. Scholastic, 2004. Ages 11–16. Italy. An eccentric grandmother devises a way to prolong her life.

Geda, Fabio. *In the Sea There Are Crocodiles*. Translated from Italian by Howard Curtis. Doubleday, 2011. Ages 14–18. Italy. Story of Enaiat Akbari who flees from the Taliban in Afghanistan across borders as told orally.

Geus, Mireille. *Piggy*. Translated from Dutch by Nancy Forest-Flier. Front Street, 2008. Ages 12–16. Netherlands. Autistic and alienated, "Dizzy" is drawn into a dangerous friendship with an outcast called "Piggy."

Greif, Jean-Jacques. *The Fighter*. Translated from German. Bloomsbury, 2006. Ages 14–18. Germany. Moshe, a poor Polish Jew, uses his physical strength as a boxer to survive the concentration camps of WWII.

Jansen, Hanna. *Over a Thousand Hills I Walk with You*. Translated from German by Elizabeth D. Crawford. Carolrhoda, 2006. Ages 12–16. Germany. Fictionalized biography of survivor of the 1994 Rwanda genocide.

Jung, Reinhard. *Dreaming in Black and White*. Translated from German by Anthea Bell. Phyllis Fogelman, 2003. Ages 12–14. Germany. Attitudes toward those living with disabilities.

Lat. *Kampung Boy*. First Second, 2006. **(GR)** Ages 14–18. Malaysia. Memoir of growing up in rural Malaysia as a Muslim boy in the 1950s. Also *Town Boy* (2007).

Mankell, Henning. *Secrets in the Fire*. Translated from Swedish by Anne C. Stuksrud. Ages 12–18. Annick, 2003. Sweden. Tragic effects of war on child victims of minefields in early 1990s Mozambique.

Miyabe, Miyuki. *Brave Story*. Translated from Japanese by Alexander O. Smith. Viz Media, 2007. Ages 11–14. Japan. Wataru lives in a suburb of Tokyo, near a haunted house with a portal to the land of Vision.

Mourlevat, Jean-Claude. *The Pull of the Ocean*. Translated from French by Y. Maudet. Delacorte, 2006. Ages 10–14. France. A modem "Tom Thumb" story. 7 brothers flee from their poor family farm led by the youngest.

———. *Winter's End*. Translated from French by Anthea Bell. Candlewick, 2008. Ages 14–18. France. 4 teens escape from an oppressive boarding school to pursue freedom and revenge for their parents' murder. Dystopia.

Orlev, Uri. *Run, Boy, Run*. Translated from Hebrew by Hillel Halkin. Houghton, 2003. Ages 11–13. Israel. Survival in the Polish countryside during the Jewish Holocaust.

Pausewang, Gudrun. *Traitor*. Carolrhoda, 2010. Ages 12–17. Translated from German by Rachel Ward. Germany. Anna finds a Russian soldier in her barn and decides to help him escape, questioning German allegiance to Hitler.

Place, Francois. *The Old Man Mad about Drawing: A Tale of Hokusai*. Translated from French by William Rodarmor. Godine, 2003. France. A boy discovers that a strange old man is a famous artist who does woodblock engraving. 1830 Edo, Japan. Reproductions of actual drawings and woodblock prints.

Pressler, Mirjam. *Let Sleeping Dogs Lie*. Translated from German by Erik Macki. Front Street, 2007. Ages 14–18. Germany. Johanna discovers her family's business was stolen from Jews during the Holocaust.

Satrapi, Marjane. *Persepolis*. Translated from French. Pantheon, 2003. **(GR)** Ages 12–15. France. Memoir of a girl struggling with oppression during the Islamic revolution in Iran. Also *Perspepolis 2* (2004).

Sharafeddine, Fatima. *The Servant*. Translated from Arabic. Groundwood, 2013. Ages 13–17.

17-year-old Faten is sent to work as a maid for a family in Beirut, but finds a way to continue her studies and escape.

Skarmeta, Antonio. *The Composition*. Illus. Alfonso Ruano. Translated from Spanish by Elisa Amado. Groundwood, 2000. **(PI)** Ages 11–14. Chile. Family loyalty or betrayal in Latin American police state.

Steinhofel, Andreas. *The Center of the World*. Translated from German by Alisa Jaffa. Delacorte, 2005. Ages 16–18. Germany. A gay teenager comes to terms with himself and his family.

Stolz, Joelle. *The Shadows of Ghadames*. Translated from French by Catherine Temerson. Delacorte, 2004. Ages 11–14. Coming of age as a Muslim girl in late 1800s Libya.

Teller, Janne. *Nothing*. Translated from Danish by Martin Aitken. Atheneum, 2012. Ages 12–14. Denmark. Teens trying to prove that life has meaning descend into mob mentality as each makes an important sacrifice.

Thor, Annika. *A Faraway Island*. Translated from Swedish by Linda Schenick. Dekorte, 2009. Ages 10–14. Sweden. Jewish sisters adopted into a Christian family in Sweden during WWII. Also *The Lily Pond* (2011).

Uehashi, Nahoko. *Morbito: Guardian of the Spirit*. Translated from Japanese by Cathy Hirano. Scholastic, 2008. Ages 10–14. Japan. Fantasy, medieval Japan, woman warrior. Also *Morbito II: Guardian of the Darkness* (2010).

Voorhoevs, Ann. *My Family for the War*. Translated from German by Tammi Reichel. Dial, 2012. Ages 12–16. Germany. Story of Franziska who was placed on the Kindertransport at the beginning of WWII.

Yumoto, Kazumi. *The Friends*. Translated from Japanese by Cathy Hirano. Farrar, 1996. Ages 11–14. Japan. 12-year-old boys interested in the concept of dying find an unexpected friend.

Zenatti, Valerie. *When I Was a Soldier*. Translated from French by Adriana Hunter. Bloomsbury, 2005. Ages 14–18. Memoir recounting 2 years of compulsory service in the Israeli Army and struggles with identity.

Related Films and DVDs

The Book Thief (2013). Author: Markus Zusak (2006). 131 minutes (Germany)

The Devil's Arithmetic (1999). Author: Jane Yolen (1988). 95 minutes. (Jewish)

The Golden Compass (2007). Author: Philip Pullman (1996). 113 minutes. (England)

Inkheart (2008). Author: Cornelia Funke (2003). 106 minutes. (Germany)

Millions (2005). Author: Frank C. Boyce (2004). 98 minutes. (England)

Miracle's Boys (2005). Author: Jacqueline Woodson (2000). 6 episodes; 133 minutes. (African American)

Persepolis (2008). Author: Marjane Satrapi (2003). 96 minutes. (Iran)

The Thief Lord (2006). Author: Cornelia Funke (2002). 98 minutes. (Germany)

Part Three

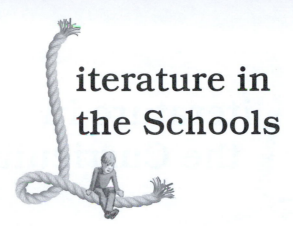

literature in the Schools

Finding compelling books for adolescents is only a first step. The ways in which you use those books can either invite adolescents to enthusiastically immerse themselves as readers or lead them to dread completing questions and worksheets once they finish reading the book. Chapters 9 and 10 focus on curriculum and teaching strategies along with the issues that arise with the use of young adult literature.

Chapter 9 begins with a discussion of the political context that influences the use of literature in schools and then explores the decisions that need to be made in planning for a literature curriculum. Different ways of organizing a literature curriculum and developing a literature unit are described along with the resources needed to support this curriculum. Questions of censorship, the relationship of young adult literature to classic canonical texts, and the teaching of literary criticism also need to be considered.

Chapter 10 highlights experiences that invite adolescents to participate in literary worlds. The chapter begins with a discussion of how teachers can create a literate environment for all readers, particularly for different types of resistant readers. Experiences with literature are organized around three types of engagements that have different purposes for readers. Reading widely for personal purposes focuses on strategies for teacher read-alouds, student independent reading, booktalks, and multimodal texts. Reading critically to inquire about the world involves in-depth consideration of a book through literature discussions, literature response engagements, drama as response, and literature across the curriculum. Reading strategically to learn about literacy and literature emphasizes explicit instruction about literacy and literature through engagements with young adult literature. Strategies for meeting the needs and interests of resistant readers are integrated throughout these sections.

Chapter Nine

Literature in the Curriculum

This chapter highlights the political context that surrounds the use of literature in classrooms as well as broader issues of planning for literature instruction. The Common Core State Standards have had a tremendous impact on the ways in which schools are planning for literature and literacy. Different organizational structures for organizing a literature curriculum with students, such as genres, themes/topics, authors, literary elements, and notable books, are overviewed along with strategies for planning literature units and for dealing with controversial issues.

The Politics of Literacy and Literature

The teaching of literacy and literature has been a controversial and contested area of debate among both educators and politicians. Calls for higher literacy standards are the focus of intense national and international interest and have led to the imposition of "one size fits all" models of national literacy standards and high stakes testing through legislation and policy initiatives. Although initiatives on literacy have long evolved from public pressure, the increasing involvement of federal and state governments in specific decisions about literacy instruction in order to raise standards is a more recent development. These public debates and government initiatives have often resulted in punitive legislation aimed at controlling teachers.

Congress created the **National Reading Panel (NRP)** in 1997 to assess the status of research-based knowledge about reading. The *Report of the National Reading Panel* (2000) was met with great controversy and skepticism because of the panel's narrow definition of scientific research that excluded the majority of research studies conducted over the preceding thirty year period and resulted in a highly skewed set of recommendations. This report narrowed the teaching of reading to instruction in phonemic awareness, phonics, reading comprehension, fluency, and vocabulary. A large body of research studies on reading aloud and independent silent reading were not included because they did not meet the NRP's narrow definition of scientific research.

The **No Child Left Behind Act (NCLB)** was passed in 2001, leading to specific reading instructional programs and requirements. By 2008, reading comprehension tests indicated that these instructional programs did *not* have statistically significant impacts on reading comprehension test scores in grades 1 through 3 and reading achievement scores for intermediate students either had not increased or were decreasing.

Accountability is a demand by government agencies and the public for school systems and teachers to improve students' school achievement as demonstrated by test scores. The NCLB Act expanded accountability by requiring annual testing of reading and mathematics achievement for all students in grades 3 to 8. NCLB also required that performance data be disaggregated according to race, gender, income, and other criteria to demonstrate progress in closing the achievement gap between students viewed as "disadvantaged" and other groups of students. These data were used to grade schools as Pass or Fail, depending on student achievement by averages for the grade and by subgroups. Schools that receive failing grades are given a period of time to improve student achievement. Failure of a school to do so resulted in reduced federal and state funding for the school, vouchers for students to attend another public school or charter school in the case of repeated failures by the school, or replacement of administrators and teachers, depending on state and local policies. States developed the actual tests, the procedures for implementation of the policy, and timetables for implementation according to federal requirements.

Critics point out that the focus on multiple choice tests has dumbed down the curriculum and led to "drill and kill" approaches to teaching isolated skills as well as to pushing low-scoring students out of public schools to boost scores. The National Association of Educational Progress tracks trends in reading achievement and issues a report called the "Nation's Report Card." Data show that reading comprehension scores for 2011 remained unchanged at grade 4 with a slight improvement at grade 8 after several years of decline that seem to be associated with NCLB. Many educators believe that the major reason for this decline was a decrease in voluntary reading among students. As a result of NCLB, a large amount of class time was spent on basic reading skills, diminishing curricular efforts in other subjects, including the enjoyment and appreciation of literature. As is often the case with policy initiatives, the failure and shortcomings of NCLB led to a new initiative based on a new set of standards and assessments.

Common Core State Standards

The current focus of national and state efforts is the ***Common Core State Standards,*** which have been adopted by most states and have influenced the standards and assessments of other states. These K–12 standards were developed by a group appointed by the National Governor's Association and the Council of Chief State School Officers. They examined research on the levels of literacy needed for success in college and careers and worked backward to determine the literacy knowledge they believed students needed to have at each grade level to be college and career ready by the end of high school. These grade-specific standards in reading, writing, speaking, listening, and language also set requirements for literacy in history/social studies, science, and technical content areas. These standards have had a tremendous impact on instruction due to state and district mandates. National performance-based assessments are under development to measure student achievement and to evaluate teachers and schools on the standards.

Aspects of the Common Core State Standards raise new possibilities for instruction, but are also accompanied by myths in how some schools are interpreting the standards and by assumptions built into the standards themselves:

- ***Possibility:*** Students will engage with more informational texts in classroom instruction, beginning in Kindergarten with a 50/50 split between literary and informational texts, increasing to a recommendation of 70 percent informational text at high school.

  - ***Myth**—Narrative and fiction are not valued in the standards.* The standards actually have a strong focus on literary fiction and argue for a better balance of the types of texts used in classrooms, not an overbalance in the other direction.

  - ***Myth**—English literature classes need to use 70 percent informational text and 30 percent literary text.* The standards call for the 70/30 split to go across the school day, a balance that is easy to reach since the majority of reading across the subject areas of math, science, and social studies is informational text.

    - ***Asssumption**—Narrative is viewed by the standards as a type of discourse that differs from the writing found in informational text; however, narrative is a text structure often used in informational books and is essential to how humans make sense of the world.

- ***Possibility:*** Students will gradually increase the complexity of texts that they are reading with continual increases across grade levels. CCSS provides a list of text exemplars for each grade level along with excerpts from these texts to demonstrate this increase in text complexity.

  - ***Myth**—These lists are core books to be read by all students.* The list is actually exemplars to help teachers consider the complexity of texts in their school, not core texts to be read by all students.

- *Myth—Text complexity is determined by quantitative measures, specifically by Lexile levels.* Text complexity in CCSS is determined by Lexile levels along with teacher judgment about the difficulty of a text related to the readers in that classroom and the task in which they are engaged.

  - *Assumption—*The focus on reading classic texts to increase complexity overlooks the importance of students reading lots of engaging contemporary novels at a range of complexity levels in order to develop fluency, flexibility, and interest as readers.

- *Possibility:* Students will engage in close reading of texts and be able to find and cite evidence in the text as they discuss key ideas and details, craft and structure, and knowledge and ideas from these texts. This kind of text analysis is viewed as bringing rigor to reading with an emphasis on higher level critical reading skills.

  - *Myth—Close reading involves asking literal level questions that can be directly answered from the text.* Instead, close reading involves inferential and evaluative thinking as students critically consider the text.

    - *Assumption—*Reader response is viewed as only focusing on sharing personal connections and not including text analysis and therefore in opposition to close reading. Reader response does begin with personal connections and interpretations, but then moves readers into analyzing their response through dialogue based on evidence from their lives and the text to develop their interpretations.

    - *Assumption—*The emphasis on close text-based reading mandates a return to narrow definitions of what and how students read. History indicates that this type of textual criticism turned off several generations to reading because it lacked purpose, meaning, and connections to ideas and issues that students cared about (Langer, 2010).

Resources to support you in meeting the Common Core State Standards are integrated throughout this text—titles of books across a range of categories, discussions of the structures and types of informational texts, information about literary elements and text structures, methods for measuring text complexity, and ways to integrate text analysis with reader response.

Even given the political context surrounding literacy and literature, young adult literature can still become a planned component of classroom life. Teachers can create a literature curriculum where instruction is planned around literature as a discipline with a focus on literary knowledge as well as the development of critical thinking and lifelong reading habits.

Planning for a Literature Curriculum

Planning for a yearlong strand of literature instruction involves choosing an approach, within which there are goals for the course of study, specific young adult books, guidelines for selection of materials, a schedule, and criteria for evaluating the course of study. Some teachers use a ***traditional approach*** to literature that focuses on mastery of content. This approach places the teacher at the center, in that the teacher decides the agenda, dispenses the information, asks the questions, and often supplies the answers. The goal of this approach is for students to learn what the teacher tells them about the literature under study.

Our focus is on an *inquiry approach,* which is grounded in problem-based learning and constructivist learning and focuses on how one learns. Teachers who choose this approach want students to be actively engaged in posing questions that are significant to them as they explore the power of literature to examine the human condition. An inquiry approach is characterized by the following:

- Students' inquiry is guided by their *own* questions related to a piece of literature— questions they find compelling and honestly care about. During the inquiry process, students revise their questions as they learn and discuss, debate, and share information with other students through collaborative learning, team projects, and small group discussions.

- Emphasis is placed on the process of how to search for and make sense of information about literature so that the knowledge gained is conceptual and has wide application.

- Teachers are facilitators rather than dispensers of knowledge who think collaboratively with students instead of providing answers.

This perspective of curriculum as inquiry affects how teachers approach ways of organizing a literature curriculum and how literature units are planned and implemented.

Ways of Organizing the Curriculum

Teachers can decide to organize a literature curriculum by genre, theme or topic, author, literary element or device, or notable book. An alternative is to create a hybrid literature curriculum by including aspects of several of these approaches in the plan.

Genre   By organizing a literature curriculum around literary genres, teachers provide a context for students to learn about various types of literature and their characteristics. An inquiry approach to genre typically begins by immersing students in a wide range of books from that genre and encouraging them to develop a list of characteristics for that genre based on their reading—for example, that works of historical fiction are always set in the past or that works of fantasy use a range of strategies to establish believability in an imaginary world. Students can then move to in-depth explorations of specific books within that genre and of the ways these characteristics play out differently across the genre. Students will begin to read with more genre awareness and will enjoy finding common elements within and differences between genres. This inquiry approach differs from traditional genre units where the characteristics for a particular genre are provided by teachers as a formula to memorize and apply, not to discover through active engagement with books.

A genre approach exposes students to a wide variety of literature across the school year and provides useful frameworks for understanding and appreciating works of different genres. This approach works well with literature circles, small groups formed around the reading of young adult books from that genre, and discussions of connections and interpretations. Since each group discusses a different book, literature circles provide a context for whole group discussions of how literary concepts and elements play out differently within that genre. Planning involves choosing a genre, gathering a range of books, and selecting several representative young adult books.

Theme or Topic   Organizing a study of literature by theme or topic is the most frequent and effective way to engage students with literature. Focusing on the multiple connections and interpretations of issues and themes in a book gives students an opportunity to relate what they learn to their own lives. Themes provide a conceptual approach to making connections across books and between their lives and broader issues, such as:

- Making a difference through involvement and activism within a community
- Belonging creates relationships and conformity
- Becoming your own person means balancing individual voice and group responsibility
- The choices we make affect our lives and health
- Difference is a resource, not a problem
- Learning through adversity produces stronger commitment

A theme approach usually involves students reading a set of books or texts related to the theme and exploring the theme through questioning, journaling, reflecting, discussing, writing, responding through drama and art, and further reading. Strategies to support discussion and response are in Chapter 10. Books can also be organized around topics like friendship, divorce, and careers as a way to support students in locating books for independent reading. Organizing by topic, however, does not facilitate discussion and thoughtful connections across books because topics stay on the surface of the book and do not engage students with issues around which they can enter into dialogue.

Another conceptual frame is to read literature organized around the social worlds of adolescents, such as peer worlds, school and sports worlds, family and romance worlds, community and workplace worlds, and virtual worlds. Students use literature and their lives to examine how language, symbols, and actions create and maintain social worlds in order to both understand and critique those worlds (Beach & Myers, 2001).

Author   The goal of a curriculum organized by author is to acquaint students with the books and writing styles of selected young adult book authors. Students may also gain knowledge of authors' lives and how those life experiences influence their works. The choice of authors will naturally be guided both by students' reading interests and the teacher's desire to introduce students to important authors and their works. The number of works chosen to represent an author will vary, but even when an author's books are lengthy, more than one work is recommended.

As a class experiences the chosen author's work, attention will be focused on trademark stylistic elements such as unusual use of words, prevalent themes, character types, or settings. Information about the author's life can be introduced through reports, audio and video recordings of interviews, book trailers, and guest appearances by the author in person or through a live internet connection. Author websites, biographies, autobiographies, and biographical reference volumes, such as *Something about the Author* (2013) and *Children's Literature Review* (2011), are good resources for information. In addition, many authors maintain active Twitter, Facebook, or online communities where they dialogue with readers, asking for advice and responding to queries. A directory of authors willing to arrange virtual visits to classrooms is found on the Skype-an-Author network (http://skypeanauthor.wetpaint.com).

Literary Element or Device   Organizing around literary elements usually refers to the elements of fiction, nonfiction, and poetry as presented in Chapters 2, 6, and 7, such as a focus on character development in a work of fiction. A *literary device* is a technique used to achieve a special effect, such as symbolism, foreshadowing, and circular plot, to add richness to stories. The goal of a literature curriculum organized by literary elements and devices is to give students a better understanding of the craft of writing so that they can read more perceptively and appreciatively and apply this knowledge to their own writing.

Careful selection of young adult books to accompany the investigation of each literary element or device is crucial. The featured element or device must be prominent and must have been used by the author with extraordinary skill to captivate readers. Books of various genres can be grouped to demonstrate the same literary element, permitting teachers to select five or six books for literature circles. Picture books sometimes provide teachers with clear examples of literary elements and devices in relatively simple contexts so that they can be understood more easily by adolescents. An excellent resource to help middle and high school teachers select picture books for this use is Hall's *Using Picture Story Books to Teach Literary Devices* (2007).

Students' acquaintance with literary elements and devices can go far beyond mere definition and include close reading of key passages. The passages can be used to examine the author's craft at developing character, establishing mood, authenticating setting, or using such devices as shifting point of view. Students can then explore these elements and devices in their own art, drama, and writing to give a personal and more complete understanding of these concepts, providing an evaluation of students' grasp of concepts.

Notable Books   Organizing around notable books can focus on young adult books that are classic or contemporary and from different genres and award-winning lists. The books can be read and analyzed for the features that contribute to their excellence, such as their relevance to readers, unique perspectives, treatment of topics, or memorable characters. Discussion of notable books can be organized by whole class, small groups, or pairs with oral and/or written responses. Novels are usually read independently, but shorter works, such as selected poems or short stories, can be read aloud in class by the teacher or students. Lists of award-winning books are in Appendix A.

Teachers who organize their literature curriculum by notable books must be careful to remain flexible in book selections from year to year so that the list of notable books reflects students' current interests and reading preferences. A list of notable books that never varies can result in a lack of student interest and stale teaching.

Developing Literature Units

Initial planning for literature units includes establishing goals for what students will explore or learn through this unit, selecting several books that will receive in-depth focus (often called touchstone books), and gathering a collection of many books related to the unit focus. For example, initial planning for a science fiction unit on future worlds could involve identifying these core books:

- Independent reading of books that are close to students' own worlds or are familiar in order to provide access to those who are new to science fiction—*The City of Ember* by Jeanne DuPrau (2003), *The House of the Scorpion* by Nancy Farmer (2002), *The Hunger Games* by Suzanne Collins (2008), *Feed* by M. T. Anderson (2002), *Double Identity* by Margaret Peterson Haddix (2005), and *Monument 14* by Emmy Laybourne (2012).

- Read-aloud touchstone texts—*The Giver* by Lois Lowry (1993) as a ground-breaking dystopian novel that will be familiar to many students and *When We Wake* by Karen Healey (2013) as a recent dystopian view of the future.
- Small group literature circles on books that are more complex dystopias so that students can work together to develop their interpretations—*The Knife of Never Letting Go* by Patrick Ness (2009), *Ship Breaker* by Paolo Bacigalupi (2010), *Little Brother* by Cory Doctorow (2008), *The 5th Wave* by Rick Yancy (2013), *Legend* by Marie Lu (2011), *Shadows Cast by Stars* by Catherine Knutsson (2012).
- Featured Author: Patrick Ness (www.patrickness.com/)

Collecting, brainstorming, and organizing literary engagements are the final steps in planning for a literature unit. Two useful tools in organizing the details of literature units are webs and lesson plans. A *web* is a graphic planning tool that reveals relationships between ideas and so creates a visual overview of a literature unit, including its focus, concepts, related book titles, and activities. A web is a map that helps teachers and students find their way to their goals and can be changed easily to encompass new ideas, be adapted for different uses, or meet special needs and circumstances. Teachers can use the web as a source for daily or weekly lesson plans as the unit unfolds.

Ideas for a web are generated through brainstorming. The main advantage of webbing is that the process clarifies and creates ideas for connections between concepts, books, and activities. Activities can be drawn across content and skill areas—writing, reading, listening, thinking, speaking, art, crafts, drama, and music. Involving students in creating webs gives them a voice in planning and can provide original ideas and relationships that the teacher had not considered.

The web in Figure 9.1 is organized around a conceptual frame of journeys as movement along a pathway that could be physical, emotional, cultural, or psychological. This frame connects to a topic of current interest, refugees, through literacy activities in an English or language arts classroom. This web could just as well be organized around concepts relating to refugees, such as facing prejudice, challenging borders and rules, experiencing the unknown, cultural transformations, the history of immigration or refugees in a particular region, or the pros and cons of immigration. As such, it could be used as a planning tool for a unit in social studies or history as well as in English or language arts. The web in Figure 9.2 is organized around concepts of taking responsibility for action and could be used to plan a unit in English, literature, or life skills.

Lesson plans vary according to the needs and experience of the teacher, but lesson plans for each day or week usually include the following components:

- *Goals or objectives* are the conceptual ideas or issues for a particular set of activities, essentially the "why" behind those activities. These goals give a focus for the activities but also leave space for students to pursue their inquiries. A teacher planning a literature unit on refugees might have the goal that students understand the complex issues surrounding the labels of legal and illegal and of securing documentation.
- *Activities and materials* indicate the preparation that the teacher needs to do for the experience, the materials needed, and the tasks or engagements for students. Teachers wanting students to understand the complex issues of documentation could read aloud the informational book, *Denied, Detained, and Deported* by Ann Bausum while students select from novels to read in small groups, such as *La Línea* by Ann

Figure 9.1   Conceptual Web on Forced Journeys, a Cross-Curricular Literature Unit
(Grades 6–8)

Journeys of Transformation

Literature circles on books about contemporary teens

Map the changes made by characters in their journeys

Under the Mesquite by Guadalupe Garcia McCall
Out of My Mind by Sharon Draper
The Steps by Rachel Cohn
The Misfits by James Howe
As Easy as Falling Off the Face of the Earth by Lynn Rae Perkins
Shakespeare Bats Cleanup by Ron Koertge

Mapping Life Journeys

Create a visual map of your life journey

Share *My Map Book* by Sara Fanelli for Ideas

Share your map with a partner

Web the kinds of journeys on your map

Analyze which journeys are forced or chosen

Forced Journeys (Picture Book Text Set)

Web the types of forced journeys and their consequences

Barbed Wire Baseball by Marissa Moss
Home to Medicine Mountain by Chiori Santiago
Michael Rosen's Sad Book by Michael Rosen
The Color of Home by Mary Hoffman
I Will Come Back for You by Marisabina Russo
I Hate English by Ellen Levine
Happy Like Soccer by Marybeth Boelts
A Storm Called Katrina by Myron Uhlberg
Show Way by Jacqueline Woodson
I Know Here by Laurel Croza

Conceptual Understandings of Journeys

Read Alouds ◄

The Island by Armin Greder
The Milk of Birds by Sylvia Whitman

Forced Journeys: Refugee Experiences

Literature Circles ◄

A Long Walk to Water by Linda Sue Park
Ask Me No Questions by Marina Budhos
Inside Out and Back Again by Thanhha Lai
The Other Side of Truth by Beverly Naidoo
A Time of Miracles by Anne-Laure Bondoux
La línea by Ann Jamarillo

Independent Reading

Current Events

Collect news stories, political cartoons, editorials on immigration issues

Research current refugee stories on the internet

Track journeys of current refugees on a large world map

► **Interviews**

Invite a community volunteer who works with refugees to share with the class

Ask students to interview an immigrant or refugee

Interview family members to trace immigration story of ancestors

Fiction
Esperanza Rising by Pam Muñoz Ryan
Out of the Dust by Karen Hesse
Lizzie Bright and the Buckminster Boy by Gary Schmidt
Now is the Time for Running by Michael Williams
The Arrival by Shaun Tan
The Good Braider by Terry Farish
All the Broken Pieces by Ann Burg
Child of Dandelions by Shenaaz Nanji

Nonfiction
Denied, Detained, Deported by Ann Bausum
Children of War: Voices of Iraqi Refugees by Deborah Ellis
Enrique's Journey by Sonia Nazario
Hope and Tears: Ellis Island Voices by Gwenyth Swain

Figure 9.2 Conceptual Web on Taking Responsibility for Action (Grades 9–12)

Going Against Societal Norms

Read books in literature circles

Create visual to show interconnection among protagonists and their decisions

Discuss ways protagonists confront the issue of responsibility

Luna by Julie Ann Peters
The Perks of Being a Wallflower by Stephen Chbosky
Little Brother by Cory Doctorow
So Yesterday by Scott Westerfeld
Big Mouth and Ugly Girl by Joyce Carol Oates

Taking a Stand on Issues

Read one of the titles, clarify the issue, and debate the two sides of the issue

Take a stand on the issue. Write an opinion paper

Create a readers' theater script and perform for the class

When We Wake by Karen Healey
Thirteen Reasons Why by Jay Asher
Legend by Marie Lu
Let Sleeping Dogs Lie by Mirjam Pressler
The Killer's Tears by Ann-Laure Bondoux

Deciding Between Right and Wrong

Read and discuss books in literature circles

Respond to prompts "If you had been the protagonist, what would you have done differently?" or "How, if ever, can one atone for a bad choice?"

Please Ignore Vera Dietz by A.S. King
One Night by Margaret Wild
Inexcusable by Chris Lynch
Twisted by Laurie Halse Anderson
Lockdown by Walter Dean Myers

Helping Others ◄

Taking Responsibility for Action

► **Becoming Yourself**

Read aloud excerpts from *Under the Mesquite* by Guadalupe Garcia McCall

Discuss (a) the issues the protagonist faces (b) whether young people should take on such responsibilities (c) what others might do in response to such situations.

Read another title

Write a personal response on: "Why does taking responsibility seem so difficult?" and "What does it mean to be responsible to yourself as well as to others?"

The 5th Wave by Rick Yancey
Monument 14 by Emily Laybourne
Antsy Does Time by Neil Schusterman
Notes from the Midnight Driver by Jordan Sonnenblick
Me and Earl and the Dying Girl by Jesse Andrews

Teacher Read Alouds on Taking Responsibility

Code Name Verity by Elizabeth Wein
Traitor by Gudrun Pausewang
The Scorpio Races by Maggie Stiefvater
Darius and Twig by Walter Dean Myers
Where Things Come Back by John Corey Whaley
The Language Inside by Holly Thompson

Choose a title to read

Consider the pressure young people face when attempting to make the right decisions for themselves rather than for others. Write about who or what might be barriers to adolescents' decision-making and who or what might be helpful in that decision-making

Write a poem that addresses the dilemma the protagonist(s) in one of the books faces when becoming an independent person

It's Kind of a Funny Story by Ned Vizzini
Out of My Mind by Sharon Draper
Waiting for No One by Beverly Brenna
Eleanor and Park by Rainbow Rowell
Does My Head Look Big in This by Randa Abdel-Fattah

Jamarillo, *Ask Me No Questions* by Marina Budhos, and *A Time of Miracles* by Anne-Aaure Bondoux.

- *Evaluation and reflection* involve plans for evaluating students' understandings around the goals and for teacher reflections on the effectiveness of the activities. *Student evaluation* can take the form of written reflections, oral questions, whole-class or small group discussions, entries in student journals, and written, oral, artistic, and dramatic responses to literature. *Self-evaluation by the teacher* can focus on student interest in the activities, student understandings related to the goals, and the plan's success in predicting time and materials needed and the effectiveness of the activities and materials. During the literature unit, teachers will want to regularly evaluate their students' understandings and questions and make adjustments in the plans.

Because literature units are several weeks long, they usually include a culminating activity that gives students an opportunity to reflect on what they have learned, review major ideas, and celebrate the focus of the unit or share their own inquiries. An overall unit evaluation is valuable to teachers, particularly if they intend to use the unit with another group of students. Online sources of lesson plans created by teachers include ReadWriteThink (www .readwritethink.org) and Web English Teacher (www.webenglishteacher.com). Students can use the internet to research topics for literature units of study, locate websites for author studies, or identify sources for further research on a theme. Students often enjoy finding books on topics of interest and reading others' comments on these books. Links to several of these sites can be found on the American Library Association's Great Sites for Kids (http:// gws.ala.org) in the Literature and Languages category.

Resources for a Literature Curriculum

An effective literature-based curriculum is based on resources that include the school library media center, bookfairs, parents, guest authors and illustrators, and local public libraries as well as a strong classroom library collection.

- *School Library Media Center.* The well-stocked, efficiently run library media center is the heart of a school. Ideally, library media specialists and teachers work collaboratively with teachers informing librarians of their resource needs and librarians identifying and locating appropriate resources, keeping teachers updated with the newest literature, and suggesting ways to present books to students. For some teens, the media center can be a haven for reading in comfortable, quiet surroundings that are not available to them elsewhere. Displays of the latest popular titles and comfortable seating areas invite teens to sit and read. Before-school and after-school hours greatly increase access and provide time to schedule book clubs around popular reading interests, such as a mystery or science fiction club.

- *Summer Reading Programs.* One way to expand traditional summer reading lists is to provide students with the option of suggesting alternative titles, subject to teacher approval, and to include recent young adult titles on the list. The main purpose of these lists is to keep students reading in their months away from school and to create a shared experience among students at the beginning of the following school year.

- *Bookfairs.* A bookfair is a book sale organized by a book vendor and held in the school building for several days. Bookfairs call attention to reading and send strong messages to adolescents and parents about a school's stance on the importance of quality literature and of book ownership.

- *Parent Partnerships.* Partnerships honor the resources and expertise of the home and the school. These partnerships might involve encouraging reading and discussing books together in the home, providing information on the public library and on sources of free audiobook and e-books, and letting families know about special literacy programs for teens at local libraries or community agencies. Instead of sending homework that interferes with family life, this type of homework encourage interactions around books.

- *Guest Authors and Illustrators.* Young adult authors and illustrators often visit schools to share about their creative processes and books. Such visits are powerful experiences that influence adolescents as readers. Publisher websites and marketing departments have information on arranging author visits in person or through electronic media.

- *Local Public Library.* Public libraries provide many services in addition to loaning books, including interlibrary loan, access to audiobooks and e-books, summertime reading programs, and various kinds of teen book clubs, poetry slams, and project groups.

- *Classroom Book Collections.* Most of the responsibility for acquiring a large and varied collection of books in your classroom will be yours. Classroom libraries usually have a permanent collection as well as a collection that is checked out from the school or public library and changes regularly to provide depth and breadth to units of study and appeal to students' interests. You can build a classroom collection by requesting funds from your principal or PTO, submitting a small grant to your school district, professional organization, or local foundations, purchasing books through paperback book clubs, frequenting library books sales, or asking for donations of used books from families. You can also establish a book exchange basket or shelf where students can donate books for others to read and take books in return that interest them.

Integrating Young Adult Literature into the Curriculum

As the field of young adult literature has matured, improved, and grown, the trend has been to include more young adult books in middle and high school reading lists. The study of adult classic works of literature still remains a tradition in American high schools, but young adult literature has increasingly been integrated into the curriculum, especially in middle schools, to meet curricular demands and engage adolescents as readers. This curricular integration raises several critical issues for teachers. One is the relationship of young adult literature to the classics that have traditionally been the staple of high school English classes. A related concern is the whether or not literary criticism can be taught using young adult literature. Finally, the issue of censorship always accompanies the use of literature regardless of its genre or the time period in which it was written.

Linking Young Adult Novels to Classics

Knowledge of our cultural heritage as found in the classics is important to have and share as citizens. But we live in a rapidly changing culture, and literature should reflect the ongoing culture as well as that of the past. Change is inevitable, and as our culture changes, so does the need for the classics that serve as a foundation for many literature classrooms. Titles often included on high school required reading lists are included in Table 9.1. This list, however, has books that are biased against women and people of color and language and writing styles that are dated and difficult for adolescents to understand because of obscure expressions and unfamiliar sentence constructions. In addition, few classics have teens as main characters, since most are adult novels. These characteristics often make many classics less relevant to adolescents. Some classics, of course, still hold appeal and, if taught in an interesting way, are enjoyed by young adults.

The decision about whether to use young adult literature or classic texts is complicated by school district requirements and by an increased emphasis on classics due to the Common Core State Standards. Many teachers pair classic works with appropriate young adult books for these reasons:

- *To serve as a bridge to understanding and appreciating the classic work.* The young adult novel is read first and, because it is more accessible, helps readers create a context for understanding the classic work and seeing its relevance to their lives.

- *To learn the vocabulary of literary criticism and to engage in thinking critically about books.* The young adult novel is read first and provides easily understandable examples of plot structure, character development, description and use of setting, development of theme, or writing style, thus preparing readers to find and understand how these elements work in the classic text.

- *To bring more diverse literature into the English curriculum.* A young adult novel with a similar plot or theme is paired with a classic text, but is written by or from the point of view of a protagonist who is not male or from a Western culture.

Table 9.1   Most Frequently Required Novels, Grades 9 through 12

Renaissance Learning Survey of Assigned Books	Goodreads Rankings from Required Reading Lists
To Kill a Mockingbird, Harper Lee	*To Kill a Mockingbird*, Harper Lee
The Crucible, Arthur Miller	*The Great Gatsby*, F. Scott Fitzgerald
Night, by Elie Wiesel	*Romeo and Juliet,* William Shakespeare
Of Mice and Men, John Steinbeck	*The Catcher in the Rye*, J. D. Salinger
Lord of the Flies, William Golding	*The Scarlet Letter*, Nathaniel Hawthorne
Macbeth, William Shakespeare	*The Crucible*, Arthur Miller
The Great Gatsby, F. Scott Fitzgerald	*The Adventures of Huckleberry Finn*, Mark Twain
Animal Farm, George Orwell	*Great Expectations*, Charles Dickens
Julius Caesar, William Shakespeare	*Lord of the Flies*, William Golding
The Adventures of Huckleberry Finn, Mark Twain	*The Grapes of Wrath*, John Steinbeck
Source: http://www.goodreads.com/shelf/show/ high-school-required-reading	*Source:* Based on Renaissance Learning, 2012. http:// www.renlearn.com/whatkidsarereading/

In planning for young adult–classic literature pairings, teachers may pair a classic work with one young adult novel or several, providing all have the required similarities. Pairing a classic work with several young adult selections allows a teacher to more effectively match students' reading abilities and interests and to investigate several different themes or several different elements of fiction. *Adolescent Literature as a Complement to the Classics* by Joan Kaywell (2010) and *From Hinton to Hamlet: Building Bridges between Young Adult Literature and the Classics* by Sarah Herz and Donald Gallo (2005) provide ideas for how classics can be paired with engaging young adult novels.

To get an idea of contemporary titles that might be paired with classics, consider the following examples, noting that many other options of young adult literature exist for these pairings:

- William Shakespeare's *Romeo and Juliet* (1597), widely taught in high schools, explores the themes of star-crossed love and prejudice. Contemporary works with a similar theme include Sharon Draper's *Romiette and Julio* (1999) (young love threatened by family prejudices and gangs), Walter Dean Myers' *Street Love* (2006) (love crossing social-class lines in Harlem), and Jenny Downham's *You against Me* (2010) (forbidden love and family loyalty). The Twilight series by Stephanie Meyer has elements of the classic *Romeo and Juliet*, but once Bella becomes a vampire the gap between the two young lovers is bridged.

- Aldous Huxley's classic, *Brave New World* (1932), investigates utopias and dystopias, bioethical issues of genetic engineering, and the importance of individuality and self-determination. It could be paired with M. T. Anderson's *Feed* (2002) (consumer-driven dystopian world in which computer feeds are implanted in brains), Suzanne Collins' *The Hunger Games* (2008) (dystopian near-future United States in which teens are pitted in gladiator-like combat), and Nancy Werlin's *Double Helix* (2004) (the perils of cloning).

- Nathaniel Hawthorne's often-assigned classic, *The Scarlet Letter* (1850), investigates the themes of alienation, acting on one's convictions, and the price of nonconformity. The same themes are found in Emily M. Danforth's *The Miseducation of Cameron Post* (2012) (alienation and acting on convictions), Joyce Carol Oates' *Big Mouth and Ugly Girl* (2002) (nonconformity), and Margaret Wild's *One Night* (2004) (pregnancy, alienation, rejection).

- Some young adult novels are explicitly written to update or mirror classics, using similar plot structures and themes, such as April Lindner's *Catherine* (2013), an update of *Wuthering Heights*; Abby McDonald's *Jane Austen Goes to Hollywood* (2013), an update of *Sense and Sensibility*; and Patrice Kindl's *Keeping the Castle* (2012), which mirrors *Pride and Prejudice*.

- Historical fiction and biography for young adults sometimes focuses on the lives of authors of frequently read classics, such as Veronica Bennett's *Cassandra's Sister* (2007) about Jane Austen; Barbara Dana's *A Voice of Her Own: Becoming Emily Dickinson* (2009); and Barbara Kerley's *Walt Whitman: Words for America* (2006).

- Classics are sometimes transformed into young adult novels using a teenage observer, such as *Ithaka* by Adele Geras (2006), which reimagines Homer's *Odyssey* through the eyes of a young companion, or into formats that appeal to young adults, such as the graphic novel format for *Beowolf* by Gareth Hinds (2007).

As is often the case, teachers do not need to choose between classics and young adult literature, but can effectively use both to build from the strengths that each offer in the lives of adolescents. Providing a more positive experience with classics through these pairings increases the possibility that students will search out other classics on their own in future reading experiences.

Teaching Literary Theory through Young Adult Literature

The study of literature generally focuses on the meaning found in a work of literature and how readers construct that meaning. In many classrooms, deep analysis through exact and careful reading is referred to as *new criticism* or *structural criticism,* but young adult readers often do not have the literary or life experience to conduct deep analyses that depend on literary allusions and historical references. We support *reader response* as asserted by Louise Rosenblatt (1938) whereby students first read for their own connections and responses to a piece of literature, have the opportunity to explore their personal responses and interpretations, and then step back and use a particular literary theory to examine the text and their response in more depth. In particular, New Historicism, rhetorical criticism, and feminist criticism are literary theories that can scaffold the ability of adolescents to analyze a text (Soter, 1999).

We selected these three literary lenses because they touch on the issues often seen in young adult literature, and these theories lend themselves to the passionate questioning of many adolescents. What should be noted is that there are multiple ways to conduct literary analysis within each of these literary lenses, and they often overlap with one another. This section provides general ideas of how these literary theories could be used with young adults.

During adolescence, many young adults question the world and their responses to it. *New Historicism* is an appropriate type of criticism that emphasizes thinking critically, learning how to analyze a text, and encouraging critical reading and question posing. New Historicism addresses questions about the social context at the time of the book's publication and how that social context and historical time period influenced the author's treatment of the text subject (mood and tone) and the reader's response to the text. Within classics, authors and readers often dialogue across a span of decades, if not centuries, and from value systems that may bear little resemblance to each other.

Using a New Historical lens, young adults can question the values found within the text and how they as readers are influenced by the way those values are represented within the text. For instance, exploring the treatment of war in Stephen Crane's *The Red Badge of Courage* (1895), James and Christopher Collier's *My Brother Sam Is Dead* (1974), Geert Spillbeen's *Kipling's Choice* (2005), Walter Dean Myer's *Sunrise over Fallujah* (2009), and Gudrun Pausewang's *Traitor* (2010) will give students a sense of the author's sentiments about war as well as the context of the time period and community and the reasons for going to war.

Often readers are asked not to impose current values on historical texts because the text is an artifact of that particular time period. In New Historicism, readers are encouraged to read from a current perspective so as to note the differences in time periods, make comparisons to current events or situations, and to comment on historical situations without excusing them. For instance, while it was legal to enslave people earlier in American history, it is illegal to do so now. By reading an historical text about such practices, readers gain insight into the thinking of that time period but are also able to comment on its immorality instead of assuming that such practices occurred without long-lasting effects on the country. New Historicism also allows for the gaps in historical thinking and writings to be highlighted, noting which voices are privileged and which are silenced, and what is missing in the chaotic path of history.

Rhetorical criticism is another literary approach to texts that engages young people in the way the text is structured: the language used within the text, the movements of the plot, and the protagonists' behaviors, as well as how the structure affects the reader's response. Interrogating the use of the particular metaphor or symbol involves young adults in examining what that metaphor or symbol means to them and the reasons the author may have used them to gain a particular response from readers. Through the use of particular language, symbols, and metaphors, an author can persuade or guide readers to a specific or intended response. By knowing this, young adults can become more critical consumers of a text.

Questions about language are especially interesting, including the use of even one word and how it affects readers' thinking. *The Book Thief* by Marcus Zuzak (2007) is narrated by death as a character and so students can investigate the rhetorical and emotional effect of using death as a narrator. This type of analysis is enlightening to adolescents and an effective way to teach literary analysis. The literary world can open up for adolescents once they discover symbolism and metaphor.

Another literary approach that engages young adults is *feminist criticism,* which examines the treatment of males and females within a text. By exploring how females and males are represented, young adults gain critical insights into how literature might reflect reality as well as how literature might affect readers and their perceptions of how males and females "should" behave. Feminist criticism also addresses who reads what and why and whether or not those preferences are based on gender. Questions that adolescents can ponder in relation to feminist criticism include queries about how the plot would change if the protagonist was the opposite sex or held a different gender location. Other questions include how the characters represent reality or stereotypes that are damaging as well as how texts influence readers' ideas about their own gendered realities and conditions.

In addition, feminist criticism explores differences in how female and male writers treat a topic, use language, and have characters behave. Juxtaposing the characters Bella and Edward from the Twilight series with the characters Katniss, Gayle, and Peeta from The Hunger Games series provides an interesting study of male and female behaviors. Both series have huge adolescent followings, and thus to look at representation in these popular novels is engaging and insightful for young adults.

By using young adult literature for literary analysis, teachers scaffold young adults' learning for the more complex texts they will encounter in the future. In addition, we find that young adults value their ability to read more deeply and appreciate their status as critical consumers of texts.

Responding to the Censorship of Young Adult Literature

Planning a literature collection involves book selection, and while students' interests and curricular requirements will naturally be a part of that selection process, there are times when teachers must also think about issues related to censorship. *Censorship* is the removal, suppression, or restricted use of reading materials on the grounds that they are objectionable, often for moral reasons (Reichman, 2001). When someone attempts to remove material from the curriculum or library, thereby restricting the access of others, it is called a *challenge.* Most book challenges occur locally, and most fail. When a challenge is successful and materials are removed from the curriculum or library, it is called a *banning,* raising the issue of denying others access to literary, artistic, or educational materials.

From its beginnings in the 1960s and 1970s, young adult literature has faced many challenges, partly because many contemporary novels focus on the real world of young people—drugs, sexuality, alcoholism, divorce, gangs, school dropouts, racism, and violence. Some people believe that these topics are unsuitable as subjects of books for adolescents. Others object to the use of profanity, mention of homosexuality, questioning authority figures, or criticism of the nation or government. The majority of censorship attempts come from individuals and groups adhering to ultraconservative political or religious beliefs. Censorship attempts also may come from the political left when there are concerns about stereotypes, bias, or misrepresentation in books about minority cultures and females.

The censorship database of the American Library Association's Office of Intellectual Freedom (OIF) indicates that the most censorship attempts in 1990–2010 came from parents (57 percent), library patrons (14 percent), and school administrators (10 percent). Of the 10,676 challenges reported to the OIF in these twenty years, 30 percent were based on material perceived to be "sexually explicit"; 25 percent were based on material perceived to have "offensive language"; and 21 percent were based on material perceived to be "unsuited to the age group." It should be noted that the OIF estimates that 75 to 80 percent of censorship attempts are not reported, so these figures are approximate.

A significant source of censorship is teachers themselves when they select books to read with students. One study found that teachers self-censor due to their fear that certain texts will create controversies leading to confrontations with parents or administrators (Freedman & Johnson, 2000). The long-term effects of continued censorship attempts, whether successful or not, can be subtle yet troubling. NCTE's Committee on the Right to Read reports that schools often remove and English teachers avoid using or recommending any book that *might* cause controversy, a practice known as "red-flagging" a book. Consequently, students are educated in a school atmosphere that is hostile to inquiry and teachers learn to emphasize their safety rather than students' needs.

Our position regarding censorship is:

- Teachers and schools have the right and the obligation to select reading materials suitable for the education of students. With this right comes the professional responsibility to select quality literature that furthers educational goals while remaining appropriate for the age and maturity level of the students.

- Parents have the right to protect their children from materials or influences they see as potentially damaging. In the instance that a parent believes that material selected by a school or teacher is potentially harmful to his/her child, that parent has the right to bring this concern to the attention of the school and request that his/her child not be subjected to this material. Parents must indicate the reason for their concern.

- The school must take the parent's objection seriously and provide a reasonable substitute for the material of concern. If an alternative procedure is necessary in the situation (for example, the student will listen to a different book in the library while the teacher is reading aloud), the alternative should respect the student and be sensitive to his/her feelings.

- The parent does not have the right to demand that the material in question be withheld from other students as this interferes with the rights and professional duty of the teacher and school to educate students. Once a student is given a reasonable alternative, the school has fulfilled its obligation and should not interfere with the First Amendment rights of other students.

As adults, we cherish our right to choose our reading material and use this right nearly every day. Middle and high school social studies and civics textbooks proudly proclaim the freedom of choice in the lives of citizens of the United States. We need to extend these rights to our children and students. A positive response to the growth of censorship attempts is to teach young people about their First Amendment rights and what is at stake, using nonfiction such as *Censorship,* essays for teens edited by Tamara Roleff (2005), and Kathleen

Krull's *A Kid's Guide to America's Bill of Rights* (1999). Young adult fiction about censorship include *Americus* by M. K. Reed (2011), *The Sledding Hill* by Chris Crutcher (2005), *The Last Safe Place on Earth* by Richard Peck (1995), and *Places I Never Meant to Be: Original Stories by Censored Writers,* edited by Judy Blume (1999). As teachers and librarians, we should do everything possible to promote books that encourage critical thinking, inquiry, and self-expression, while maintaining respect for the views of others.

The American Library Association's Office of Intellectual Freedom monitors the challenges made against books for children and young adults in the United States. Most adults and young adults who have read the highly regarded books that often appear on these "most challenged books" lists find the reasons given for the challenges perplexing. The following young adult titles appeared on the ALA list of the Most Challenged Books of 2012 and 2011:

- *The Absolutely True Diary of a Part-Time Indian* by Sherman Alexie.

  Reasons: Offensive language, racism, sexually explicit, unsuited for age group

- *Thirteen Reasons Why* by Jay Asher.

  Reasons: Drugs/alcohol/smoking, sexually explicit, suicide, unsuited for age group

- *Looking for Alaska* by John Green.

  Reasons: Offensive language, sexually explicit, unsuited for age group

- *Hunger Games* by Suzanne Collins.

  Reasons: Anti-ethnic, anti-family, offensive language, occult, violence

Of the OIF's *Most Frequently Challenged Books of the 21st Century (2000–2009),* over half are books for children or young adults, including the Harry Potter series by J. K. Rowling, *The Chocolate War* by Robert Cormier (1974), *The Giver* by Lois Lowry (1993), and *The Perks of Being a Wallflower* by Stephen Chbosky (1999). The top challenged classics include *The Great Gatsby* by F. Scott Fitgerald (1925), *The Grapes of Wrath* by John Steinbeck (1939), *To Kill a Mockingbird* by Harper Lee (1960), *Beloved* by Toni Morrison (1987), and *1984* by George Orwell (1949).

Often, individuals challenge books on the basis of a single word or phrase, or on hearsay, and have not read the book. Teachers and library media specialists have found a written procedure is helpful in bringing order and reason into discussions with those who want to censor school materials. Most procedures call for teachers and librarians to give would-be censors a complaint form and ask them to specify their concerns in writing. There are advantages to this system in that both teachers and parents are given time to reflect on the issue and to control their emotions; and would-be censors are given time to read the book in its entirety. This system for dealing with censorship attempts works best when administrators know the process and pertinent laws and are supportive and involved. Developing written procedures and complaint forms are important tasks for a school's literature curriculum committee. Figure 9.3 presents a form produced by the National Council of Teachers of English (NCTE) for reconsideration of a work of literature.

Another strategy that can prevent censorship attempts by parents is for teachers to send a permission slip home with students. This form states the titles and nature of titles to be assigned for reading in school and at home, and parents sign to indicate their consent to let their child read these books. Information about assigned reading can also be placed on a website for parents to read several weeks in advance of the actual assignment, so that there is time to find an acceptable alternative for a particular student.

Figure 9.3 Citizen's Request for Reconsideration of a Work

Author _____ Paperback _____ Hardcover _____

Title _____

Publisher (if known) _____

Request initiated by _____

Telephone _____

Address _____ City _____ Zip Code _____

Complainant represents

_____ Himself/Herself

_____ (Name organization) _____

_____ (Identify other group) _____

1. Have you been able to discuss this work with the teacher or librarian who ordered it or who used it? _____ Yes _____ No

2. What do you understand to be the general purpose for using this work?

   a. Provide support for a unit in the curriculum? _____ Yes _____ No

   b. Provide a learning experience for the reader in one kind of literature? _____ Yes _____ No

   c. Other _____

3. Did the general purpose for the use of the work, as described by the teacher or librarian, seem a suitable one to you? _____ Yes _____ No

   If not, please explain. _____

   _____

4. What do you think is the general purpose of the author in this book? _____

   _____

5. In what ways do you think a work of this nature is not suitable for the use the teacher or librarian wishes to carry out? _____

   _____

6. Have you been able to learn the students' response to this work? _____ Yes _____ No

7. What response did the students make? _____

   _____

8. Have you been able to learn from your school library what book reviewers or other students of literature have written about this work? _____ Yes _____ No

9. Would you like the teacher or librarian to give you a written summary of what book reviewers and other students have written about this book or film? _____ Yes _____ No

10. Do you have negative reviews of the book? _____ Yes _____ No

11. Where were they published? _____

12. Would you be willing to provide summaries of the reviews you have collected?
    _____ Yes _____ No

13. What would you like your library/school to do about this work?

    _____ Do not assign/lend it to my child.

    _____ Return it to the staff selection committee/department for reevaluation.

    _____ Other: Please explain _____

    _____

14. In its place, what work would you recommend that would convey as valuable a picture and
    perspective of the subject treated? _____

    _____

    _____

Signature _____ Date _____

Source: Committee on the Right to Read. The students' right to read. Urbana, IL: National Council of Teachers of English. http://www.ncte.org/positions/statements/righttoreadguideline. Courtesy of National Council of Teachers of English.

Learning how to select books that are of good quality and appropriate for young people is the responsibility of teachers and librarians. Teachers must make book selections that are responsible choices on the bases of literary quality and knowledge of adolescent development and psychology. The NCTE guidelines, while stating that teachers are best qualified to make decisions about books, suggest that parents and community members be included on review committees, and, in addition, that schools develop written rationales for book selections to respond to challenges. This practice can prevent attacks on books because parents are involved in the process. If your school does not have such a policy, make a practice of noting the reason for your choice of a book and how it supports your curricular goals, and keep these notes in a file in the event of an objection.

The political context of teaching in today's world is full of perils and complexity for teachers as they balance their goals and the needs of their students against the pressures of standards and tests and the demands of parents and administrators. It's no wonder that many choose to base their curriculum around mandates and to teach only the required canonical texts. The problem, of course, is that the engagement and learning of adolescents is negatively affected as is the goal of creating lifelong readers who value literature in their lives. Our intent in this chapter is to provide options and resources and to argue that the decision is not whether to choose mandates and classic texts *or* innovation and young adult literature. The decision is not either/or but instead involves thoughtful consideration of the approach that best fits your students and curriculum and also addresses mandates.

References

Abdel-Fattah, R. (2007). *Does my head look big in this?* New York: Scholastic.

Alexie, S. (2007). *The absolutely true diary of a part-time Indian*. New York: Little, Brown.

American Library Association. (2012). *Frequently challenged books of the 21st century*. Retrieved from www.ala.org/issuesadvocacy/banned/frequentlychallenged/21stcenturychallenged/index.cfm.

Anderson, L. H. (2007). *Twisted*. New York: Viking.

Anderson, M. T. (2002). *Feed*. Cambridge, MA: Candlewick.

Andrews, J. (2012). *Me and Earl and the dying girl*. New York: Amulet.

Asher, J. (2011). *Thirteen reasons why*. New York: Razorbill.

Bacigalupi, P. (2010). *Ship breaker*. New York: Little Brown.

Bausum, A. (2009). *Denied, detained, deported*. New York: National Geographic.

Beach, R., & Myers, J. (2001). *Inquiry-based English instruction*. New York: Teachers College Press.

Bennett, V. (2007). *Cassandra's sister*. Cambridge, MA: Candlewick.

Blume, J. (Ed.). (1999). *Places I never meant to be: Original stories by censored writers*. New York: Simon & Schuster .

Boelts, M. (2012). *Happy like soccer*. Illus. L. Castillo. Somerville, MA: Candlewick.

Bondoux, A. L. (2007). *The killer's tears*. New York: Delacorte.

———. (2009). *A time of miracles*. New York: Delacorte.

Brenna, B. (2011). *Waiting for no one*. Markham, ON, Canada: Red Deer Press.

Budhos, M. (2006). *Ask me no questions*. New York: Atheneum.

Burg, A. (2009). *All the broken pieces*. New York: Scholastic.

Chbosky, S. (1999). *The perks of being a wallflower*. New York: MTV Books.

Children's literature review: Excerpts from reviews, criticism, and commentary on books for children and young people, vols. 1–182. (1976–2013). Detroit: Thomson Gale.

Cohn, R. (2003). *The steps*. New York: Simon & Schuster.

Collier, J. L., & Collier, C. (1974). *My brother Sam is dead*. New York: Scholastic.

Collins, S. (2008). *The hunger games*. New York: Scholastic.

Committee on the Right to Read. (1982). *The students' right to read*. Urbana, IL: NCTE.

Cormier, R. (1974). *The chocolate war*. New York: Knopf.

Crane, S. (1895). *The red badge of courage*. New York: Appleton.

Croza, L. (2010). *I know here*. Illus. M. James. Toronto: Groundwood.

Crutcher, C. (2005). *Sledding hill*. New York: HarperCollins

Dana, B. (2009). *A voice of her own: Becoming Emily Dickinson*. New York: HarperTeen.

Danforth, E. M. (2012). *The miseducation of Cameron Post*. New York: Balzer and Bray.

Doctorow, C. (2008). *Little brother*. New York: Tor.

Downham, J. (2010). *You against me*. London : David Fickling.

Draper, S. (2010). *Out of my mind*. New York: Atheneum

———. (1999). *Romiette and Julio*. New York: Atheneum.

DuPrau, J. (2003). *The city of Ember*. New York: Random.

Ellis, D. (2009). *Children of war: Voices of Iraqi Refugees*. Toronto: Groundwood.

Fanelli, S. (1995). *My map book*. New York: HarperCollins.

Farish, T. (2012). *The good braider*. New York: Skyscape.

Farmer, N. (2002). *The house of the scorpion*. New York: Atheneum.

Fitzgerald, F. S. (1925). *The Great Gatsby*. New York: Scribners.

Geras, A. (2006). *Ithaka*. New York: Harcourt.

Greder, A. (2008). *The island*. Sydney/Chicago: Allen & Unwin.

Green, J. (2006). *Looking for Alaska*. New York: Speak.

Haddix, M. P. (2005). *Double identity*. New York: Simon & Schuster.

Herz, S., & Gallo, D. (2005). *From Hinton to Hamlet: Building bridges between young adult literature and the classics.* Westport, CN: Greenwood.

Hall, S. (2007). *Using picture storybooks to teach literary devices: Recommended books for children and young adults* (Vol. 4). Santa Barbara, CA: Libraries Unlimited.

Hawthorne, N. (1850). *The scarlet letter.* New York: Ticknor, Reed, and Fields.

Healey, K. (2013). *When we wake.* New York: Little, Brown.

Hesse, K. (1997). *Out of the dust.* New York: Scholastic.

Hinds, G. (2007). *Beowolf.* Cambridge, MA: Candlewick.

Hoffman, M. (2002). *The color of home.* Illus. K. Littlewood. New York: Dial.

Howe, J. (2001). *Misfits.* New York: Simon & Schuster.

Huxley, A. (1932). *Brave new world.* London: Chatto & Windus.

Jaramillo, A. (2006). *La línea.* New York: Roaring Brook.

Kaywell, J. F. (2010). *Adolescent literature as a complement to the classics.* Lanham, MD: Rowan & Littlefield.

Kerley, B. (2006). *Walt Whitman: Words for America.* Illus. B. Selznick. New York: Scholastic.

Kindle, P. (2012). *Keeping the castle.* New York: Viking.

King, A. S. (2012). *Please ignore Vera Dietz.* New York: Ember.

Knutsson, C. (2012). *Shadows cast by stars.* New York: Atheneum.

Koertge, R. (2003). *Shakespeare bats cleanup.* Somerville, MA: Candlewick.

Krull, K. (1999). *A kid's guide to America's Bill of Rights.* New York: HarperCollins.

Lai, T. (2011). *Inside out and back again.* New York: Harper.

Langer, J. (2010). *Envisioning literature.* New York: Teachers College.

Laybourne, E. (2012). *Monument 14.* New York: Feiwel & Friends.

Lee, H. (1960). *To kill a mockingbird.* New York: Lippincott.

Levine, E. (1995). *I hate English.* Illus. S. Bjorkman. New York: Scholastic.

Lindner, A. (2013). *Catherine.* New York: Little Brown.

Lowry, L. (1993). *The giver.* New York: Houghton.

Lu, M. (2011). *Legend.* New York: Putnam.

Lynch, C. (2005). *Inexcusable.* New York: Atheneum.

McCall, G. G. (2011). *Under the mesquite.* New York: Lee & Low.

McDonald, A. (2013). *Jane Austen goes to Hollywood.* Cambridge, MA: Candlewick.

Morrison, T. (1987). *Beloved.* New York: Knopf.

Moss, M. (2013). *Barbed wire baseball.* Illus. Y. Shimuzu. New York: Abrams.

Myers, W. D. (2013). *Darius and Twig.* New York: Amistad/HarperCollins.

———. (2010). *Lockdown.* New York: Amistad/HarperCollins.

———. (2006). *Street Love.* New York: Amistad/HarperCollins.

———. (2009). *Sunrise over Fallujah.* New York: Scholastic.

Naidoo, B. (2001). *The other side of truth.* New York: HarperCollins.

Nanji, S. (2008). *Child of dandelions.* Honesdale, PA: Boyds Mills.

National Association of Educational Progress (2011). *The Nation's Report Card: Reading 2011* Washington, DC: National Center for Education Statistics, Institute of Education Sciences, U.S. Department of Education.

Nazario, S. (2006). *Enrique's journey.* New York: Random House.

Ness, P. (2009). *The knife of never letting go.* Cambridge, MA: Candlewick.

Oates, J. C. (2002). *Big Mouth and Ugly Girl.* New York: HarperCollins.

Orwell, G. (1949). *1984.* London: Secker & Warburg.

Park. L. S. (2010). *A long walk to water.* New York: Clarion.

Pausewang, G. (2010). *Traitor.* Translated from German. Minneapolis, MN: Carolrhoda.

Peck, R. (1995). *The last safe place on earth.* New York: Delacorte.

Perkins, L. R. (2010). *As easy as falling off the face of the earth.* New York: Greenwillow.

Peters, J. A. (2006). *Luna.* New York: Little, Brown.

Pressler, M. (2007). *Let sleeping dogs lie.* Translated from German. New York: Front Street.

Reed, M. K. (2011). *Americus.* New York: First Second/Roaring Brook.

Reichman, H. (2001). *Censorship and selection.* Chicago: American Library Association.

Renaissance Learning (2012). *What kids are reading: The book reading habits of students in American schools.* Wisconsin Rapids, WI: Renaissance Learning.

Roleff, T. (2005). *Censorship.* Chicago: Greenhaven.

Rosen, M. (2008). *Michael Rosen's sad book.* Illus. Q. Blake. Somerville, MA: Candlewick.

Rosenblatt, L. M. (1938). *Literature as exploration.* Chicago: Modern Language Association.

Rowsell, R. (2013). *Eleanor and Park.* New York: St. Martin's Griffin.

Roy, J. (2006). *Yellow star.* Tarrytown, NY: Marshall Cavendish.

Russo, M. (2011). *I will come back for you: A family in hiding during World War II.* New York: Schwartz & Wade.

Ryan, P. M. (2000). *Esperanza rising.* New York: Scholastic.

Santiago, C. (2002). *Home to Medicine Mountain.* Illus. J. Lowery. San Francisco: Children's Book Press

Schmidt, G. (2004). *Lizzie Bright and the Buckminster boy.* New York: Clarion.

Shakespeare, W. (1597). *Romeo and Juliet.* London: Thomas Creede.

Schusterman, N. (2008). *Antsy does time.* New York: Dutton.

Something about the author, Vols. 1–245. (1971–2013). Detroit: Thomson Gale.

Sonnenblick, J. (2006*). Notes from the midnight driver.* New York: Scholastic.

Soter, A. (1999). *Young adult literature and the new literary theories.* New York: Teachers College Press.

Spillebeen, G. (2005). *Kipling's choice.* Translated from Dutch. New York: Houghton.

Steinbeck, J. (1938). *The grapes of wrath.* New York: Viking.

Stiefvater, M. (2012). *The Scorpio races.* New York: Scholastic.

Swain, G. (2012). *Hope and tears: Ellis Island voices.* Honesdale, PA: Calkins Creek.

Tan, S. (2006). *The arrival.* New York: Scholastic.

Thompson, H. (2013). *The language inside.* New York: Delacorte.

Uhlberg, M. (2011). *A storm called Katrina.* Illus. C. Bootman. Atlanta, GA: Peachtree.

Vizzini, N. (2006). *It's kind of a funny story.* New York: Miramax.

Wein, E. (2013). *Code name Verity.* New York: Disney-Hyperion.

Welin, N. (2004). *Double helix.* New York: Puffin.

Westerfeld, S. (2004). *So yesterday.* New York: Penguin.

Whaley, J. C. (2012). *Where things come back.* New York: Atheneum.

Whitman, S. (2013). *The milk of birds.* New York: Atheneum.

Wild, M. (2004). *One night.* New York: Knopf.

Williams, M. (2011). *Now is the time for running.* New York: Little, Brown.

Woodson, J. (2005). *Show way.* Illus. H. Talbott. New York: Putnam.

Yancy, R. (2013). *The 5th wave.* New York: Putnam.

Zusak, Markus. (2007). *The book thief.* New York: Knopf.

Chapter Ten

Experiencing Literature

Engagement with literature highlights the potential of a book to capture the attention of adolescents and invite their participation in a literary world. Authentic, well-written books are the first step, but they must be supported by significant experiences that bring adolescents and books together for a variety of purposes. These experiences include reading widely for personal purposes, reading critically to inquire about the world, and reading strategically to learn about literacy and literature. Balancing these experiences supports the learning and development of adolescents as each serves a different purpose and highlights different books and roles. These experiences need to occur within a literate environment that is particularly supportive of resistant readers.

Creating a Literate Environment for All Readers

The teacher is the key element in creating a classroom environment and so can exert a powerful influence on students and their view of literature and of themselves as readers. A supportive teacher creates an atmosphere in which students feel comfortable and safe to share their reading interests, reactions, and insights with the teacher and other students. A caring teacher knows that students want to succeed and be good readers and therefore sets high expectations for all students and builds their trust so they can meet those expectations.

A respectful classroom environment encourages the exchange of ideas among students so that they feel safe in taking risks to publicly share their perspectives and ask questions. Respect also involves learning how to contest each other's ideas without personal insults or put-downs. In respectful classrooms teachers accept the students' free reading choices and differences in their reading habits, including the right to decide not to finish a book selected for independent reading. Teachers can encourage independent reading by showing an interest in what students choose to read, reading some of what their students are reading (even books that they typically would not select to read) in order to have conversations with students. Teachers who accept that some students read more slowly and read much less than others send a message that they are pleased to see all students reading. Effective teachers guide students to good young adult literature but do not force it on them.

Table 10.1 summarizes key research studies on the characteristics of classroom environments that engage the interest and learning of adolescents through young adult literature.

Adolescents Who Resist Reading

Even when teachers create literate environments that immerse students in many experiences with well-written and compelling young adult books, some students will resist any engagement with books or reading. Adolescents who are struggling readers have difficulty with cognitive competencies, such as reading comprehension, study skills, fluency, and word recognition. They are tired of struggling after spending years in special reading programs and their insecurity leads them to avoid situations where they might fail in front of peers. Their experiences in middle and high schools lead to further disengagement due to a greater emphasis on textbook reading, more teacher control, loss of student choice, focus on competition, and lack of instruction on content area reading strategies (Guthrie & Davis, 2003). They gradually become disengaged and develop resistance.

Students learning English as a second language sometimes encounter difficulties in reading because they lack strong English vocabularies and well-developed sentence structures to draw on when encountering English language texts. They are also often asked to read texts that portray unfamiliar experiences and cultural norms. This group is large and growing so teachers need to be familiar with books that are more supportive with strong visuals, less print, and predictable language patterns as well as books from global cultures that reflect their cultural experiences.

Resistant readers also include readers who can read but choose not to. Often they are alienated from reading due to factors such as ineffective literacy instruction, or they may not have been encouraged to read for their own enjoyment by the adults in their lives. Resistant readers may be those who have not yet found the right book that will launch them into lifelong reading or have been forced to read fiction when their preference is nonfiction.

Table 10.1	Important Studies on Engagement and Young Adult Literature	
Researcher(s)	**Subjects**	**Findings**
Ivey and Johnston (2013)	Interviews of 71 eighth graders from four classrooms, biweekly observations, teacher interviews	Implemented a student-selected, self-paced reading curriculum with young adult literature. Students indicated that this approach led them to: • become engaged readers who talk about books. • make changes in relationships, identities, social imagination, and social and personal agency. • increase their intellectual stance, knowledge, and critical reading. Students identified the causes of these changes as time to read, choice, teacher read-alouds and recommendations, and edgy compelling books.
Fullterton and Colwell (2010)	Content analysis of multiple studies on literature discussion, 1989–2009	Identifies the benefits of small group discussions, the role of the teacher, and the influence of gender and student power and status on discussion
Albright and Ariail (2005)	141 middle grade teachers in a Texas school district	Teachers in the survey: • read aloud mainly to help students gain information from textbooks. • read from a limited variety of types of texts. • rarely read aloud nonfiction chapter books.
Strommen and Mates (2004)	Survey of 151 students in grades 6 and 9 on reading attitudes	Identified factors associated with love of reading: • Discussions of books with other readers • Active members of a community of readers • Family members prioritize reading for pleasure • Access to many varied reading materials • Value imagination and thinking from books
Worthy, Patterson, Salas, Prater, and Turner (2002)	24 struggling, resistant readers	Most effective factor in increasing a student's motivation to read was a teacher who tailored instruction to the student's needs, found materials that fit the student's needs and interests, and took time to inspire the student to read.
Ivey and Broaddus (2001)	1,765 sixth-graders in 23 diverse schools in mid-Atlantic and northeastern United States	Students were asked what made them want to read in school and ranked the following as most important: • Free reading time and teacher read-alouds • Quality and diversity of reading material • Choice in selecting reading materials Favored free reading material included magazines, adventure books, mysteries, scary stories, joke books, and nonfiction about animals

continued

Table 10.1 *(continued)*

Researcher(s)	Subjects	Findings
Cope (1997) Follow-up study to Carlsen and Sherrill	272 twelfth-graders from advanced, general, and remedial-level English classes, including resistant readers	Love of reading in students is promoted by: • self-choice of books they find interesting. • interesting books for assigned reading. • being read to by a good reader. Dislike of reading is promoted by: • required reading of uninteresting books, mainly classics, before students are developmentally prepared for them. • overanalysis of any single work. • book reports. • being forced to read aloud in class.
Stewart, Paradis, Ross, and Lewis (1996)	49 developmental reading students (scored below grade level on a standardized reading test) in grades 7, 8, and 9	After three years in a literature-based reading program, students strongly believed that they read better in terms of speed, fluency, comprehension and retention, and overall school performance because of the program. The attributes of the program that the students found most helpful: • Choice over what they read • Interest in what they read • Being given time in school to read • Reading practice
Carlsen and Sherrill (1988)	College students who were committed readers	Conditions that promoted a love of reading: • Freedom of choice in reading material • Availability of books and magazines • Family members who read aloud • Adults and peers who model reading • Role models who value reading • Sharing and discussing books • Owning books • Availability of libraries and librarians
Fielding, Wilson, and Anderson (1986)	Middle graders	Students who read a lot at home showed larger gains on reading achievement tests.
Fader, Duggins, Finn, and McNeil (1976)	Boys, ages 12 to 17	Classrooms full of high-interest books and print for self-selected reading significantly improved low-achieving students' attitudes toward school, learning, and reading as well as their verbal proficiency and language comprehension.

A steady diet of textbook and assigned reading has led many resistant readers to view reading as school work, lacking relevance and value in their lives, and so they only read when forced to do so for school.

Some adolescents resist reading because the books they are asked to read do not depict their lives or the lives of those who are significant to them in their families and communities. Young adult books are more multiculturally and globally diverse today than in years past, but books that reflect the true range of cultural diversity of our society are still underrepresented in schools. Unless adults make a conscious effort to search out books reflecting a range of cultural identities, adolescents may not find themselves in books and so resist reading because they see these books as threatening and demeaning to their identities and irrelevant to their lives.

Boys who resist reading may do so in part because of the preponderance of female teachers in U.S. schools who tend to select reading materials that do not always appeal to boys. Their resistance to reading also may stem from the perception that reading, because it is quiet and passive, is a female activity, or because teachers ask them to read silently from fiction when they prefer to interact socially with peers around an informational book. Some boys are avid readers, but of materials that schools do not traditionally recognize, such as magazines, internet websites, and informational books (Wilhelm & Smith, 2002; Sullivan, 2009).

When Reeves (2004) asked adolescent readers why they resist reading, many responded that they can and do read in particular circumstances. Schools often only define reading as the fiction novels in English/language arts classrooms and so adolescents who read a great deal in other contexts from non-school reading materials are labeled as resistant. While text difficulty can be a barrier to reading, a lack of interest in assigned and independent reading materials is commonly mentioned as a reason for resistance. According to Strommen and Mates (2004) avid readers who were inundated with textbook reading became reluctant to read for pleasure, and many students noted that they valued their outside reading more highly than the reading connected with school.

For most adolescents, their ability as readers is *not* the reason for their resistance. They resist because the materials they are asked to read are not interesting, and the gap between their reading preferences and those of the school grow each year. Their reading choices reflect their own interests, often related to issues of identity and enjoyment, factors rarely considered in school reading. Finally, issues of agency are critical as adolescents lament the loss of choice in their reading materials and the loss of control over their reading pace (Lenters, 2006). Students want time to read in school, but they want to read materials of personal interest and they want a voice in selecting those materials.

Struggling readers can become resistant readers quite quickly and vice versa. Thus, there is a need to create literacy and literary opportunities for all types of readers to prevent the detrimental effects that non-reading can have on students academically and personally. Bridging adolescents' outside reading interests with in-school reading practices is one way to connect with resistant readers, and utilizing young adult literature allows for such linkage.

Reading aloud, independent reading, and the use of multimodal texts are ways to bring literature to life for many young adults. A classroom library that contains all types of reading materials—both written and visual—builds a reading environment that responds to all readers. The social nature of adolescence means that adolescents are motivated by working with others and so respond positively to literature circles, drama activities, book clubs, and reading buddies. Classroom engagements that support students in taking risks to diversify their reading interests and draw on their passions along with discussions with peers can pull in even the most resistant of readers.

Reading Widely for Personal Purposes

Reading literature widely for personal intentions highlights choice. Extensive reading for purposes significant to adolescent's lives can range from enjoyment to personal inquiries on topics of interest. Reading widely involves engagement and demonstration; students are not focused on writing or talking about the book or using it for an activity. They immerse themselves in reading alongside other readers. The goal is to create a lifelong habit of reading for purposes that matter to the reader—not because the teacher said so. Nancy Atwell's seminal work *In the Middle* (1987), and her more recent book, *The Reading Zone* (2007), offer real-life examples of creating these experiences.

Ivey and Broaddus (2001) asked middle school students what makes them want to read in school. Their responses overwhelmingly indicated that they wanted time for reading in school, personally interesting materials, choice in selecting those materials, and teacher read-alouds. The students also indicated that rarely were these practices available in school, especially books that interested them.

Students should have the opportunity to choose from a wide range of reading materials. Wide reading provides adolescents with a broad background from which to develop comprehension and interpretation strategies, promotes positive attitudes about reading, and encourages the development of lifelong reading habits. Many adults stop engaging with books once they leave school and view reading as boring because of the lack of choice in schools. In addition, reading many materials with ease increases fluency and the integration of reading strategies.

The experiences that encourage reading widely for personal purposes include reading aloud, independent reading, and the use of multimodal texts. The role of the teacher is to provide a regularly scheduled time for reading and a variety of materials from which students can select.

Reading Aloud by Teachers

Reading aloud to students is an important teaching strategy for English/language arts teachers and teachers of other content areas. Read-alouds are usually associated with primary and elementary children, but many of the same benefits of reading aloud apply to middle and high school students. Foremost among these is motivation for students to read by engaging them in reading that is entertaining and rewarding. Other important reasons to read aloud to young adults include:

- Building knowledge and interest in topics and issues related to classroom inquiries and units of study.
- Engaging students in the world of a story to build motivation for reading independently or for whole group discussion.
- Introducing students to authors and genres they might like to read independently. Sometimes you can read a carefully selected passage from a book, poem, or short story to give students a taste of what is in store for them if they choose to read the book in its entirety.
- Demonstrating fluent, expressive reading to students and encouraging critical thinking through discussion. If you are not a strong expressive oral reader, use audio books recorded by professional readers.

- Presenting examples of good writing (e.g., description, dialogue, expository writing) and new vocabulary. Students' writing can be positively influenced by the characteristics of the stories they hear and discuss.

Teachers can use a short read-aloud of a picture book or an excerpt as a way to introduce students to the focus of a class session and transition them into the class. Teachers can also read aloud from a novel related to an instructional unit, reading a chapter at each class session. Reading aloud short excerpts is also an effective strategy for introducing students to a variety of genres, formats, and topics to consider for independent reading.

Readers who struggle often have a higher listening comprehension than reading comprehension and so can interact with higher-level reading materials through read-alouds or audiobooks. Reading aloud provides a way to encourage the development of critical thinking for these students.

Book Selection   Read through the books, poems, and short stories that you are considering as read-aloud choices so you can determine whether they will be enjoyable to students, appropriate in terms of theme, language, and conceptual difficulty, and accessible to various types of student response. Reading materials ahead of time develops your reading fluency and expression and allows you to check for examples of content, literary devices, or good writing to call to students' attention.

Over a school year, vary your read-aloud selections by genre, author, mood, and setting, as well as by the background, gender, and cultural identity of protagonists. Books, poems, and short stories of varying degrees of difficulty should be selected with the understanding that complex but worthy works may require some discussion with teachers to be fully appreciated by students. Keep adding new works to your read-aloud list and choose works that students have not heard or read before to keep both your own and your students' interest in read-aloud selections strong. For suggested read-aloud titles see the Excellent Books to Read Aloud lists included in Chapters 3 through 8.

Preparation   Establishing a routine for read-aloud sessions and engaged listening will provide an effective context for a successful experience. The context should signal, *we are taking valuable class time for this activity because it is important and worthy of your attention.* Once the class is ready to listen to a new selection, briefly introduce it by providing a historical context, showing the geographical setting on a large map, or mentioning other works by the author that might be familiar to students. Announce the title and author's name and share some brief information about the author's background related to the book's content before beginning to read. This information can usually be found on the jacket flap, an author's note or afterword, or the author's website. In subsequent read-aloud sessions of the same book, a brief reminder of what was happening in the story when the previous session ended helps orient students and pull them back into the book.

Reading Aloud Effectively

- Think of reading as a type of dramatic performance. Use different voices for different characters. Try accents, when appropriate. Use your voice to emphasize various moods suggested in the story, and employ pauses to heighten suspense.

- Maintain eye contact with students. Not only will this help to keep listeners' attention, but it also will inform you when a word of explanation is necessary.
- Use body language and facial expressions to enhance the drama of the reading. Leaning forward during a suspenseful part of a story or chuckling during a funny part conveys your involvement in the story to your audience.
- Read the chapter or selection from beginning to end without interruption. When a word occurs during read-aloud that you suspect may be unfamiliar to students, simply pause and give a synonym that students know and continue reading. You might want to call attention to a passage because it is an excellent example of a type of writing or is pivotal to the story. In this case say something like "That was an excellent description; I'll reread it." Do so, and then continue reading. In general, keep interruptions to a minimum.
- A brief discussion of two or three minutes after each read-aloud session provides time to ask questions, clarify plot developments, share brief responses to story developments, or predict future plot developments.
- If the read-aloud is being used to introduce a particular theme or concept or to focus on a specific aspect of language or literature, bring that aspect of the text to students' attention *after* the reading and brief discussion. Interrupting the reading for a prolonged discussion or inserting multiple brief comments during the reading takes students out of the book and interrupts their understanding and enjoyment of the story.

When reading a novel aloud over several weeks, these practices can keep students engaged:

- Create a chart or diagram of characters and their relationships and roles, especially if the story has a large number of characters, and post where students can easily see it.
- Draw and display a map of the story setting to track plot events in sequence. Maps are particularly helpful in quest fantasies.
- Develop a time line, placing dates in intervals above the line and story events below the line at the appropriate date. If relevant, historic events are noted on a third tier. A time line can serve as a mnemonic device for the story line as well as for historic events of the era.

Booktalks

A *booktalk* is an oral presentation about a book that invites interest. Booktalks are not analyses of the author's style or the old-fashioned book report that discusses characters, setting, theme, and plot. Booktalks on five to ten books each week from the school library media center can entice students to read and experience good literature. Some teachers have students give booktalks to encourage other students to read the suggested books. These tips will support more effective booktalks:

- Read the book before giving a booktalk.
- Choose books that you like or think your students will enjoy. Sincere enthusiasm is infectious.
- Show the book to the students during the booktalk. Format aspects such as cover illustrations, length, and size influence choice and can be weighed by students only if they can see the book.

- Keep the booktalk brief, generally no more than two or three minutes. Do not tell too much about the book or the students will see no reason to read it; usually four to six sentences will suffice.
- State the topic and something about the action in the story, but *do not detail the plot*. Focus on a scene or character at the heart of the story, but do not discuss a scene that gives away the ending.
- Booktalk a group of books that share the same theme, talking briefly about each book and how it fits with the others.
- For more tips on booktalks, see www.thebooktalker1.com and www.nancykeane.com/booktalks.

The following is a booktalk on *The Scorpio Races* by Maggie Stiefvater (2011):

> Imagine an island where wild horses rise out of the sea, and in their rising, wreak havoc on the land, destroying property and people who attempt to capture them. Further imagine that you can capture and race these horses for money and honor. In this fantasy, *The Scorpio Races* by Maggie Stiefvater, tough men capture and race the wild horses—the *capaill uisce*—along the shore of Thisby Island. Not only are the horses uncontrollable but they are also meat-eaters. Some riders live. Many die. Sean is the best rider in the isle, but he seems bored with the races; however, this year will have a surprise—Puck, a girl, has decided to join the race on her own, very ordinary horse. As Sean and Puck get to know each other, they realize that only one of them can be the winner. Filled with mystery and adventure, you will enjoy finding out what happens at *The Scorpio Races*.

After the booktalk, make the book available to students to peruse and consider. Give booktalks on a variety of books at different levels of reading difficulty, on different topics, and with male and female protagonists from many cultures in order to reach out to the wide range of interests and abilities that exist among students.

Independent Reading by Students

Another way for students to experience good literature is to create opportunities for independent reading. Indeed, the ultimate goal of a literature program is to turn students into readers who voluntarily select and read good literature with enjoyment, understanding, and appreciation while becoming lifelong readers. Setting aside some time each week for students to read silently is particularly important because the demands on students' time outside school often leave them with little or no time for reading. If possible, schedule regular independent reading periods throughout the week. The length of time periods may vary, but there must be enough time for students to get well into their books and to gain some level of satisfaction from the reading. This practice is important for *all* students regardless of reading proficiency. Students who are unaccustomed to independent reading may need shorter sessions at first until they develop the stamina to read longer texts (Johnson, Freedman, & Thomas, 2007).

A classroom collection is essential to supporting wide reading, consisting of paperback books collected from a range of sources. This collection should include informational books, graphic novels, trivia books, and magazines since these materials are particularly supportive of resistant readers. The American Library Association (www.ala.org) creates an annual list, Quick Picks for Reluctant Young Adult Readers. Scholastic Book Club provides monthly specials of affordable paperback books for the classroom and for students to purchase for their own reading (https://clubs2.scholastic.com).

Some middle schools have instituted sustained silent reading (SSR) programs on a school-wide basis to promote reading habits in students (Pilgreen, 2000). In these SSR programs a certain time each day is set aside for all students, teachers, librarians, coaches, principals, custodians, and office and kitchen staff to take a "reading break." The philosophy behind SSR programs is that students need to see adults who read and place a high priority on reading. In SSR programs, students read materials of their own choosing and are not required to write book reports or give oral reports.

Many schools have purchased ***computerized reading incentive programs*** to motivate students to read more widely. Programs such as Accelerated Reader (AR) pretest students to determine their reading levels, then assign each student to a level of books with predetermined numbers of points according to difficulty. After students finish reading a book silently, they complete multiple-choice tests to assess literal comprehension to earn points based on the score. Students can then earn prizes according to their performance. Reports on the success of such programs are mixed. Many teachers and schools report concerns about their impact on students' interest in reading:

- Levels to which books are assigned seem arbitrary to students.
- Extrinsic rewards diminish the desire of students to read for the pleasure of reading.
- Testing students' literal comprehension emphasizes inconsequential information, thus demeaning both the story and the reading act.
- Students find ways to gain the rewards without reading the books by, for example, asking other students for answers, skimming books for facts, or finding information online.
- Personal enjoyment of literature is often deemphasized.

Teachers can design their own programs to avoid these drawbacks and invite students to read independently. Students can keep a record of their independent reading, respond to books in a variety of ways, and work to achieve individual silent reading goals set in negotiation with the teacher. Rewards, such as a celebration party, are given to the whole class for total number of pages or books read as a group to avoid the negative consequences of highly competitive programs.

Tips for successful independent reading include:

- Give booktalks so students are aware of books that might interest them.
- Provide time for students to share briefly with each other in small groups at the end of an independent reading time or to give occasional booktalks to the class.
- Have short story collections and magazines available for students who forget to bring their independent reading books to class or finish them during class.
- Encourage attentiveness to books rather than other classwork during independent reading time.
- Demonstrate your own passion for reading by being engrossed in your own book.
- Be knowledgeable about and interested in the books the students are reading.

Another way to encourage independent reading is to integrate it into homework requirements. Reading at home for a prescribed number of minutes from free-choice materials might involve asking students to read 20 minutes each school night or 80 minutes a week, providing extra credit for those who read more. Content area teachers can support independent reading by asking students to read from a list of books related to the class focus of study or by providing related books for check-out by students. Students might be asked to keep a reading journal in which they record responses to their independent reading through writing, webs, charts, or drawings or through a written dialogue with the teacher once they complete a book. Some teachers ask for a parent's signature to provide accountability for independent reading completed at home.

Experiencing Literature as Multimodal Texts

Adolescents are immersed in mass media—video games, iPods, the internet—that provide them with interactive digital, visual, auditory, and dramatic texts. Young adult literature is increasingly available in a range of media, providing important points of access for many adolescents, especially resistant readers. These multimodal texts include audiobooks, films, and digital books.

Audiobooks of young adult literature provide readings by well-known actors and professional readers. Audiobooks are an excellent teaching tool. The class can listen to an audiobook instead of using a teacher read-aloud, and audiobooks can be an effective way to engage resistant readers during independent reading times. When assigning homework reading, students who struggle with more complex texts can be offered the option of listening to the audiobook while following along in the written copy. Students who otherwise would be unable to participate in class discussions are then able to contribute. Free audiobooks can be accessed through websites such as http://librivox.org; and www.gutenberg.org. The American Library Association (www.ala.org) names an annual list of audiobooks, Amazing Audiobooks for Young Adults.

Films based on young adult books provide students with a multimedia experience of a story. Teachers can engage students in comparing how film is similar to and different from text. Both have plots, characters, settings, themes, styles, and points of view. Both are edited and both can have dialogue and narration. However, film differs from text in that it has sound (spoken words, music, and sound effects) and photography (color or black and white, angles, close-ups, and panoramas). Additionally, films have actual people or animated characters inhabiting the character roles and actual settings, whereas books ask readers to form their own images of characters and settings.

With this quick background in the elements of cinema, students can become better "readers" of film, equipped to discuss or write their personal responses to films based on literature. Films that support or contradict the content of the book may be suitable for classroom use depending on the teacher's intent. Usually teachers show a film after the book has been read and discussed. The film then provides an opportunity to compare and contrast with the book while considering the advantages and limitations of the two media. For some students the movie experience may be motivation to read the book or others in the same series or by the same author.

Teachers will want to select films based on young adult books that are appropriate to the age level and connected to classroom inquiries. The American Library Association has an award for videos for young people, the Andrew Carnegie medal, which is given to the producer of a video.

Some other sources for films, videos, and DVDs are as follows:

- *The Video Source Book* (Syosset, NY: National Video Clearinghouse), published by Gale Research, Detroit, MI. This annual reference lists media and provides sources for purchase and rental.
- *Fabulous Films for Young Adults* (http://www.ala.org/yalsa/fabfilms)
- The Internet Movie Database (www.imdb.com) is a large film database with production, ratings, and other movie details with links to external reviews.

Digital books are an increasingly popular format for accessing literature. Digital books are available on websites such WaveCloud.com (www.wavecloud.com) and OpenRoad.com (www.openroadmedia.com) which have books available from a range of publishers and include biographies of authors and other resources of interest to young adults. Scholastic has developed Storia, with interactive applications for e-books, a trend by other publishers as well.

Electronic book (e-book) readers are growing in popularity and will be integrated into classrooms as the technology becomes more affordable. E-books are generally cheaper than paper books, take up less space, are environmentally less wasteful to produce, and are more easily distributed. They have the potential to make the concept of an out-of-print book obsolete and to make virtually any book available to readers who have access to the internet. Access to full-text books is also possible on smartphones. Providing access not only to books, but to newspapers, magazines, and blogs, e-readers can be an important source of informational materials.

With such devices, teachers have greatly expanded choices of reading materials for students and literature for text sets and in-class reading. A disadvantage of some e-book readers is the lack of color graphic capability, making picture books, illustrated informational books, and graphic novels using color ineffective as e-books.

Capabilities of e-book readers that may facilitate reading include:

- A built-in dictionary so that readers can get a definition of a word by clicking on it
- Automatic searching and cross-referencing of text for finding earlier references to characters or events
- Nonpermanent highlighting
- Text-to-speech software that can automatically convert e-books to audiobooks

Interactive books and websites provide ways for readers to move between platforms, websites, and print books. Cross-format books by authors such as Patrick Corman direct readers to listen to audio, view a video, or read a short story on a mobile device at particular points in the text in order to continue the story. Some publishers are putting quick response (QR) codes that link to online sources in books that lead to background information, music playlists, various kinds of media, and related maps, photos, or videos. Still other authors have built extensive interactive websites around a particular book series.

The significance of independent reading and reads-alouds is often discounted in schools and seen as "filler" or "frills" that waste instructional time. Ivey and Johnston (2013) report on research in a middle school where the eighth-grade teachers moved to student-selected, self-paced reading. Each class session began with substantial time for student reading, followed by a teacher read-aloud of a young adult book and time for student writing. Students also had many informal conversations about their reading and developed dialogic relationships with characters as well as each other. Not only did the test scores rise, but students reported changes in their identities, sense of agency, relationships, moral understandings, and knowledge. Students became engaged critical readers who read continuously in and out of school, talked about books with peers, and acted with greater personal and social agency. They believed they could make a difference.

Reading Critically to Inquire about the World

Reading literature critically to inquire about the world involves reading to consider issues and ideas in adolescents' lives, the broader society, and the content areas. These experiences support teens in becoming critical and knowledgeable readers and thinkers. Readers are encouraged to engage deeply with the text and then to step back to share their connections and reflect critically with others about the text and their responses through a close reading of both the text and their interpretations.

This intensive reading of a few books to think deeply and critically balances the extensive reading of many books. The books chosen for intensive reading have multiple layers of meaning and invite readers to linger longer. These books invite social interaction and discussion, as students need others to think with as they struggle with interpretation and understanding.

When students experience a story, they often want to respond or express their reactions to the experience in some way. Sharing their responses can involve thinking about the experience through a new form or medium; they develop a better understanding of what they experienced by organizing and deepening their feelings and thought, and they discover that other readers' experiences with the same book may have been different. Although it is important to give students opportunities to respond to books, not every book needs or merits a lengthy response. Rosenblatt (1938) reminds us that no two people have the same life experiences and that it is the transaction that occurs between the text, the reader, and the present context that provokes a particular response.

In addition, adolescents can engage with literature as part of thematic studies or inquiries within content areas, such as math, science, and social studies. They read critically to compare information and issues across these books, learn facts about the topic, and consider conceptual issues. Literature becomes a tool for understanding the world and considering broader social and scientific issues, as well as a means of facilitating their interest in a topic.

Literature Discussion

Whole class discussion can accompany a read-aloud or a text read by the entire class, a common practice in secondary classrooms. These discussions initially center on the personal connections and perspectives of readers about the book, characters, events, themes, and outcome, asking students to share, "What are you thinking?" Read-alouds are often short selections used to introduce a particular focus and so the discussion may end there. When the text is a literary work that the class is reading for close literary analysis, the discussion will move from personal connections and interpretations into a focused analysis of the text and student interpretations. Since only a few students have an opportunity to express their viewpoints in whole group discussions, moving between small group and whole class sharing increases engagement and deepens thinking.

Literature circles involve students meeting in small groups to discuss a book they have read as a group. One of the goals of literature circles is for adolescents to learn to work and think with one another and to value the opinions and views of others. The small group format is student led and provides more opportunities for dialogue. These literature circles can be a discussion of a whole class novel or piece of literature where students move between talking in small groups, sharing out their thinking, and then returning to additional small group work.

Another option is for each group to read a different book related to a broad theme. For example, some secondary teachers organize a round of literature circles with adolescent novels either before or after they have read and discussed an assigned novel from the canon, such as John Steinbeck's *The Grapes of Wrath* (1938). Teachers gather **shared book sets,** multiple copy sets of five or six copies of different adolescent novels that build from themes and issues introduced in the assigned text but bring those issues into their lives through adolescent literature.

A third option is for students to read from **text sets,** ten to fifteen conceptually related informational texts or sophisticated picture books, or a set of five or six conceptually related chapter books or short stories (see Table 10.2). Each small group has a different text set built around a specific issue that is related to a broad theme or issue that is the class focus. The difference is that each student in a group is reading a different book and so the discussion focuses on comparing and contrasting the books to examine the issue, rather than discussing different interpretations of the same book as occurs in shared book discussions. These text sets can highlight different perspectives, encouraging critical thinking.

Text sets and shared book sets of adolescent literature can be created around themes, characters, and issues in an English language arts curriculum or in a particular content area, such as history or science. In these cases, the books are often selected as a supplement to the textbook chapter so that students first read the chapter to get an overview of the scientific or historical concept or event and then break into small groups to more deeply consider a range of differing perspectives, information, and conclusions. Examples of shared book sets and text sets around themes of forced journeys and taking responsibility for action are found in Figures 9.1 and 9.2 in Chapter 9.

The following features are typically found in literature circles:

- Students are organized into heterogeneous groups of four to six, based on their interests. They are introduced to the options through booktalks. They indicate their top three choices on a ballot so that the teacher can then form the groups.

- Students read the books and prepare for literature discussion. One option is to have students determine how many pages to read a day in order to finish the book within a particular period of time (e.g., one to two weeks), through both in class and out of class reading. Students meet in a mini-circle for ten to fifteen minutes daily to check in with each other on their reading goals and share connections and confusions. Students who are struggling with the book can partner with another student from the group or listen to an audio book.

  - As students read, they respond by writing or sketching their connections, questions, and concerns to be ready to share with group members. The responses may be in a literature log, on sticky notes placed in the book, or on a graffiti board.

Table 10.2 Examples of Text Sets by Genre, Theme, or Topic	
Genre, Theme, or Topic	**Titles**
Escape into imaginary worlds	*The Amazing Maurice and His Educated Rodents* by Terry Pratchett *Inkheart* by Cornelia Funke *Seraphina* by Rachel Hartman *Larklight* by Philip Reeve *The Wand in the Word: Conversations with Writers of Fantasy* by Leonard Marcus
Perspectives on war	*A Long Way Gone: Memoirs of a Boy Soldier* by Ishmael Beah *Sunrise over Fallujah* by Walter Dean Myers *Purple Heart* by Patricia McCormack *Bamboo People* by Mitali Perkins *The War to End All Wars* by Russell Freedman
Finding oneself	*Bucking the Sarge* by Christopher Paul Curtis *Solace of the Road* by Siobhan Dowd *The Lucy Variations* by Sara Zarr *The Tequila Worm* by Viola Canales *What Are You? Voices of Mixed-Race Young People* by Pearl Gaskins
The search for answers	*The Butterfly Clues* by Kate Ellison *Me, the Missing, and the Dead* by Jenny Valentine *Looking for Alaska* by John Green *Sonny's House of Spies* by George Ella Lyon *Forensics* by Richard Platt
The struggle to be free	*Incarceron* by Catherine Fisher *Winter's End* by Jean-Claude Mourlevat *The Girl with Borrowed Wings* by Rinsai Rossetti *Five Thousand Years of Slavery* by Marjorie Gann *After Gandhi: One Hundred Years of Nonviolent Resistance* by Anne O'Brien
The need for story	*Here Lies Arthur* by Philip Reeves *The Book Thief* by Markus Zusak *Storyteller* by Edward Myers *Bad Boy: A Memoir* by Walter Dean Myers *Writing Magic: Creating Stories That Fly* by Gail Carson Levine

- Encourage students who finish reading ahead of the rest of the group to read an independent reading book thematically related to their literature circle books.
- Teachers can use closed internet networks to have students share their responses to literature or to encourage student journaling about books.

- Students complete the book and meet in literature circles for extended discussions. These discussions typically occur after students have read the entire book. Students may need to meet in literature circles along the way if a chapter book is particularly difficult or if students are struggling readers or English language learners. Literature circles typically last anywhere from two days to two weeks, depending on the length of the book and the depth of the discussion about the book. The discussions are open-ended and provide time for readers to share their initial responses with each other and then dialogue about several issues in more depth.

- Students create a web or consensus board to brainstorm the issues that they could explore further, based on their initial sharing.
- Students identify a focus that they want to inquire about together as a group through a careful analysis of the text and of their interpretations.
- Students prepare for the discussion of the identified issue by rereading sections of the book, writing or sketching in their logs, marking relevant quotations with sticky notes, engaging in further research, or using a particular response engagement.
- Students share their ideas and connections related to the identified issue and engage in dialogue around differing interpretations and perspectives.
- Students can continue their literature circles by returning to their web multiple times to identify another issue for discussion.

- Text set discussions begin with each student reading one or two books from the set and meeting to share their books. Students often move between reading and sharing for a week or two and then webbing the connections and differences across the books in their set. They choose one of these issues to discuss in greater depth through inquiry and critique.
- Teachers do not need to be in a group, but if they join a group, they participate as a reader and group member, sharing their thoughts.
- When students complete their literature circles, they can present the key ideas from their discussions to the class by pulling together their thinking about the book or text set.
  - They may share informally by talking about their book and showing their web of connections and issues to the class.
  - They can prepare a formal presentation by listing the most important ideas to share about their book and brainstorming ways to present these ideas (murals, skits, posters, dioramas, etc.). They choose the one that best fits the ideas they want to share.
  - They can create a classroom newsletter/newspaper in which each literature group writes about the books they are reading and includes visual sketches, webs, or charts.

The discussions in literature circles are more complex and generative if teachers embed these circles within a broad class theme, such as identity or sense of place, around which they have planned a range of engagements, including class read-alouds and browsing of other books on that theme.

When students have the opportunity to converse and dialogue about what they are reading, they explore their "in-process" understandings, consider alternative interpretations, and become critical inquirers. Literature circles support reading as a transactional process in which readers actively construct understandings of a text by bringing meaning to, as well as from, that text. They come to understand that there is no one meaning to be determined, but many possible interpretations to explore and critique. The primary intent of these discussions is to provide a space for readers to think about life from multiple perspectives, not to learn about literary elements or comprehension strategies.

Literature Response Engagements

Requiring students to list the author, title, date, genre, setting, main characters, and summary of the plot seldom leads students to delve more deeply into literature. Students usually view traditional book reports as tedious busywork and as a punishment for reading a book. Although teachers assign book reports to get students to read, students often report that they never read the book, but instead read the bookflap and a page or two at the beginning and end or read online book summaries.

So-called literature response forms, worksheets, and literature units have been published or are available online for teachers. These worksheets are often little more than disguised book report forms with a focus on low-level comprehension rather than higher level critical thinking and interpretation.

Readers deepen and extend their interpretations of literature when they respond in a variety of ways. When readers move from reading to writing, art, or drama, they take a new perspective on a book. In the process of exploring their thinking about a book through various sign systems, they discover new meanings and expand their understandings of that book. Resistant readers are often uncomfortable with verbal and written responses to a book, preferring graphic and artistic responses.

The following response engagements provide structures to encourage students to push their thinking about a book. These engagements stand in contrast to activities where students write a summary, retell a book, answer comprehension questions, or make a "cute" art project. Response engagements challenge students to identify and explore the issues that they find significant within a book, rather than answer the teacher's questions about the book. *Creating Classrooms for Authors and Inquirers* by Kathy G. Short and Jerome Harste (1996) provides more information on these engagements.

- *Freewrites.* At the beginning of a group meeting, set a timer for five minutes and ask students to write continuously about their thoughts on the book, then turn and talk in the group. If the group is still not sure how to begin, one person can read aloud all or part of their freewrite. The group discusses the ideas in that freewrite and then moves on to the next person.

- *Post-ful Thinking.* Students put sticky notes on pages where they have a significant connection as they read and jot a quick comment. They share these with the group and use them to find issues to discuss together. Notes can also be used to revisit the book when the group decides to examine a specific issue by marking relevant pages to prepare for the discussion.

- *Literature Logs.* Students stop periodically as they read and respond to what they are thinking about, including questions and connections. These entries can take the form of a written response, a sketch, a web, a chart, quotes to remember, and so on. Students reread their literature logs right before beginning a group discussion so the issues are fresh in their minds.

- *Collage Reading/Text Rendering.* Students mark quotes that are significant to them as they read. In collage reading, group members read aloud quotes to each other.

One person reads a quote, then someone else reads another quote, and the reading continues in no particular order. Readers choose when to read a quote in order to build off of what someone else has read, but no comments are made about the quotes. Text rendering is similar, except readers state why they chose the quote. There is no discussion until after the text rendering is finished.

- **Graffiti Boards.** Put a large sheet of paper on the table. Each group member takes a corner of the paper to write, web, and sketch their thoughts about the book or text set. The comments, sketches, quotes, and connections are not organized; the major focus is on recording initial responses during or immediately after reading a book. Group members share from their graffiti to start the discussion. Webbing or charting can then be used to organize the connections.

- **Save the Last Word for Me.** As students read, they note passages or quotes that catch their attention because they are interesting, powerful, confusing, or contradictory and put the quote on a 3 × 5 inch card. On the back of the card, they write why they found that particular passage noteworthy. In the group, one person shares a quote and the group briefly discusses their thinking while the initial person remains silent. When the discussion dies down, the person who chose the quote tells why he/she chose it. That person has the last word, then the group moves on to the next person.

- **Sketch to Stretch.** After reading a book, students make a sketch (a quick graphic/symbolic drawing) of what the story meant to them or their connections to the book (not an illustration of the story). In the group, they share their sketches and discuss symbols and ideas. After sharing the sketches, they choose issues to explore in more depth as a group.

- **Webbing What's on My Mind.** After sharing initial responses to a book, a group brainstorms a web of issues, themes, and questions that could be discussed from the book or text set. Using the web, the group decides on the one issue that is most interesting or causes the most tension to begin discussion. The discussion is continued by choosing from other ideas on the web. New ideas are added as they develop from the discussion.

- **Consensus Board.** Divide a large board into four sections with a circle in the middle. The circle contains the book's title or key theme. In the individual sections, each student writes or sketches personal connections to the book or theme. The group discusses these individual connections and comes to consensus on the issues or big ideas to explore further. These are written in the middle of the board for further discussion.

- **Comparison Charts/Venn Diagrams.** Students read a text set and discuss similarities and differences across the books. From these discussions, broad categories are identified that the group wants to compare more closely across the books. A chart with the books listed on the side and the categories across the top is constructed. Both pictures and words are used to make the comparisons in the boxes. A Venn diagram (two circles that overlap in the center) focuses the comparison on one major issue at a time.

- **Story Ray.** Each person receives a three-foot narrow strip of paper (a ray) on which to create a visual essence of a selected chapter using colors, images, and a few words with various art media and little or no white space. The rays are shared in the group by explaining their symbolism. The rays are then assembled on a large mural or wall in the shape of sun rays to reflect the unfolding of the novel.

- *Mapping.* Maps provide a way to organize thinking and explore relationships among ideas, people, and events. They can take a range of forms to show visual relationships, explore processes and change, and record movement of people or ideas. Maps can show:

  - The journey of change for a character within a book or of an idea/issue over the course of the book.
  - Symbols that show the heart (the values and beliefs) or the mind (the thoughts and ideas) of a particular character.
  - A cultural "x-ray" in the shape of a person that show a character's inner values and beliefs and outer actions and qualities.
  - A flowchart that explores how certain decisions made by a character create particular consequences.

- *Time Lines and Diagrams.* Time lines can help students explore how particular historical events influenced the characters in a book. Draw a line on a long strip of paper, placing the dates below the line on scaled intervals. Note the story events above the line and the events from history below the line. Time lines are also useful with text sets of historical sources.

- *Jackdaws.* Jackdaws are collections of artifacts or copies of objects from a particular historical period or event. The term "jackdaw" refers to a European bird that collects colorful objects for its nest and refers to a teaching tool that connects historical books with the real events through concrete objects (Dodd, 1999). Jackdaws are made by collecting a wide array of related materials in their original forms or in reproductions, such as maps, time lines, diary entries, recipes, newspaper clippings, music, clothing, artwork, letters, advertisements, photographs, and books of the era. The objects are placed in a decorated box with labels and explanations. The jackdaw can be used as an extension activity for a book read in class as well as for building background. Many teachers enlist students in the development of jackdaws. The Library of Congress provides access to primary sources at www.loc.gov/teachers as does Primary Source, http://www.primarysource.org/, which has online curriculum units with documents and photographs.

Students who are new to working in groups often find that working in pairs is an easier way to become comfortable with discussion. Any of the response engagements may be used with partners, rather than in a small group. There are also several response engagements that are particularly designed for partners.

- *Say Something.* Two people share the reading of a short story. The first person reads aloud a chunk of text (several paragraphs or a page) to the other person. When the reader stops, both of them "say something" by making a prediction, sharing personal connections, asking questions, or commenting on the story. The second person then reads aloud a chunk of text and again both "say something." The two readers continue alternating the reading of the story, commenting after each reading, until the story is completed.

- *Written Conversation.* Have a silent conversation by talking on paper. Two people share a piece of paper and a pencil, talking about a book by writing back and forth to each other. No talking is allowed, except with young children, who often need to write and then read what they have written aloud in order for the other child to write back.

Drama as Response

Creative drama is informal drama that involves the reenactment of story experiences (Mc-Caslin, 1990). It is improvisational and involves the actors creating dialogue and movement as they engage in the drama. Props may be used, but not scenery or costumes. Because of its improvisational nature and simplicity, creative drama places importance on the experience of the participants, not on performance for an audience.

A picture book, short story, or single scene from a chapter book may be dramatized. The most suitable stories to start with are relatively simple, involving two to six characters and high action. The steps in guiding creative drama in the classroom are:

- Students select a story they want to act out, and listen to or read it independently several times, paying attention to the characters and story scenes.
- Students list the characters and the scenes on the chalkboard or on chart paper.
- Students assign parts to actors. If enough students are interested in dramatizing the same story, two or more casts of actors can be assigned. Each cast of characters can observe the performances of the others and learn from them.
- Each cast uses the list of scenes to review the plot, ensuring that all actors recall the events. Discuss the characters, describing the actions, dialogue, and appearance for each.
- Give the cast of characters a few minutes to decide how to handle the performance. Then run through it several times to work out the bumpy parts. Lines are improvised, not memorized.

The Fantastic Plays for Kids website (www.childdrama.com) has useful ideas and lesson plans for creative drama.

Dramatic inquiry, also known as *drama in education,* involves the use of drama to create an imaginative space or drama world around critical moments in a story, rather than acting out a story (Edmiston & McKibben, 2011). Students develop characters and situations and take on diverse perspectives that go beyond the book. Discussion supports readers in standing back and talking about events that happened to other people in a different world. Dramatic inquiry puts students in the middle of events and within the world of the story as they explore their tensions and issues. Students explore multiple perspectives within and beyond the story boundaries through strategies such as the following:

- *Tableaus.* Each small group of students creates a frozen image without talk or movement to represent an idea or moment related to the story.
- *Writing-in-Role.* Students assume the identity of a character and write a text from that perspective, such as a reflection on events or a journal entry.
- *Hot Seat.* Students take on the roles of different characters and sit on the hot seat to respond to questions about their perspective on an issue from the story.
- *News Program.* Students take on the role of television or newspaper reporters and interview characters from the book to retell an event from a range of perspectives.
- *Perspective Switch.* Each student shifts perspectives, trying out the perspectives of characters who are opposed, supportive, or ambivalent to an issue.

These drama strategies take readers beyond reenactments of a story to their own drama worlds, giving them a lens for critically examining the events and margins of a story. *Action Strategies for Deepening Comprehension* (Wilhelm, 2002) offers examples of these drama strategies in responding to literature.

Literature across the Curriculum

Students may also experience good literature in content-area classes when teachers supplement or replace textbooks with fiction and nonfiction literature for instruction. *Literature across the curriculum* refers to using literature as the content reading in social studies, health, science, and mathematics courses. Literature provides more interesting and well-written accounts and perspectives on historical events and scientific information. In addition, textbooks often superficially cover large amounts of information, whereas nonfiction literature focuses on a particular topic in more depth, providing a context for inquiry into broader social and scientific issues. Students who struggle as readers can benefit from attractively illustrated and more accessible nonfiction literature. A collection of nonfiction literature of varying lengths and difficulties can meet the needs of students at different reading levels, unlike textbooks written on a single readability level.

The stories and narrative in literature are often more understandable, real, and memorable than the expository language of textbooks. Works of historical fiction present historical events from a young person's point of view and feature well-defined characters and settings, and student interest in the narrative can later move to an interest in the history itself.

Literature often addresses issues or perspectives omitted from textbooks, which tend to express a dominant culture view. Books can fill in these gaps and permit students to read multiple perspectives on an event or issue. The roles of women and various cultural groups in U.S. history, for example, are often given short shrift in history textbooks. Students can compare and contrast information from a range of sources, encouraging critical thinking and challenging them to verify facts across different sources. Books present political and social events in terms of the moral issues related to them. Reading these books, adolescents can see how historical events affected the lives of ordinary people and can better understand the beliefs and values underlying the choices made by political leaders.

Teachers benefit from using literature across the curriculum because their course materials are richer, more interesting, more complete, and, particularly in the area of science, more up-to-date. When courses become more interesting, students are likely to become more engaged as learners.

A strategy teachers use when selecting text sets around a topic is to purposely look for books that contradict one another with different information or viewpoints. Students may start with the textbook and then research the events or issue from other books, or read a work of fiction and then seek to verify to what extent the facts within the story are accurate or complete.

In studying the history of the nineteenth-century westward expansion in the United States, a history teacher could select trade books that present the perspectives of American Indians who were displaced by the European settlers, focus on the roles of women pioneers, tell the contributions of the Chinese Americans in building the transcontinental railway, and detail the more harrowing aspects of pioneers' lives. Generally, history textbooks either downplay the roles of women and minority groups in U.S. history or omit them altogether and present overviews rather than detailed accounts.

The following trade book selections are appropriate for such a unit:

Gabriel's Story by David A. Durham (2002) African-American teen and violence in the West

Dragon's Gate by Laurence Yep (1993) Chinese Americans' contributions to railroad

Black Storm 'Coming by Diane Wilson (2005) Biracial family, wagon train, Pony Express

Best Shot in the West by Patricia McKissack (2012) Famous African-American cowboy

The Legend of Bass Reeves by Gary Paulsen (2008) Legendary African-American law man

The Game of Silence by Louise Erdrich (2004) Ojibwa family displaced by white settlers

Hattie Big Sky by Kirby Larson (2006) Women homesteaders in Montana

Sacajawea by Joseph Bruchac (2008) Shoshone companion to Lewis and Clark

Rodzina by Karen Cushman (2003) Orphan train to California

Boston Jane series by Jennifer Holm (2001) Women pioneers

Students can read one of these titles, comparing what they learn from these books with their textbooks and pointing out any omissions or contradictions in the two sources. For example, the U.S. government's Manifest Destiny policy of the 1840s (the belief of European-Americans that it was their mission to extend the "boundaries of freedom" to others by appropriating more land), usually addressed in history textbooks, could be contrasted with the resulting disenfranchisement and loss for American Indians as addressed in selected books. Debates, essays, and stance papers are particularly appropriate response forms for honing students' critical thinking about history.

By incorporating recent real-life stories of immigrant experiences in the United States, such as An Na's *A Step from Heaven* (2001), Firoozeh Dumas' *Funny in Farsi* (2004), Marina Budhos' *Remix: Conversations with Immigrant Teenagers* (2007), and Thanhha Lai's *Inside Out and Back Again* (2011), teachers help students relate to the topic of immigration by showing that it is happening today in their world. These stories not only help students empathize with recent immigrants by revealing the difficulties of assimilating to a new culture, they often throw light on the political problems in the characters' home countries that necessitated the immigration.

Sometimes a single book, rather than a text set, encourages critical thinking. Avi's *Nothing but the Truth* (1991), written from several viewpoints about a boy's attempt to argue for his freedom of speech, could be read in a literature or history class. Some readers will take the boy's side or his homeroom teacher's side, but they will find that some of their peers view events differently than they did. Another example is *How to Save a Life* by Sara Zarr (2011), in which alternating voices convey the conflict between a pregnant teen and the daughter of the woman who wants to adopt her baby. These books encourage readers to question sources of information, look at the whole picture before deciding on what is true, and consider the possible consequences of actions.

Teachers can ask students to compare facts presented in their textbooks with those found in various books on the same topic. This strategy is particularly helpful in keeping course material up-to-date, given the rapidity of progress and change in scientific fields. Textbook information on global warming, for example, can be compared to facts in David Laurie and Cambria Gordon's *The Down-to-Earth Guide to Global Warming* (2007) and *How We Know What We Know about Our Changing Climate* by Lynne Cherry and

Gary Barusch (2008), while Karen Healey's *When We Wake* (2013) features a girl who is brought back to life 100 years after she is killed to find that the effects of global warming have devastated her country. For ideas on planning units incorporating trade books, fiction and nonfiction, see the lists of Recommended Books at the end of Chapter 5, "Historical Fiction," and the biography lists in Chapter 6, "Nonfiction," which are organized by historical era, the planning webs in Figures 9.1 and 9.2, and the examples of text sets in Table 10.2.

Content-area reading is the ability to read to acquire, understand, and connect to new content in a particular discipline. In content-area classes students are often assigned textbooks, a type of expository text, which they frequently have more difficulty reading and understanding than narrative texts. When students enter schools with departmentalized organizations, the teaching of reading is often neglected, even though the demands of reading increase with the specialized vocabulary, abstract ideas, more complex syntax, and the need for prior knowledge required by textbooks. Content-area teachers feel more responsibility to impart knowledge about the particular subject matter in which they specialize and may ignore the need to assist students in their literacy development. This perspective is slowly shifting in content area classrooms with the help of resources, such as Chris Tovani's *Do I Really Have to Teach Reading?* (2004).

Not surprisingly, by the time students in the United States enter middle school, their reading achievement levels, on average, begin to fall. Allington (2002) reasoned that textbooks written at many students' frustration levels are partially to blame. He found that exemplary teachers avoid this problem by using multiple instructional resources written at varying levels of difficulty and then offer their students some choice in their assigned content-area reading. Teachers can make reading textbooks easier if they teach students how such texts are structured and explain their specialized features. In Chapter 6, the elements and structures of informational texts are explained with examples.

Reading Strategically to Learn about Literacy and Literature

Reading literature to learn about literacy creates strategic readers who reflect on their reading processes and text knowledge. Teachers can help adolescents develop a repertoire of strategies to use when they encounter difficulty, either in figuring out words or in comprehending, and to gain knowledge of text structures, genres, and literary elements. Adults guide adolescents' reflections on their reading processes by teaching these strategies and structures and by having students read literature that highlights particular reading strategies or text structures. Students who have a range of effective reading strategies and text knowledge can problem solve when encountering difficulty so as to develop reading proficiency. Reading strategies can be effectively taught within the context of reading a book for meaning and then pulling back to talk about the strategies students used to make sense of that book.

Struggling readers often need support to develop a greater repertoire of comprehension strategies to use in constructing meaning. Most readers intuitively engage in these processes, but struggling readers often have spent so much time on phonics and decoding that they are unsure about how to read for meaning. Two useful resources are *I Read It But I Don't Get It* by Chris Tovani (2001) and *Shades of Meaning* by Donna Santman (2005).

Often literary instruction takes the form of worksheets where students list literary elements and devices, such as character, conflict, metaphors, and symbolism rather than thoughtfully considering how these elements influence meaning. Author studies, in which students immerse themselves in reading and examining an author's whole body of work, are a meaningful context in which students can examine particular literary elements and genres to learn about literature. Genre studies also provide a way for students to explore literary elements and genres within a meaningful context.

Writing often provides an effective way for students to explore language and text structures, particularly if they use literary works as writing models or mentor texts. When adolescents read and listen to stories, they accumulate vocabulary, sentence structures, stylistic devices, story ideas and text structures. Teachers can show examples of clear, lively writing in nonfiction and call attention to the use of captions, graphs, tables, figures, and authentic photographs as ways to effectively present information.

Table 10.3 provides suggestions for books that can be used as mentor texts. Also, much of the fan fiction on the internet provides venues for young adults to gain

Table 10.3   Using Literary Works as Writing Models

Literary Device or Element	Suggested Books
Characterization	*Dodger* by Terry Pratchett *Daniel Half Human: And the Good Nazi* by David Chotjewitz *Out of My Mind* by Sharon Draper *The One and Only Ivan* by Katherine Applegate
Dialogue	*Ruby Holler* by Sharon Creech *Going Bovine* by Libba Bray *Why We Broke Up* by Daniel Handler *Period 8* by Chris Crutcher
Metaphor	*Lizzie Bright and the Buckminster Boy* by Gary Schmidt *Green Angel* by Alice Hoffman *Kira-Kira* by Cynthia Kadohata *Chime* by Franny Billingsley
Mood	*The Killer's Tears* by Anne-Laure Bondoux *The Scorpio Races* by Maggie Stiefvater *Second Chance Summer* by Morgan Matson *A Monster Calls* by Patrick Ness
Journal writing	*The Diary of Pelly D.* by L. J. Adlington *Witch Child* by Celia Rees *Maata's Journal* by Paul Sullivan *We Were Here* by Matt de la Peña
Point of view	*Eleanor and Park* by Rainbow Rowell *How to Save a Life* by Sara Zarr *Nothing but the Truth* by Avi *Keesha's House* by Helen Frost
Flashbacks	*Who Is Jesse Flood?* by Malachy Doyle *Hush* by Jacqueline Woodson *A Northern Light* by Jennifer Donnelly *The Perfect Shot* by Elaine Alphin

experience as writers. Students can use young adult books as mentor texts through experiences such as:

- Creating a new episode using the same characters.
- Writing a new conclusion of what might have happened if the protagonist had made a different decision or if some external force had been different.
- Taking the perspective of a character other than the protagonist and writing reflections on the situation. Rainbow Rowell's *Eleanor & Park* (2013) is an example of changing points of view where the same story is told from the perspectives of a girl and a boy who are neighbors.
- Writing the synopsis of a ***prequel*** (a story in which events precede those detailed in an earlier work) to a story.
- Taking a story set in the past and recasting it in a modern-day setting and writing a plot summary of this new work. Or a character can be taken from historical fiction and become a visitor in modern times by describing how this character would be likely to react.

Often teaching about literacy and literature occurs as isolated skills instruction, away from actual engagement in reading a book that matters to the reader. Rosenblatt (1938) reminds us that a focus on strategies and literary knowledge should occur *after* readers have an opportunity to read and immerse themselves in the world of that text and share their understandings with other readers. We do not read to search for metaphors or opening lines but because literature adds to our lives. Once readers have a chance to consider the significance of a book, then they can pull back to examine the strategies used by the author to engage them as readers or the strategies they can use to dig more deeply into a book.

Many cultures view reading as necessary to a well-ordered society and to the moral well-being of the individual. Engagement with literature invites adolescents to make meaning of texts in personally significant ways in order to facilitate learning of content and to develop positive lifelong reading attitudes and habits. In addition, adolescents gain a sense of possibility for their lives and for society, along with the ability to consider others' perspectives and needs. Engagement with literature thus allows them to develop their own voices and, at the same time, go beyond self-interest to an awareness of broader human consequences.

References

Adlington, L. J. (2005). *The diary of Pelly D.* New York: HarperCollins.

Allington, R. (2002). You can't learn much from books you can't read. *Educational Leadership, 60*(3), 16–19.

Alphin, E. (2005). *The perfect shot.* Minneapolis, MN: Carolrhoda.

Applegate, K. (2012). *The one and only Ivan.* New York: HarperCollins.

Atwell, N. (1987). *In the middle.* Portsmouth, NH: Heinemann.

———. (2007). *The reading zone.* New York: Scholastic.

Avi. (1991). *Nothing but the truth.* New York: Orchard.

Beah, I. (2007). *A long way gone: Memoirs of a boy soldier.* New York: Farrar.

Billingsley, F. (2011). *Chime.* New York: Dial.

Bondoux, A. (2006). *The killer's tears.* New York: Delacorte.

Bray, L. (2009). *Going bovine.* New York: Ember.

Bruchac, J. (2000). *Sacajawea.* San Diego: Silver Whistle.

Budhos, M. (2006). *Ask me no questions.* New York: Atheneum.

———. (2007). *Remix: Conversations with immigrant teenagers.* Eugene, OR: Wipf & Stock.

Carlsen, G. R., & Sherrill, A. (1988). *Voices of readers: How we come to love books.* Urbana, IL: NCTE.

Cherry, L. (2008). *How we know what we know about our changing climate.* Photographs by G. Barusch. New York: Dawn.

Chotjewitz, D. (2004). *Daniel half human: And the good Nazi.* Translated from German. New York: Atheneum.

Collins, S. (2008). *The hunger games.* New York: Scholastic.

Cope, J. (1997). Beyond *Voices of Readers:* Students on school's effects on reading. *English Journal, 86*(3), 18–23.

Creech, S. (2002). *Ruby Holler.* New York: HarperCollins.

Crutcher, C. (2013). *Period 8.* New York: Greenwillow.

Curtis, C. P. (2004). *Bucking the Sarge.* New York: Random House.

Cushman, K. (2003). *Rodzina.* New York: Clarion.

de la Peña, M. (2009). *We were here.* New York: Delacorte.

Dodd, E. (1999). Echoes of the past. *Childhood Education, 75*(3), 136–141.

Donnelly, J. (2003). *A northern light.* New York: Houghton Mifflin Harcourt.

Dowd, S. (2009). *Solace of the road.* London: David Fickling.

Doyle, M. (2002). *Who is Jesse Flood?* New York: Bloomsbury.

Draper, S. (2010). *Out of my mind.* New York: Atheneum.

Dumas. F. (2004). *Funny in Farsi.* New York: Random House.

Durham, D. A. (2002). *Gabriel's story.* Norwell, MA: Anchor.

Edmiston, B., & McKibben, A. (2011). Shakespeare, rehearsal approaches, and dramatic inquiry. *English in Education, 45*(1), 86–101.

Ellison, K. (2012). *The butterfly clues.* New York: Egmont.

Erdrich, L. (2005). *The game of silence.* New York: HarperCollins.

Fader, D., Duggins, J., Finn, T., & McNeil, E. (1976). *The new hooked on books.* New York: Berkley.

Fielding, L. G., Wilson, P. T., & Anderson, R. C. (1986). A new focus on free reading: The role of trade books in reading instruction. In T. Raphael (Ed.), *The contexts of school-based literacy,* pp. 149–160. New York: Random.

Fisher, C. (2007). *Incarceron.* New York: Dial.

Freedman, R. (2010). *The war to end all wars: World War I.* New York: Clarion.

Frost, H. (2003). *Keesha's house.* New York: Farrar.

Fullteron, S. K., & Colwell, J. (2010). Research on small-group discussions of literature: An analysis of three decades. In Jimenez, R., Risko, V., Hundley, M., & Rowe, D., *59th Yearbook of the National Reading Conference* (pp. 57–74). Oak Creek, WI: NRC.

Funke, C. (2003). *Inkheart.* Translated from German. New York: Scholastic.

Gann, M., & Wilson, J. (2011). *Five thousand years of slavery.* Toronto: Tundra.

Gaskins, P. (Ed.). (1999). *What are you? Voices of mixed-race young people.* New York: Holt.

Green, J. (2006). *Looking for Alaska.* New York: Speak/Penguin.

Guthrie, J. T., & Davis, M. H. (2003). Motivating struggling readers in middle school through an engagement model of classroom practice. *Reading and Writing Quarterly, 19,* 59–85.

Handler, D. (2011). *Why we broke up.* New York: Little, Brown.

Hartman, R. (2012). *Seraphina.* New York: Random.

Healey, K. (2013). *When we wake.* New York: Little, Brown.

Hoffman, A. (2003). *Green angel.* New York: Scholastic.

Holm, J. (2001). *Boston Jane: An adventure.* New York: HarperCollins. (Others in the series: *Boston Jane: Wilderness days,* 2002; *Boston Jane: The claim,* 2004.)

Ivey, G., & Broaddus, K. (2001). "Just plain reading": A survey of what makes students want to read in middle school classrooms. *Reading Research Quarterly, 36,* 350–377.

Ivey, G., & Johnston, P. (2013). Engagement with young adult literature: Outcomes and processes. *Reading Research Quarterly, 48*(3), 255–275.

Johnson, H., Freedman, L., & Thomas, K. F. (2007). *Building reading confidence in adolescents.* Thousand Oaks, CA: Corwin.

Kadohata, C. (2004). *Kira-Kira.* New York: Atheneum.

Katin, M. (2006). *We are on our own.* Montreal: Drawn & Quarterly.

King, A. S. (2012). *Please ignore Vera Dietz.* New York: Ember.

Lai, T. (2011). *Inside out and back again.* New York: Harper.

Larson, K. (2006). *Hattie Big Sky.* New York: Delacorte.

Laurie, D., & Gordon, C. (2007). *The down-to-earth guide to global warming.* New York: Orchard.

Lenters, K. (2006). Resistance, struggle, and the adolescent reader. *Journal of Adolescent & Adult Literacy, 50*(2), 136–146.

Levine, G. C. (2006). *Writing magic: Creating stories that fly.* New York: HarperCollins.

Lyons, G. E. (2004). *Sonny's house of spies.* New York: Atheneum.

Marcus, L. (Ed.). (2006). *The wand in the word: Conversations with writers of fantasy.* Somerville, MA: Candlewick.

Matson, M. (2012). *Second chance summer.* New York: Simon & Schuster.

McCaslin, N. (1990). *Creative drama in the classroom* (5th ed.). New York: Longmann.

McCormack, P. (2009). *Purple Heart.* New York: Balzer & Bray.

McKenna, M., Ellsworth, R., & Kear, D. (1995). Children's attitudes toward reading: A national survey. *Reading Research Quarterly, 30,* 934–957.

McKissack, P. (2012). *Best shot in the West: The adventures of Nat Love.* San Francisco: Chronicle.

Myers, E. (2008). *Storyteller.* New York: Clarion.

Myers, W. D. (2001). *Bad boy: A memoir.* New York: Amistad.

———. (2009). *Sunrise over Fallujah.* New York: Scholastic.

Na, A. (2001). *A step from heaven.* Asheville, NC: Front Street.

Ness, P. (2011). *A monster calls.* Illus. by J. Kay. Somerville, MA: Candlewick.

O'Brien, A. (2009). *After Ghandi: One hundred years of nonviolent resistance.* San Francisco: Chronicle.

Paulson, G. (2006). *The legend of Bass Reeves.* New York: Wendy Lamb.

Perkins, M. (2010). *Bamboo people.* Watertown, MA: Charlesbridge.

Peters, J. A. (2006). *Luna.* New York: Little, Brown.

Pilgreen, J. (2000). *The SSR handbook: How to organize and manage a Sustained Silent Reading Program.* Portsmouth, NH: Heinemann.

Platt, R. (2005). *Forensics.* New York: Houghton.

Pratchett, T. (2001). *The amazing Maurice and his educated rodents.* New York: HarperCollins.

———. (2012). *Dodger.* New York: HarperCollins.

Rees, C. (2001). *Witch child.* Cambridge, MA: Candlewick.

Reeve, P. (2008). *Here lies Arthur.* New York: Scholastic.

———. (2006). *Larklight: A rousing tale of dauntless pluck in the farthest reaches of space.* New York: Bloomsbury.

Reeves, A. R. (2004). *Adolescents talk about reading: Exploring resistance to and engagement with text.* Newark, DE: International Reading Association.

Rosenblatt, L. M. (1938). *Literature as exploration.* Chicago: Modern Language Association.

Rossetti, R. (2013). *The girl with borrowed wings.* New York: Dial.

Rowell, R. (2013). *Eleanor & Park.* New York: St. Martin's Griffin.

Santman, D. (2005). *Shades of meaning: Comprehension and interpretation in middle school.* Portsmouth, NH: Heinemann.

Schmidt, G. (2004). *Lizzie Bright and the Buckminster boy.* New York: Clarion.

Short, K., & Harste, J. (1996). *Creating classrooms for authors and inquirers.* Portsmouth, NH: Heinemann.

Sís, P. (2007). *The wall: Growing up behind the iron curtain.* New York: Farrar.

Smith, M. W., & Wilhelm, J. D. (2002). *Reading don't fix no Chevys: Literacy in the lives of young men.* Portsmouth, NH: Heinemann

Steinbeck, J. (1938). *The grapes of wrath.* New York: Viking.

Stewart, R. A., Paradis, E. E., Ross, B. D., & Lewis, M. J. (1996). Student voices: What works in literature-based developmental reading. *Journal of Adolescent & Adult Literacy, 39*(6), 468–478.

Stiefvater, M. (2011). *The Scorpio races.* New York: Scholastic.

Strommen, L. T., & Mates, B. F. (2004). Learning to love reading: Interviews with older children and teens. *Journal of Adolescent & Adult Literacy, 48,* 188–200.

Sullivan, M. (2009). *Connecting boys with books 2.* Chicago: American Library Association.

Sullivan, P. (2003). *Maata's journal.* New York: Atheneum.

Tovani, C. (2004). *Do I really need to teach reading?* Portland, ME: Stenhouse.

———. (2000). *I read it, but I don't get it: Comprehension strategies for adolescent readers.* Portland, ME: Stenhouse.

Valentine, J. (2008). *Me, the missing, and the dead.* New York: HarperTeen.

Wilhelm, J. (2002). *Action strategies for deepening comprehension.* New York: Scholastic.

Wilson, D. (2005). *Black storm comin'.* New York: M. K. McElderry.

Woodson, J. (2002). *Hush.* New York: Putnam.

Worthy, J., Patterson, E., Salas, R., Prater, S., & Turner, M. (2002). "More than just reading": The human factor in reaching resistant readers. *Reading Research and Instruction, 41*(2), 177–202.

Yep, L. (1993). *Dragon's gate.* New York: HarperCollins.

Zarr, S. (2011). *How to save a life.* New York: Little, Brown.

———. (2013). *The Lucy variations.* New York: Little, Brown.

Zusak, M. (2007). *The book thief.* New York: Knopf.

Appendix A

Book Awards

The awards listed in this appendix were established at different times, but we have included only the award winners from 2000 to 2013. The full list of previous award winners can be found on the website of the sponsoring organization for that award. Some programs, such as the Boston Globe–Horn Book Awards and the Coretta Scott King Awards, confer separate awards for text and picture books. We provide only the text awards in this appendix.

Michael L. Printz Award for Excellence in Young Adult Literature

The Michael L. Printz Award is an award for a book that exemplifies literary excellence in young adult literature. It was established by the Young Adult Library Services Association of the American Library Association in 2000. The award is sponsored by Booklist, a publication of the American Library Association.

2013 *In Darkness* by Nick Lake. Bloomsbury. (Realistic fiction, ages 14–18.)

HONOR BOOKS

Aristotle and Dante Discover the Secrets of the Universe by Benjamin Alire Sáenz. Simon & Schuster. (Realistic fiction, ages 14–18.)

Code Name Verity by Elizabeth Wein. Hyperion. (Historical fiction/World War II, ages 14–18.)

Dodger by Terry Pratchett. HarperCollins. (Fantasy, ages 14–18.)

The White Bicycle by Beverley Brenna. Red Deer Press. (Realistic fiction, ages 14–18.)

2012 *Where Things Come Back* by John Corey Whaley. Atheneum. (Realistic fiction, ages 12–16.)

HONOR BOOKS

Why We Broke Up by Daniel Handler. Little, Brown. (Realistic fiction, ages 14–18.)

The Returning by Christine Hinwood. Dial. (Historical fantasy, ages 14–18.)

Jasper Jones by Craig Silvey. Knopf. (Realistic fiction, ages 13–18.)

The Scorpio Races by Maggie Stiefvater. Scholastic. (Fantasy, ages 14–18.)

2011 *Ship Breaker* by Paolo Bacigalupi. Little, Brown. (Dystopia/Science fiction, ages 14–18.)

HONOR BOOKS

Stolen by Lucy Christopher. Chicken House. (Realistic fiction, ages 12–16.)

Please Ignore Vera Dietz by A. S. King. Knopf. (Magical realism, ages 14–18.)

Revolver by Marcus Sedgwick. Roaring Brook Press. (Realistic fiction/survival, ages 13–18.)

Nothing by Janne Teller. Atheneum. (Realistic fiction, ages 15–18.)

2010   *Going Bovine* by Libba Bray. Delacorte. (Fantasy, ages 13–18.)

HONOR BOOKS

Charles and Emma: The Darwins' Leap of Faith by Deborah Heiligman. Holt. (Historical, ages 12–17.)

The Monstrumologist by Rick Yancey. Simon & Schuster. (Historical fantasy, ages 12–17.)

Punkzilla by Adam Rapp. Candlewick. (Realistic fiction, ages 14–18.)

Tales of the Madman Underground: An Historical Romance, 1973 by John Barnes. Viking. (Realistic fiction, ages13–17.)

2009   *Jellicoe Road* by Melina Marchetta. HarperCollins. (Realism, ages 14–18.)

HONOR BOOKS

The Astonishing Life of Octavian Nothing, Traitor to the Nation, **Volume II:** *The Kingdom on the Waves* by M. T. Anderson. Candlewick. (Historical fiction/U.S. Revolutionary War, ages 15–18.)

The Disreputable History of Frankie Landau-Banks by E. Lockhart. Hyperion. (Realism, ages 14–18.)

Nation by Terry Pratchett. HarperCollins. (Fantasy/survival, ages 14–18.)

Tender Morsels by Margo Lanagan. Knopf. (Fantasy, ages 15–18.)

2008   *The White Darkness* by Geraldine McCaughrean. HarperCollins. (Realism/survival, ages 12–16.)

HONOR BOOKS

Dreamquake: Book Two of the Dreamhunter Duet by Elizabeth Knox. Farrar. (Fantasy, ages 15–18.)

One Whole and Perfect Day by Judith Clarke. Front Street. (Realism, ages 14–16.)

Repossessed by A. M. Jenkins. Harper-Collins. (Fantasy, ages 14–18.)

Your Own, Sylvia: A Verse Portrait of Sylvia Plath by Stephanie Hemphill. Knopf. (Biography/poetry, ages 14–18.)

2007   *American Born Chinese* by Gene Luen Yang. First Second. (Mixed genre graphic novel, ages 12–18.)

HONOR BOOKS

The Astonishing Life of Octavian Nothing, Traitor to the Nation, **Volume I:** *The Pox Party* by M. T. Anderson. Candlewick. (Historical fiction/U.S. Revolutionary War, ages 15–18.)

An Abundance of Katherines by John Green. Dutton. (Realistic fiction, ages 15–18.)

Surrender by Sonya Hartnett. Candlewick. (Realism/psychological thriller, ages 15–18.)

The Book Thief by Markus Zusak. Knopf. (Historical fiction/Nazi Germany, ages 14–18.)

2006   *Looking for Alaska* by John Green. Dutton. (Realistic fiction, ages 15–18.)

HONOR BOOKS

Black Juice by Margo Lanagan. EOS/HarperCollins. (Fantasy/short stories, ages 15–18.)

I Am the Messenger by Marcus Zusak. Knopf. (Realism/mystery, ages 15–18.)

John Lennon: All I Want Is the Truth by Elizabeth Partridge. Viking. (Biography, ages 15–18.)

A Wreath for Emmett Till by Marilyn Nelson. Illustrated by Philippe Lardy. Houghton. (Nonfiction/poetry, ages 15–18.)

2005   *How I Live Now* by Meg Rosoff. Random House. (Dystopia/Science fiction, ages 14–18.)

HONOR BOOKS

Airborn by Kenneth Oppel. HarperCollins. (Fantasy, ages 12–16.)

Chanda's Secrets by Allan Stratton. Annick. (Realistic fiction, ages 14–18.)

Lizzie Bright and the Buckminster Boy by Gary D. Schmidt. Clarion. (Historical fiction/Maine, 1912, ages 13–16.)

2004 *The First Part Last* by Angela Johnson. Simon & Schuster. (Realism/African-American, ages 14–18.)

HONOR BOOKS

A Northern Light by Jennifer Donnelly. Harcourt. (Historical fiction/United States, 1906, ages 14–18.)

Keesha's House by Helen Frost. Farrar. (Realism/poetry, ages 14–18.)

Fat Kid Rules the World by K. L. Going. Putnam. (Realism, ages 14–18.)

The Earth, My Butt, and Other Big Round Things by Carolyn Mackler. Candlewick. (Realism, ages 13–16.)

2003 *Postcards from No Man's Land* by Aidan Chambers. Dutton. (Realism, ages 15–18.)

HONOR BOOKS

The House of the Scorpion by Nancy Farmer. Simon & Schuster. (Science fiction, ages 11–15.)

My Heartbeat by Garret Freymann-Weyr. Houghton. (Realism, ages 14–18.)

Hole in My Life by Jack Gantos. Farrar. (Autobiography, ages 13–18.)

2002 *A Step from Heaven* by An Na. Front Street. (Realism/Korean-American, ages 14–18.)

HONOR BOOKS

The Ropemaker by Peter Dickinson. Delacorte. (Fantasy, ages 13–16.)

Heart to Heart: New Poems Inspired by Twentieth-Century American Art by Jan Greenberg. Abrams. (Poetry, ages 11–18.)

Freewill by Chris Lynch. HarperCollins. (Realism/mystery, ages 14–18.)

True Believer by Virginia Euwer Wolff. Atheneum. (Realism, ages 14–18.)

2001 *Kit's Wilderness* by David Almond. Delacorte. (Magical realism, ages 12–16.)

HONOR BOOKS

Many Stones by Carolyn Coman. Front Street. (Realism, ages 14–18.)

The Body of Christopher Creed by Carol Plum-Ucci. Harcourt. (Realism/mystery, ages 13–18.)

Angus, Thongs, and Full Frontal Snogging: Confessions of Georgia Nicolson by Louise Rennison. HarperCollins. (Realism, ages 12–16.)

Stuck in Neutral by Terry Trueman. HarperCollins. (Realism, ages 11–16.)

2000 *Monster* by Walter Dean Myers. Harper-Collins. (Realism, ages 15–18.)

HONOR BOOKS

Skellig by David Almond. Delacorte. (Magical realism, ages 11–13.)

Speak by Laurie Halse Anderson. Farrar. (Realism, ages 14–18.)

Hard Love by Ellen Wittlinger. Simon & Schuster. (Realism, ages 14–18.)

National Book Award for Young People's Literature

The National Book Award for Young People's Literature, sponsored by the National Book Foundation, is presented annually to recognize the outstanding contribution to children's literature in terms of literary merit, published during the previous year. The award committee considers books of all genres written for children and young adults by U.S. writers. The award carries a $10,000 cash prize.

2012 *Goblin Secrets* by William Alexander. Margaret K. McElderry. (Fantasy, ages 12–16.)

2011 *Inside Out & Back Again* by Thanhha Lai. Harper. (Realistic fiction, ages 12–16.)

2010 *Mockingbird* by Kathryn Erskine. Philomel. (Realistic fiction, ages 12–16.)

2009 *Claudette Colvin: Twice Toward Justice* by Phillip Hoose. Farrar. (Biography, ages 12–18.)

2008 *What I Saw and How I Lied* by Judy Blundell. Scholastic. (Realism/mystery, ages 14–18.)

2007 *The Absolutely True Diary of a Part-Time Indian* by Sherman Alexie. Little, Brown. (Fictionalized autobiography, ages 14–18.)

2006 *The Astonishing Life of Octavian Nothing, Traitor to the Nation,* **Volume I:** *The Pox*

Party by M. T. Anderson. Candlewick. (Historical fiction, ages 15–18.)

2005 *The Penderwicks: A Summer Tale of Four Sisters, Two Rabbits, and a Very Interesting Boy* by Jeanne Birdsall. Knopf. (Realism, ages 9–13.)

2004 *Godless* by Pete Hautman. Simon & Schuster. (Realism, ages 13–18.)

2003 *The Canning Season* by Polly Horvath. Farrar. (Realism, ages 12–15.)

2002 *The House of the Scorpion* by Nancy Farmer. Atheneum. (Science fiction, ages 11–15.)

2001 *True Believer* by Virginia Euwer Wolff. Atheneum. (Realism, ages 14–18.)

2000 *Homeless Bird* by Gloria Whelan. Harper-Collins. (Realism/India, ages 12–15.)

Newbery Medal

The Newbery Medal, sponsored by the Association for Library Service to Children division of the American Library Association, is given to the author of the most distinguished contribution to children's literature published during the previous year. Only U.S. citizens are eligible for this award. Books appropriate for both children and young adults are included in this award.

2013 *The One and Only Ivan* by Katherine Applegate. HarperCollins. (Fantasy, ages 12–15.)

HONOR BOOKS

Splendors and Glooms by Laura Amy Schlitz. Candlewick. (Historical thriller, ages 12–14.)

Bomb: The Race to Build—and Steal—the World's Most Dangerous Weapon by Steve Sheinkin. Roaring Brook Press. (Information/history, ages 12–18.)

Three Times Lucky by Sheila Turnage. Dial/Penguin. (Realistic/humorous, ages 12–15.)

2012 *Dead End in Norvelt* by Jack Gantos. Farrar. (Realistic fiction/humorous, ages 12–14.)

HONOR BOOKS

Inside Out & Back Again by Thanhha Lai. HarperCollins. (Historical fiction, ages 12–14.)

Breaking Stalin's Nose by Eugene Yelchin. Holt. (Historical fiction/Russia, ages 12–14.)

2011 *Moon over Manifest* by Clare Vanderpool. Delacorte. (Historical fiction, ages 12–14.)

HONOR BOOKS

Turtle in Paradise by Jennifer L. Holm. Random House. (Historical fiction, ages 11–14.)

Heart of a Samurai by Margi Preus. Amulet. (Historical fiction, ages 12–15.)

Dark Emperor and Other Poems of the Night by Joyce Sidman. Illustrated by

Rick Allen. Houghton Mifflin. (Poetry, ages 12–14.)

One Crazy Summer by Rita Williams-Garcia. Amistad. (Historical fiction, ages 12–16.)

2010 *When You Reach Me* by Rebecca Stead. Wendy Lamb. (Historical fantasy, ages 12–15.)

HONOR BOOKS

Claudette Colvin: Twice Toward Justice by Phillip Hoose. Melanie Kroupa. (Biography, ages 12–18.)

The Evolution of Calpurnia Tate by Jacqueline Kelly. Holt. (Historical fiction, ages 12–16.)

Where the Mountain Meets the Moon by Grace Lin. Little, Brown. (Fantasy/Chinese folklore, ages 12–14.)

The Mostly True Adventures of Homer P. Figg by Rodman Philbrick. Blue Sky Press. (Historical fiction, ages 12–15.)

2009 *Graveyard Book* by Neil Gaiman. Illustrated by Dave McKean. HarperCollins. (Fantasy, ages 12–15.)

HONOR BOOKS

The Underneath by Kathi Appelt. Illustrated by David Small. Atheneum. (Magical realism, ages 10–14.)

The Surrender Tree: Poems of Cuba's Struggle for Freedom by Margarita Engle. Holt. (Poetry, ages 11–18.)

Savvy by Ingrid Law. Dial. (Fantasy, ages 12–15.)

After Tupac & D Foster by Jacqueline Woodson. Putnam. (Realism/African-American, ages 12–16.)

2008 *Good Masters! Sweet Ladies! Voices from a Medieval Village* by Laura Amy Schlitz. Illustrated by Robert Byrd. Candlewick. (Monologues/dialogues, ages 10–15.)

HONOR BOOKS

Elijah of Buxton by Christopher Paul Curtis. Scholastic. (Historical fiction/African-American, ages 10–14.)

The Wednesday Wars by Gary D. Schmidt. Clarion. (Realism, ages 11–14.)

Feathers by Jacqueline Woodson. Putnam. (Realism/African-American, ages 10–14.)

2007 *The Higher Power of Lucky* by Susan Patron. Illustrated by Matt Phelan. Simon & Schuster. (Realism, ages 10–13.)

HONOR BOOKS

Penny from Heaven by Jennifer L. Holm. Random. (Historical fiction/1950s America, ages 11–14.)

Hattie Big Sky by Kirby Larson. Delacorte. (Historical fiction/1918 Montana, ages 14–18.)

Rules by Cynthia Lord. Scholastic. (Realistic, ages 10–13.)

2006 *Criss Cross* by Lynne Rae Perkins. Greenwillow. (Realism, ages 11–15.)

HONOR BOOKS

Whittington by Alan Armstrong. Illustrated by S. D. Schindler. Random. (Animal fantasy, ages 10–14.)

Hitler Youth: Growing Up in Hitler's Shadow by Susan Campbell Bartoletti. Scholastic. (Nonfiction, ages 11–15.)

Princess Academy by Shannon Hale. Bloomsbury. (Fantasy, ages 11–15.)

Show Way by Jacqueline Woodson. Illustrated by Hudson Talbott. Putnam. (Picturebook/African-American, ages 8–11.)

2005 *Kira-Kira* by Cynthia Kadohata. Atheneum. (Realism/Japanese-American, ages 11–14.)

HONOR BOOKS

Al Capone Does My Shirts by Gennifer Choldenko. Putnam. (Realism, ages 11–14.)

The Voice That Challenged a Nation: Marian Anderson and the Struggle for Equal Rights by Russell Freedman. Clarion. (Biography, ages 11–14.)

Lizzie Bright and the Buckminster Boy by Gary D. Schmidt. Clarion. (Historical fiction/Maine, 1912/African-American, ages 13–16.)

2004 *The Tale of Despereaux: Being the Story of a Mouse, a Princess, Some Soup, and a Spool of Thread* by Kate DiCamillo. Illustrated by Timothy Basil Ering. Candlewick. (Animal fantasy, ages 8–12.)

HONOR BOOKS

Olive's Ocean by Kevin Henkes. Greenwillow. (Realism, ages 11–14.)

An American Plague: The True and Terrifying Story of the Yellow Fever Epidemic of 1793 by Jim Murphy. Clarion. (Information/history, ages 12–18.)

2003 *Crispin: The Cross of Lead* by Avi. Hyperion. (Historical fiction, ages 11–15.)

HONOR BOOKS

The House of the Scorpion by Nancy Farmer. Atheneum. (Science fiction, ages 11–15.)

Pictures of Hollis Woods by Patricia Reilly Giff. Random House. (Realism, ages 10–13.)

Hoot by Carl Hiaasen. Knopf. (Realism, ages 9–12.)

A Corner of the Universe by Ann M. Martin. Scholastic. (Realism, ages 11–14.)

Surviving the Applewhites by Stephanie S. Tolan. HarperCollins. (Realism, ages 12–16.)

2002 *A Single Shard* by Linda Sue Park. Clarion/Houghton. (Historical fiction, ages 10–14.)

HONOR BOOKS

Everything on a Waffle by Polly Horvath. Farrar. (Realism, ages 12–14.)

Carver: A Life in Poems by Marilyn Nelson. Front Street. (Poetry/biography, ages 12–14.)

2001 *A Year Down Yonder* by Richard Peck. Dial. (Historical fiction, ages 10–15.)

HONOR BOOKS

Because of Winn-Dixie by Kate DiCamillo. Candlewick. (Realism, ages 8–12.)

Hope Was Here by Joan Bauer. Putnam. (Realism, ages 12–14.)

Joey Pigza Loses Control by Jack Gantos. Farrar. (Realism, ages 9–12.)

The Wanderer by Sharon Creech. HarperCollins. (Realism, ages 12–14.)

2000 *Bud, Not Buddy* by Christopher Paul Curtis. Delacorte. (Historical fiction/African-American, ages 9–12.)

HONOR BOOKS

Getting Near to Baby by Audrey Couloumbis. Putnam. (Realism, ages 10–13.)

26 Fairmount Avenue by Tomie dePaola. Putnam. (Biography, ages 7–9.)

Our Only May Amelia by Jennifer L. Holm. HarperCollins. (Historical fiction/United States, 1899, ages 10–14.)

YALSA Award for Excellence in Nonfiction for Young Adults

The YALSA Award for Excellence in Nonfiction is given for the best nonfiction book published for young adults during the previous year. It was established in 2010.

2013 *Bomb: The Race to Build—and Steal—the World's Most Dangerous Weapon* by Steve Sheinkin. Roaring Brook Press.

FINALISTS

Steve Jobs: The Man Who Thought Different by Karen Blumenthal. Feiwel & Friends.

Moonbird: A Year on the Wind with the Great Survivor B95 by Phillip M. Hoose. Farrar.

Titanic: Voices from the Disaster by Deborah Hopkinson. Scholastic.

We've Got a Job: The 1963 Birmingham Children's March by Cynthia Levinson. Peachtree.

2012 *The Notorious Benedict Arnold: A True Story of Adventure, Heroism, & Treachery* by Steve Sheinkin. Square Fish.

FINALISTS

Sugar Changed the World: A Story of Magic, Spice, Slavery, Freedom and Science by Marc Aronson and Marina Budhos. Clarion.

Bootleg: Murder, Moonshine, and the Lawless Years of the Prohibition by Karen Blumenthal. Flash Point/Roaring Brook Press.

Wheels of Change: How Women Rode the Bicycle to Freedom (with a Few Flat Tires Along the Way) by Sue Macy. National Geographic.

Music Was IT: Young Leonard Bernstein by Susan Goldman Rubin. Charlesbridge.

2011 *Janis Joplin: Rise Up Singing* by Ann Angel. Amulet Books.

FINALISTS

They Called Themselves the KKK: The Birth of An American Terrorist Group by Susan Campbell Bartoletti. Houghton Mifflin Harcourt.

Spies of Mississippi: The True Story of the Spy Network that Tried to Destroy the Civil Rights Movement by Rick Bowers. National Geographic.

The Dark Game: True Spy Stories by Paul Janeczko. Candlewick.

Every Bone Tells a Story: Hominin Discoveries, Deductions, and Debates by Jill Rubalcaba and Peter Robertshaw. Charlesbridge.

2010 *Charles and Emma: The Darwins' Leap of Faith* by Deborah Heiligman. Square Fish.

FINALISTS

Almost Astronauts: 13 Women Who Dared to Dream by Tanya Lee Stone. Candlewick.

Claudette Colvin: Twice Toward Justice by Phillip Hoose. Farrar.

The Great and Only Barnum: The Tremendous, Stupendous Life of Showman P. T. Barnum by Candace Fleming. Schwartz & Wade.

Written in Bone: Buried Lives of Jamestown and Colonial Maryland by Sally M. Walker. Carolrhoda.

Sibert Award: Informational Books

The Robert F. Sibert Informational Book Award was established by the Association for Library Service to Children (ALSC) in 2001 and is awarded annually to the author(s) and illustrator(s) of the most distinguished informational book published in the United States in English during the preceding year. Only the award winners are listed here; three to four honor books were also named for each year.

2013 *Bomb: The Race to Build—and Steal—the World's Most Dangerous Weapon* by Steve Sheinkin. Roaring Brook Press.

2012 *Balloons over Broadway: The True Story of the Puppeteer of Macy's Parade* by Melissa Sweet. Houghton Mifflin.

2011 *Kakapo Rescue: Saving the World's Strangest Parrot* by Sy Montgomery. Photographs by Nic Bishop. Houghton Mifflin.

2010 *Almost Astronauts: 13 Women Who Dared to Dream* by Tanya Lee Stone. Candlewick.

2009 *We Are the Ship: The Story of Negro League Baseball* by Kadir Nelson. Disney-Jump at the Sun.

2008 *The Wall: Growing Up behind the Iron Curtain* by Peter Sís. Farrar/Frances Foster.

2007 *Team Moon: How 400,000 People Landed Apollo 11 on the Moon* by Catherine Thimmesh. Houghton.

2006 *Secrets of a Civil War Submarine: Solving the Mysteries of the H. L. Hunley* by Sally M. Walker. Carolrhoda.

2005 *The Voice That Challenged a Nation: Marian Anderson and the Struggle for Equal Rights* by Russell Freedman. Clarion.

2004 *An American Plague: The True and Terrifying Story of the Yellow Fever Epidemic of 1793* by Jim Murphy. Clarion.

2003 *The Life and Death of Adolf Hitler* by James Cross Giblin. Clarion.

2002 *Black Potatoes: The Story of the Great Irish Famine, 1845–1850* by Susan Campbell Bartoletti. Houghton Mifflin.

2001 *Sir Walter Ralegh and the Quest for El Dorado* by Marc Aronson. Clarion.

Orbis Pictus Award

The Orbis Pictus Award promotes and recognizes excellence in the writing of nonfiction for children. The title commemorates the work of Johannes Amos Comenius, Orbis Pictus—The World in Pictures (1657), considered to be the first book actually designed and published for children. Only the award winners are listed here; three to four honor books were also named for each year.

2013 *Monsieur Marceau: Actor without Words* by Leda Schubert. Illustrated by Gérard DuBois. Roaring Brook Press.

2012 *Balloons over Broadway: The True Story of the Puppeteer of Macy's Parade* by Melissa Sweet. Houghton Mifflin Books for Children.

2011 *Ballet for Martha: Making Appalachian Spring* by Jan Greenberg and Sandra Jordan. Illustrated by Brian Floca. Roaring Brook Press.

2010 *The Secret World of Walter Anderson* by Hester Bass. Illustrated by E. B. Lewis. Candlewick Press.

2009 *Amelia Earhart: The Legend of the Lost Aviator* by Shelley Tanaka. Illustrated by David Craig. Abrams Books for Young Readers.

2008 *M.L.K. Journey of a King* by Tonya Bolden. Abrams Books for Children.

2007 *Quest for the Tree Kangaroo: An Expedition to the Cloud Forest of New Guinea* by Sy Montgomery. Photographs by Nic Bishop. Houghton Mifflin.

2006 *Children of the Great Depression* by Russell Freedman. Clarion Books.

2005 *York's Adventures with Lewis and Clark: An African-American's Part in the Great Expedition* by Rhoda Blumberg. HarperCollins.

2004 *An American Plague: The True and Terrifying Story of the Yellow Fever Epidemic of 1793* by Jim Murphy. Clarion Books.

2003 *When Marian Sang: The True Recital of Marian Anderson: The Voice of a Century* by Pam Muñoz Ryan. Illustrated by Brian Selznick. Scholastic.

2002 *Black Potatoes: The Story of the Great Irish Famine, 1845–1850* by Susan Campbell Bartoletti. Houghton Mifflin.

2001 *Hurry Freedom: African Americans in Gold Rush California* by Jerry Stanley. Crown.

2000 *Through My Eyes by Ruby Bridges,* Margo Lundell. Scholastic Press.

Carnegie Medal: Great Britain

The Carnegie Medal, sponsored by the Chartered Institute of Library and Information Professionals, is given to the author of the most outstanding children's book first published in the United Kingdom during the preceding year. Books appropriate for both children and young adults are included in this award.

2013   *Maggot Moon* by Sally Gardner. Hot Key. (Dystopia/Science fiction, ages 13–18.)

2012   *A Monster Calls* by Patrick Ness. Walker. (Fantasy, ages 12–16.)

2011   *Monsters of Men* by Patrick Ness. Walker. (Dystopia/Science fiction, ages 12–16.)

2010   *The Graveyard Book* by Neil Gaiman. Bloomsbury. (Fantasy, ages 12–16.)

2009   *Bog Child* by Siobhan Dowd. David Fickling. (Realistic fiction, ages 12–16.)

2008   *Here Lies Arthur* by Philip Reeve. Scholastic. (Fantasy, ages 12–16.)

2007   *Just in Case* by Meg Rosoff. Penguin. (Magical realism, ages 15–18.)

2006   *Tamar* by Mal Peet. Walker. (Realism/mystery, ages 14–18.)

2005   *Millions* by Frank Cottrell Boyce. Macmillan. (Realism, ages 11–14.)

2004   *A Gathering Light* by Jennifer Donnelly. Bloomsbury. (Historical fiction/United States, 1906, ages 14–18.) (U.S. edition entitled *A Northern Light*)

2003   *Ruby Holler* by Sharon Creech. Bloomsbury. (Realism, ages 9–13.)

2002   *The Amazing Maurice and His Educated Rodents* by Terry Pratchett. Doubleday/HarperCollins. (Fantasy, ages 12–16.)

2001   *The Other Side of Truth* by Beverly Naidoo. Puffin/HarperCollins. (Realism, ages 12–15.)

2000   *Postcards from No Man's Land* by Aidan Chambers. Bodley Head. (Realism, ages 14–18.)

Boston Globe–Horn Book Awards

The Boston Globe–Horn Book Awards are given to an author for outstanding fiction or poetry for children, to an illustrator for outstanding illustration in a children's book, and, since 1976, to an author for outstanding nonfiction for children. Only the awards for fiction are listed here.

2013   Fiction: *Eleanor & Park* by Rainbow Rowell. St. Martin's Griffin. (Fiction, ages 13–17.)

2012   Fiction: *No Crystal Stair: A Documentary Novel of the Life and Work of Lewis Michaux, Harlem Bookseller* by Vaunda Micheaux Nelson. Illustrated by R. Gregory Christie. Carolrhoda. (Fictionalized biography, ages 13–18.)

2011   Fiction: *Blink & Caution* by Tim Wynne-Jones. Candlewick. (Realistic thriller, ages 12–16.)

2010   Fiction: *When You Reach Me* by Rebecca Stead. Lamb/Random. (Historical fantasy, ages 12–16.)

2009   Fiction: *Nation* by Terry Pratchett. HarperCollins. (Fantasy, ages 13–18.)

2008   Fiction: *The Absolutely True Diary of a Part-Time Indian* by Sherman Alexie. Little, Brown. (Fictionalized autobiography, ages 14–18.)

2007   Fiction: *The Astonishing Life of Octavian Nothing, Traitor to the Nation,* **Volume I:** *The Pox Party* by M. T. Anderson. Candlewick. (Historical fiction/U.S. Revolutionary War, ages 15–18.)

2006   Fiction: *The Miraculous Journey of Edward Tulane* by Kate DiCamillo. Illustrated by Bagram Ibatoulline. Candlewick. (Fantasy, ages 8–11.)

2005   Fiction: *The Schwa Was Here* by Neal Shusterman. Dutton. (Realism, ages 12–16.)

2004   Fiction: *The Fire-Eaters* by David Almond. Delacorte. (Historical fiction/England, 1962/Cuban missile crisis, ages 12–16.)

2003   Fiction: *The Jamie and Angus Stories* by Anne Fine. Illustrated by Penny Dale. Candlewick. (Fantasy, ages 5–7.)

2002   Fiction: *Lord of the Deep* by Graham Salisbury. Delacorte. (Realism, ages 11–15.)

2001   Fiction: *Carver: A Life in Poems* by Marilyn Nelson. Front Street. (Biography/ Poetry, ages 12–14.)

2000   Fiction: *The Folk Keeper* by Franny Billingsley. Atheneum. (Fantasy, ages 11–15.)

Governor General's Literary Awards: Canada

The Governor General's Literary Awards has separate prizes for children's literature (text and illustration) for books published in Canada. Only the awards for text are listed here.

2012   *The Reluctant Journal of Henry K. Larsen* by Susan Nielsen. Tundra.

2011   *From Then to Now: A Short History of the World* by Christopher Moore. Tundra.

2010   *Fishtailing* by Wendy Phillips. Coteau.

2009   *Greener Grass: The Famine Years* by Caroline Pignat. Red Deer.

2008   *The Landing* by John Ibbitson. Kids Can.

2007   *Gemini Summer* by Iain Lawrence. Delacorte.

2006   *Ingrid and the Wolf* by André Alexis. Tundra.

2005   *The Crazy Man* by Pamela Porter. Groundwood.

2004   *Airborn* by Kenneth Oppel. HarperCollins.

2003   *Stitches* by Glen Huser. Groundwood.

2002   *True Confessions of a Heartless Girl* by Martha Brooks. Groundwood.

2001   *Dust* by Arthur Slade. HarperCollins Canada.

2000   *Looking for X* by Deborah Ellis. Groundwood.

Book of the Year for Older Readers Award: Australia

The Children's Book Council of Australia sponsors five awards for excellence in children's books: The Picture Book of the Year Award; the Book of the Year for Early Childhood; the Book of the Year for Younger Readers Award; the Book of the Year for Older Readers Award; and the Eve Pownall Award for Information Books. Only the Book of the Year for Older Readers Award is listed here.

2012   *The Dead I Know* by Scot Gardner. Allen & Unwin.

2011   *The Midnight Zoo* by Sonya Hartnett. Viking.

2010   *Jarvis 24* by David Metzenthen. Penguin Group Australia.

2009   *Tales from Outer Suburbia* by Shaun Tan. Allen & Unwin.

2008 *The Ghost's Child* by Sonya Hartnett. Candlewick.

2007 *Red Spikes* by Margo Lanagan. Knopf.

2006 *The Story of Tom Brennan* by J. C. Burke. Random House.

2005 *The Running Man* by Michael Gerard Bauer. Omnibus.

2004 *Saving Francesca* by Melina Marchetta. Viking.

2003 *I Am the Messenger* by Markus Zusak. Pan Macmillan Australia.

2002 *Forest* by Sonya Hartnett. Viking.

2001 *Wolf on the Fold* by Judith Clarke. Allen & Unwin.

2000 *48 Shades of Brown* by Nick Earls. Penguin.

Coretta Scott King Awards

The Coretta Scott King Awards commemorate Dr. Martin Luther King Jr. and Coretta Scott King for their work in promoting peace and world brotherhood. They are given to an African-American author and an African-American illustrator whose children's books, published during the preceding year, made outstanding inspirational and educational contributions to literature for children and young people. The awards are presented annually by the Coretta Scott King Committee of the American Library Association. Only the author awards are listed here.

2013 *Hand in Hand: Ten Black Men Who Changed America* written by Andrea David Pinkney. Illustrated by Brian Pinkney. Jump at the Sun/Disney.

2012 *Heart and Soul: The Story of America and African Americans* written and illustrated by Kadir Nelson. Balzer + Bray/HarperCollins.

2011 *One Crazy Summer* by Rita Williams-Garcia. Amistad.

2010 *Bad News for Outlaws: The Remarkable Life of Bass Reeves, Deputy U.S. Marshal* by Vaunda Micheaux Nelson. Illustrated by R. Gregory Christie. Carolrhoda/Lerner.

2009 *We Are the Ship: The Story of Negro League Baseball* by Kadir Nelson. Hyperion.

2008 *Elijah of Buxton* by Christopher Paul Curtis. Scholastic.

2007 *Copper Sun* by Sharon Draper. Atheneum.

2006 *Day of Tears: A Novel in Dialogue* by Julius Lester. Jump At the Sun/Disney.

2005 *Remember: The Journey to School Integration* by Toni Morrison. Harcourt.

2004 *The First Part Last* by Angela Johnson. Simon & Schuster.

2003 *Bronx Masquerade* by Nikki Grimes. Dial.

2002 *The Land* by Mildred D. Taylor. Fogelman/Penguin Putnam.

2001 *Miracle's Boys* by Jacqueline Woodson. Putnam.

2000 *Bud, Not Buddy* by Christopher Paul Curtis. Delacorte.

Pura Belpré Award

The Pura Belpré Award honors Latino writers and illustrators whose work best portrays, affirms, and celebrates the Latino cultural experience in a work of literature for youth. This award is sponsored by the Association for Library Service to Children and the National Association to Promote Library Services to the Spanish Speaking. Until 2008, the award was given biennially, but it is now given annually. Only the author awards are listed here.

2013 *Aristotle and Dante Discover the Secrets of the Universe* by Benjamin Alire Sáenz. Simon & Schuster.

2012 *Under the Mesquite* by Guadalupe Garcia McCall. Lee and Low.

2011 *The Dreamer* by Pam Muñoz Ryan. Illustrated by Peter Sís. Scholastic.

2010 *Return to Sender* by Julia Alvarez. Knopf.

2009 *The Surrender Tree: Poems of Cuba's Struggle for Freedom* by Margarita Engle. Holt.

2008 *The Poet Slave of Cuba: A Biography of Juan Francisco Manzano* by Margarita Engle. Illustrated by Sean Qualls. Holt.

2006 *The Tequila Worm* by Viola Canales. Random.

2004 *Just a Minute: A Trickster Tale and Counting Book* by Yuyi Morales. Chronicle.

2002 *Esperanza Rising* by Pam Muñoz Ryan. Scholastic.

2000 *Under the Royal Palms: A Childhood in Cuba* by Alma Flor Ada. Atheneum.

1998 *Parrot in the Oven: Mi Vida* by Victor Martinez. HarperCollins.

1996 *An Island Like You: Stories of the Barrio* by Judith Ortiz Cofer. Orchard.

Mildred L. Batchelder Award

The Mildred L. Batchelder Award commemorates Batchelder's belief in the importance of good books for children in translation from all parts of the world. The award is given to an American publisher for a children's book considered to be the most outstanding of those books originally published in a foreign language in a foreign country, and subsequently translated into English and published in the United States. Given annually to a publisher for a book published in the preceding year.

2013 Dial, *My Family for the War,* written by Anne C. Voorhoeve, translated from German by Tammi Reichel.

HONORS:
Graphic Universe, *A Game for Swallows: To Die, to Leave, to Return* written and illustrated by Zeina Abirached, translated from French by Edward Gauvin.

Eerdmans, *Son of a Gun* by Anne de Graaf, translated from Dutch by the author.

2012 Eerdmans, *Soldier Bear* by Bibi Dumon Tak, illustrated by Philip Hopman, translated from Polish by Laura Watkinson.

HONOR:
Delacorte, *The Lily Pond* by Annika Thor, translated from Swedish by Linda Schenck.

2011 Delacorte, *A Time of Miracles* by Anne-Laure Bondoux, translated from French by Y. Maudet.

HONORS:
Namelos, *Departure Time* by Truus Matti, translated from Dutch by Nancy Forest-Flier.

Atheneum, **Nothing** by Janne Teller, translated from French by Martin Aitken.

2010 *Delacorte*, **A Faraway Island** by Annika Thor, translated from Swedish by Linda Schenck.

HONORS:

Farrar, Straus and Giroux, **Eidi** by Bodil Bredsdorff, translated from Danish by Kathryn Mahaffy.

Enchanted Lion, **Big Wolf and Little Wolf** by Nadine Brun-Cosme, illustrated by Olivier Tallec, translated from French by Claudia Bedrick.

Arthur A. Levine, **Moribito II: Guardian of the Darkness** by Nahoko Uehashi, illustrated by Yuko Shimizu, translated from Japanese by Cathy Hirano.

2009 *Arthur A. Levine*, **Moribito: Guardian of the Spirit** by Nahoko Uehashi, translated from Japanese by Cathy Hirano.

HONORS:

Eerdmans, **Garmann's Summer** written and illustrated by Stian Hole, translated from Norwegian by Don Bartlett.

Amulet, **Tiger Moon** by Antonia Michaelis, translated from German by Anthea Bell.

2008 *VIZ Media*, **Brave Story,** written by Miyuki Miyabe, translated from Japanese by Alexander O. Smith.

HONORS:

Milkweed, **The Cat: Or, How I Lost Eternity** by Jutta Richter, illustrated by Rotraut Susanne Berner, translated from German by Anna Brailovsky.

Phaidon, **Nicholas and the Gang** by René Goscinny, illustrated by Jean-Jacques Sempé, translated from French by Anthea Bell.

2007 *Delacorte*, **The Pull of the Ocean** by Jean-Claude Mourlevat, translated from French by Y. Maudet.

HONORS:

Delacorte, **The Killer's Tears** by Anne-Laure Bondoux, translated from French by Y. Maudet.

Hyperion/Miramax, **The Last Dragon** by Silvana De Mari, translated from Italian by Shaun Whiteside.

2006 *Arthur A. Levine*, **An Innocent Soldier** by Josef Holub, translated from German by Michael Hofmann.

HONORS:

Phaidon, **Nicholas** by René Goscinny, illustrated by Jean-Jacques Sempé, translated from French by Anthea Bell.

Bloomsbury, **When I Was a Soldier** by Valérie Zenatti, translated from French by Adriana Hunter.

2005 *Delacorte/Random House*, **The Shadows of Ghadames** by Joëlle Stolz, translated from French by Catherine Temerson.

HONORS:

Farrar, Straus, and Giroux, **The Crow-Girl: The Children of Crow Cove** by Bodil Bredsdorff, translated from Danish by Faith Ingwersen.

Richard Jackson, **Daniel Half Human: And the Good Nazi** by David Chotjewitz, translated from German by Doris Orgel.

2004 *Walter Lorraine/Houghton Mifflin*, **Run, Boy, Run** by Uri Orlev, translated from Hebrew by Hillel Halkin.

HONOR:

Chronicle, **The Man Who Went to the Far Side of the Moon: The Story of Apollo 11 Astronaut Michael Collins** by Bea Uusma Schyffert, translated from Swedish by Emi Guner.

2003 *The Chicken House/Scholastic*, **The Thief Lord** by Cornelia Funke, translated from German by Oliver Latsch.

HONOR:

David R. Godine, **Henrietta and the Golden Eggs** *by Hanna Johansen, illustrated by Käthi Bhend, translated from German by John Barrett.*

2002 *Cricket/Carus,* **How I Became an American** *by Karin Gündisch, translated from German by James Skofield.*

HONOR:

Viking, **A Book of Coupons** *by Susie Morgenstern, illustrated by Serge Bloch, translated from French by Gill Rosner.*

2001 *Arthur A. Levine/Scholastic,* **Samir and Yonatan** *by Daniella Carmi, translated from Hebrew by Yael Lotan.*

HONOR:

David R. Godine, **Ultimate Game** *by Christian Lehmann, translated from French by William Rodarmor.*

2000 *Walker,* **The Baboon King** *by Anton Quintana, translated from Dutch by John Nieuwenhuizen.*

HONORS:

Farrar, Straus, and Giroux, **Collector of Moments** *by Quint Buchholz, translated from German by Peter F. Neumeyer.*

R&S Books, **Vendela in Venice** *by Christina Björk; illustrated by Inga-Karin Eriksson, translated from Swedish by Patricia Crampton.*

Front Street, **Asphalt Angels** *by Ineke Holtwijk, translated from Dutch by Wanda Boeke.*

Margaret A. Edwards Award

The Margaret A. Edwards Award honors an author's lifetime achievement for writing books that have been popular over a period of time. The annual award is administered by the Young Adult Library Services Association of the American Library Association and is sponsored by School Library Journal. It recognizes an author's work in helping adolescents become aware of themselves and addressing questions about the importance of and their role in relationships, society, and the world.

2013	Tamora Pierce
2012	Susan Cooper
2011	Sir Terry Pratchett
2010	Jim Murphy
2009	Laurie Halse Anderson
2008	Orson Scott Card
2007	Lois Lowry
2006	Jacqueline Woodson
2005	Francesca Lia Block
2004	Ursula K. Le Guin
2003	Nancy Garden
2002	Paul Zindel
2001	Robert Lipsyte
2000	Chris Crutcher

Phoenix Award

The Phoenix Award, sponsored by the Children's Literature Association, is given to the author of a book first published twenty years earlier. The book must have been originally published in English and cannot have been the recipient of a major children's book award.

2013 *The Frozen Waterfall* by Gaye Hiçyilmaz. Faber and Faber.

2012 *Letters from Rifka* by Karen Hesse. Holt.

2011 *The Mozart Season* by Virginia Euwer Wolff. Holt.

2010 *The Shining Company* by Rosemary Sutcliffe. Farrar, Straus, and Giroux and Bodley Head.

2009 *Weetzie Bat* by Francesca Lia Block. HarperCollins.

2008 *Eva* by Peter Dickinson. Delacorte.

2007 *Memory* by Margaret Mahy. McElderry.

2006 *Howl's Moving Castle* by Diana Wynne Jones. Greenwillow.

2005 *The Catalogue of the Universe* by Margaret Mahy. Atheneum.

2004 *White Peak Farm* by Berlie Doherty. Orchard.

2003 *The Long Night Watch* by Ivan Southall. Methuen.

2002 *A Formal Feeling* by Zibby Oneal. Orion.

2001 *Seventh Raven* by Peter Dickinson. Penguin.

2000 *The Keeper of the Isis Light* by Monica Hughes. Atheneum.

Appendix B

Magazines

The following list includes some of the most popular magazines available to young adults.

Art

Scholastic Art. Themed issues featuring lessons, reproductions, posters, and artist profiles to supplement the art curriculum. Ages 13–18. Six issues/year. Order at http://classroommagazines.scholastic.com/products/choices.

Drama

Plays, the Drama Magazine for Young People. Scripts for plays, skits, puppet shows, and round-the-table readings (a type of readers' theatre). Ages 6–17. Seven issues/year; eight to ten scripts per issue. Order at www.playsmagazine.com/.

Languages

Each of these magazines includes teen-interest articles and features interviews with pop culture personalities and sports figures as well as teen perspectives on other countries and cultures; extension lessons on reading, grammar, and vocabulary skills; read-aloud plays; and free language CDs for pronunciation skills. Ages 12–18. Six issues/year. Order at http://teacher.scholastic.com/products/classmags.

French

Allons-Y (beginners); *Bonjour* (advanced beginners); *Ça-Va?* (intermediate); *Chez Nous* (advanced). Order through www.classroommagazines.scholastic.com/products/allons-y.

German

Das Rad (beginners); *Schuss* (advanced beginners). Order through www. http://classroommagazines.scholastic.com/products/das-rad.

Spanish

¿Qué Tal? (beginners); *Ahora* (advanced beginners); *El Sol* (intermediate and advanced). Order through www.classroommagazines.scholastic.com/category/title/-qu-tal.

Language Arts and Literature

Cicada. Stories and poems written by outstanding adult authors and teens. Ages 14–18. Six issues/year. Order at www.cricketmag.com.

Claremont Review. Literary magazine that showcases inspiring young adult writers, aged 13–19. They publish poetry, fiction, drama, and art twice per year, spring and fall. Subscribe at http://www.theclaremontreview.ca/.

Scholastic Action. High interest–low reading level (third to fifth grade). Readers' theatre plays, true teen nonfiction, celebrity profiles, debate prompts, language arts skill-builders for struggling and resistant readers. Ages 12–18.

Fourteen issues/year. Order at http://www
.scholastic.com.

Scholastic Scope. Readers' theatre plays, classic and
contemporary literature, nonfiction, first person
true teen stories, reading comprehension
activities, vocabulary builders, writing prompts.
Ages 12–18. Seventeen issues/year. Order at
www.scholastic.com/Scope.

*Stone Soup: The Magazine by Young Writers and
Artists.* Stories, poems, book reviews, and art
by young people. Ages 8–13. Six issues/year.
Order at www.stonesoup.com.

Teen Graffiti. Teen writers writing for and about
teenagers and teen issues. Ages 13–17. Six
issues/year. Order at http://www.magazines
.com/teen-graffiti.

Teen Ink. A national teen magazine, book series,
and website devoted entirely to teenage
writing and art. Ages 12–18. Ten issues/year.
Order at www.teenink.com.

Mathematics

Scholastic Math Magazine. Math problems,
computation, statistics, consumer math,
real-life applications, career math, critical
reasoning. Ages 12–15. Twelve issues/year.
Order at www.scholastic.com/Math.

Recreation and Entertainment

Black Beat. Urban music news and trends,
hip-hop culture, gossip. Ages 15–20. Six
issues/year. Order at www.magazine-agent
.com/black-beat/magazine.

BMX Plus! Reviews and tests of bikes and
equipment, worldwide race coverage,
interviews with top personalities.
Ages 11–18. Twelve issues/year. Order at
www.bmxplusmag.com.

Boys' Life. News, nature, sports, history, fiction,
science, comics, Scouting, colorful graphics,
and photos. Published by the Boy Scouts of
America. Ages 8–18. Twelve issues/year.
Order at www.boyslife.org.

GamePro. Video game magazine for serious
gamers. Reviews and previews of video

games plus tips and strategies. Ages 11–18.
Twelve issues/year. Order at www
.magazine-agent.com/GamePro/Magazine.

Neo. Manga, anime written by experts in the
United Kingdom, Japan, and the United
States. Ages 12–18. Order from http://www
.magazines.com/neo.

New Moon Girls. An international magazine by
and about girls. Designed to build
self-esteem and promote a positive body
image. Ages 8–15. Six issues/year. Order at
www.newmoongirls.magazines.com/.

Right On! Entertainment news and celebrity
profiles for black teens. Ages 11–18. Six
issues/year. Order at www.magazine-agent
.com/Right-On/Magazine.

Seventeen. Fashion, health, beauty, celebrity
interviews for female teens. Ages 14–18.
Twelve issues/year. Order at www
.seventeen.com.

Sports Illustrated. Sports news, analysis, and
personality profiles. Ages 14–18. Fifty-six
issues/year. Order at www.si.com/subscribe.

Teen Voices. A print (two issues/year) and online
(monthly) social justice magazine publishing
essays and articles by teens on their lives, their
world, and the issues affecting them. Provides
an educational forum that challenges media
images of women and serves as a vehicle of
change. Order at www.teenvoices.com.

Science and Health

Choices. Articles and activities to teach and
promote family and consumer sciences,
prevention of drug abuse, personal
responsibility, careers, and health.
Ages 13–18. Six issues/year. Order at
www.scholastic.com/Choices.

Current Health 2. Articles and news about
nutrition, fitness, personal health, and the
harmful effects of drugs and alcohol.
Optional: Human Sexuality Newsletter.
Ages 12–18. Eight issues/year. Order at www
.subscriptionaddiction.com/magazines/.../
current-health-2-magazine.

Current Science. News in science, health, and technology; science activities. Ages 12–16. Sixteen issues/year. Order at www .weeklyreader.com.

Science World. Articles, experiments, and news to supplement the science curriculum. Ages 12–16. Fourteen issues/year. Order at http://www.scienceworld.scholastic.com/.

Social Studies and History

Calliope. Articles, stories, interviews, time lines, maps, and authentic photos to generate an interest in world history. Themed issues. Ages 9–14. Nine issues/year. Order at www.cricketmag.com.

Cobblestone. Articles about U.S. history. Themed issues. Ages 9–14. Nine issues/year. Order at www.cricketmag.com.

Career World. Practical advice and information on career awareness, college planning, and vocational/technical opportunities. Ages 12–18. Six issues/year. Order at www .magazine-agent.com/Career-World/ Magazine.

Current Events. Important national and world news; debates on topics relevant to students' lives; maps, charts, diagrams. Ages 11–16. Twenty-five issues/year. Order at www .weeklyreader.com.

Junior Scholastic. Features U.S. and world current events, world cultures, map skills, geography, plays, and debates. Ages 11–14. Eighteen issues/year. Order at http://www.scholastic .com/Junior.

Muse. Nonfiction articles, photoessays, and jokes relating to history, science, and art. Ages 10–18. Nine issues/year. Order at www.cricketmag.com.

New York Times Upfront. Current national and international news, debates on issues, op-ed pieces, essays by teens, eight-page teacher edition. Ages 15–18. Fourteen issues/year. Order at http://www.upfront.scholastic.com/.

Skipping Stones. An international, multicultural children's magazine. Articles by, about, and for children about world cultures and cooperation. Multilingual. Ages 7–17. Five issues/year. Order at www.skippingstones.org.

Index to Children's Books and Authors

Page numbers followed by *f* or *t* indicate figures or tables, respectively.

Subject Index

Page numbers followed by *f* or *t* indicate figures or tables, respectively.

Credits and Acknowledgements

Text Credit

Page 106: Kirby, D.L., & Kirby, D. (2010). *Contemporary memoir: A 21st-century genre ideal for teens.* English Journal, 99 (4), 22-29. (p. 22)

Page 138: "The Leopard of Loneliness," from *A Fury of Motion: Poems for Boys by Charles Ghigna.* Copyright 2003 by Charles Ghigna Published by WordSong, an imprint of Boyds Mills Press, Inc. Used by permission.

Page 138: "Evolution," Copyright and by Holbrook, S. (2003). Evolution. In S. Holbrook, *By definition: Poems of feelings.* Honesdale, PA: Boyds Mills Press.

Page 140: "Sonnet" by Rossetti, C. (1998). Sonnet. In M. Rosen, *Classic poetry: An illustrated collection.* Illustrated by Paul Howard. Cambridge, MA: Candlewick.

Page 140: "Matsuo Basho," by Matsuo Basho.

Page 141: "Even When" by Hemp, C. (1993). Even when. In P. B. Janeczko, Ed., *Looking for your name.* New York: Orchard. © Christine Hemp.

Page 141: "SOS," Copyright 1974 by Robert Froman. First appeared in *Seeing Things,* published by Thomas Y. Crowell. Reprinted by permission of Curtis Brown, Ltd.

Page 202: Table 9.1. Source: Based on Renaissance Learning, 2012. http://www.renlearn.com/whatkidsarereading/

Page 208: Figure 9.3. Committee on the Right to Read. The students' right to read. Urbana, IL: National Council of Teachers of English. http://www.ncte.org/positions/statements/righttoreadguideline. Courtesy of National Council of Teachers of English.

Design Image Credits

Part and chapter opener drop caps: Kittisak Taramas/Fotolia

Chapter opener background and A-head child icons: David Wiesner

Excellent Books to Read Aloud icon: Verte/Fotolia

Notable Authors and Illustrations icon: Okalinichenko/Fotolia

Recommended Books icon: Anterovium/Fotolia

References icon: Fotokalle/Fotolia

Related Films and DVDs icon: Cobalt/Fotolia